Social Scientists

and

Farm Politics

in the

Age of Roosevelt

RICHARD S. KIRKENDALL

Social Scientists and Farm Politics in the Age of Roosevelt

IOWA STATE UNIVERSITY PRESS
AMES • IOWA

To the Memory of My Parents,

Roland P. Kirkendall

and

Marjorie Monfort Kirkendall

HD
1761
.K5
1982

Printed by The Iowa State University Press, Ames, Iowa 50010

This paperback edition is an unabridged republication of the work originally published by the University of Missouri Press in 1966, to which has been added a Foreword prepared especially for this reprint edition.

First edition © 1966 by the Curators of the University of Missouri

Foreword © 1982 by The Iowa State University Press

Reprint edition, 1982

Library of Congress Cataloging in Publication Data

Kirkendall, Richard Stewart, 1928–
    Social scientists and farm politics in the age of Roosevelt.

    Reprint. Originally published: Columbia: University of Missouri Press, 1966.
    Bibliography: p.
    Includes index.
    1. Agriculture and state—United States—History—20th century. 2. Social scientists in government—United States—History—20th century. 3. United States—Economic policy—1933-1945. 4. United States—Politics and government—1933-1945.
    I. Title.
HD1761.K5   1982   338.1′873   82–14949

ISBN 0-8138-1681-5

CONTENTS

ACKNOWLEDGMENTS

As do all historians, I have accumulated many debts. I must emphasize my debt to Merle Curti. During more than a decade of association with him, he has been a major source of inspiration and encouragement for me. This study originated in his seminar at the University of Wisconsin and emerged first as a dissertation that he directed. Throughout my period of work on the social scientists in farm politics, I have benefited greatly from his many writings on the intellectual in America.

Although, as do most studies in recent United States history, this one draws heavily on published primary sources, particularly on articles in periodicals (with the *Journal of Farm Economics* leading this list), the available and relevant unpublished sources are also very rich. Of these, the most important are the manuscripts in the National Archives in Washington, D.C., notably the records of the Secretary of Agriculture and the Bureau of Agricultural Economics. In other words, the United States Department of Agriculture's unusually liberal policies governing access to documents made this study a possibility. In working through these extensive collections, I profited from the industrious and imaginative assistance of several people, especially Helen Finneran, Vivian Wiser, Harold T. Pinkett, and Stanley Brown.

Several collections—the papers of Franklin D. Roosevelt in the

Roosevelt Library, of Harry S Truman and Clinton P. Anderson in the Truman Library, of M. L. Wilson in Montana State College, and of George Peek in the University of Missouri, and the Historical Files of the Department of Agriculture—supplemented the manuscripts in the National Archives in major ways. As is true of all who have worked in the Presidential libraries, I was served splendidly by their directors, Herman Kahn, Elizabeth Drewry, and Philip C. Brooks, and by staff members, especially Robert Jacoby, J. V. Deyo, Philip D. Lagerquist, and Harry Clark, Jr. Much help came from Rita McDonald of the archives of Montana State College in Bozeman and from Jane R. Berry and Nancy C. Prewitt of the Western Historical Manuscripts Collection at the University of Missouri in Columbia. And I am grateful also to Gladys L. Baker, Wayne D. Rasmussen, and Vivian Wiser for allowing me to see and for helping me to use the extremely valuable collection that they have developed in the Department of Agriculture and for their assistance in other ways.

Interviews with participants in the agricultural politics of the 1930's and 1940's supplemented and illuminated the work in other sources. Interviewing is a research technique in which I have a great deal of confidence and on which all students of recent history must rely heavily. The major shortcomings of the technique are known to every researcher, but they can be overcome if the researcher can interview a number of persons with different points of view and can check the interviews against various manuscripts. Fortunately, I was able to do both. Thus, my interviews produced many benefits: valuable leads on events and sources, helpful views on the participants' conceptions of the relative significance of various developments, and important information that could not be found in the written records. I am grateful to the people who gave generously of their time to talk with me about their experiences. Special thanks are due M. L. Wilson, who not only made himself and the hospitality of his home available to me on many occasions and allowed me to use the typescript of his Columbia oral history interview but also brought me into association with other helpful men.

I must express gratitude also for the excellent work conducted for Columbia University's Oral History Collection by Dean Albertson, now of the University of Massachusetts. His lengthy interviews of M. L. Wilson and Howard Tolley are rich in detail and interpretation and of major significance for my study. The other oral history interviews that were relevant and available varied greatly in value for me, but all of them made contributions.

As I hope the study shows, I have learned much from the many historians and political scientists who have published articles and books on the New Deal and farm politics. Of this group, I am especially thankful to Gilbert Fite of the University of Oklahoma. He not only produced many publications that I found useful but also helped me in several other important ways.

This list of helpful people would be incomplete if it did not include my colleagues in the Department of History of the University of Missouri. A fine group who place high value on both teaching and research, they have supplied intellectual stimulus and practical suggestions of the sort needed by an inexperienced scholar.

I wish to express my gratitude for the grants and fellowships that I have received from several institutions: the Research Committee of Wesleyan University, the Research Council of the University of Missouri, the American Philosophical Society, and the Truman Library Institute of National and International Afairs. Without their financial assistance, I could not have conducted this study, for the sources are scattered widely throughout the country, I found them in twenty cities ranging from Cambridge, Massachusetts, to South San Francisco, California.

Finally, let me thank James J. Galbreath for his help in my work in the Federal Records Center, the staff of the Bancroft Library for calling my attention to the papers of Charles C. Teague, Rexford G. Tugwell for the opportunity to see his valuable diary, Boris I. Bittker for permission to consult the Jerome Frank Papers, Mrs. Earl A. Orye for her cooperative spirit and excellence as a typist, the many librarians who have assisted me, and the thoughtful people who have opened their private papers to the inquiring eyes of historians.

In this new edition, the basic contents of the book remain what they were when it first appeared in 1966. Nevertheless, I now wish to acknowledge the help of an additional group of people: those who have given the book a chance for renewed life. The suggestion for a second edition originated with my friend and colleague, Richard Lowitt, who then championed the proposal. I am grateful also to James W. Wallace, William G. Murray, and Lauren Soth for their support of the proposal and to Soth for his thoughtful and informed introduction to this edition. I wish as well to thank Merritt Bailey, the director of Iowa State University Press, and Carl Hamilton and the Press manuscript committee for their decision to bring the book out again. I wish also to express my gratitude to Edward King, the director of the University of Missouri Press, the book's first publisher, for his cooperation. And I am pleased that Judith Gildner and others of Iowa State University Press devoted talent and time to this enterprise. The efforts of all of these people strengthen my convictions that the book continues to be a significant contribution to the field of agricultural history and has relevance to present-day concerns.

R.S.K.

Iowa State University
July, 1982

FOREWORD

The New Deal, its opponents charged, was an American version of the statism sweeping Europe. According to the Liberty League, it was an ideological revolution that threatened to overturn the historic private-enterprise capitalism of "the American Way." But Franklin Delano Roosevelt's unprecedented government interventions in economic affairs after 1932 appear in retrospect anything but a coordinated ideological movement. And far from being a crusade to rout capitalism, most historians now agree the New Deal saved capitalism from self-destruction.

The New Deal had no theme, no political philosophy, just rough and ready pragmatism—a throwing off of the inhibitions of the past about what is proper for government to do and what is not. FDR said he would confront the economic emergency like a quarterback: if one play did not work, he would try another. And he did.

The uniqueness of the New Deal was its experimental approach. FDR was not the first president to call upon intellectuals—professors, scholars, writers, researchers—to help make policy. But his Brain Trust and ensuing staff appointments went far beyond previous practice in using intellectuals for practical government jobs; he intended the execution of policy as well as the formulation of it. Opponents attacked the New Deal on just that ground: theoretical professors were superseding realistic business men and politicians in trying to run the country. Cartoonists loved to draw pictures of long-haired, wild-eyed individuals wearing mortar boards and gowns and labeled "New Dealers."

No department of government so well epitomized the trial-and-error method and the reliance on intellectuals as the United States Department of Agriculture. This was an irony, considering the traditional skepticism of "book farming" by the department's farmer clientele. The USDA and the Land Grant colleges and universities were gradually establishing a climate of respect for science and learning, but in 1933, "practical farmers" remained dubious about advice from professors.

The reason for the turn to intellectuals by the USDA was the new young secretary of agriculture. Henry Agard Wallace, scion of an Iowa family noted for its promotion of scientific agriculture, brought to the top a new cadre of scholars: economists, sociologists, and political scientists. Wallace himself had established a reputation as an economist as well as crop researcher and geneticist. He had begun publishing economic information and analysis in *Wallaces' Farmer* when his father, Henry Cantwell Wallace, was secretary of agriculture in the early twenties. He was one of the first farm editors to publish hog-corn price ratios and other market comparisons to help farmers plan their operations. Henry C. Wallace, with help from his son, Henry A., initiated and encouraged agricultural outlook program research and education by the USDA and the agricultural colleges. "H.A.," as he was known to distinguish him from "H.C.," maintained close liaison with the farm economists of the USDA and the colleges. I well remember his conferences with A. G. ("Al") Black, head of economics at Iowa State College (now University) when I was a student there. So it was only natural that the new secretary of agriculture in 1933 recruited the economists, including Al Black, who became prominent New Deal farm administrators and policymakers.

Richard Kirkendall's study of the social scientists in the agricultural phase of the New Deal is a perceptive review of a period about which I possess personal experience and knowledge, including a year in the old Bureau of Agricultural Economics. I knew most of the actors—mostly from afar, some, such as Al Black, Howard Tolley, and Louis Bean, rather intimately. Kirkendall has told their story well. This paperback edition of his book, by the Iowa State University

Press, will enlarge readership at a time when the lessons from a period of bold innovation in social policy are especially cogent. The successes and failures of early "supply management" efforts and the reasons why, should inform food-agriculture policymakers of today. The ideologists of the Reagan "revolution" in the eighties may benefit from a study of the nonideological trouble-shooting in the thirties.

Within the New Deal social-planning fraternity of the USDA a rift quickly developed between the practical agricultural-college, agribusiness draftees and the idealistic, reform-minded, urban lawyers and economists. The former were typified by Chester Davis, a Montana agricultural official and later Federal Reserve banker, and George Peek, a farm machinery manufacturing executive. The latter group included Rexford Guy Tugwell, the Columbia University professor of economics and FDR favorite, and Jerome Frank, urban liberal lawyer, later judge. The practical men were mainly interested in organizing production control and helping commercial farmers get on their feet. The urban liberals paid more attention to the poverty sector of rural America, especially the blacks who were being displaced by cotton-acreage cutbacks and denied their legal share of the benefits of the new program. They concerned themselves with southern tenant problems, housing, small farms, migratory labor and race discrimination. The southern congressmen and farm leaders, who were the strongest backers of the acreage control programs, objected loudly to this kind of activity.

Henry Wallace, M. L. Wilson, and Howard Tolley were moderators of mediators. They wanted to get on with what they saw as the main issue—revival of commercial agriculture—but not at the sacrifice of needed reforms. Eventually, however, Wallace got rid of some of the reformers in order to keep the larger program going. Kirkendall's book reminds us once again of the political practicality of the Wallace New Deal in agriculture.

After nearly a decade of innovations—crop acreage control, price support, rural electrification, soil conservation assistance, farm credit changes, aid for low-income farmers—the movement slowed to a creep. The coming of World War II brought it to a halt. Political assassination of long-range planning signaled the end of New Deal reforms in agriculture.

The reaction against the very word "planning" was ideological:

planning was associated with socialism and central government control; the Soviet Union's Gosplan was reviled by all true believers in free enterprise. Therefore County Agricultural Planning, undertaken briefly under the BAE, carried a poor connotation. The setting of production goals in Washington made many farmers and farm organization leaders nervous. I have always thought, too, that the improvement in farm income occurring under the farm programs turned some early New Deal supporters into conservative opponents of government "meddling" in their affairs. In the military buildup just prior to World War II, when County Agricultural Planning began, the "try anything" mood of 1932–1934 had nearly vanished. People who had been saved from disaster by government loans and subsidies began to feel they had done it all by themselves.

But the planning program was upset largely for more practical political reasons. The American Farm Bureau Federation feared County Agricultural Planning as a potential rival farmer organization, and for good reason. The bureau itself had grown to power as a quasiofficial arm of the federal-state Agricultural Extension Service, actually receiving and dispensing public funds in many states.

Leaders of the bureau, notably Edward A. O'Neal of Alabama, the longtime president of the national organization, were foremost backers of the New Deal, including crop acreage control, price supports, the entire business. Other farm organizations, the Farmers Union and the Grange, were reluctant at first. The union wanted "cost of production" guarantees; the grange feared "socialist intervention." The Farm Bureau increased membership rapidly through its tie-in with government. The first farm adjustment programs were largely administered through the extension service and even after being legally divorced they remained under Farm Bureau influence in many areas, especially in the South.

As the country Agricultural Adjustment Act committees drew away from extension and established their own organizational camaraderie, the Farm Bureau took alarm that this might be the beginning of a farm organization in competition for political influence. This concern contributed to the growing antigovernment sentiment in the bureau.

When County Agricultural Planning committees were placed under BAE (rather than extension which did the fieldwork), Ed O'Neal and his colleagues saw another threat that a new "Farm Bureau" might arise. Since they were losing enthusiasm for some of the New Deal programs as economic conditions improved, the need for "planning" seemed doubtful. If any planning was to be done, it should be done by nongovernmental farmer organizations, which the Farm Bureau considered itself to be, though it still had legal ties with state governments in many states.

With "Mr. Win the War" displacing "Mr. New Deal," as FDR said, it was easy to rout the agricultural planners.

As the war came on, of course, there was more and more government planning of agriculture, including the allocation of production supplies, rationing, subsidies, price controls, and other state interventions never dreamed of by the County Agricultural Planning enthusiasts. They were interested primarily in encouraging better land-use planning on a voluntary, locally managed basis. Some of the planning leaders saw this movement as a way to reduce the national government role in crop acreage adjustments. The opponents saw it as a U.S. Gosplan for farming.

Kirkendall rightly emphasizes the planning motivation behind many of the New Deal farm programs and their designers, particularly Minburn L. Wilson. "M.L." Wilson was a philosophical partner of Henry A. Wallace from pre–New Deal days. He did much to convince Roosevelt and Wallace of the merits of the "domestic allotment plan," the foundation of the first Agricultural Adjustment Act. He and Howard Tolley had high hopes for County Agricultural Planning under the BAE.

The thirties were exciting times in the formerly staid Department of Agriculture. For seventy years it had been a developmental and educational agency. Now it was becoming an action agency. The "Old Dealers" in the bureaucracy were left in their offices with little to do while the USDA expanded around them and new idea men took over. John D. Black of Harvard University, Theodore W. Schultz of Iowa State University, and other original thinkers from the academic world were often seen in the halls of the South Building and in the conference rooms. The BAE set up a production goals committee, with Orris V. Wells as chairman, on which I served. We published a pamphlet on yardsticks for long-range planning for foreign trade, consumer requirements, soil conservation, and farm family income. Nobody paid much attention, but it reflected the interest in the planning idea in the top echelon of the USDA.

Another innovation in which I had a small part was the designing of the first crop insurance plan by a BAE committee chaired by Roy Green. FDR submitted the plan to Congress and it passed.

It was a thrilling time. The breakthroughs in mobilizing intellectual power for social purposes, I believe, have been lasting. County Agricultural Planning died, but the concept of national charting of food and agricultural production and distribution within a free-enterprise system survives. This book is helpful in revealing the process.

Lauren Soth

February 1982

INTRODUCTION

The Rise
of the
Service Intellectual

This is a study of one of many significant and controversial features of the New Deal: the role of intellectuals in its development. The study deals with the rise of the social sciences and the entry of social scientists into politics. It provides an illustration of one type of intellectual life, a "service" type, a type that American colleges and universities were producing abundantly by the beginning of the twentieth century. Rejecting alienation, the ivory tower, and the left bank, as well as assumptions about the inherent impracticality of academic men, the service intellectual insists that society needs men of academically trained intelligence who will deal actively and directly with affairs of great importance and interest to men outside the academy and also that some intellectuals have an obligation to define their role in terms of active service to their society.

As with other features of the New Deal, the service intellectual did not suddenly appear upon the American scene in 1933. He had been taking shape for many years, stimulated by the problems and opportunities of life in the New World as well as by the advice and practice of Old World intellectuals like Francis Bacon and Herbert Spencer and institutions such as the German universities. European precedents existed for the service intellectual; American conditions encouraged his full development.[1]

The role of the intellectuals in the New Deal had major sources in the transformation of American higher education in the late nineteenth and early twentieth century and in the participation of intellectuals in the Progressive Movement. Before the Civil War, American colleges had frequently been criticized as undemocratic and impractical; in the first half-century after the war, the institutions of higher learning changed rapidly and significantly. The curriculum was enlarged; science became much more important; colleges and enrollment increased rapidly. The role of government in higher education grew as new state colleges and universities were established and old ones were expanded. State governments played the larger part, but the national government, with its system of land grants and other aids, also promoted these developments. The colleges and universities now attempted to serve the aspirations of large numbers of individuals and groups, especially their hopes for economic progress, and the transformation reflected the growing importance of science in American life and also the influence of democracy and business. The farm business was included; among the new institutions were the agricultural colleges. They assumed that farmers too could and should be served by higher education, and they tried to make farming more successful by making it more scientific.[2]

The new institutions of higher learning produced service intellectuals; the Progressive Movement provided opportunities for them to serve in government, and intellectuals who were involved in that movement provided theoretical justification for their political participation. The philosopher John Dewey, to take a major example, regarded the mutual distrust between intellectuals and other people as a carry-over from the class societies of the Old World that should be discarded. Attempting to alter the association of the intellectual with aristocracy, this philosopher criticized the assumptions that intellectual ability is confined to a small group and that the ivory tower is the proper abode for intellectuals. By putting their knowledge to work for the reform of society, they could promote both intellectual and social progress. Denying that the change would mean "a surrender of the business of thought, for the sake of getting busy at some so-called practical matter," Dewey insisted that the new relationship would "signify a focusing of thought and intensifying of its quality by bringing it into relation with issues of stupendous meaning."[3]

Closely related to the philosophy of John Dewey was the new social science of Lester Frank Ward, Richard T. Ely, Simon Nelson Patten, Thorstein Veblen, and others. Rebelling against the speculative or deductive approach, they insisted that the study of man and society must become scientific and must tackle pressing social problems. Developing an evolutionary view of human affairs, they rejected the theory that man could not control evolution and argued that government action, based upon scientific knowledge, could shape the evolutionary process and promote the general welfare.[4] In line with the theory, the new social scientists willingly accepted governmental positions. By the end of the first decade of the twentieth century, according to one economist, "the appointment of economists in tax commissions, industrial commissions and labor commissions has become so common as now to be taken for granted even in the United States, where it is a very recent development."[5] "In the Progressive era," Richard Hofstadter writes, "the estrangement between intellectuals and power . . . came rather abruptly to an end."[6]

The tendency of academic intellectuals to enter government service appeared most conspicuously in the state of Wisconsin during the Progressive period. As the historian of Wisconsin progressivism has pointed out, "there was hardly a phase of the movement in Wisconsin in which one or more members of the University faculty did not perform some significant function or serve in some important capacity."[7] The president of the institution in the early years of the twentieth century, Charles Van Hise, called attention to the use of scholars by German governments and urged that his faculty be employed in this way, arguing that the professors had knowledge that could help the state solve its problems. Van Hise himself served in as many as five government positions at one time.[8]

One of the best-known exponents of this point of view was the economist John R. Commons, a leader in the development of labor history as a field of study and institutional economics. He drafted Wisconsin's Civil Service and Industrial Commission laws and served as one of the first commissioners on this very important agency. Even before his arrival in Wisconsin in 1904, he had worked for the United States Industrial Commission, which he later described as "the first governmental agency to bring together a staff of trained economists for its work" and as "the original 'brain trust.'"[9] In the state, he found even greater opportunities:

Here . . . was a unique university — utilitarian, idealistic and free. Here investigation accompanied action. Here the people seem to think that democracy must be efficient if plutocracy is to stay out.[10]

Commons did not believe that scientists should manage society; he believed that they should simply be one of the influential groups. They needed to cooperate with "practical" men drawn from business and labor organizations and the like, for the "experts" could contribute indispensable technical knowledge while other groups could supply essential suggestions drawn from practical experience. Each group had its contributions to make, each its shortcomings.[11]

The economist did not expect that those he advised would accept all that he supplied. Political leaders and leaders in other areas had experiences that he did not have and ran risks that he did not run. Only the leader could tell how much of the economist's material he could use and when and how he should use it. "Hence, I always accepted philosophically what they rejected of my hard work, and stuck to them nevertheless," he wrote in his autobiography. "They were leaders. I was an intellectual."[12] As this was written in 1934, it was obviously offered as advice to his former students who were following in his footsteps. "Now some thirty or more of my former students are at Washington in several of the organizations of the New Whirlwind."[13]

Wisconsin's progressive governor, Robert M. La Follette, encouraged the movement of academic men into government service. He had been educated at the state university in the 1870's where he had come under the influence of President John Bascom and his conception of the social service character of public institutions of higher learning. Bascom was recognized, Curti and Carstensen have written, "as the pioneer of the Wisconsin idea, especially insofar as the faculty of the University undertook to give their service as experts to promote the well-being of the people." "I made it a . . . policy," La Follette wrote in his autobiography,

in order to bring all the reserves of knowledge and inspiration of the university more fully to the service of the people, to appoint experts from the university wherever possible upon the important boards of the state . . . a relationship which the university has always encouraged and by which the state has greatly profited.[14]

"La Follette, perhaps more than any other figure in twentieth century political history," David A. Shannon has written, "was responsible for the now generally accepted practice of government officeholders seeking the advice and drawing upon researches by academic experts."[15] And Professor Hofstadter agrees:

La Follette enjoys a special place; though less a scholar or an intellectual than some of his contemporaries, he must be credited with the origins of the brain-trust idea, both because of the effective union he achieved, as governor of Wisconsin, between the University of Wisconsin and the state government, and because of the efficient, research-minded staff he brought with him to Washington during his senatorial days.[16]

The conservation movement of the Progressive period provided another illustration of the drawing together of scientific knowledge and governmental practice. Van Hise, for example, a distinguished geologist, was a leading promoter of conservation as an adviser to Theodore Roosevelt, as a member of the state conservation agencies, and as the author of an influential and very useful book.[17] Even more important, Gifford Pinchot, the most prominent individual in the movement, studied the scientific management of forests in Europe and returned home to apply those scientific principles in American forests, while serving as chief of the Forestry Division and Forestry Service of the United States Department of Agriculture from 1898 to 1910.[18] One historian has argued recently that the conservation movement was essentially a scientific movement.[19]

The intellectuals who dominate the pages that follow represented the service type. As social scientists who advocated large-scale government action in economic affairs, these New Dealers had ties with the developments, institutions, and men that have been mentioned — with the new universities, including the land-grant schools and the University of Wisconsin; with the Progressive Movement, including the Wisconsin and conservation phases of it; with John R. Commons, John Dewey, and other early exponents of this view of intellectual life. The New Deal careers of these social scientists testify to the links between the New Deal and long-term developments in American history that had their origins years before 1933. Those careers indicate that by the 1930's the social scientists had established themselves as one of the influential groups in American politics. The careers disclose the complexity of American attitudes toward intellectuals, for some people in the 1930's seemed to reject the basic assumption of the service intellectuals — the assumption that their training enabled them to be "practical" men — while other Americans obviously believed at the time that these intellectuals could participate successfully in the political process on its higher levels.

The New Deal careers of these social scientists also call attention to difficult questions involved in the relations between intellectuals and other people. The theory of the service intellectual implies that those relations should be close. But how close should they be? Who should define the terms of service? What people should be served? Loren Baritz, in a very important study of social scientists who worked in American industry, concludes that those men became mere "servants of power," the servants of "the industrial elite," and that they abandoned "the wider obligations of the intellectual who is a servant of his own mind."[20] Those social scientists who participated in farm politics certainly often worked closely with the power groups there and tried frequently to promote the interests of those groups. But those social scientists tried to accomplish much more; they did not serve slavishly the interests of the power groups. The social scientists tried to alter the behavior of those groups and to promote the interests of others — the rural poor and the consumers of farm products. The social scientists even tried to reform the power structure of farm politics by attempting to draw new groups into it and to promote new political alliances. The intellectuals experienced frustrations, however, in their efforts to be more than mere servants of power.

The social scientists' sense of frustration suggests that they were not guilty of what Professor Hofstadter defines as the characteristic failure of their kind.

The characteristic failure of the expert who advises the powerful is an unwillingness to bring his capacity for independent thought to bear as a source of criticism. He may lose his capacity for detachment from power by becoming absorbed in its point of view. For American intellectuals, so long excluded from places of power and recognition, there is always the danger that a sudden association with power will become too glamorous, and hence intellectually blinding.[21]

Their association with power did not drive them to the conclusion that they "no longer had any connection with the intellectual community" and that their responsibilities were to power alone.[22]

This study deals with but one group of actors on the New Deal stage and but one group of social scientists operating in a relatively brief period of time: the social scientists who played major roles in efforts to promote agricultural planning in the United States from

1930 to 1946. I have focused my attention upon agricultural planning chiefly because a rather large number of social scientists had an interest in it and because their interest led them into some illuminating activities. The years 1930 and 1946 were important in those activities. In 1930, several social scientists, led by M. L. Wilson and Howard Tolley, cooperated with a Minnesota congressman, Victor Christgau, to introduce a bill that outlined their ambitions. In 1946, Tolley resigned as chief of the Bureau of Agricultural Economics and thereby symbolized the frustrations that he and his associates had experienced.

The study explores the character, extent, and explanations of the influence of the social scientists upon the development of agricultural policies. The story, in bold outline, is one of expanding influence and rising hopes from 1930 to 1940 and of increasing frustration from 1940 to 1946. The chief problem is to explain this change in the fortunes of the social scientists, and this problem has forced me to explore the nature of farm politics and to look at farm leaders, politicians, and businessmen as well as at social scientists. Although the solution to the problem is found largely in the changing relations between the New Deal and the most powerful farm organization, the American Farm Bureau Federation, pressure groups did not monopolize power in farm politics during the "Age of Roosevelt." Politicians and bureaucrats were also significant. Change in the relations of the social scientists with the Secretary of Agriculture ranked very high on the list of factors producing the change in the fortunes of these men of knowledge. Also important were President Roosevelt's belief in the value of intellectuals and his swing away from the matters that most concerned these social scientists when the country moved into World War II.

PART ONE

Preparations for Planning

CHAPTER 1

Outlining Hopes and Ambitions

Preparations for planning were well under way before the Roosevelt Administration came to power in 1933. One sign of those preparations was the Christgau bill, which a young Minnesota congressman introduced in the first year of the great depression and which had been prepared by two social scientists, Howard Ross Tolley and Milburn Lincoln Wilson. The chief significance of the bill lay, not in its immediate consequences, but in the evidence that it provided about the minds of men who would play leading roles in the agricultural planning programs of the New Deal. The bill revealed a complex pattern of values involving science, business, and democracy. Scientific and democratic methods were to be called upon to produce profit for the business of farming, to plan more efficient use of the land, and to serve the interests of both producers and consumers of farm products.

The complexity of the pattern is the feature that must be emphasized. Neither those who interpret farm policy as involving only governmental efforts to provide higher prices for commercial farmers nor those who see land planning as simply the application of science to American politics receive support from an analysis of the thought and action of Tolley and Wilson in the years just before the New Deal.[1]

11

These social scientists, who were to become important New Dealers, hoped that their program would raise prices, but they also had other goals in mind. These agricultural economists hoped to bring their discipline to bear upon the problems of agriculture, but Tolley's and Wilson's activities as planners were influenced also by values that they shared with other groups in American society and that were derived from many experiences, not just from the development of agricultural economics.

Farms and colleges had shaped Wilson's growth and convinced him that science should be carried to the farmers. Born in 1885 and raised on a prosperous, family-sized farm in the rich corn-belt country of Iowa, he developed, with help from the writings of "Uncle Henry" Wallace in *Wallaces' Farmer*, an interest in scientific agriculture and a desire to attend the agricultural college in Ames. He completed that school's four-year course in agriculture, receiving a degree in 1907. His training had emphasized the natural sciences and had given him a scientific turn of mind, a strong interest in the new field of farm management, and a desire to bring the knowledge of the colleges into the lives of the farmers.

He also had a strong urge to succeed in farming, and so, soon after graduation he turned down offers of jobs in scientific agriculture and headed west as his ancestors had been doing for more than a century. Confident that his knowledge would enable him to do well, he farmed first in Nebraska and then, lured by reports of new money-making opportunities, in Montana.

As the reports had been much too optimistic, Wilson soon looked for methods of farming to meet the needs of a land so unlike the humid Midwest. After joining the staff of Montana State College, he participated in the experiments in dry-land farming that were being conducted there and became the state's first county agent and county agent leader. Although he paid some attention to progressive politics, he devoted most of his time to the educating of farmers in the management of their farms.

By the fall of 1919, however, Wilson had become troubled by the shortcomings of his own education and decided to explore the social sciences and philosophy. During the next four years, he earned a master's degree in agricultural economics at the University of Wisconsin, attended a number of graduate courses at the University of Chicago and at Cornell, and acquired stronger convictions about the value of organization for economic groups and of government action in economic affairs.[2]

Faced with major problems in Montana — declining rainfall and skidding prices — and major developments in agricultural technology, but confident that farming could become prosperous on the northern plains, Wilson stepped up his efforts to discover and promote the most efficient ways to use land and machinery in that dry country. A most important effort to discover the changes Montana farmers should make was undertaken by the Fairway Farms Corporation, a nonprofit educational institution that went into operation under Wilson's management in 1924. Henry C. Taylor supplied the basic ideas; John D. Rockefeller provided the financial support; and other economists and financiers plus Chester C. Davis, the Montana Commissioner of Agriculture, contributed a good deal of help. The corporation experimented in tenant rehabilitation and agricultural adjustment, hoping to help tenants make the transition to ownership on farms with the acreage, manpower, horsepower, machinery, methods, crops, and livestock needed to operate at a profit on Montana land. By receiving much publicity, the corporation established Wilson as a leading authority on the experimental method of research in agricultural economics.[3] To one enthusiastic observer, Fairway seemed "the most revolutionary experiment in economic agricultural research ever attempted." It was "a scientific and carefully planned effort to transfer the industrial efficiency of modern factory methods to the farm. . . ."[4]

In these activities, Wilson displayed a keen awareness of the problems of the relations in a democracy between scientists and other people. His teachers in Madison, Chicago, and Ithaca, including John R. Commons, James Tufts, and George Warren, were leading exponents of the idea that intellectuals should participate actively in the affairs of their communities. Just as Commons and his colleagues had been involved in the Progressive Movement, Tufts, according to Wilson, "was as much concerned in how he applied ethics in labor industrial relations as he was in the theoretical side of ethics."[5] Tufts was a close associate of John Dewey, a philosopher Wilson admired greatly and regarded as the chief source of his own philosophy.[6] Wilson's presidential address before the American Farm Economics Association in 1925 reflected the point of view of these men. While expressing a hope that science would become more and more influential in the shaping of policy, he pointed out that a program could not become a reality until it had the approval of public opinion. Consequently, more attention should be given to the methodology of formulating policies and the means of developing them in the minds of rural people. Economic facts needed to be given to farm people so that agricultural policies would be to a large degree an expression of the farmers themselves. Fortunately, several states had already begun "interesting experiments . . . in the democratic formulation of local, regional, and state programs . . . ," involving "the joint efforts of farmers and extension and research workers."[7]

In 1927, Wilson put his view of democracy into operation in Montana. On January 5, a group of leading farmers, stockmen, and representatives of business and industry of the state came to Bozeman to discuss ways to present to the people the information that had been gathered by the experiment station and other agencies and that could be of value in planning the future course of Montana agriculture. After dividing the state into six districts, the group appointed representative men and women in each district to serve on commodity committees; it called upon the committees to make reports at agricultural conferences in the districts. About twelve hundred men and women participated in the conferences and produced recommendations for programs of agricultural development that called for "adjustments in production, in the business organization of individual farms and in the general practices of definite communities." Wilson had great confidence in these procedures:

Agricultural programs such as these being undertaken at these Montana conferences are developed by successful farmers and by scientific and research agencies. They represent the best judgment of the community. When such programs are developed in each community, and when each community can be better informed as to its advantages, its competitors, and its place in the whole scheme of agricultural production, then all farmers will be able to make sounder judgments as to what and how much to produce, and how the farm as a whole may best serve the needs of society and still be a successful business unit returning an income which will enable the farm family to get its share of the good things of life.

In the next few years, Wilson made other efforts to work with farmers in the development of farm programs.[8]

Wilson also spent a brief period in the mid-twenties in the United States Department of Agriculture, serving as head of the Division of Farm Management and Costs in the recently established Bureau of Agricultural Economics. One of his tasks was to help a rising member of that agency, Howard Tolley, get acquainted with the people in the agricultural colleges. Wilson knew these people, and Tolley needed to get to know them if he was to succeed, for they worked closely with the BAE on problems in agricultural economics and farm management.[9]

Although he was a product of the rural Midwest, having been born on an Indiana farm in 1889, Tolley's role in farm politics grew initially out of his skills as a mathematician, not as a farmer. He spent much of his childhood and youth on farms but yearned for an urban occupation. Educated chiefly at Indiana University, he taught school for several years and then in 1912 went to work for the Coast and Geodetic Survey, hoping that life in Washington would be more exciting than in a small town. His talents as a mathematician encouraged William J. Spillman, a pioneer in the study of farm management, to lure the young man away from a rather unsatisfying job and into that branch of agricultural economics. He was to train Tolley in this "coordinating science" that brought together the results of research and knowledge from the other sciences and studied them in hopes of "determining how to organize the farmer's resources . . . so as to obtain the maximum economic return . . . from their use."[10] Only after going to work for the Department of Agriculture's Office of Farm Management in 1915 did Tolley become aware of and very interested in agricultural problems and begin his efforts to help the farmer become a successful businessman.[11]

Tolley worked briefly at the beginning of the 1920's in the Division of Agricultural Engineering, studying the value of tractors in farming, but he spent most of the decade in the Bureau of Agricultural Economics, joining it in 1922 as head of the Division of Farm Management. In the new agency, he associated with and was educated by leading agricultural economists, including, in addition to Wilson and Spillman, Henry C. Taylor, formerly a professor at the University of Wisconsin and the first chief of the BAE, and John D. Black, a Wisconsin-trained professor, at the University of Minnesota and Harvard University. Tolley contributed to efforts to enlarge the perspective of farm management, improve its methods, and make it more effective. These involved attempts to study more than the individual farm; to see the farm in its relations with its region, competing regions, the general agricultural situation, and the total economic picture; to draw upon statistical theory and methods in determining the relations between "input" and "output" in different types of farming and in forecasting the movement of prices for agricultural commodities; and to devise farm management plans that would enable farmers to develop profitable relations between their operations on the farm and the conditions in the market.

With more efficient and profitable ways to farm as the practical aims of the research, more than research was required. The results had to be made known to the farmer before he could make the necessary adjustments in his operations, and thus the BAE, soon after its formation in 1922, developed the "outlook program," a major attempt to unite science and business — the science of agricultural economics and the business of farming. By the late 1920's, the program had grown to the point where, as John Black described it,

once each year, all the forces in the Department of Agriculture are mobilized around the one question of determining as nearly as is possible, on the basis of existing information and analyses, what the present condition is with respect to production, consumption and prices of the farm products, what developments are under way with respect to all these, and what adjustments the producers should make in order to meet these impending developments.[12]

Tolley provided much of the leadership in the growth of the program. With his special skill for directing group research projects, he advanced rapidly in the bureau, becoming head of the Division of Farm Management and Costs in 1926, assistant chief in charge of research two years later, and executive secretary of the "outlook" committees. He worked to make the information more accurate and dependable and to develop the program into a service that would operate throughout the year.[13]

The programs in which Tolley and Wilson were involved tried to promote adjustments in farming operations, but as the general economic situation descended into depression in 1929 and as the plight of the farmer worsened, the economists were far from satisfied with their work. While the experiment at Fairway Farms had reduced costs, it had not produced profits, for wheat prices were too low;[14] the outlook program, in spite of the steady efforts to improve it, had failed to influence production in a substantial fashion. In fact, to many men who had entered the BAE in its early, optimistic days, the bureau and its outlook program now seemed to be suffering from the more limited goals of Nils Olsen, its chief, and of Arthur Hyde, the Secretary of Agriculture. Thus, early in 1930, Tolley departed for California to direct the new Gianinni Foundation in agricultural economics at Berkeley. To Tolley, Hyde, who had been an automobile dealer and the governor of Missouri, seemed quite ignorant of and not very interested in agriculture; Olsen, who was one of Tolley's old friends, seemed to have become Hyde's disciple and to be supplying uninspired leadership for the bureau. Unlike his former post with a department that seemed unlikely to accomplish anything, the position at the University of California promised great opportunities. The appointment also reflected Tolley's stature in his profession.[15]

The agricultural situation, as a number of economists saw it, demanded greater efforts to discover what adjustments were needed and to encourage farmers to make those changes. Not enough time and money were being devoted to efforts to help the farmer answer questions of basic importance in his business, and only a few farmers were being reached by the outlook program.[16] Furthermore, experience with that program was revealing the immensity of the task of determining the most profitable production program for a particular farm. F. F. Elliott, one of Tolley's lieutenants, had argued in 1928 that blanket recommendations for the "average" farmer were too indefinite and likely to be misleading. Farmers needed to be divided into specific groups according to size of farms and type of farming areas so that economists could appraise the needs of typical groups and interpret the effect which changing economic conditions were likely to have upon them. "Until the outlook is localized in this way and interpreted to the individual farmer in terms of an organization with which he is familiar," Elliott suggested, "its meaning may not be sufficiently definite to be helpful to him."[17]

Tolley, in a speech delivered shortly after he left the bureau, called for a program of the sort that Elliott had recommended. Noting that workers in the outlook program had talked frequently about "localization of the outlook and its application to the different regions of the country and to different sections within a state," he insisted that national and state outlook reports were not enough. The work, "to have real and permanent value, must be carried to the point where the results and reports will indicate . . . what changes and adjustments are likely to prove profitable on the farms in different areas and under different producing conditions."[18]

At this time, however, the Federal Farm Board embarked upon a program that was quite unlike the one that Tolley and others had in mind. The board, reflecting the serious agricultural situation at the moment and the interest in agricultural adjustment that had been developing for a decade, began to call for general reductions in the output of major crops. Tolley, Wilson, and some of their associates, while welcoming this action because it publicized the adjustment approach to the farm problem, criticized the board's efforts as crude and as being based upon inadequate research.[19]

Wilson and Tolley joined forces with Congressman Victor Christgau to propose an alternative way of solving the farmer's problems. This first-term congressman, a Republican from southern Minnesota, had a rural, midwestern, progressive point of view that featured a strong interest in the plight of the farmer and a belief that the government should attempt to solve the farmer's basic problems. The Congressman's viewpoint had been shaped not only on a Minnesota farm but also in the graduate school of his state university, where, as a student of agricultural economics, he had come under the influence of a leading advocate of the adjustment approach, John D. Black. Consequently, Christgau, the first agricultural economist to serve in Congress, knew of the discussions that had been going on in the profession about the problems and possibilities of agricultural adjustment and had an interest in the subject. He viewed the agricultural situation, Wilson noted, "more or less in economic terms" and thus was a logical choice for the task that Tolley and Wilson had in mind.[20] Elmer Starch brought the men together. Starch was one of Wilson's associates at Fairway Farms and had studied with Christgau at the University of Minnesota. Now, in the summer of 1930, the Congressman introduced a bill that Tolley and Wilson, assisted by other economists, had produced.[21] As Christgau later explained, he introduced the bill "after consulting with agricultural economists from various sections of the country interested in the problem." [22]

The bill called for an agricultural adjustment program designed to lead to highly efficient and profitable farms. Farmers in the different agricultural regions were to be given help to determine what commodities they could produce to the greatest advantage so that production could be brought into line with the demands of present economic conditions and techniques of production and could be constantly readjusted as changes took place. Thereby, the farmer would always produce commodities that he was equipped to produce, do so in the most efficient manner, and grow no more of them than could be sold at an adequate price. Farms in areas of very poor land would be abandoned; commercial farming would become the occupation only of those who had a chance to succeed in it, and the farm business would be made profitable and remain so.[23]

The bill proposed a great expansion of research and education in economics in order to develop a successful adjustment program. Costs, prices, techniques of production, farm organizations, land-use practices, present and prospective supply and demand, markets, and other items would be explored, and the great complexity and diversity of American agriculture would be recognized in these explorations. In fact, one of the first tasks of the Secretary of Agriculture under the new program would be to designate the boundaries of the principal production or "type-of-farming" regions in the country. Then the researcher would be able to study the different regions and their relations with one another and with farming regions outside the United States so as to determine the systems of farming that could most profitably use the resources of each region. Furthermore, the recommended systems of farming would be tested under actual farm conditions so as to determine the feasibility of the systems. Finally, to guarantee that increases in research would result in adjustments on the farm, the bill called for an enlarged educational program designed to bring the results of the research to the attention of the farmer.

Established agencies would play important roles in these activities. As individual farmers could not provide for themselves comparable elaborate research staffs and information services that big corporations provided, public agencies had to supply the research and information that farmers needed. With the United States Department of Agriculture, the land-grant colleges, the extension services, and the experiment stations already in operation, the Christgau bill proposed that these agencies would participate in the adjustment program.

The bill, however, had provisions for new as well as old agencies. Some of the experimentation was to be conducted by new regional research corporations of the Fairway type that would be created throughout the country. Other new agencies would implement Wilson's conception of democracy. Regional research and planning councils, staffed by directors of the experiment stations and officials of the BAE, would be set up by the Secretary of Agriculture in each of the principal production regions. Assisting the councils would be advisory boards, composed of representatives of the farmers, cooperatives, processors, distributors, bankers, and the general public. The planning councils, which would "carefully study the outlook facts, both of national and local significance, and develop a production program for the type-of-farming area,"[24] were evidence, as one student of Wilson's activities has pointed out, of the latter's "emphasis on economic democracy through the people participating and growing in understanding of their problems."[25] Planning, Wilson insisted, "must be developed democratically and be brought about by 'the will of the people.' "[26]

Actually, several significant dimensions of the economist's planning theories were revealed in the organizational scheme that the bill envisioned. In addition to the emphasis upon broad participation, the planning program involved a degree of decentralization. Wilson, Russell Lord observed, "did not care for the sort of overhead planning he had seen in Russia" in 1929.[27] Furthermore, the scheme lacked a system of powerful controls. Planning agencies would simply present their program to the farmers and seek to persuade them to fit themselves into it, leaving each farmer free to determine to what extent the program for his type of farm could be applied to his particular farm.[28] Quite optimistically, the planners assumed that good advice would encourage the farmer to change his ways and would enable him to obtain a satisfactory standard of living. "We are still essentially a democratic country, living under a democratic system of government," Christgau explained.

We cannot dictate to the farmers what they shall produce, but we can lead them along certain lines and supply them with information. If we can give the farmers complete information regarding economic problems they will advance as far in economic planning as they have in the techniques of production.[29]

Wilson and Tolley looked upon the bill as a means of extending and revitalizing the outlook program and of converting it into a permanent and effective adjustment program. Existing machinery failed to use all of the agencies and people in the farming regions that could help to make adjustment programs successful. Furthermore, as the outlook had only administrative status, it could easily be killed by administrative action. Lacking confidence in the Hoover Administration, the planners believed that the chances of securing adequate support for an adjustment program would be increased substantially by special legislation.[30] John Black regarded the bill as a very important part in the development of the outlook method and predicted that the method would "grow until some day we shall simply look at it and say: This is the national agricultural policy of the United States."[31]

The Christgau bill focused upon the use of good farm land but suggested that farms in areas of very poor land should be abandoned, and Wilson developed this suggestion in other legislation that he proposed in the early 1930's. His proposal drew heavily upon work in the BAE that had been directed by another Wisconsin-trained economist, Lewis Cecil Gray. Gray had received a Ph.D. degree from that university just before World War I, after studying chiefly with Richard T. Ely and Henry C. Taylor, pioneers in land and agricultural economics. He had come away convinced that government must attack social and economic problems, including problems in the use of natural resources, and that intellectuals must devote themselves to affairs of great importance and interest to people outside the academy, serving in government posts when necessary. He remained in academic posts only until 1919 when he became the first head of the Department of Agriculture's Division of Land Economics, an agency which became part of the Bureau of Agricultural Economics in 1922.

By the beginning of the depression, Gray had rejected both classical economics with its advice to let nature take its course and the nation's traditional emphasis upon expanding the supply of agricultural land and multiplying the number of farms. Instead, he advocated government planning based upon scientific knowledge. The idea that the unrestricted sway of individual competition works out to the maximum advantage of the public, he advised the Chief of the BAE, "has been responsible for the fact that our forests have been wastefully sacrificed, our soils needlessly impaired, and the entire fabric of our rural civilization has come to manifest serious depreciation." He was especially critical of the Bureau of Reclamation and its supporters, who harmed farmers by sustaining the traditional tendency for agriculture to expand more rapidly than the market demand would justify. He proposed a new national land policy involving the coordination of the efforts of all government agencies dealing with the land. "Only by such unity of policy and execution," he insisted, "can ill-considered and excessive expansion and rapid but wasteful utilization be supplanted by deliberate selection, careful economy, and constructive development with due reference to the long-time requirements of the nation." Involved in his proposed system of national land-use planning was a great expansion in the role of scientists, including social scientists, in making decisions about the use of the land.[32]

Wilson's proposed federal land policy bill resembled Gray's suggestions. As the main object of the bill, Wilson listed "a more efficient utilization of all of the lands of the United States but especially those not adapted to private ownership. . . ." The Montana economist called for "a truly national program" that would "develop, clarify and coordinate existing policies and administrative activities of federal agencies dealing with land use" and would coordinate federal and state land policies, leaving to the states and regions matters that they could handle more adequately than the federal government. The latter should take the lead in the development of a national land inventory, various fact-finding surveys, and fundamental research on the national and international implications of land use and should embark upon a nationwide educational program to supplement the scientific activities. The federal government should also cooperate with the states, regions, and local areas in the development and financing of land-use programs, especially in problem areas, transfer control of the public domain to the Department of Agriculture, establish machinery for the administration of that domain in cooperation with state land-use boards, and embark upon a modest program of land acquisition as part of well-developed, long-term regional land programs. In addition, the federal government should coordinate its reclamation and drainage policies in a national land-use program and give direction to land settlement and the "back-to-the-land" movement. Along this line, Wilson proposed that the new land policy bill should begin with repeal of the homestead and other national land laws that enabled individuals to obtain public lands and use them for agricultural purposes. "Certainly the time has arrived," he insisted, "when we must reverse our traditional historic land policy from that of expansion to one of adjustment and perhaps of contraction of the tilled area." [33]

The proposed bills could make the farm business more profitable, but the social scientists hoped to serve more than the interests of established commercial farmers. Wilson and his associates paid some attention to the needs of the rural poor. While Gray believed that withdrawing submarginal land from agriculture would in the long run help to make commercial farming more profitable, he stressed other goals in recommending such a program, including the conversion of poor farmlands to other and better uses and the elevation of the standard of living of the rural poor by removing them from poor farms and resettling them in locations with greater opportunities.

For good farm land, Gray advocated what he termed a democratic system of farm ownership and defined as a wide diffusion of farm ownership. As social and economic forces could no longer be counted upon to preserve such a system, he called for new policies deliberately designed to insure the maintenance of a democratic system of tenure.[34]

Wilson's list of proposals included the decentralization of industry and subsistence farming. He believed that many farmers on poor land and unemployed wage earners in the city should be provided with part-time farms and jobs in new industries. He looked upon the large industrial cities as "failures" in which the working people had "lost security and the opportunity for the constructive use of their leisure time." The Mormon villages of Utah provided a desirable alternative. Thus, he advocated the decentralization of industry and the development of a new type of suburban industrial community in which people lived on small plots of land that would provide much of their food and worked in factories to produce industrial goods for sale. As he saw this proposal, it could provide people with the security that had been destroyed by the machine age and with opportunities for the use of their leisure time, and it could provide the nation with a large part of the answer to the problems of relief and unemployment. He hoped that his suggestion could "offer to a great group of people who now seem to be stranded in the present industrial city or on hopeless submarginal land, the opportunity of dignified, wholesome, abundant living." Behind the suggestion lay assumptions about the "psychological and philosophical values which attach to the soil" and the superiority of rural life.

Although Wilson placed a high value on contact with the soil, he wished to avoid an increase in the number of commercial farmers. The people in his proposed "subsistence homesteads" would not become commercial farmers but would earn their money in industrial pursuits. There were limitations on the amount of food people could consume, Wilson pointed out, but none on industrial products. Thus to live abundantly people must be able to produce abundantly those things which can be consumed abundantly.

Wilson denied that his proposal represented a retreat from the age of machinery and science. In fact, products of that age, such as electricity and the automobile, would provide bases for the type of community he planned and would enable one to spread over a ten- or fifteen-mile area. He criticized those agrarians who advocated the reorganization of rural America into a system of small, nearly self-sufficient farms involving little use of science and machinery. On the other hand, he criticized those who would reorganize agriculture in such a way as to close rural America to all but commercial farmers who would operate only the best lands and employ the most scientific and efficient methods. While he hoped for a commercial agriculture that would be organized and operated in these ways, he envisioned a rural America containing other patterns of life as well. All of the ways would employ science and machinery, but some of them would not involve the production of farm products for commercial purposes and would place their emphasis upon security and the cultural and spiritual aspects of life.[35]

Although proposals such as these could change rural America, they seemed unlikely to produce the change that most interested commercial farmers in the early 1930's: a quick rise in the prices of farm products. By 1932, Wilson had another plan — the Voluntary Domestic Allotment Plan — that he believed could accomplish this price increase. The plan rejected proposals of farm groups of an earlier day designed to change the practices of big business[36] and called upon farmers to imitate one of the methods of the most successful businessmen. The method was production control, and the goal was higher and more stable prices for the commercial farmer, the rural businessman. To accomplish these things, the power of government was to be brought to the aid of the farmer, helping him to behave as many urban business leaders had been behaving for more than a generation and to establish a profitable balance between supply and demand.

Social scientists, not farm groups nor political leaders, produced this scheme for farm relief. In fact, the creators of the allotment plan were influenced by a sense of the inadequacies of the main programs of the farm groups and the Hoover Administration. Before Wilson began to devote a good deal of attention to the plan, two of his friends — Spillman of the BAE and Black of Harvard — played the major roles in the development of it, publishing their suggestions in Spillman's *Balancing the Farm Output* (1927) and in Black's *Agricultural Reform in the United States* (1929).

After the general depression hit and Hoover's Farm Board failed to check the flood of commodities flowing from the nation's farms, Wilson became the leading advocate of the allotment plan. Under his leadership and with help from other economists, especially Black,

Tolley, and Mordecai Ezekiel, and also from men in the legal profession and the business world, including Stanley Reed, the Solicitor for the Farm Board, and Henry I. Harriman, a Boston businessman, the scheme moved beyond the versions contained in the Spillman and Black books, adding new ways to control production and to finance and administer the program. The revisions bore the imprint of Wilson's pragmatic mind. During the 1920's, he had often discussed Spillman's and Black's ideas with those economists and others, and in 1929 he had taken a trip to Russia to advise the Russians on large-scale, mechanized agriculture. His observations had strengthened his concern about the declining opportunities in European markets for American farmers and his doubts about the McNary-Haugen plan that he had supported earlier. This plan, the leading farm relief proposal of the 1920's, promised to solve the economic problems of the American farmer by dumping his surplus crops in foreign markets. Now, in the early 1930's, convinced that such a plan could not work in a world in which Russians and others were expanding farm production and European countries were building trade barriers against American farm products, Wilson looked for effective ways of reducing agricultural production, especially in the wheat country that he knew so well.[37]

Wilson concluded that, to solve the farmer's problems, government needed to do more than conduct educational campaigns in rural America. It needed to employ new means of enabling farmers to adjust production to effective demand as industrialists did. At the same time, farmers should not rely solely upon the federal government. In giving thought to the means of administering the program, Wilson drew upon his own experiences of working closely with farmers, including his efforts to organize them into farm bureaus and seed loan committees, and upon programs of close cooperation between government and farm cooperatives that John R. Commons had discussed with Wilson and that he had seen in operation in Saskatchewan. In addition, late in 1931 he learned of the techniques of an imaginative tax assessor in a Montana county. They strengthened the economist's conviction that farmers should have an important part in administration. Therefore, he suggested that the producers of each commodity, after holding meetings in their communities to discuss the situation, should vote to determine whether or not a production plan should be applied to the commodity. Following an affirmative vote, farmer committees, elected by the cooperating farmers, should be formed in the counties to decide upon the allotment for each producer, dividing allotments that had been devised by federal officials for the state and by state officials for the counties. Later the committees would check up on the performance of the participants.[38]

These features of Wilson's proposal differed significantly from the administrative arrangements outlined by Spillman and Black, and to Wilson the differences represented improvements of great value. They involved a system of administration that was decentralized, non-bureaucratic, and democratic and a new system of cooperation — co-operation between government and the farmers. A chain of authority would run in a two-way direction between Washington and the farm. Implied also was increased cooperation between economists serving in the federal government and the agricultural colleges and farmers. They would help one another make informed judgments as to what was necessary, desirable, and possible in agricultural policy.[39] These mechanisms resembled the aspects of the Christgau bill that reflected Wilson's democratic values.

Although these values played a part in Wilson's proposal, its chief aim was improvement in the business situation of the farmer. Like Spillman and Black, he believed that schemes like the McNary-Haugen plan contained a fatal flaw. Failing to think of anything more than raising farm prices, they would stimulate production and thus worsen the farmer's situation. In the early 1930's, severe reductions in demand for American agricultural products made reductions in output necessary. In the existing situation, production should be limited to the effective demands of the domestic and foreign markets and no efforts should be made to dump surpluses abroad, for dumping would force other countries to push their tariff walls even higher. "From a theoretical standpoint," Wilson suggested,

the solution of the farm surplus problem lies in the restoration and development of international trade and in the modification and reduction of all tariffs. An economic dictator might accomplish this, but we in the United States have now gone so far along the isolation route that it will take some time to slacken the speed, reverse the engines, and begin to move in the opposite direction. Until we can move in the other direction, we must think about a new balance between supplies and demands for the exportable commodities or, if you please, production control.

Wilson hoped that a national policy of tariff adjustment would be enacted and that the present emergency would only be of two or three years' duration. But if nationalism persisted in Europe and America, it might be necessary to continue the domestic allotment plan as a more or less semi-permanent institution.[40] That plan would regulate production in such a way as to "supply the domestic needs" and "export in the world markets an amount which can be sold to an advantage."[41]

The existing situation demanded production control, and the alternatives to the allotment plan struck Wilson as incapable of meeting the demands of the situation effectively. These alternatives included the Spillman-Black proposals and also the efforts by the Hoover Administration to encourage farmers to reduce output, efforts that emphasized persuasion and rejected stronger methods of control. Secretary Hyde, for example, regarded the adjustment of production to market requirements as the fundamental need of American agriculture. He urged the farmer to imitate the practice of successful industrialists. ". . . the United States Steel Company was built up and grew out of exactly the same conditions which afflict agriculture now," he informed one farmer. "If you, and such as you, would get in line and do for yourselves what industry does for itself by bringing your industry and your application within the beneficial application of the law of supply and demand, profits could be secured."[42] Adjustments had to be voluntary. "There exists no power in the government or elsewhere" to compel the farmer, Hyde insisted. "Indeed there ought not to be any power to compel him."[43] The chief role of the government was to supply advice to farmers so that they could devise sound production plans.

Although Hyde adhered to the voluntary method, he lacked complete confidence in it. He recognized that there were "direct methods of enforcing cooperation which would go to the heart of the problem," but he doubted that the country could afford to use them. "What will have happened to our theories and principles of government, to all of our ideas of liberty and freedom of action when we have got to the point of telling a farmer he shall not cultivate more than fifty per cent of his land?" Hoover's lieutenant asked. Recognizing "the undoubted public good of a balanced production and a long train of human betterment that will follow it," he wavered, but he held to the position "that balanced production must be attained by voluntary association of farmers in their own organizations. . . ."[44]

Wilson proposed that the government do more than talk to the farmers. It should employ its taxing and spending powers to promote reductions in output. His plan involved a tax on farm commodities to be paid by the processors when they handled those products and to be used to finance a system of payments to farmers who agreed to adjust production. Each farmer would be free to refuse to participate in the program but would be encouraged to participate not merely by the promise of higher prices in the market but by payments to him from the government.[45] The plan, in short, clearly advocated production control and sought to provide more effective means of accomplishing this than the Hoover Administration advocated. At the same time, Wilson's plan avoided the legal compulsion involved in some of the production plans being proposed at the time.[46]

Even the allotment plan had certain major weaknesses from Wilson's point of view. He admitted that it could "retard adjustments which are more or less inevitable."[47] By simply proposing general reductions in acreage, the plan did not guarantee that the most efficient use would be made out of the land. The Montana economist insisted that ultimately production should be upon the best land and in the area of greatest comparative advantage.[48] This farm relief scheme, in other words, shared a basic weakness of the Farm Board's adjustment program. Thus the allotment plan did not have wide support from economists.[49] They were more enthusiastic about the Christgau bill, which one of them termed a valuable beginning in the development of collective engineering.[50]

Wilson believed that the bad tendencies of the plan could be offset in time by agricultural planning as proposed by the Christgau bill and a new land policy bill.[51] In fact, he assumed that the farm relief scheme could lead to these other programs. As the scheme appeared to offer a quick and effective way to raise prices, it had a chance to gain support from groups that were interested in farm relief. By calling upon the farmers to reduce the acreage that they devoted to certain crops, the plan offered a way to "stimulate a great lot of discussion and talk about planning and agricultural readjustment."[52] Wilson was particularly interested in the plan because he believed it would stimulate thought in the matter of production adjustments as no other proposal had.[53] "My personal scheme," Wilson informed Ezekiel early in 1932, "is to throw allotment in with the expectation that it will get a good emotional response and act as a cat's paw which at least will drag into the discussion the principles of the Christgau bill and a new land policy bill."[54]

Social scientists had developed a scheme to get farmers to imitate the practices of successful businessmen. A genuine interest in making the business of farming profitable was, however, only one of the motives of the men who developed the allotment plan. They hoped that it would lead to more complex programs that would make rural life more scientific and more democratic as well as more profitable.

Although historians have paid much attention to the allotment plan and to the Montana economist's role in shaping and promoting it, they have failed to point out that he had important reservations about the plan and that he valued it, in part, because it seemed to open the way for the long-range programs in which he had greater confidence.[55] The Christgau bill indicated, as Russell Lord has written, "that Wilson's principal initial interest in farm legislation was not simply to raise farm income; he saw it primarily as a device for national planning, with the people participating and growing in understanding on a grand scale."[56] Wilson and Tolley did hope to raise farm income and make farming profitable. But as scientific students of agriculture, they could not rely upon any conceivable device to accomplish this purpose. The social scientists wanted to employ methods that would also promote a more efficient use of the land. Furthermore, they did not believe that scientists could nor should simply dictate how the land would be used. Influenced by democratic themes in their culture, these social scientists concluded that the nation needed to develop new machinery that would bring scientists and other people together in the planning process.

CHAPTER 2

Building
Support

To fulfill their ambitions, Wilson and his associates needed to gain support for their proposals from men of power in farm politics, including the leaders of pressure groups as well as the politicians. Wilson played the leading role in the efforts to build support, revealing as he proceeded that he was not an ivory tower intellectual and that he could operate skillfully in the political arena. His activities there also indicated that the organized commercial farmers were not the only group interested in farm relief. Certain urban business groups shared that interest. In fact, during the early months of Wilson's campaign for the allotment plan, he had greater success with businessmen than with farm leaders. Most important, however, he established ties with the man who was moving rapidly to the center of the American political stage, Franklin D. Roosevelt.

Beginning in 1930, Wilson, along with Tolley, Christgau, Black, and Ezekiel, campaigned for the Christgau bill. Aware of the growing interest in planning and agricultural adjustment, they hoped to tap that interest and provide direction for it. Convinced that only planning, not "laissez-faire or the old methods" could "give all of the population of the United States plenty of food and clothing and give every farmer on the land the minimum standard of living, security and comforts which are included in a healthful family budget," Wilson welcomed the "new and vital interest" in planning. He pointed out, however, that most of the talk about it failed to provide specific proposals on methods. "As yet," he suggested in 1931, "the only definite specific proposals with which I am acquainted are those based on the philosophy which Mr. Tolley outlined a year ago and the procedure described in the Christgau bill." [1] The campaign did produce interest in the bill among some groups, including the United States Chamber of Commerce,[2] but not enough to secure passage of it. In 1932 Christgau introduced it once again, but, as in 1930, Congress failed even to give it a hearing.

What the social scientists needed first of all was to sell their proposal that was designed to provide a quick solution to the business problems of agricultural interests. That proposal was, of course, the allotment plan. An obstacle in Wilson's path, however, was the commitment of the leading farm organizations to schemes that he was criticizing as unrealistic ways of dealing with the problem of low farm prices. In early 1932, the American Farm Bureau Federation supported the McNary-Haugen plan; the National Grange, the export debenture plan; and the National Farmers Union, a scheme to ensure to the farmer cost of production plus a reasonable profit.

At this time, Wilson had support from only one small farm organization, the Montana Farm Bureau Federation, but he worked hard to "get hooked up with the National Farm Bureau and the National Grange." [3] Operating shrewdly, he stressed the support from the Montana group in order to make his plan appear as the proposal of "a group of farmers, not an academic college professor." [4] Actually, however, he had persuaded the group to endorse the plan.[5] The organization's leader, W. L. Stockton, a former advocate of McNary-Haugen who had been converted by Wilson, worked closely with him, campaigned strenuously for the plan in the wheat country, attempted to get the national organization to back the plan, and proposed and sent out the invitations to an important meeting in Chicago on April 19, 1932, that discussed the plan and took steps designed to gain support for it. Wilson hoped to work through the farm organizations as much as possible, so that they would not feel that his group sought to get around them. He believed that, if farm representatives attended the Chicago meeting, the public would regard the bill as a farm relief measure that had been developed by farmers and had gained support from other interests.[6] In writing to the leaders of the Grange and the Farm Bureau in April, he explained:

the economists are anxious to be of the greatest public service to the leaders of the farm organizations and we naturally think we can be of much more service to them in the future than we have been in the past if we could get the proper hook-up.[7]

The farm leaders, however, did not appear eager to make "the proper hook-up" and were "conspicuous by their absence" from the Chicago meeting.[8]

Wilson seemed to threaten further weakening of the farm forces. Hurt by the difficulties they had in agreeing upon a farm plan, farm leaders were struggling to achieve unity in the political arena, and they feared that Wilson would promote disunity. To Earl Smith, the president of the most powerful of the state farm bureaus, the Illinois Agricultural Association, it seemed that the allotment plan would "only operate to bring forth more confusion rather than the much needed crystallization of sincere thought" behind the McNary-Haugen plan.[9]

Furthermore, farm leaders like Smith and George Peek, a leader in the development and promotion of the McNary-Haugen plan, had doubts that Wilson's plan could operate effectively. In addition to their doubts about the possibility and desirability of controlling production, these leaders argued that the machinery to administer the plan was much too cumbersome and complicated. Schemes that promised to raise farm prices without calling upon the farmer to change his practices avoided these difficulties.[10] As Wilson had indeed given special attention to administrative problems, these criticisms troubled him, and he attempted to persuade Farm Bureau leaders that his novel scheme for decentralized administration would work.[11] Other advocates of the plan joined him in these efforts to gain support from the farm leaders.[12] Success, however, eluded the Wilson group during most of 1932. This hampered their efforts to get support from Congress for the plan.[13]

Although Wilson's failure to gain support from farm leaders complicated the task of interesting other people in his plan, he did obtain significant support from leading businessmen who advocated farm relief as a means of promoting economic recovery and of preventing farmers from moving in radical political directions. Both economic and political motives were at work. "You would be surprised," Wilson informed another economist, "how much the business interests are now het up over so-called farm relief." As a result, the promoters of the allotment plan were "in a position . . . to bring in a certain type of businessman in the east which was not the case in the McNary-Haugen fight."[14] That fight had helped to acquaint such businessmen with farm problems and with the need for action to deal with them.[15] Vigorous criticism of groups like the United States Chamber of Commerce by leaders in the Hoover Administration as well as by farm organizations also put pressure on business leaders to break with their negative attitude toward farm relief schemes and to demonstrate an interest in finding solutions to farm problems.[16]

Some business leaders liked Wilson's suggestion that farmers should imitate industrialists by controlling production, a much more attractive proposal to them than the traditional agrarian demands for "trust-busting" that reflected a fear of business power and insisted that business leaders change their ways.[17] No doubt Wilson's "practical experience," his ability to speak in nonacademic terms, and his hostility toward radical critics of the business system helped him in developing good relations with business leaders.[18] Stockton's close ties with Gerard Swope of General Electric, a leading advocate of economic planning, also contributed to the growth of support among important industrialists for the allotment plan.[19] Walter McCarthy of the Capitol Elevator Company of Duluth financed the reprinting of Black's discussion of the plan, which provided wide publicity for it and generated interest in it among a number of business groups.[20] McCarthy, Henry I. Harriman, George and Burton Peek of the farm machinery industry, Louis S. Clarke, the president of the Nebraska Mortgage Bankers Association, R. R. Rogers, the assistant secretary of the Prudential Life Insurance Company, and H. G. Harrison, an Omaha representative of Prudential, participated in the Chicago meeting; and Rogers and Clarke served on the five-man committee established by the meeting to gain support for the plan.[21] A number of other business leaders and groups, which, as Wilson explained, had "a little money" and were "vitally dependent upon the farmer's income,"[22] were drawn into the campaign.[23]

Although many business leaders helped, Harriman and Rogers were Wilson's most important allies in the business world. Harriman, the chairman of the board of the New England Power Association, the owner of a large Montana ranch, and, beginning in May, 1932, the president of the United States Chamber of Commerce, rallied behind the allotment plan because of his economic position and his general ideas about ways of dealing with the depression. He and Wilson had met in 1930 after the economist addressed the agricultural committee of the chamber, and soon Wilson became a member of that committee.[24] The businessman shared the professor's interest in Montana farm land, and Wilson could appeal to Harriman's concern about the distressed condition of his farm holdings besides the more general factors that interested many businessmen: the apparent ability of the plan to restore agricultural purchasing power and to prevent the growth of agrarian radicalism.[25] Furthermore, the plan harmonized with the general ideas on economic planning that Harriman and some other businessmen were pushing in 1932. "If you have given much study to the various types of national planning that are put before the country," Wilson wrote to another economist,

you will see that there is a great similarity between the Domestic Allotment proposal and the proposal of the National Chamber of Commerce and Swope. In other words the Domestic Allotment is proposing to do in agriculture about what those plans propose to do in industry. It is for this reason that the men like Mr. Harriman of the National Chamber of Commerce Committee on Continuity and Stability, are very much interested in the Domestic Allotment Plan.

Harriman hoped to root out remnants of individualism in the business world, organize it more completely, and establish central control of production and prices. Wilson emphasized the organization of farmers into committees for the administration of the allotment plan; Harriman advocated the organization of businessmen into trade associations. Involved in his proposal were modifications of the antitrust laws so that they would cease to hamper efforts at collective action.[26]

Harriman shared Wilson's misgivings about the other farm relief proposals. Believing such proposals would only produce higher tariffs abroad, Harriman hoped that farm leaders could be persuaded to drop their own pet schemes and to unite behind the production control program. "What we need," he insisted, "is . . . a plan which will substantially balance production and consumption to the home requirement with, of course, such exports as can be properly made under world conditions at fair prices." Besides endorsing the allotment plan, Harriman also endorsed the economist's ideas on retiring submarginal lands, restricting reclamation, and closing government lands to homesteaders.[27]

In seeking to sell the allotment plan, Harriman functioned as an energetic liaison between agriculture and industry and between East and West.[28] Among other matters, he helped Wilson to develop closer working relations with and a substantial amount of support from the Chamber of Commerce. While serving on the organization's agricultural committees, Wilson worked closely during 1932 and early 1933 with farm leaders like Earl Smith and with many business leaders interested in agriculture, including Robert E. Wood of Sears, Roebuck and Company, a vigorous participant in farm politics, who looked upon farm purchasing power as a factor of basic importance and worked to promote cooperation between businessmen and farmers. Wilson "greatly admired" Wood's attitude on agricultural problems, believing he had "grasped the relationship between agriculture and industry much more clearly than most businessmen in the country." [29]

Rogers of Prudential played a role second only to Harriman's among the businessmen behind Wilson. This "spokesman of the life insurance interests" provided most of the money behind Wilson's efforts to influence politicians and pressure groups, brought him into contact with other insurance men and bankers, and battled against other businessmen who opposed the plan. The Montana college professor and the New Jersey businessman admired each other's contributions to the growth of support for the crop control scheme.[30]

Rogers' interest in farm relief grew out of his role in the life insurance industry. Having learned of Wilson's work in Montana and in Russia and having become acquainted with him while both were serving on the agricultural committee of the chamber, the businessman had turned to the economist for advice when the depression hit the insurance companies, then the dominant source of farm mortgage money.[31] "I understand that the fifteen largest life insurance companies have $1,400,000,000 invested in farm loans," Wilson informed a friend. Thus they had "some little interest in what is prosaically called the agricultural situation." [32] (One executive of a Minnesota insurance company campaigned for the plan from "Canada to the Gulf and Coast to Coast.") [33] The companies, with Rogers as their leading spokesman on farm matters, sought a solution to the farm problem that would solve the problem of the companies and accomplish this "without disrupting still further our entire economic structure. . . ." [34]

Wilson recognized that worries among the life insurance people would give him a chance to gain significant support. In warning Rogers and others of the possibility of debt repudiation, Wilson suggested that they must support a farm program in order to avoid this. "It is perfectly clear," he advised Rogers in the summer of 1932, "that we must have elevation in prices or else we are going to have debt repudiation on a scale which will ruin the moral fiber of millions of people and terribly disrupt if not ruin the financial structure." [35] And the professor continued to fear and warn of "a great growth of debt repudiation and general economic disorganization unless something can be done reasonably soon." [36] Thus he pictured the allotment plan as a device that could improve the economic situation of these businessmen and prevent radical behavior by the farmers. Simultaneously, he worked to get farm and political leaders to accept the insurance executive's argument that efforts should be made to raise farm prices so that the farmer could pay his debts and could avoid repudiation and demands upon government for loans at low interest rates. [37] In short, Wilson regarded his plan as capable of uniting major groups in rural and urban America.

While Wilson's relations with these business leaders indicated that at least one intellectual knew how to get along with such people, he did not gain as much support from them as he had hoped to receive. In large part because of Wilson's difficulties with the farm organizations, Rogers could not get as much money as the promoters felt they needed. [38] Many businessmen seemed reluctant to jeopardize the possibility of cooperation between farm and business organizations by appearing to push a farm program in which farm groups had little interest. In the insurance companies, many men waited for farm groups, particularly the Farm Bureau, to endorse the plan. [39]

To complicate Wilson's political problems still more, the support that he did have from business leaders hampered his efforts to obtain help from the farm groups. Still believing that if they were united in support of the plan "they could send it over in a whoop," [40] he learned that they were "passing rather bad stories . . . to the effect that this plan came from the National Chamber of Commerce, the big insurance companies, Wall Street and so forth." [41] Even George Peek, a Midwestern businessman who had become a farm leader, feared that Wilson had been influenced too much by Eastern industrialists and

financiers. "I imagine from what I read in the papers," Peek wrote
to a close associate, "that those groups are pretty well discredited
in Washington and I hope that M. L. [Wilson] will not be too much
influenced by them although we should all welcome their cooperation." [42] And some of the leaders of the Farm Bureau, a group that
had often cooperated with business groups, expressed traditional
agrarian doubts about the wisdom of allowing business leaders to
play a major role in the formation of farm policy.[43] The "heir of
agrarian radicalism," the Farmers Union, voiced even stronger opposition to Wilson and his associates. The group distrusted his academic position as it had doubts about the political orientation of
the agricultural colleges, doubts that seemed to be confirmed by his
ties with big businessmen. As John A. Simpson, the fiery president
of the organization, wrote to one of Wilson's colleagues:

I deny the right to any except farm organizations to offer plans to solve farmers' problems. I resent it as an insult by those offering it in assuming that
farmers do not have sufficient intelligence to know what they need. I believe
you are sincere in the matter, but I do not believe Wilson is. I think he is
financed by big business.[44]

And Simpson warned Franklin Roosevelt that the allotment plan
was "a United States Chamber of Commerce scheme to muddy the
water." [45]

Quite obviously, as Wilson recognized, his political situation was
extremely complex. Some friction prevailed in the relations between
farm and business groups, with certain business leaders — somewhat
unsure about their political and economic future and rather sophisticated in their approach to politics — more interested in cultivating
farm support than farm leaders were in seeking political aid from
businessmen. Wilson had feared that his urban ties might antagonize
rural leaders, but he saw businessmen as the only leaders not committed to other farm proposals and the only ones in 1932 with the
money needed to finance a campaign for a new one.[46]

Not all businessmen welcomed Wilson's efforts. The processors
and distributors, who had large sums invested in facilities designed
to handle farm products, opposed the idea of cutting back on farm
production and feared the impact of the processing tax on their businesses. Thus, the millers, grain traders, meat packers, and cotton
dealers and manufacturers quickly became the most vocal and vigorous opponents of the allotment plan. Some of them emphasized
plans for the expansion of sales, suggesting that the government

should stop its efforts to promote higher farm prices; it should allow
prices to drop and should either work to reduce barriers to international trade or dump products abroad. Some also advocated a program of marketing agreements that would exempt processors from
the antitrust statutes, enable them to work out agreements to pay
higher prices to farmers, and allow these businessmen to enlarge their
profits by charging consumers higher prices.[47]

These hostile groups attacked both the professors and the businessmen who promoted the plan. The attack upon the first group
challenged one of their basic assumptions, the assumption that intellectuals could be "practical" men, and employed a theory that ex-
alted businessmen. Harriman and other businessmen were advised
to rely upon those who had "spent their lives in the accumulation of
expert knowledge of the handling, processing and marketing of the
country's grain crops — those engaged in the highly specialized business of grain marketing, and who know most about it" and to reject
"theories evolved by pedagogues who are undoubtedly sincere in their
intentions and beliefs but who are without practical experience in
handling grain, nor are possessed of any comprehension of the diver-
gence from theory involved in the actual transaction of business of
this kind."[48] The attack also appealed to theories concerning the
proper relations between government and business. "It appears in-
consistent to us," the president of the Millers' National Federation
wrote to Harriman,

that you, either as an individual or as president of the U. S. Chamber of Commerce, an organization definitely committed to a policy opposed to Government interference with business, should sponsor directly or indirectly such
a radical plan contrary to those principles for which the United States Chamber of Commerce stands.[49]

Harriman, according to these critics, not only departed from the
traditions of the chamber but also packed one of its special committees with champions of the allotment plan in hopes of forcing the
organization to endorse it.[50]

These critics troubled Wilson. They had political power; they
kept alive the charge that the plan would be difficult, if not impossible, to administer; and they raised the troublesome claim that the
plan was unconstitutional because it would tax processors (and ultimately consumers) in order to pay producers. Wilson tried to convince these businessmen that his was the most conservative and
constructive of the proposed solutions to the farm problem.

At the same time, the attacks by the processors and distributors contained some benefits for Wilson. As these "middlemen" had for years been distrusted by the farmer, their attacks on the allotment plan and its supporters created problems for those who tried to make it appear to be a "Wall Street" scheme to prevent the farmers from getting a workable program.[51]

At the same time that Wilson worked in the complex world of pressure-group politics, he also dealt directly with the politicians who could translate his proposals into law. Although the Hoover Administration accepted the suggestions of some social scientists, its leaders did not give much encouragement to him. In November, 1931, the Administration, following advice from Gray, had sponsored a National Conference on Land Utilization that made recommendations resembling proposals he had been making for several years. One product of the conference was a National Land-Use Planning Committee. As executive secretary, Gray played the major role in the work of the committee, and it publicized the point of view and doctrines that he had developed. Many members of the Administration, including the President, hoped to put the committee's ideas into action. Hoover persuaded the Republicans to include in their platform a plank concerning submarginal lands, and during the campaign, he promised to support the program. Speaking in Des Moines, Iowa, he called attention to the research on land-use problems in the Department of Agriculture and to the subsequent conference that had been called "to formulate practical means of action." "The broad objective of such a program," the campaigner explained, "is to promote the reorganization of agriculture so as to divert lands from unprofitable to profitable use, and to avoid the cultivation of lands the chief return of which is the poverty and misery of those who live on them."[52]

The Hoover Administration did not demonstrate the same enthusiasm for the Christgau bill. In fact, the Administration was moving in the opposite direction from the one that the bill proposed. At the National Conference on Land Utilization, Tolley had publicly denounced the 1931 outlook reports as "woefully lacking in information that will be helpful in planning production" and as "outlook reports in name only."[53] Black and Ezekiel also criticized the outlook for departing from the practices that had developed under Tolley's leadership;[54] Congressman Christgau suggested that someone "higher up," not the BAE, had forced the change in practices; an editorial in *Wallaces' Farmer* pinned the blame on an old enemy of the Wallaces, Herbert

Hoover.[55] The President and other leaders in the Administration, disturbed by pessimistic forecasts from the BAE that contradicted optimistic pronouncements from the White House, had placed restrictions upon the program.[56] As the small program of the early 1930's had upset the Administration, it could not be expected to develop an interest in a bill that proposed a vast expansion of the outlook.

Proponents of the allotment plan tried to get the Hoover Administration to endorse it. They stressed its links with the Administration's efforts to curtail production and the need to check the revolt of the Midwestern farmers against the Republican party. Wilson received a great deal of encouragement from the chairman of the Farm Board, James Stone, and a small amount from the Republican platform, which contained a cautious plea for production control.[57]

Two Republican congressmen now added to Wilson's list of accomplishments. The April meeting in Chicago had established a committee composed of Louis S. Clarke, Rogers, W. R. Ronald, the editor of the Mitchell, South Dakota, *Evening Republican*, Henry A. Wallace, and Wilson, with the latter selected as chairman. The committee devoted most of its attention to efforts to sell the plan in Washington and in Congress. Helped especially by Ronald's friend Senator Peter Norbeck, a South Dakota Republican, Wilson was able to explain his plan to congressmen. Assisted by Ezekiel and Black and the legislative drafting bureaus of the House and Senate, Wilson prepared a bill that was introduced early in July by Norbeck and Representative Clifford Hope, a Republican from the Kansas wheat region.[58] Both Hope and Norbeck praised Wilson for his work on the plan, which they regarded as superior to its competitors, and stressed the need for production control and the Wilsonian means of accomplishing it. In discussing the measure before the House and Senate, these congressmen emphasized the similarity between the proposal and long-established practices in industry and exaggerated the amount of support that the plan had from farm organizations.[59] Although Congress failed to take action on the Hope-Norbeck bills, Wilson was not disappointed, for he regarded them as educational bills that had helped him to "preempt a little of the field of farm legislation and begin to get national consideration along with other farm relief plans."[60]

President Hoover, however, dashed whatever hopes Wilson had for support from the Administration. He announced in his acceptance speech that he would oppose any farm relief plans involving subsidies and bureaucratic control of production, and he rejected advice that he endorse the plan in his major campaign speech on farm policy. He had frequently urged farmers to reduce their production, but he feared any methods of promoting this, other than advice and persuasion.[61] "The President absolutely refused to accept proposals by which farmers would be forced to reduce production," two of his lieutenants have written. "To him this meant sheer Fascism." He placed the allotment plan in this category.[62]

Franklin Roosevelt proved more receptive. He had already developed the habit of drawing upon intellectuals for advice, including advice on the kinds of questions that most interested Wilson. Influenced by the conservation movement during the Progressive period, FDR had developed an interest in promoting changes in land-use practices, and as governor of New York, he developed an ambitious land program. One of Wilson's teachers, Professor George F. Warren of Cornell, a pioneer in farm management and agricultural economics, played a leading role in these efforts to plan the use of the land. Roosevelt was, one student of his thought has suggested, "more interested in regional planning and a long-range program for agricultural betterment than he was in the short-run problems of depression relief for farmers."[63] So was Wilson, and he responded enthusiastically to Roosevelt's work. The economist regarded the Governor's speech to the 1931 Conference of Governors as the "most striking and . . . as far as public opinion is concerned, one of the most important statements that has yet been made on *planning*. . . ." Wilson viewed the work that Warren and his colleagues were doing for Roosevelt as "almost identical" to the type of program that Tolley and he were advocating, and he had confidence that the Governor would be willing to "go the limit" in the readjustment of farms and the retirement of submarginal land.[64] In March, 1932, Wilson wrote to Roosevelt, praising his pamphlet *Acres Fit and Unfit* as "a classic in its line" and asking that copies of it be provided for the Montana groups that were meeting frequently to discuss land utilization.[65] A month later, in a nationwide radio speech advocating land-use planning, Wilson applauded New York's efforts.[66]

Roosevelt reflected his belief in the value of intellectuals by forming his "brain trust" to help him with his campaign for the Presidency. The leader of this group, Raymond Moley, recognized a similarity between production control in agriculture and his own general interest in economic planning; and thus, although his point of view and experience were largely urban, he played a very important part in shaping the ideas on agricultural policy that Roosevelt presented to the nation in 1932. Moley's most important contribution here was in reducing the candidate's dependence on Cornell economists and in replacing them with an economist from Columbia, Rexford Guy Tugwell, as top adviser on farm relief. The Cornell group emphasized monetary reform as the chief means of raising farm prices; Tugwell introduced Roosevelt to Wilson and his production control scheme.[67]

Roosevelt's political beliefs and procedures, however, meant that an intellectual needed more than a chance to advise a candidate in order to sell a program. While the farm groups pressed FDR to accept schemes promising higher prices without demanding any changes in farm operations, he hesitated to supply the farmers with a plan and announced that he would accept any one upon which the farm leaders could agree.[68]

Tugwell had little confidence in these leaders and protested against this willingness to follow them in a rather passive fashion. He believed they could not invent anything new and could agree only on a farmer-biased piece of legislation, and he advised Roosevelt to first adopt a plan and then get the farm groups to support it by presenting it as a means of escaping the political weaknesses resulting from disunity.[69] Although Tugwell had been born on a farm in western New York, he was an outsider in the world of farm politics. Having joined the march to the city, he received his education and taught chiefly in eastern private universities, Pennsylvania and Columbia, rather than in land-grant colleges. His lack of confidence in farm groups extended to those colleges and their extension services, agencies that seemed to be identified with upper-class groups in rural America.[70]

Tugwell disliked the agrarian philosophy that many farmers and farm leaders endorsed.[71] They talked of the fundamental importance of agriculture and the superiority of agriculture as a way of life; he insisted that the United States had become fundamentally an industrial nation, and he did not regret the change. In fact, he talked of absorbing "a very large number of persons from farms into our general industrial and urban life."[72] He had been thrilled by the tremendous increase in the productive capacity of American industry during the 1920's. His major book during that decade, *Industry's Coming of Age*, sought to explain this development. Referring to it enthusiastically as the "Second Industrial Revolution," he wrote:

We are merely bringing to bear in industry a combination of common sense, inherited processes and inventions, and heightened human efforts, such as never existed in any other time. It is of utmost moment that all intelligent persons should concern themselves not only with the encouragement and furthering of this already appearing trend but should assist in controlling its direction and results in the interest of human welfare.[73]

Again and again he advised men to cooperate with rather than oppose the growth of industry. "Industry can lay the basis for any higher life; and no higher life can be built without an industrial basis," the future Assistant Secretary of Agriculture had written in the 1920's; ". . . it can free mankind for whatever life seems to men most good."[74]

Although Tugwell's philosophy had this urban industrial cast, it was not designed to comfort the urban businessmen. In fact, he believed they had failed as leaders of the American economy and should be replaced as leaders by economists who would "say what the economic system of America can and should do and . . . point the true path toward new goals."[75] Rejecting classical economics and disliking classical economists, he admired economists who participated in politics and who did so with confidence in the ability of government to plan the economic development of the nation. "It cannot be said that I have neglected my first real opportunity to join in social experimentation," he wrote in his diary late in 1932. Because he believed industrial advance made some form of collectivism necessary, he advocated economic planning by the national government with a strong system of controls. He castigated the business leaders and the individualistic philosophies that stood in the way of the establishment of national economic planning.[76]

Tugwell, like Wilson and Tolley, had become a leading advocate of economic planning during the 1920's and early 1930's. Influenced by Simon Nelson Patten, Thorstein Veblen, and John Dewey, the Columbia economist had reached the conclusion that economic planning involving government controls offered the only way to derive the maximum benefits from industrialism. Planning would carry the consolidation or coordination process to its logical conclusion and would enable industry to run more smoothly than it did under business control. Planning, as he viewed it, required strong control of investment and of prices so as to balance production and consumption. Only planning, not competition, could achieve this balance; government officials, not corporation executives, could provide the planning that was needed.[77] The ideas that Tugwell brought into politics implied, as he defined them, "a harsh, relentless discipline . . . a heavy hand had to be laid on the very citadel of faith — business — and . . . it had to be rigorously directed and disciplined."[78]

As to agriculture, Tugwell believed that fundamental changes had to be made. To accomplish them, the country could not depend upon "the clumsy mechanisms of unregulated price determination" nor upon "the ordinary business system of rewards and penalties" because of the "unresponsiveness of agricultural production to price changes." Agriculture needed governmental action concerned for the public welfare and aimed at increased technical efficiency, lower costs and prices, and the conservation of society's interest in the land. Uncontrolled private enterprise in agriculture meant a tragically wasteful and destructive use of the land. He believed that government should promote the consolidation and rationalization of agriculture, reorganizing it along the lines that industry had followed. The area of land in production should be limited so that the system would include only the most efficient farmers operating the best land, and the cities and factories should absorb a very large number of people from the farms.[79]

One of the Columbia professor's first tasks as adviser to the rising New York politician in the spring of 1932 was to analyze the various farm plans. During the 1920's, Tugwell had become sympathetic with the farmers' efforts to get the national government to embark upon a positive farm program and had concluded that some attempt to control production should be made. "The first step," he had written in 1928, "is to make farming profitable. And for this it is necessary to adjust production to the amount which will be consumed at prices which are higher than present (not future) costs."[80] As Professor Bernard Sternsher has written, Tugwell "had not quite arrived at the domestic allotment idea by 1928. But he was moving in that direction."[81] In the spring of 1932, Beardsley Ruml told the brain truster about the development of the allotment plan. Soon he was in contact with Wilson, and then in June Tugwell attended a conference of economists at the University of Chicago where he learned more about the plan and the serious interest in it by talking to Wilson, Wallace, Black, Tolley, Ezekiel, and others. Tugwell came away convinced that the plan fitted the economic and political situation better than its competitors. The proposal to have elected county committees, rather than the national government, enforce the crop quotas struck him as "a remark-able contribution." [82]

Tugwell did have two major reservations about the plan. In terms of broad social welfare, he believed, production should be adjusted upwards. Inadequate purchasing power, however, prevented this, for industry's price and production policies had reduced employment and, hence, the demand for agricultural products, making it necessary for the farmer to cut back on his production. "The adjustment downward of production," Tugwell has written, "was an emergency measure, one of desperation." [83] If industry would reform and expand, then the farmer could increase his output once again, taking advantage of the new demands. [84] In industrial America, the behavior of the farmers needed to conform to industrial patterns.

Furthermore, like Wilson, Tugwell was unhappy that the plan would merely take a part of each field or farm out of production. "There is no recognition in it of the basic conditions that ought to determine the use of the land," he complained. "It adjusts supply to the moment's market, but it neither conserves the land nor makes provision for permanently bettering farmers' lives." However, also like Wilson, he hoped that the emergency efforts would gradually evolve into a program of complete control and efficient utilization. "Such a system," he suggested, "would envisage a commercial agriculture made up of the most efficient farmers operating the best of our lands, with the remaining land being used in other ways and the remaining farmers devoting their time to other occupations." [85]

Consequently, Tugwell introduced the allotment plan into the Roosevelt camp. Right after the Chicago meeting with Wilson, Tugwell won his first victory in his efforts to get Roosevelt to choose a specific farm program. As the Democratic convention was about to meet, Tugwell and Moley were hard at work on the acceptance speech. Thanks to the former's persistent urging and despite Roosevelt's doubts on political grounds, the candidate agreed to put the principle of the allotment plan into the speech. He did not go as far as the professor wanted, however, for Tugwell could not assure Roosevelt that the plan would be widely accepted. "What was really being asked of him," Tugwell has recalled, "was that Roosevelt should modify his principle of demanding preliminary agreement among all concerned. I wanted him, now that we had found a workable formula, to espouse it and to coerce the farm leaders into its acceptance by going over their heads to the farmers themselves."[86]

Roosevelt would not accept Tugwell's advice on strategy, but the speech, given dramatic emphasis by Roosevelt's unprecedented flight to the convention on July 2, testified that he had moved some distance toward Wilson[87] and led to Wilson's recruitment by the Roosevelt forces. With Moley and Tugwell urging FDR to get the details of the plan from Wilson, the latter, immediately after the convention, came to Albany. There on July 6, under vigorous questioning by the candidate and in the presence of other advisers, including Tugwell and Moley, Wilson explained his plan and the other farm relief proposals and discussed their economic and political possibilities. While this discussion strengthened Roosevelt's convictions on the economic possibilities of the allotment plan, he still held some reservations on political grounds. Nevertheless, Tugwell, Moley, and Roosevelt urged the Montana professor to prepare the first draft of the agricultural speech to be given in Topeka, Kansas, on September 14.[88]

Wilson eagerly accepted this new opportunity, discussed the project with a number of his associates, and prepared a draft. It paid careful attention to political factors, apparently hoping to overcome Roosevelt's reservations as well as the farmers'. A basic aim was to tempt farmers to desert the Republican party without driving urban groups away from the Democrats. The draft pictured Roosevelt as one who understood and sympathized with the farmers, while Republican leaders, with the exception of a few true but frustrated friends of the farmer, were portrayed as largely responsible for the farmer's plight. Those leaders had fought against the "Equality for Agriculture" movement with which Roosevelt now identified himself. Similarly, Wilson urged FDR to praise the agricultural colleges, to speak of his cooperation with "farm economists, farm leaders and . . . those liberal-minded businessmen who agree that something . . . must be done to give agriculture purchasing power" and to explain "why many of our business leaders are saying that there cannot be economic recovery nor a basis for a sound economic situation in this country until agriculture is rehabilitated." Purchasing power was emphasized in order to show that aid to the farmer was not a narrow class issue. Finally, care was taken to convince the listeners that the allotment plan was workable and earnestly proposed.[89]

Many advisers contributed to the final draft of the Topeka speech. The list included Peek's associate Hugh Johnson and Wilson's colleague Henry A. Wallace.[90] The speech was obviously more than just a polished version of Wilson's draft. Nevertheless, it repeated many of Wilson's suggestions, especially those based on his political calculations, and endorsed his plan, although somewhat vaguely.[91]

In their July meeting, Roosevelt and Wilson had also discussed their ideas on other subjects, and in his Topeka speech, the candidate drew upon the economist's advice in outlining proposals for "national planning in agriculture." First on Roosevelt's list of proposed "permanent measures" was the reorganization of the United States Department of Agriculture so as to create "the administrative machinery needed to build a program of national planning." Second was "a definite policy looking to the planned use of the land." Roosevelt argued that, because the population had stopped expanding rapidly and because agriculture was becoming more efficient, the country had more than enough tilled land to meet its needs for many years to come and that great areas of relatively poor land provided undesirable competition for better land and unnecessary expenses for the whole society. To correct this situation, he called for a survey that would lead to improvements in the use of land and the distribution of population.

Wilson had warned against devoting too much of the speech to New York's experiences in land planning, fearing that many Westerners had little interest in them and that Roosevelt might give the impression that he hoped to solve the farm problem simply by extending this program to the entire country.[92] In a carefully worded paragraph, the candidate described New York's efforts to turn unprofitable marginal farm lands to the growing of trees for lumber and pulp. He pointed out that the wheat and corn belts had little need for such a program but suggested that "this Eastern program is not only good for the East but is also of value in that it removes the competition of marginal hill farms from your own crops in the West."

The speech paid some attention to the redistribution of population, a subject in which Roosevelt as well as Wilson was interested. Planning designed "to gain a better and less wasteful distribution of agricultural productive effort" would point the way "to readjustments in the distribution of the population in general," FDR argued. In one of his favorite images, he suggested that the "pendulum" was "swinging back from the intense concentration of population in the cities." Quickly he pointed out that this "did not mean a 'back-to-the-land' movement in the ordinary sense of a return to agriculture." Instead, this involved "definite efforts to decentralize industry." Many groups, including commercial farmers, would benefit, for millions of people would obtain "cheaper and more wholesome living" and the commercial farmer would find "a considerable part of his market closer to his own dooryard."[93]

Wilson was delighted with the Topeka speech. Roosevelt's words convinced him that, as President, the New Yorker would back the economist's efforts to reorganize the Department of Agriculture and to coordinate national, state, and local agencies in the fashion envisioned in the Christgau bill. "Governor Roosevelt is sold on agricultural planning," Wilson informed Christgau early in October. "The paragraph in his speech which talked about agricultural planning had your bill in mind."[94] The economist was also convinced that the speech committed the candidate to the allotment plan.[95] Wilson had urged Roosevelt to avoid a more clear-cut endorsement. Hesitant to let his relations with the candidate come out into the open and thereby antagonize the opponents of the plan and provide them with a clearly defined target, Wilson had agreed with Roosevelt that he should simply set forth the specifications for a plan but not mention it by name. Rather than say Roosevelt had endorsed the plan, the strategy was to argue that it was the only proposal that met his specifications.[96] Wilson had a more cautious approach to politics than Tugwell did.

"It is not often," the readers of *Wallaces' Farmer* were informed, "that presidential candidates commit themselves as far as Roosevelt did at Topeka."[97] The farm leaders recognized that Roosevelt had become very interested in the allotment plan and also that he was very popular in rural America. Consequently, they became less hostile to the plan and began to talk of accepting it if ways to simplify it could be found. This development received additional stimulus from the processors, who brought their opposition to the plan into the open at the same time that Roosevelt made his Topeka speech. Farm leaders called upon Wilson and his associates to discuss the plan with them and thereby gave its advocates a chance to insist that legislation must harmonize with Roosevelt's specifications and that only the allotment plan did so.[98]

To further these encouraging developments, proponents of the plan worked to strengthen the candidate's commitment. Although Wilson believed that Roosevelt seemed quite likely "to stand pat with us," the proponents worried that the farm groups might force him to change his mind. If Roosevelt stood firm, the Wilson group assumed, then — and only then — the farm organizations would support production control. Thus he must continue to insist that farm legislation meet his requirements.[99] Early in November, W. R. Ronald, one of the many midwestern Republicans who deserted their party to support Roosevelt, pointed out to him that the sharp division among the farm leaders made it necessary that he "show the way." The South Dakota newspaperman advised that in drafting his farm program Roosevelt must rely upon economists "if it is to prove practical and successful. . . . If a small group of economists and legal advisers could come to conclusions as to the specific form in which the plan should be worked out for legislative action, you would then have something of a check sheet for use in passing upon any proposals for change by the farm leaders," Ronald concluded. "I am confident that it would be possible, under your leadership, to bring into virtual agreement most of those who are especially interested in agriculture."[100]

Although Roosevelt's desire to keep all farm groups behind him still influenced him and Wilson's and Tugwell's fears that those groups would not support production control persisted,[101] Roosevelt had committed himself sufficiently to promote some willingness among the farm groups to accept production control as at least one way to attack the farm problem.[102] He had, in short, helped Wilson solve his greatest political problem. As a consequence, Roosevelt's large victory over Hoover on November 8, 1932, opened the door to congressional endorsement of the plan.

To Wilson and Tolley, Roosevelt's victory promised even more than the enactment of the allotment plan. Speaking before the American Farm Economics Association in December, 1932, Wilson called attention to Roosevelt's plea for land planning in his Topeka speech and to his "great personal interest in initiating and carrying out the New York State land-use program." Referring to the latter as "a milestone on the road of land planning," Wilson predicted that the President-elect would "manifest the same personal interest as President of the Nation in land policy matters as he did as Governor of the State of New York."[103] Tolley also believed that the proposals for which he had been battling would now be translated into action.[104] These social scientists were prepared for and welcomed the coming of a New Deal.

CHAPTER 3

Achieving a Partial Victory

Roosevelt's support of the allotment plan led to victory for its proponents. Before the end of Roosevelt's first hundred days as President, Congress authorized the Administration to establish a system of production control for the nation's farmers. The President's support, however, had limits. Consequently, the Wilson group achieved only a partial victory. As Roosevelt's political methods sought to rally all possible groups behind him, the advocates of the allotment plan had to share their victory with others. Farm legislation included more than that plan.

Following the election, with Roosevelt's support of the plan becoming somewhat more obvious,[1] two of the three leading farm organizations moved closer to Wilson. Late in November, the Grange indicated that it was willing to add the plan to the list of proposals that the organization would support, and early in December, after listening to speeches by Wilson and Wallace, the Farm Bureau endorsed the plan. Only the Farmers Union held out.[2]

The Farm Board soon provided further encouragement, with Ezekiel, as the economic adviser to that agency, playing a key role in this important development. Obviously disturbed by the strong criticism of the board coming from farm and business groups and eager to remain the most important administrative agency in the field of farm policy, the board had considered making a recommendation to Congress that the allotment plan be adopted and that the board, rather than the Department of Agriculture, administer it.[3] Just before the election, Wilson had suggested to Ezekiel that, if Roosevelt were elected, the board should come out for the plan about as clearly as Roosevelt had in the Topeka speech. "From the standpoint of agricultural political strategy," Wilson advised, "I would say that they would make a mistake if they didn't come out pretty strongly and clearly for the plan."[4] Soon after the election, Ezekiel informed the board members that their stabilization program had failed because they had no power to adjust production. "The Farm Board, in spending $300,000,000 of public money on stabilization, has demonstrated that farm prices cannot be increased, so long as farmers continue to produce more than the market will take," the economist suggested. "The voluntary domestic allotment plan provides a public agency through which farmers can coordinate their planting and adjust production so as to eliminate the surpluses and also receive immediate benefit payments to help carry them through the process."[5]

On December 7, the board publicly admitted that it had failed. In line with Ezekiel's suggestions, it announced that prices could not be held at a fair level without effective production control. Although no specific plan was endorsed, the statement was interpreted by observers to mean that the board advocated the allotment plan.[6]

When the congressmen returned to Washington, several of the leading proponents of production control — Wilson, Tugwell, Ronald, Harriman, and Ezekiel — stepped up their campaign in the capital, confident that a major triumph lay ahead. Working chiefly with the chairman of the House Committee on Agriculture, Marvin Jones, a Texas Democrat, and with farm leaders, the proponents were able to achieve agreement on an "agricultural adjustment" bill that satisfied them. Meetings on December 12, 13, and 14 combined Tugwell's desire for leadership by the Roosevelt forces with the President-elect's idea that he should accept a proposal upon which the farm leaders could agree and with their demand that they should be allowed to draft the program. While John Simpson of the Farmers Union continued to criticize production control, he did not attempt to prevent agreement on it. Edward A. O'Neal and Earl Smith of the Farm Bureau and Louis J. Taber of the Grange agreed to support the bill.

Behind the progress lay the widely held belief that Roosevelt supported the plan, a belief strengthened by the assumption that Tugwell
represented the President-elect.[7]

The strongest tribute to the political skill and influence of the intellectuals came in the complaints of a leading opponent of production
control, George Peek. He complained that the "farm leaders were
being led off by economists" and that the farm people had gone "along
with Tugwell against their judgment." This veteran of the battles of
farm politics resented the appearance of "a new group . . . who had
never been active in our farm fight" but had moved in when success
seemed just around the corner.[8]

In spite of the progress, success eluded the proponents of the allotment plan in the lame-duck session. Congressman Jones battled vigorously for the bill in committee and on the floor of the House after it
was introduced on January 3.[9] Among the farm leaders, O'Neal fought
especially hard for it, testifying before the agricultural committees,
sending open letters to the senators, appealing to the nation over the
radio, and warning of the possibility of revolution if Congress failed
to provide relief for the farmers.[10] Simpson, on the other hand, openly
fought production control once again, pushing his cost-of-production
program as a substitute.[11] Some confusion prevailed in the Roosevelt
ranks as Henry Morgenthau and one of his advisers from Cornell,
Professor William I. Myers, were also in Washington discussing alternatives to the allotment plan, which they disliked, while the President-
elect failed to allocate clearly the responsibility for managing the
legislation and in other ways generated some uncertainty concerning
his opinion of the bill.[12] The processors and distributors battled strenuously against the legislation. Representatives of General Mills, the
American Institute of Food Distributors, the Millers National Federation, the American Institute of Meat Packers, the American Cotton
Shippers Association, the Cotton Textile Institute, the American and
the National Cotton Manufacturers Associations, the Silk Association
of America, and other similar groups took advantage of every opportunity to publicize their views, making special efforts to promote a
sense of identity between their interests and those of wage earners
and urban consumers by arguing that the processing tax would promote unemployment in the processing plants and increase the cost of
living.[13] Proponents of the plan made special efforts to combat this
troublesome and effective argument,[14] emphasizing the importance
to urban groups of farm purchasing power, and achieved some suc-

cess, especially in gaining support from Republican Congressman Fiorello La Guardia of New York City.[15]

Subjected to powerful and conflicting pressures, Congress disappointed the champions of the plan. The House changed the measure substantially, producing a bill that, in Wilson's words, "did not square with the philosophy of the allotment plan."[16] Then the chairman of the Senate Agricultural Committee, Ellison D. ("Cotton Ed") Smith of South Carolina, revealed that he was determined not to be pushed around by Roosevelt and disappointed those who hoped that the Senate would improve upon the bill. To complicate the situation still more, Smith introduced a bill of his own that dealt only with cotton, a step that infuriated O'Neal, for it threatened to shatter the degree of unity that had been achieved in December.[17] For a time the only hope seemed to be the passage of a bill that Hoover could veto and thereby increase farm support for the plan. Hoover proposed a land-leasing program as an alternative, denounced the allotment plan as "unworkable" and certain to "do far more harm than good to agriculture," and indicated clearly that he would not accept a bill involving that plan.[18] Congress, however, did not force the President to carry out his threat and left Wilson and his associates to console themselves with the thought that agitation of the issue had fulfilled the need for further political education.[19]

For Wilson, the behavior of Congress had been discouraging if not demoralizing. He had looked upon Congressman Jones's bill as a "good bill" because "it contained most of the fundamental elements of the voluntary domestic allotment plan" and "was based on the fundamental principle that no farmer should receive benefits unless he adjusted production." The treatment of the bill convinced him that only a few congressmen "accepted the fundamentals of the present agricultural situation." Most of them thought only of raising prices and neglected the need for adjustments in production. The economist suggested, however, that one "could not expect a proposal embodying as many new elements as the domestic allotment plan to be understood or accepted . . . in the very short time it has been under consideration."[20]

In spite of the frustrations of the lame-duck session, the plan's proponents were confident that even the opposition of the processors and distributors would weaken once Roosevelt took office, and then Congress would accept the plan or at least some kind of production control.[21] An especially encouraging development before March 4 was the selection of Henry A. Wallace as Secretary of Agriculture for the incoming Administration. Wilson and Tugwell had worked hard to persuade Roosevelt that he should choose this Midwestern farm journalist. His reputation in an important agricultural section that had supported Roosevelt, but which might return to its Republican traditions in later elections, and his strong support from major farm leaders, especially those in the Farm Bureau, encouraged Roosevelt to accept this advice. Significantly, Wallace's leading competitors included Morgenthau and Peek, two opponents of the allotment plan, while Wallace had been urging farmers since the early 1920's to reduce their production, had concluded before 1932 that McNary-Haugen would hurt farmers by producing greater production in the United States and higher tariffs abroad, and had helped Wilson promote interest in the allotment plan. To gain support from advocates of the McNary-Haugen plan, Wallace talked of allotment as "the 1932 model of the McNary-Haugen bill, especially designed to increase prices without bringing about an overproduction" and "almost exactly the same as the old McNary-Haugen idea, except that the tariff benefits go to those who sign an agreement to control their acreage." While he hoped that eventually vigor would be restored to international trade, he looked upon the allotment plan as necessary in the existing situation. Furthermore, he not only endorsed the plan but also was enthusiastic about national agricultural planning of the Wilson-Tolley type.[22]

As had his father before him, Wallace believed that economists should participate significantly in the shaping of farm policy. Henry C. Wallace had been Secretary of Agriculture in the early 1920's. Under his leadership, the BAE had taken shape. Its establishment in 1922 had reflected his interest in the economic side of agriculture and his convictions that the department should give as much attention to the market conditions that faced the farmer as it did to efforts to help him with production problems and that the farmer needed to understand economics in order to free himself from domination by business and industry and to compete on equal terms with them in the contest for wealth.[23] His son was repelled by the negative approach to public policy of many economists and admired those who thought of economics as "not merely theoretical and academic, but something living, moving, active and directional in the world of affairs." As he believed that the nation must learn to live more and more with social controls, he regarded the duty, privilege, and opportunity of the economists as "greater than they have hitherto been willing to admit." Some of their number had to become more than mere technicians, the younger Wallace maintained; "they must rise beyond their interest in supply and demand curves and become concerned with the world of intangible values and with ultimate direction."[24]

As his economic adviser, Wallace selected an economist who agreed with him about production control and the role of economists. His choice was Mordecai Ezekiel. Drawn together by their strong interest in statistics, the two men had been friends for several years. Ezekiel had learned a great deal from his Farm Board experience about the ways an economist must operate in order to be useful to decision-makers, and he insisted that economists could and should be important figures in the policy-making process. ". . . it seems to me that this, if ever, is the time when economists have some advice to give as to the fundamental difficulties in the present situation and what might be done to correct them," he wrote to another economist. The solutions, he believed, "necessarily involve political action in the national field," a subject that he did not regard as "outside the field of professional economists."[25]

An economist who agreed with Ezekiel and Wallace was selected as Assistant Secretary of Agriculture. Wilson, who had been considered as a possible Secretary of Agriculture, was asked by Wallace to be his assistant. Wilson declined, saying that he wanted to devote his attention to wheat. Wallace then encouraged Wilson to come to Washington to help in the development of the legislation and to establish the wheat program. Asked for his opinion of Tugwell as Assistant Secretary, Wilson endorsed the suggestion.[26] Although they disagreed on monetary policy, Wallace liked Tugwell and his ideas on most matters and urged him to accept the post. The economist agreed, although he had some doubts that a professor should take on an administrative job and that a New Yorker should move into a top spot in agriculture.[27] He welcomed the chance that the post provided for constructive activities. According to Professor Sternsher, "Tugwell was not the first professor to serve in the USDA, but his appointment was unique in that it broke with the tradition of choosing professors from state agricultural institutions."[28] The historians of the department have written:

Selection of a professor of economics from east of the Alleghenies without land-grant college connections, who had a reputation for brilliant and unorthodox ideas, symbolized change in the Department of Agriculture that was to plunge it into the swift moving current of controversial economic and social reforms.[29]

Wallace, Ezekiel, Wilson, and Tugwell represented the commitment to national action that characterized the new Administration. On March 8, only four days after inauguration, Roosevelt accepted a suggestion from Wallace and Tugwell to push for immediate farm legislation and thus take advantage of the tremendous support for the new President. Congress was in an unusual mood, seemingly willing to grant Roosevelt all the authority he needed to deal with the economic crisis, and there seemed to be a way to escape the political problems that still plagued the promoters of production control. They decided, and Roosevelt agreed, that Congress should be freed of any need to choose one of the proposals for farm relief and that the responsibility for reconciliation and choice should be passed on to the President and his Secretary of Agriculture. At Roosevelt's request, Wallace called the farm leaders to Washington for a conference on March 10 and 11. They agreed on their way to the capital that the President should be given a broad grant of authority to deal with the farm problem, and, as essential groundwork had been laid in December, the conferees reached agreement rather quickly. While fairly specific provisions concerning production, the regulation and supervision of marketing and processing, and the processing tax were included in the recommendations to Roosevelt, they also contained the provision that "in the drafting of a bill to carry out these recommendations, all powers necessary to the successful carrying out of the purpose to be achieved shall be included." In the conference and the drafting sessions that followed, Tugwell and Ezekiel along with other advocates of the allotment plan played important roles. Wilson devoted most of his energies to conversations with farm leaders, hoping to get and maintain their support.[30]

In spite of the high degree of unity that had been achieved between the Administration and the farm groups, Congress resisted the desire for quick action and took nearly two months to pass the legislation. Senator Smith, John Simpson, and the "middlemen" continued to cause trouble. The intellectuals who supported the allotment plan were attacked as impractical and radical, with Ezekiel's name providing an additional basis for attacks upon him. The promise of new freedom from the antitrust laws helped to reduce the fears of the processors and distributors somewhat, and the vigorous efforts of Secretary Wallace blocked an attempt to add Simpson's cost-of-production amendment to the bill, a proposal that Wallace regarded as unworkable but one that had the support of Senator George Norris and other Midwestern and Western legislators. Wallace's arguments infuriated Simpson, but they followed advice that Ezekiel and other economists had provided. The Administration applied a large amount of pressure to both the House and the Senate, and the bill finally passed by wide margins. Roosevelt signed the Agricultural Adjustment Act on May 12, bringing to an end the biggest battle of the "Hundred Days." Wallace and Tugwell went to the White House to watch the President sign their bill.[31]

The social scientists in farm politics had won a great victory! The Agricultural Adjustment Act included major Wilsonian features: production control, voluntary participation encouraged by rental or benefit payments, self-financing through processing taxes, and a role for farmers in administration. The act also included a modification of the Wilson plan that Tugwell had suggested at the December meeting with the farm leaders and that had changed the goal somewhat. While Wilson sought to "make the tariff effective" for the farmer, paying him the amount of the tariff on a commodity in order to get him to reduce his production of it, the act sought to raise farm prices high enough to give agricultural commodities the purchasing power they had in the 1909–1914 period. Before market prices reached that level, the payment to the farmer would equal the difference between the current market price and the "parity price" — the price needed to give commodities the purchasing power they had had in the base period. This parity price idea had been the basis for Peek's original "Equality for Agriculture" proposal but had been dropped for reasons of political strategy. Wilson, reflecting his tendency to think in terms of the political implications of economic ideas, did not like the return to the old basis, for he believed that the idea to "make the tariff effective" had strong appeal among the protectionist-oriented farmers of the Middle West.[32]

Because FDR had not followed Tugwell's advice about the role of the leader, the social scientists had to share their victory with one of the most active businessmen in farm politics. In the new legislation, the chief competitors of the allotment plan were two programs with which George Peek was most closely associated. One was his proposal to dispose of surpluses abroad, by dumping if necessary. The act would allow the administrators to use funds from the processing tax to promote the expansion of foreign markets. This feature had been included in spite of Ezekiel's objections that the provision would create "a great temptation to use the processing taxes for this purpose instead of going ahead and using the funds for the control of production. . . . This proposal appears to be one more step in the continuous campaign to change the Administration's farm relief plan over into the old McNary-Haugen plan," he had warned Wallace.[33] In addition, the act included a program that Peek and other proponents of the McNary-Haugen plan and also the processors and distributors had been pushing. This program would place the responsibility for raising farm prices on these businessmen and the marketing cooperatives. The legislation authorized marketing agreements whereby the agencies that were handling farm products would promise the government to pay agreed-upon prices to the farmers. If under the agreements, prices failed to reach the desired level ("parity") then the difference between the fair price and the market price would be paid to the farmer by the government, and the Treasury would be reimbursed by the tax on the processors.[34]

Thus, the "agricultural adjustment" section of the New Deal farm law amounted largely to a combination of the ideas of Wilson and Peek, a combination that did not satisfy the latter. This former farm implements manufacturer disliked the idea of reducing output, arguing instead that the emphasis should be placed on expanding sales. The farm leaders, he believed, eager to try anything in the emergency, had allowed the professors and the economists to dominate the creation of the farm program.[35]

The Farm Bureau, eager to claim credit for gaining this legislation for the nation's commercial farmers, did not choose to look upon itself as dominated by professors and economists. The organization deserved credit in the sense that it was the leading pressure group in the battle that led to the passage of the act. Social scientists and businessmen, however, had played the chief creative roles in the development of the ideas embodied in the legislation.[36]

The passage of this measure, then, amounted to a partial victory for the social scientists. Roosevelt's support played a crucial role in this development. On the other hand, his political strategy, which sought to maximize support for him from the farm organizations, had prevented the Wilson group from gaining the clear-cut victory they desired. Nevertheless, the intellectuals had demonstrated that they were men of considerable skill in the political arena, capable of matching wits and also of working with so-called "practical men." The intellectuals had entered politics and had gained a significant amount of support from important business, farm, and political leaders for a farm relief scheme that had originated with economists, not farm leaders.

To understand this political success story, however, one point must be recognized. The production control program harmonized at many points with basic assumptions of powerful farm and business groups. Thus, the intellectuals were not forced to challenge those assumptions but needed only to persuade these men of power in the American political process that the allotment plan would accomplish what they desired. The business and farm leaders simply had to be led to believe that production control could do for farming what it had often done for manufacturing.

Apparently, most farmers were less enthusiastic about production control in 1933 than were farm and business leaders like O'Neal and Harriman. Some farmers were ready to accept this program as an emergency measure. "For years the cotton and tobacco producers," Theodore Saloutos has pointed out, "were nurtured on a philosophy of farm relief which the new administration finally adopted and elaborated upon." [37] Many farmers, however, preferred the cost-of-production principle. One "dirt farmer" wrote Roosevelt that "80% of the dirt farmers of this land will be against the allotment plan if they understand it." The trouble, according to this man, was that Wilson was "college bred" and thus did not know anything about dirt farmers and could not even sympathize with them. Farmers did not want any "college professor" to solve their problems.[38] In similar fashion, an Eastern farm journal criticized the program that Roosevelt had obtained from "a few college professors" and reported that "voluntary letters from practical farmers" indicated that they knew what was needed.[39] An Eastern newspaperman concluded from a trip through the agricultural states that the allotment plan was "a politicians' and theorists' remedy, without support from the practical farmers."[40] And support for such views comes from a leading agricultural historian, who suggests, after looking at a large volume of evidence on farm opinion in early 1933, "that the agricultural planners in Washington made the basic decisions and that grass-roots opinion was more revered in theory than in practice by policy-makers."[41]

In addition to the many doubts that farmers had about production control, one should note that the planners like Wilson and Tugwell and the representatives of the farm organizations who participated in the formation of AAA had their eyes on different objectives. The farm organizations were interested chiefly in the elevation of farm prices, while the economists were interested, most of all, in establishing a permanent program of agricultural planning that would promote adjustments in agriculture to meet new situations as they developed.[42] ". . . few if any of the farm leaders see the underlying significance of the voluntary domestic allotment plan especially in that it injects the planning and the group organization feature," Wilson informed Tugwell.[43] The latter justified the short-run program as a necessary means to eliminate "price disparities" between agriculture and other sectors of the economy but called attention to the "wider implication." "This is an attempt to plan." [44] The social scientists were making progress along paths that they wanted to take but were operating in a political environment in which not all of the significant participants accepted every one of the intellectuals' ideas.

PART TWO

Social Scientists
in
Power

CHAPTER 4

Elevating
Production Control

Now that the Agricultural Adjustment Act was the law of the land, two major tasks faced the social scientists. One of these was to make the allotment plan the major form of farm relief. Before the end of 1933, this task was accomplished. To some extent, this accomplishment grew out of the labors of Wilson and Tugwell. Of major importance, however, was the support that their ideas received from key men in the political process, especially Secretary Wallace and President Roosevelt. Congress, encouraged by many of the farm leaders, had given those officials the power to put these ideas into practice. As 1933 moved forward, Roosevelt and Wallace used that power.

The new farm law authorized the employment of several alternative policies, and the selection of the people to administer it became a crucial matter. Here, Wilson's ties with Wallace were significant, for, even before Congress had passed the law, Wallace had promised Wilson that he could administer the part of the program that interested him most — the part that dealt with wheat. While Congress debated, Wilson turned his attention to the application of the bill to this commodity, and after Congress and the President had turned the bill into law, Wilson became the chief of the new Wheat Section of the

Agricultural Adjustment Administration. Strong support for him from the organized farmers, especially in the wheat country, helped to compensate for the opposition to him from some opponents of the allotment plan. Thus he gained a chance to promote a reduction of output in the first commodity to which the new law was applied and to influence the development of the entire farm program.[1]

Other advocates of production control were recruited. The group included one of John D. Black's former students, Albert G. Black of Iowa State College, who became chief of the Corn-Hog Section, and Wilson's good friend Howard Tolley of the University of California, who took a similar position in the Special Crops Section, an assignment that gave him an additional opportunity to serve the interests of the groups which whom he had been working in California.[2] The law was passed too late for control to be applied to the production of such commodities as cotton, tobacco, and hogs in 1933, and administrators were forced to resort to such devices as the campaigns to slaughter pigs and to plow up cotton and tobacco, but officials were able to get most farmers, especially the larger operators, to agree to cut back on production in 1934.[3]

Recognizing that they needed time to succeed in their efforts to raise prices by reducing production, the advocates of this approach warned against the development of alternative programs that could lessen the willingness of farmers to cut back on their production. Warnings were issued against encouraging farmers to believe that monetary policy was a universal cure-all for to depend heavily upon government purchases of farm products. Widespread demands for a quick increase in farm income limited the effectiveness of these warnings.[4]

One leading advocate of production control, Mordecai Ezekiel, battled strenuously and with some success to place economists in influential positions in the operation of the farm program. Obviously confident that these social scientists would promote the adjustment approach, he at times criticized the appointment of other people. In August, for example, when a job was created to deal with the switching of production from one crop to another, he protested against the selection made for the job, arguing that "there is no work in the Adjustment Administration which is of more fundamental and long-time importance," that the appointee had "no special competence for this job," and that the Department should seek "the best man available for the job, rather than . . . someone . . . whose selection has been dictated by other considerations." His choice was F. F. Elliott, a man with "infinite knowledge" of "farm conditions throughout the country developed in his study of particular farms" and an economist of "outstanding ability."[5] Ezekiel also defended the use of economists in the development of the farm program. When a critic complained about the role of "impractical theorists," Ezekiel pointed to the increase in farm income and asked: "I wonder if you feel that this increase in income is due to impractical theorists."[6]

Agricultural economists obviously welcomed such opportunities. Almost all of them contributed in one way or another to the development of farm programs during the 1930's. "The events of the past year," one of these economists reported proudly late in 1933,

have demonstrated that in periods of emergency it is from the body of research workers that administrators and advisers are recruited. They alone often times possess the detailed, accurate and timely knowledge necessary to grapple successfully with important problems. While the transfer of such men weakens research, it constitutes its strongest justification.[7]

Not everyone welcomed the economists. Farmers who desired large acreage allotments complained about the size of the allotments that the economists in the program specified.[8] George Peek became so unhappy at one point with Ezekiel's efforts that Peek told the economist that he would approve no more appointments from him covering people who were to be put in the job of opposing the Agricultural Adjustment Administration.[9] Peek headed that agency, an assignment which guaranteed that controversy would flourish in the development of the farm program.

Peek's selection had been dictated chiefly by notions about the realities of farm politics. Roosevelt and Wallace wanted an administrator whose practical experience and prestige in farm circles would satisfy farm and business leaders and congressmen and gain their cooperation with the bold new farm program; even Tugwell, in spite of his skepticism about the wisdom of business leaders, his opposition to Peek's ideas on farm policy, and his fears that Peek would dominate the agricultural program, saw some value in selecting a man who could work with the established men of power in farm politics. Peek, sharing the fears of a number of politicians, farm leaders, and businessmen that Tugwell and Ezekiel, seemingly radical, impractical, and close to the President, would dominate Triple-A, wanted the job so that his ideas rather than those of the "theorists" would control the program. Peek and Wallace disagreed from the begin-

ning on the relations that the Administrator should have with the
Secretary and the President, but Roosevelt gave Peek enough satisfaction on this point to bring him into office. Peek later suggested that
he had been chosen as mere "window dressing" to gain the support
of political and economic leaders while the "secret plans" of Wallace
and Tugwell for "regimented production" could be matured.[10]

As administrator, Peek sought to give various urban business
groups a leading role in the program and to emphasize marketing
agreements as the means of raising farm prices. When Tugwell insisted that the government should write the regulations that would
govern the operations of the businessmen who came under the law,
Peek replied that only businessmen knew the intricacies of their industries. He called upon such businessmen as Charles Brand of the
National Fertilizer Association, Glen McHugh of the Equitable Life
Insurance Company, and W. L. Westervelt of Sears, Roebuck and
Company to take key administrative jobs; he sought advice from his
old friend Bernard Baruch; and he organized agencies, such as the
Food Industries Advisory Board, composed of leading processors and
distributors. To raise farm prices, Peek worked out agreements with
these business groups to purchase a certain volume of farm products
at a price acceptable to the groups and to the administrators of the
program.[11]

While Peek's tendency to work so closely with businessmen disturbed others in the Administration, the lawyers who entered the
Triple-A troubled Peek and his associates. Tugwell chose the legal
philosopher and lawyer Jerome Frank as counsel for the AAA, and
Frank turned to the leading law schools to find professors and recent
graduates for his staff. The result was a youthful, hard-working, intellectually vigorous group, eager for public service and embracing
broad concepts of the role of a lawyer and of their own responsibilities under the Agricultural Adjustment Act. While their superiors
and the nation later discovered that a few of these lawyers were Com-
munists, most of them were interested simply in reforming capitalism
and more interested in the general welfare than in the special interests of the commercial farmers. To the Peek group, these lawyers
appeared distressingly inexperienced, radical, urban, and Jewish;
Peek used his own money to employ Fred Lee, a lawyer who had long
been involved in farm politics. Finally, Peek unsuccessfully called
upon Wallace to dismiss Frank, then appealed over the Secretary's
head to the President, urging him to fire the lawyer. When the latter

learned from Tugwell that Peek had filed a list of complaints against him with the President, Frank suggested to Wallace that "my real offense is that I concurred in your judgements on certain important issues." [12]

With arguments reflecting distrust of the business leaders with whom Peek worked, Tugwell and Frank justified their recruitment policies. Lawyers of the Triple-A, these intellectuals insisted, should be able to match wits with the clever legal staffs of the corporations with which the government worked. While Tugwell and Frank assumed that business interests needed to be controlled and reformed by the government, Peek assumed that the government could rely upon their cooperative spirit. His critics, acknowledging that marketing agreements could raise farm prices, believed that that rise would come at the expense of urban consumers, thereby reducing the purchasing power of this essential group and making no contribution to recovery. They battled to give AAA the power to control prices and profits so as to protect the interests of the consumers of farm products, arguing that farmers could not enjoy prosperity if city people could not afford those products. [13]

Thus tension prevailed in the administration of the farm program during its first six months. As early as May, the press noted the battle between the "intellectuals" and the "practical men." One focal point of conflict was production control. While the emergency — and Wallace and Roosevelt, who insisted that the allotment plan should be tested — forced Peek to accept some cutbacks in production, he did so reluctantly, resisted efforts to make this the main feature of the program, and continued to seek ways to sell the surplus. Wallace, on the other hand, believed that when marketing agreements were divorced from production control they could make only limited contributions to increased farm purchasing power. In the fall, Wallace publicly criticized Peek's agreements; Peek challenged Wallace's authority to control Triple-A; and Wallace and Tugwell vetoed Peek's plan to dump butter on the European market and pressed the President for a decision that would indicate clearly where authority lay. He found himself forced at last to make a choice between representatives of different farm policies. He tried, however, to find a way to move Peek out of AAA without alienating him and his powerful friends. Peek therefore moved in mid-December to a new post as special adviser to the President on foreign trade, thereby finding a chance to try to eliminate the need for production control.

To replace Peek, Wallace selected Chester Davis and so put Triple-A under the direction of a man who believed in production control. Although he had been Peek's top lieutenant in the McNary-Haugen fight, Davis had concluded that the growth of extreme economic nationalism had invalidated that plan and that the United States must reduce its cropland. He had become an advocate of the allotment plan in 1932. On entering Triple-A in its early days as chief of the Production Division, he had promoted production control, believing that it should be given major emphasis. Now, under his vigorous leadership, which was to last until 1936, marketing agreements would remain as a feature of the farm program but in a subordinate position, and production control would emerge clearly and explicitly as the central feature. Davis accepted Wallace's view that production adjustment was basic to the success of the farm program and that marketing agreements could serve only as a supplement to the more fundamental adjustments in output.[14]

Following the change in personnel, Paul Appleby, Wallace's principal adviser on administrative organization[15] and a warm admirer of Tugwell and Frank, assured a friend who had been concerned about the "turmoil in the Department" that the situation would now clear up; and Wallace assured him that Triple-A would work "with much less friction than formerly."[16] Wallace had established himself as the administrative and philosophical leader of the new program;[17] he had crushed Peek's attempt to make Triple-A an independent agency, free from control by the Secretary and subordinate only to the President. Wallace had avoided the situation that had faced his predecessor, Arthur Hyde, after the creation of the Federal Farm Board, a situation in which the major farm program operated outside the Department of Agriculture.

From the point of view of the social scientists in farm politics, Wallace's victory was extremely important. It meant that by the end of 1933 a man who admired them and was highly receptive to their ideas was clearly in control of farm policies while another man who tended to distrust these people as impractical and radical had been forced out of power. One can understand why one of the intellectuals, Rex Tugwell, tried so hard to push Peek from his lofty position. Tugwell obviously recognized all that was at stake in the battle. He distrusted this businessman in farm politics; he admired Wallace. The economist has written of Roosevelt's choice for Secretary of Agriculture: "He settled on none of the heads of the farm organizations but on the one acknowledged intellectual among all those who had a right to be considered." [18] Following the election of 1932, Tugwell had encouraged Roosevelt to select the Iowa farm journalist; and now, late in 1933, Tugwell once more promoted Wallace's advance.

By the end of 1933, the situation that faced the social scientists was a very favorable one. Although production control was not the only means being used by the Roosevelt Administration to increase the income of commercial farmers, this method occupied the most prominent position in the attempts to accomplish this. Wilson and Tugwell had contributed in major ways to the elevation of the production control program. Most important, their ideas had the support of the Secretary of Agriculture and the President, and those men were willing to remove from office an opponent of those ideas, even a man of great stature in the world of farm politics. The power situation within the Administration provided encouragement for those who hoped to establish a long-range planning program.

CHAPTER 5

Moving Toward
the Long-Range Programs

The second major task facing the social scientists when they came to power in 1933 was the promotion of long-range programs that involved far-reaching changes in the ways the nation used the land. Even before they had accomplished the first task, that of making the allotment plan the major form of farm relief, they began to push forward on the second. Before the end of the New Deal's second year, they accomplished much here also. Again, support from Roosevelt and Wallace was extremely important.

Prior to the passage of the Agricultural Adjustment Act, Roosevelt authorized Wilson and Tugwell to work with Wallace on the reorganization of the department to make of it an instrument for national planning. In authorizing this step, the President provided additional evidence that he shared the economists' point of view on matters of fundamental importance to them. He gave these men an additional opportunity to promote their strong interests in agricultural planning and in the long-range planning of land utilization.[1]

In August, after having established the wheat program, Wilson turned to another of his strong interests, subsistence homesteads. The Subsistence Homesteads Division had been established in the Department of Interior, and Roosevelt called upon Wilson to run it. The President had earlier put pressure upon Congress to get the legislators to authorize the experiment. Other individuals also helped Wilson obtain this opportunity. His close friend from the business world, Henry Harriman, who admired New England village life, labored to promote interest in the program; and a Southern progressive Democrat, Senator John H. Bankhead of Alabama, who had learned of subsistence homesteads from other promoters and who looked upon the project both as a relief measure and as a way to restore a small yeoman class, "the backbone of every great civilization," led the fight for the appropriation. Groups like the Catholic Rural Life Congress and individuals such as the publicist Bernarr Macfadden supported the Senator's efforts.[2] Reflecting the experiment's dependence upon the stimulus of the depression, the new division was part of the public works program established by the National Industrial Recovery Act and administered by Harold Ickes, the Secretary of Interior. Calling for "the redistribution of the overbalance of population in industrial centers," the NIRA provided $25,000,000 for the development of subsistence homesteads. Wilson later explained that "the long-time program of the Subsistence Homesteads Division aims at a redistribution of population in the interest of providing greater economic stability and a higher standard of living for working men's families." His projects, however, attempted to rehabilitate the rural poor as well as impoverished wage earners.[3]

Wilson believed that the division belonged in the Department of Agriculture, and in his new duties he worked closely with that department, striving to avoid conflict with AAA. Agricultural authorities insisted that the communities must produce farm products only for their own use and must provide adequate part-time nonfarm employment so that the needed cash income could be obtained without engaging in the commercial production of farm products. The aim was avoidance of the absurdity of attempting to reduce farm surpluses with one program and encouraging their production with another, and the success of the experiment depended chiefly on the development of industries capable of providing employment for the residents of the communities.[4]

Although Wilson had enthusiastic supporters,[5] his experiences were far from pleasant. Richard T. Ely was favorably impressed, regarding work along this line as a necessary part of any sound and permanent recovery program;[6] and Gray's lieutenant, O. E. Baker, looked upon the experiment as one way to retard the declining birth rate, a problem of major proportions in his eyes. Baker suggested to Wilson that

Gandhi's habit of retiring an hour each day, or a day each week, for meditation, is really worth consideration by a man supervising this pioneer effort at relocating the nation's population. I speak with no exaggeration when I say that the future of the nation lies in no small part in your hands.[7]

Spokesmen in Congress for private enterprise, however, blocked an effort to develop manufacturing in the projects with government funds. Labor leaders, worried about the difficulties of organizing workers in a decentralized industrial system and convinced that industrialists would dominate and exploit the workers in the communities, criticized the program, as did farm leaders and others associated closely with agriculture who grew concerned about the loss of markets when workers produced their own food and about the possibility that "subsistence" farmers would actually ship a substantial volume of goods to market. Conservative journalists criticized the whole scheme as impractical, and Tugwell was inclined to agree.[8]

Wilson did not know how he should respond to his critics. When the *Saturday Evening Post* carried an especially critical story on one of his projects, he wrote to another proponent of community building:

The facts have been so completely disregarded in the whole story that I can say I am not especially concerned. The *Post* apparently is enrolled in the effort to belittle every experimental effort undertaken in the interest of finding a way out of the mess the country has been in.[9]

But to Bernarr Macfadden, Wilson expressed more concern about the inaccuracies and "skillful innuendo" in the article. "I believe that if the matter stands unchallenged it will do great harm to the true subsistence homesteads idea." Thus he urged the publisher to investigate some of the projects. "If on the basis of the investigation Liberty Magazine would see fit to print an article setting forth the true situation . . . ," he advised, "I believe that it would perform a great service for the cause to which you have made such great contributions in the past."[10]

Secretary Ickes, skeptical of a program that he believed had been imposed upon him, proved even more troublesome. Because of his characteristic fear that government money would be wasted or stolen and he would be criticized for it, he kept a close watch on the projects and criticized Wilson — often in front of others — for the way in which the projects were being managed. In line with his interest in decentralized planning, Wilson established separate local corporations for each project. Ickes, however, fearing that this would prevent him from controlling something for which he would be held responsible, changed the system. He established one general corporation which sent out for each project managers who were directly responsible to Washington, and he placed some of Wilson's duties in the hands of one of Ickes' trusted subordinates. The Secretary concluded that Wilson had made a "mess" of the work, that he was "not a good executive," and that he "did not know how to pick the right kind of personnel." Ickes came to look upon the experiment as "nothing but a headache," one administrative unit for which he "felt apologetic," and "the only activity where I feel that I did not really make good." [11]

Believing in a chain of command, Ickes also resented Wilson's ties with the White House. Not only the President but also his wife and Louis Howe had strong interests in the work and participated in it. Howe, in fact, took it upon himself to make a decision about housing for one of the projects, which turned out to be very unsatisfactory. This was only his largest blunder! [12]

Wilson found working for Ickes much less satisfying than life with Henry Wallace. The economist looked upon the Secretary of Interior as an urbanite who knew nothing about farmers and who feared unjustifiably that they would engage in the same kind of graft to which he had been exposed in Chicago politics. Wilson resigned in June, 1934, with the complaint that Ickes had not given him "a great deal of freedom in the administration of ideas" and had not allowed him to do many things as he thought they should be done. [13]

In spite of the difficulties, some progress was made under Wilson's leadership. Thirty-two communities were planned, and funds were advanced to twenty-seven of them. No houses were occupied, but fifty were close to completion by June. Nearly 14,000 applicants were considered, and more than 750 approved, at least tentatively. [14] Two months after he departed, the division had passed the slow, preliminary stage of organization and planning and had entered the period when its work could be measured and displayed in houses constructed and in families living and working on their homesteads. [15] By November, more than fifty families were living in the communities, and more than one hundred additional homes were under construction. [16]

The division continued to function for a year after Wilson's departure and concentrated during that period chiefly upon the construction of the communities that he had initiated. Nearly 700 houses were completed, and more than 1,300 others were begun. The experiment, however, was constantly plagued by legal and administrative delays, and less than one-third of the original appropriation was spent.[17] This small amount of progress did not cause Wilson to lose faith. He continued to devote a share of his attention to the encouragement of the decentralization of industry and the development of "a rurban pattern of life in America — a life based upon a combination of industrial employment and agricultural activities."[18] He had looked upon the program of the division as an experiment, had believed that a new way of life could take shape only in a slow fashion, and had hoped that his experimentation would encourage others to conduct bigger experiments of this type.[19]

At the same time that the subsistence homesteads program was taking shape, the planners were promoting other significant developments. In the summer of 1933, Wallace, Tugwell, and Ezekiel became alarmed at the great expansion in reclamation that seemed likely to take place under the public works program, and they protested against the prospect of a great increase in agricultural land. Wallace warned that the reclamation projects would "open us up to very heavy political attack throughout the middle-west, as long as we are engaged in acreage control." He welcomed a suggestion that "at every step to bring new land into use, there should be a corresponding move to take marginal land out of use to such an extent as to balance productive powers." Drawing upon estimates supplied by Gray, the Secretary suggested that the 30,000,000 poorest acres of crop land could be acquired for about $250,000,000. He urged the President to authorize him and Secretary Ickes to establish a joint committee to prepare a program dealing with the general aspects of the problem of taking old land out of agriculture and bringing new land into it.[20] At the same time, Wallace indicated to Ickes that he hoped they could "do something really effective along this line and, in this way, heal the breach between Elwood Mead and the Bureau of Agricultural Economics which has caused so much discord in the past."[21]

Roosevelt discussed the question with the two cabinet officers and indicated in a press conference on July 27 that he and Ickes had accepted Wallace's suggestions. According to the President, each time the Public Works Administration allotted funds for a reclamation program another allotment would be made to retire poor land of equivalent productivity. By this process the administration would avoid a net increase in productive acreage and would remove from agriculture land that should not be used for farming.[22] The President authorized the creation of a joint committee of the two departments to plan the procedures of the new program. Wilson served as one of the representatives of Interior; Ezekiel and Gray represented Agriculture. Tugwell also made contributions as plans for the operations took shape. Among other matters, the planners decided that for each dollar spent on reclamation another should be used to purchase submarginal land.[23]

After extended consideration of the methods that could be employed to carry out the policy, a significant step forward was taken. On December 28, the Public Works Administration authorized the Federal Employment Relief Administration to use $25,000,000 for the purchase of land. For the first time, the national government had funds that it could use to buy submarginal farms.[24]

Besides trying to develop a submarginal land program, planners in the Department of Agriculture were also trying to coordinate reclamation with their production control program. Wallace suggested that the new policy "reconciled the ancient conflict of interest between the farmers of the middle west and the people of the far west." Zealous advocates of reclamation, however, did not applaud. They looked upon the new policy as a burden and upon Wallace as an enemy. While he denied that he was hostile to reclamation, he, like Gray, obviously wanted to give the Department of Agriculture some degree of control over reclamation so that it would fit into a consistent, overall land policy.[25]

To help develop such a policy, a new Land Planning Committee was formed in the fall of 1933 as an adjunct of the recently established National Planning Board. Quite logically, Wilson, who was acquainted with land problems in both Interior and Agriculture, was chosen as chairman. Tugwell, Ezekiel, and Gray were also included in this new committee, which carried on the work of the National Land-Use Planning Committee and, like it, attempted to coordinate the activities of the established agencies and had power only to make recommendations. The committee devoted its attention to submarginal agricultural areas, reclamation, and grazing and homesteading on the public domain.[26] Illustrative of its labors, the committee provided encouragement for a movement in which Gray, Wilson, and the National Land-Use Planning Committee, as well as others, had been involved and which led to the passage of the Taylor

Grazing Act in 1934. Gray and Ezekiel drafted a recommendation, which the committee endorsed, calling for the closing to farming of all public lands that could not support a farm family and for the use of these lands for other purposes. This recommendation reflected the economists' interests in restricting agricultural expansion and in promoting the conservation of national resources.[27]

In a major statement of policy at the end of 1933, Tugwell indicated clearly just what the planners in Agriculture hoped to accomplish. Drawing upon the work of Gray's Division of Land Economics and speaking before the American Farm Economics Association, he suggested that in the future the federal government would perform two functions in relation to the land. It would hold and administer all lands which could not be effectively operated under private ownership and would devote them to the uses for which they were best suited. In addition, the government would control the use of land which remained in private ownership to whatever extent was necessary to provide for continuous productivity. Department planners hoped that the land purchase policy announced at this time would merely be an early step toward putting into action the general program outlined by Tugwell and that land purchase would serve a multitude of purposes, not merely the reduction of agricultural surpluses.[28]

Developments such as these provided a good deal of encouragement for Gray. In midsummer he had been somewhat uncertain about "the views of the existing Powers as to how the Planning Committee will fit into the new scheme of things,"[29] but by late summer, he was convinced that his work under Hoover was to go forward under Roosevelt, that the National Land-Use Planning Committee had "served to crystallize interest," and that partly as a result of its activities land-use planning was emerging "as a definite element in agricultural policy."[30] On November 11, that committee issued its final report. After summarizing its work and expressing satisfaction with the new Administration, the committee recommended that it cease to exist, suggesting that it had "accomplished the work it was adapted to perform and that the Committee could not function effectively as a Federal coordinating agency under the conditions that have developed during the past six months." The Land Planning Committee of the Planning Board was now recognized as the successor of the earlier committee. Gray's membership in both committees guaranteed that the land planning movement could go forward without interruption despite the change in organization.[31]

An especially important step followed the appointment of Chester Davis as Administrator of Triple-A. He established a new division in that agency, a Program Planning Division. He had more confidence in economists than Peek did, liked their ideas about agricultural adjustment and planning, and believed that some people in the agency needed to be free of administrative chores so as to have time to think about the weaknesses of the farm program and to evaluate and devise proposals for change. And around him were people he respected, like Wallace, Ezekiel, Wilson, and Tolley, urging him to think along these lines. While serving as director of the Production Division, he had called upon Tolley to appraise the adjustment program. Now he gave the social scientists a chance to use this program as a means of moving in directions that were more desirable from their point of view. For nearly five years, the division was to function as the main planning agency in a department that for the first time had authority to plan a national agricultural program and to put the program into effect.[32]

Wallace and Davis could have placed the new assignment in the hands of the Bureau of Agricultural Economics, but their relations with the chief of that agency, Nils Olsen, were not fully satisfactory. His bureau had suffered for a time from the economy drive of the early months of the Roosevelt Administration and continued to suffer from the drafting of his men to staff Triple-A and from the pressure to serve the research needs of the farm programs. This pressure tended to divert the attention of the BAE away from the basic work in which it was interested and from other service work it was required by law to perform. Olsen feared that the character of the bureau might be changed, that it might be drawn into political controversies and would cease to be an effective research and service institution. In addition, much of the New Deal displeased him. While he applauded the developments in land policy, regarding them as outgrowths of efforts he had been making for several years, he was quite skeptical of the major efforts to raise farm prices, believing that an emphasis upon the restoration of international trade would be more desirable. His economists displeased some of the administrators by criticizing their programs, arguing, for example, that AAA's cotton program was reducing the exports of American cotton.

In time, relations between BAE and Triple-A would improve. In April, 1935, Olsen resigned to enter the business world as director of the Farm Investment Department of the Equitable Life Assurance Society. To replace him, Wallace selected Al Black, an economist with a friendlier attitude toward the farm programs and a strong conviction that economists should take advantage of the kinds of opportunities for service that the New Deal was opening to them. Relations between the bureau and the Secretary now returned to a condition they had not enjoyed since the days of the first Wallace and Henry Taylor, and relations between BAE and AAA improved.[33]

In December, 1933, however, rather poor relations with the bureau encouraged Wallace and Davis to establish a new agency and to place a critic of the BAE, Howard Tolley, in charge of this Planning Division. Admired by his superiors, interested in planning, and experienced in the direction of group research, Tolley was an excellent choice for the assignment. After having established one of the Triple-A programs, instead of returning to California as planned he had accepted Davis' request to join the Production Division as chief economist and had devoted his attention to the problems that were arising in connection with the production control program. Now Tolley moved into a spot that gave him a chance to promote the ideas that had been involved in the Christgau bill. He was granted a great deal of freedom in the development of his activities and was given a chance to try to move the farm program beyond the reduction in production, the specific marketing agreements, and the small efforts under way to distribute the surplus to the unemployed. He tried to substitute the idea of adjustment as distinguished from reduction in the thinking of everybody concerned, including the farm people. Soon he was publicly criticizing Triple-A, arguing, as did Wilson and Tugwell, that it was not producing the most desirable changes.[34]

Tolley's top lieutenants had long shared his interest in planning. Gray became chief of the division's Land Policy Section. He remained as head of BAE's Division of Land Economics, which continued its basic research at the same time that it worked closely with Gray's new agency. The latter attempted to determine the total area of land needed for the production of farm and forest products, the acreage that should be withdrawn from agriculture or used less intensively, and the use of areas withdrawn from farming. Gray devoted much of his attention to land of questionable value for agricultural production, and Elliott, as chief of the Production Planning Section, shaped plans for changes in the use of good farm land in the major agricultural areas. Like Gray, Elliott had significant personal experience to draw upon. He was noted for his mapping of types-of-farming areas, a subject that now became increasingly important as the planners attempted to attack adjustment problems regionally.[35]

The new division ranged widely over the national and international economy in its efforts to develop a comprehensive, long-range plan for agriculture that would raise rural standards of living, supply farmers with a fair share of the national income, and also serve the interests of the consumers of farm products.[36] Following a suggestion made by Ezekiel and Louis Bean, another economist from the BAE who was advising the Secretary, Tolley established the Agricultural-Industrial Relations Section and placed Bean in charge, as he had long specialized in this area. The section collected information on present and prospective industrial and financial developments and explored their relations to the welfare of farmers, seeking clues to trends in industrial employment, in the demand for farm products, and in the migration of labor to and from the farms. Other sections studied farm and city people on relief, migratory workers, sharecroppers, and other low-income groups. Reflecting the planners' hopes for a revival of international trade and their fears about the political as well as economic consequences of a fully nationalistic economic system, the Import-Export Section estimated and planned the nation's international trade in agricultural products.[37]

Plans for reorganizing agriculture so that it could supply all Americans with a proper diet provided a significant illustration of the thinking that was taking place in the division. Scientists had been learning more about the role of vitamins, and critics of production control were insisting that policy should emphasize efforts to increase consumption. In 1933, Wallace had suggested to Dr. Louise Stanley, the chief of the Bureau of Home Economics, that the country needed to know more about minimum food requirements and maximum possibilities of healthful consumption. Since 1930, Dr. Hazel K. Stiebeling of BHE had been conducting investigations of the diets of various population groups in the United States, and now she prepared recommendations for four diets at different levels of nutritive content and cost. Tolley organized a study conducted by Elliott's section which converted the diets into their implications for agricultural production. In 1934, Tolley placed on his office wall a chart portraying the relations between acres and diets, and he and others in the department publicized the conclusions of the study, which indicated that when prosperity and better knowledge of nutrition allowed Americans to consume the diet recommended as best, the United States would need more, not less, land in production and would need to change the ways in which farm lands were used. These conclusions exerted a great influence on the thinking of the planners and revealed that they were trying to enlarge the role of science in the shaping of decisions about production and were interested in much more than higher prices for commercial farmers.[38]

The diet studies represented the planners' emphasis upon "planned" or "balanced abundance," a concept that implied that the long-run solution to the "farm problem" depended heavily upon efficient industrial production, low industrial prices, full employment, and high wages. Although the planners continued to talk of the importance of expanding farm purchasing power, they placed increasing emphasis upon the theory that farmers depended heavily upon urban markets.[39]

Ezekiel, who by 1934 was associate director of the Planning Division besides being economic adviser to the Secretary, was the leading promoter of this rejection of what has been called "agricultural fundamentalism" and has been defined as "a widespread, deep-seated persistent conviction that agriculture is *par excellence* the fundamental industry, and that farmers are, in a peculiar sense and degree, of basic importance in society."[40] As he later explained, his work in agriculture drove him into work on the industrial problem in an effort to find a lasting solution to the agricultural problem.[41] "The farm problem created by heavy unemployment in the cities, cannot be solved on the farm," he concluded.[42] Many new opportunities in urban areas had to be developed in an expanded industrial system that would absorb the surplus rural population and the crops of those who continued to farm. Expansion of industry and migration to the cities, not back-to-the-farm schemes, would produce high standards of living for the American people. To accomplish these changes, Wallace's adviser insisted, the government should function as planner and promoter, helping rural people to move into the cities and expanding production and purchasing power — the keys to the good life. In line with his theories, Ezekiel frequently battled for the protection of consumer interests.[43]

Even though some farm leaders looked upon Ezekiel as too interested in consumers and not sufficiently vigorous in promoting the interests of producers,[44] Wallace both encouraged the economist's work and was influenced by it.[45] The Secretary's report to the Executive Council in April, 1934, illustrated this point of view. Stating that a complete revival in agriculture depended upon "a restoration of purchasing power and an abundant flow of industrial products at relatively low prices" and that the department could not "map out" its "long-time agricultural program providing for the full utilization of our agricultural resources and an adequate national diet" until a definite outline of an industrial program took shape, Wallace called upon the Administration to take action to expand industrial production and to achieve full employment.[46]

To accomplish its broad objectives, the Planning Division worked closely with numerous agencies in hopes of coordinating their activities and of getting them to serve the needs of the adjustment program. "In my opinion," Tolley announced late in 1934, "the farmers of the country as well as those charged with the administration of the Agricultural Adjustment Act or its successor, will expect research in agricultural economics and related fields in the future to be so organized that more and more of the results will serve as a basis of action in agricultural adjustment and related fields."[47] From the beginning, agricultural economics had had a problem-solving orientation, and now Tolley, stimulated by the New Deal, was trying to make his profession even more useful.[48]

Gray's post as chief of the Land Policy Section gave him a chance to begin to convert into an action program the body of knowledge concerning land-use that had been accumulating in the Division of Land Economics, the National Land-Use Planning Committee, and elsewhere. After the land purchase program was authorized, Ezekiel advised Wallace that the department must be given responsibility for the planning phase of this program. The economist looked upon the program as offering the first opportunity for real action in connection with land utilization and recognized that this was a field in which the department had been developing a basis for action over the past ten years. He feared that if planning were turned over to other agencies to handle, this might "produce further danger of conflicting objectives between different Government agencies such as existed in the past between Interior and Agriculture, and . . . still exists on reclamation policies." If the department became the planner, then there would be "complete consistency between the operations in controlling agricultural production and in controlling land use."[49]

Wallace followed Ezekiel's advice. On the one hand, he took steps designed to prepare the department to make important contributions, urging his bureau chiefs to give Tolley prompt and complete cooperation in his efforts to centralize the contribution of the department toward a unified land program for the federal government. On the other, he took action to see that his economists, including Ezekiel and Tugwell, had a chance to influence the development of the land purchase program. "In cooperating in work necessary to expend this money, and in developing a broad general plan for the expenditure of further sums for the same purpose," he announced, "the Department has been given the first real opportunity to work out ideas it has been developing for many years." [50]

In line with Ezekiel's advice, Gray's section became the planning agency for the program. The section did not buy land nor resettle and rehabilitate people; those were the responsibilities of Harry Hopkins' Federal Employment Relief Administration. The Land Policy Section selected the lands that should be withdrawn from agricultural production and the land onto which the displaced farmers were to be moved and contributed to the determination of the other ways in which the lands involved in the program were to be used. Older policies of public land acquisition had involved selecting land with the intention of converting it to a specific use, such as forestry; now Gray had several alternatives available to him, and he attempted to find the best way to use each parcel of land that was purchased. [51]

Thus Gray's section had two major responsibilities. Its basic work was to develop a long-term national plan for the better use of the land. Its more immediate task was to plan and develop specific land retirement projects. [52] Gray, as one of his younger associates of those days recalled,

was a lovable, gentle, thoughtful man who seemed to belong more in a library than in charge of the planning of a great program of land retirement. Yet he inspired his staff to perform endless hours of extra labor in their efforts to meet deadlines. [53]

Gray recognized that $25,000,000 would enable him to make only a very small beginning in dealing with a very large problem, but he assumed that the acquisition of any amount of poor farm land would represent progress and thus was pleased with what was taking place. "The establishment of the Land Policy Section, together with the allocation of twenty-five million dollars by the Public Works Administration for submarginal land purchases, marks a definite entrance of the Administration on a land program of far reaching scope," he informed another promoter of land-use planning. "This development really represents the culmination of the work of the old Land-Use Planning Committee." [54]

At the same time, Gray worked with Tugwell and Ezekiel on legislative proposals designed to move beyond the $25,000,000 program and to obtain clear congressional authorization for their long-range ambitions. Wallace backed their suggestions, and Tugwell discussed them with the President. The Director of the Budget, Lewis Douglas, however, blocked action at this point, suggesting that "Tugwell's proposed bill" would commit the government to "a long-time land policy, the scope and annual cost of which is wholly indeterminate" and "directly in conflict with the Administration's financial program." [55]

Roosevelt, nevertheless, sought other ways to move forward. Helped by a major drought, he obtained additional funds from Congress to purchase submarginal farms and resettle their occupants. [56] In a speech in June at Yale University, he defended a major feature of land planning — the government's use of experts — and called attention to the links between his programs and the conservation movement of the Progressive period, stating that Gifford Pinchot "started me on the conservation road." "From that time on, . . . we have gone ahead by a slow process of education until today the whole country . . . is thoroughly familiar with the purpose of the great national plan for the better use of land and water. . . ." [57] In a message to Congress on June 8, he indicated that he hoped to be able to present to the next Congress "a carefully considered national plan covering the development and the human use of . . . natural resources." [58] At the end of the month, he established the National Resources Board to replace the National Planning Board and authorized the new agency to prepare a report for him by December 1 on the development and use of the nation's resources. [59]

As chairman of the board's Land Planning Committee, Wilson played a major role in the preparation of the report. He returned to the Department of Agriculture in July, happy to be back and to be free of his ties with Ickes. In replacing Tugwell as assistant secretary when the latter moved into the new post of under secretary, Wilson accepted major responsibilities for the development of the department's efforts to establish new national land policies and a long-term adjustment program. The preparation of the report gave him another chance to shape a program that had been on his mind when he came to Washington in 1933. [60] He hoped to develop a national land policy that would

at least, start the American people to thinking in the direction of better use of our land resources and in shifting people from the submarginal lands and . . . retiring out of use those lands that are not sufficiently productive to give a stable standard of human life.[61]

He did not look upon this land policy as a substitute for Triple-A's efforts at production control but as a supplement, designed to deal with a different problem. As the submarginal lands contributed little to production, withdrawing them would not solve the surplus problem. But if the two million farm families who occupied such land tried to remain farmers, they could hurt the other four million. The poor land could not provide a decent income for a farm family unless the government forced farm prices to an unreasonably high level. This would cause consumers to rebel and would lead to drastic reductions in production that would harm the farmers "employing good lands, good systems of farm management and capable of earning a good income with fair instead of exorbitant prices." [62]

Although no complete inventory of the nation's resources had previously been attempted, the Land Planning Committee completed its work in less than five months. As the committee's director for this task, Gray played the most active role. He was able to draw upon the great mass of scientific data which had been collected by the various research agencies over a long period of years. While his Land Policy Section and Land Economics Division did much of the work, important contributions were also made by many other agencies, including the agricultural colleges and experiment stations. The procedure itself, involving local and state as well as national agencies, was a source of satisfaction to him.

On the basis of this work, the committee urged a reversal of old attitudes of heedless and planless exploitation of land resources and called for a national policy affecting land ownership and use that would serve the public welfare and not only private advantage. As had the Land-Use Planning Committee of the Hoover Administration, Roosevelt's committee also hoped to promote a coordinated attack upon land problems. The committee provided inventories of available land and estimates of future requirements and proposed policies to correct maladjustments in land use, recommending acquisition by the federal government of 75,000,000 acres of submarginal farm land in the next fifteen years and expansion of public forests, recreational areas, Indian reservations, and wildlife refuges. The proposals would affect 450,000 families on poor land and emphasized the improvement of their condition, not the reduction of crop land.[63]

The recommendations promoted further progress. The Resources

Board adopted them, and Roosevelt submitted the board's report to Congress on January 25, 1935. "For the first time in our national history we have made an inventory of our national assets and the problems relating to them," he informed the congressmen. "For the first time we have drawn together the foresight of the various planning agencies of the Federal Government and suggested a method and a policy for the future." He hoped that the report would be the foundation for "a permanent policy of orderly development in every part of the United States."[64] In the months that followed, the Land Planning Committee continued to function with Wilson as chairman and Gray and Ezekiel included in the membership. It developed an extended supplementary report on land-use problems, attempted to coordinate the land purchase activities of all federal agencies, and was pleased to see many of its recommendations of 1934 translated into action.[65]

The land program had both friends and foes. Opposition came from newspapermen, businessmen, and others who worried that their areas would be depopulated, their businesses would collapse, or their public agencies would be deprived of needed tax revenues. Opposition came also from farmers who had ties of sentiment with their locations, despite their suffering, and had no desire to move. But the leaders of the organized farmers and a number of congressmen and businessmen were enthusiastic about the kind of work in which Gray was involved.[66]

Gray's work moved forward but not without difficulties. Tension existed in the relations between the Department of Agriculture and the Relief Administration. Officials in the department feared that the resettlement program under Hopkins' control might add to the farm surpluses and tried hard to prevent resettled farmers from engaging in commercial agriculture. Some of the officials believed that those in charge of relief, as a consequence of their limited experience with agricultural problems, had some strange ideas about the ways in which rural life should be organized and consequently should no longer be in charge of any rural activities. Members of FERA, on the other hand, criticized Triple-A on the grounds that it was promoting a displacement of tenant farmers, forcing them to turn to the relief agency for help.

Confusion marked the relations between land purchase and resettlement. Relief officials charged that Gray had little interest in people on poor land and was interested only in moving them from it, giving little thought to where they would go. The criticism was unfair. He accepted the view, which was a new view in the federal government, that whenever it bought land the government acquired an obligation to help the people find a new location. He believed that proper provision for the families involved was the most important aspect of the land program. Thus, he and his staff worked hard to take care of the farm families whose land was to be purchased. They reached an agreement with FERA that the Land Policy Section was responsible for the selection and development of submarginal land projects while the Relief Administration was in charge of resettlement. Representatives of the two agencies met frequently to try to find ways to coordinate land purchase and resettlement, but while land buying proceeded at a rapid pace, few families were relocated.[67] Wilson and Tolley tried to accelerate resettlement. "The land purchase program is making such rapid progress," the Assistant Secretary reminded the official responsible for resettlement early in 1935, "that we fear we shall find ourselves seriously embarrassed . . . unless provision for this important step can be promptly accomplished."[68]

Many factors contributed to the lack of coordination. Rapid land buying was stimulated by budgetary considerations as the appropriation for it would be available only until June 30, 1935. A shortage of money, on the other hand, hampered the development of an adequate settlement program. Furthermore, plans for rural rehabilitation were much more complicated than land purchase plans and required more time to perfect.[69]

A quite different situation characterized the relations between land purchase and reclamation. In June, 1934, Gray publicly criticized the rapid rate of reclamation development. He indicated that he believed in reclamation but not the type that was forced by pressure group activity. He wanted reclamation to be an "integral segment of national land planning and policy," an important part of the effort to shift population from poor to good land and to expand production as demand expanded, but he criticized "the great expansion of reclamation activity at a time when our cultivated acreage is clearly excessive in relation to demand." Since 1932, the government had allocated to reclamation nearly as large a sum as had been spent in all the years since the initial reclamation act was passed. "The necessity for providing employment has been a ready recourse for those who have sought to defend the policy," he noted caustically, "and in the case of specific projects, various local advantages have been offered in support. I have heard no one, however, offer a substantial argument in support of the present program on general grounds of national welfare."[70]

Gray continued his efforts to restrain Mead and received encouragement from Wallace, who remained troubled by the conflicting aims of the Department of Agriculture and the Bureau of Reclamation. In March, 1934, for example, a department committee headed by Gray recommended that ultimately the department should control all "programs of land use for all lands chiefly valuable for the production of organic resources" and that thus the Soil Erosion Service, the Subsistence Homesteads Division, the General Land Office, the National Park Service, and the Bureau of Reclamation should be transferred from Interior to Agriculture.[71]

By the end of June, 1935, all but $4,000,000 of the $25,000,000 originally allotted for land retirement had been used, as over 5,000,000 acres had been optioned and nearly 400,000 purchased, but reclamation had moved forward much more boldly. "Commissioner Mead, of course, is always in favor of any reclamation project," Ickes had informed Roosevelt. "That is his job."[72] Gray estimated that in order to conform to the original agreement on the coordination of land purchase and reclamation an additional $50,000,000 for land retirement "would be justified to offset the potential increase of productivity of land that will result from funds already allotted for reclamation projects."[73] On this issue, Gray was battling for a lost cause.[74]

Nevertheless, although land programs still lacked the coordination that Gray had long sought, progress was taking place. "When the history of these times is written," Dean Ladd of the New York College of Agriculture suggested to Wallace in 1935,

I believe that one of the great achievements of your administration as Secretary of Agriculture will be the initiation of a sound land-use program for the United States. Franklin D. Roosevelt coined the term "land use." It is fitting that his Secretary of Agriculture should be the man responsible for putting a land-use program into practical effect.[75]

"Fortunately we have a President with a deep knowledge of land problems who has had the experience of pioneering a land policy in a great state with intricate land problems of its own," Wilson announced late in 1934.[76] While he regretted that the load that FDR was carrying prevented him from giving land questions as much attention as they deserved, the economist was optimistic. "The fact that we have in the President someone who has a genuine interest in this subject means that we have at least a substitute for the apathetic leaders at the top," he wrote to Richard Ely. ". . . all in all, there are more hopeful signs today than at any time in the past."[77] ". . . land planning," Gray wrote a short time later, "has received greater emphasis and support since 1932 than ever before in the history of the country."[78]

The social scientists had called upon the farmer to imitate the methods of the industrialist so as to bring profit to the business of farming, but they had not stopped at this point. Accepting more than business values, they thought in terms of the interests of a number of groups, including urban consumers and farmers on poor land, and they attempted to bring about a better use of the land, hoping not only to improve upon the land-use practices that prevailed before 1933 but also upon those promoted by Triple-A. By the beginning of 1935, the social scientists' ideas on production control and long-run planning figured prominently in the New Deal.

CHAPTER 6

Facing Pressures
from Left and Right

During 1934, hostility toward the New Deal mounted rapidly. To some critics, the Roosevelt Administration seemed to be moving the country in dangerously radical directions, destroying the traditional political and business systems. To others, not enough change was taking place; like regimes of the past, the new one seemed subservient to business interests. The social scientists in farm politics, especially Tugwell, and their ideas, including production control, provided targets for many critics. In this political context that threatened their ambitions, the social scientists tried to protect the production control program, but they disagreed with one another on how they should deal with the realities of farm politics. Wilson, especially, struggled to develop and maintain the support from farm and business groups that had helped him achieve his earlier successes. Tugwell, on the other hand, doubted the wisdom of relying on these groups.

Included in the efforts to develop and maintain support were arguments reminding businessmen and others of the similarity between the agricultural program and the practices of large corporations. This line, which the Wilson group had employed in 1932, was developed in elaborate fashion in 1934 by one of Wallace's advisers, Gardiner

Means, the Columbia University economist who had collaborated with Adolf Berle on the outstanding study, *The Modern Corporation and Private Property*, published in 1932. Means's studies of industrial prices revealed the ways in which giant corporations used their power to control production in order to uphold prices and disclosed the weaknesses of the farmer in such an economic system. The more individualistic farmer could not exercise the same control over production and thus "administer" his prices. For him, in contrast with the corporation, price rather than production was the flexible factor. Furthermore, the farmer suffered from the industrialist's ability to restrict production not only because it led to higher industrial prices but also because the practice reduced the demand for agricultural products. Factories working at less than full capacity needed fewer agricultural products, and unemployed wage workers had little purchasing power.[1]

Means's work was highly regarded and frequently drawn upon by members of the Department of Agriculture, including Wallace, Tugwell, Ezekiel, and Wilson.[2] They argued that developments in the distribution of power within the economy had placed the farmer in a disadvantageous position, and thus he needed help from the government that would enable him to imitate industrial practices. Triple-A was satisfying the farmer's need for "the centralizing powers of government to achieve the same results industries achieve through corporate organization."[3] If industrialists could adjust production to demand, was it wrong to use government power to help farmers do the same? Had not the industrialist, by cutting back on his production and thereby reducing the demand for farm products, forced the farmer to reduce output? In response to critics, Tugwell pointed out that the cotton textile manufacturers had ordered a 25 per cent reduction in output and employment in order to sell at higher prices. "The Tories did not suggest," he argued,

that the wise and manly thing for the cotton manufacturers to do would be to go bankrupt in the good old American way and thereby reduce their prices to a point at which their goods could be sold. . . . It is only when the farmers do it that it suddenly becomes wrong, unnatural, and un-American to try to control their economic destinies through cooperation.[4]

A similar argument compared the farm program with the protection that industrialists had long received from the tariff. Department officials suggested that political action of this type had affected the income of various groups and that through the operations of Triple-A farm production "for the first time has been placed on a position of something like equality with industries producing manufactured products protected by high tariffs." "If there is one thing the AAA has succeeded in doing," Ezekiel suggested, "it is in making the farmers conscious of the benefits industry previously got through the tariff, and given farmers a similar vested interest in the domestic market. . . . If the protected interests do not like it," he added, "then let them take off their tariffs."[5]

The arguments suggested that production control was not a radical program. Farmers were simply being advised to behave like urban businessmen. The arguments also suggested that the program was not being imposed upon the farmers by a group of "impractical" intellectuals, as many charged.

Some of the social scientists promoted other ways of answering the latter charge. Cooperation with farm leaders in drafting legislation, as in December, 1932, and March, 1933, was one way. It pleased men like O'Neal, who argued that "instead of forcing a policy upon agriculture, the Administration has called in the recognized leaders of agriculture and then asked them to write their own program."[6] In this frame of mind, he provided strong support for the farm program. "A great deal of credit should be given to Ed O'Neal of the Farm Bureau, who is always Johnny on the spot when it comes to fighting battles in defense of these policies," Wilson informed a friend.[7]

Wilson's ideas about the roles that farmers should play in the administration of the program formed part of the same pattern. Although the Adjustment Act authorized the formation of committees of farmers, the need for quick action encouraged Wilson and others in 1933 to rely chiefly upon the already existing and experienced extension services of the agricultural colleges to operate the program on the local level. "Extension" had agents in nearly every agricultural county, and those agents knew how to work closely with the farmers. The Farm Bureau encouraged this move to rely upon the county agents; some Democratic politicians in the Middle West opposed it, fearing the Republican ties of those officials. Tugwell opposed it on somewhat different grounds; he feared the close ties between the extension services and the large commercial farmers.[8] Leaders in the extension services also had some fears. They believed that their institutions could be harmed by being drawn into administration and away from their traditional emphasis upon education. On the other hand, the new responsibilities offered extension a way of dealing with the demands that were being made, often in the name of economy in government, that the services be reduced sharply or even abolished. By playing a crucial role in the attack upon the agricultural crisis, the extension services could demonstrate their utility and not only survive but grow. Furthermore, by accepting the responsibility, they could prevent the development of another organization to administer the program that could replace extension in many counties. The college leaders accepted the request that they assist in the administration of the farm program, and the county agents soon conducted the educational and promotional work needed to establish the program in the rural areas and assumed major administrative responsibilities.[9]

As quickly as possible, however, state and local farmer committees were formed throughout the country. State committees were appointed by the Secretary; temporary county and community committees were named but often replaced by elected committees as soon as election machinery was provided. As Wilson explained in July, 1933, "the fundamental close-to-the-soil work of making the plan operate in the township and on the farm will be up to the farmers themselves." There county organizations will "make the allotments and carry out the essential task of determining whether each man has fulfilled his agreement."[10] He provided leadership in the development of the committees. Soon 1,450 county committees were operating in the wheat country and more than 4,200 throughout rural America.[11] The results delighted most of the social scientists and also Henry Wallace. Tugwell, on the other hand, had doubts that the growth of the committees represented the growth of democracy.[12]

The formation of the farmer committees did not eliminate the extension services from the administration of the farm program. The county agents frequently organized the county committees and then served as their secretaries. Agents who were not secretaries commonly served as advisers to the committees. The state directors of extension often served as chairmen of the state committees. In the cotton South, extension played an especially large role: The directors handled most of the administrative tasks, selected the farmers to serve on the committees, and used them chiefly in an advisory capacity. As a reward for their labors, the extension services received a great deal of Triple-A money that enabled them to expand their staffs and the areas and number of people they served.[13]

During 1934 and early 1935, some efforts were made to reduce the role of the extension services in the administration of the farm program. Desires to encourage the farmers to play a more active role and to return the county agents to their educational activities were involved. The efforts were influenced also by doubts about extension's loyalty to and interest in the farm program and fears that the close ties between this organization and the Farm Bureau in many states would enable that group to dominate the program and cause farmers who did not belong to the Farm Bureau to refuse to cooperate with Triple-A. Al Black, as head of the Corn-Hog Section, worked especially hard to reduce the power of both the extension services and the Farm Bureau in the administration of the program. Wilson, after his appointment as assistant secretary, became the department's leading man in handling the troublesome question of the relations with extension.[14]

While some Farm Bureau leaders disliked Black and protested against his activities,[15] most of these men in the Middle West and South liked the administrative arrangements in Triple-A. That agency helped these men to expand the size and power of their organization, and they in turn played influential roles in the development and operation of the agency's committees.[16] In 1934, President O'Neal pointed out in a nationwide radio speech that the farmers themselves were being organized into committees and that Wallace had advised that these committees should be coordinated. "What a challenge and an opportunity this is to us in the Farm Bureau. Our Farm Bureau leaders should take the lead in organizing and coordinating these production control committees and associations," O'Neal declared. "The Farm Bureau is ideally fitted for this task, because of its fundamental set-up to speak for all farmers, and its long experience of close cooperation with the Agricultural Extension Service, the Land-Grant Colleges and the Agricultural Experiment Stations."[17]

Other farm groups, however, were not as happy with the administration of Triple-A. One foe of the Farm Bureau, the Missouri Farmers Association, which had not been represented at the conference of farm leaders in March, 1933, protested that "Wallace has . . . placed the farm bureau crowd and the county agents overwhelmingly in the saddle!"[18] Even before 1933, the leader of the M.F.A., William Hirth, had complained that Roosevelt had surrounded himself "with Professors and hairsplitters who are long on theories, but who don't know what it means to have a bloody head as I have from daily contact with closed banks and the marketing of millions of dollars worth of farm commodities."[19] Now, with the social scientists in power, Hirth objected to "the visionary schemes of the so-called 'brain trust' who want to make the Country over" and "babble about a 'planned society.' . . . Policy making," Hirth insisted, "must depend chiefly upon men who bear ugly scars which they have acquired in the 'bull pen' of practical experience, rather than upon those who are fascinated by 'major social experiments.' . . . The job of getting agriculture back on its feet calls not for well-meaning theorists," he argued, "but for double-fisted practical men who still have faith in our institutions." [20] Other critics also complained about the large role that professors were playing in the farm program, contending that the Agricultural Adjustment Act was "being administered in entirely too theoretical and 'professorial' a manner" and that "the 'brain trusters' who contrived the AAA . . . were no better qualified to manage the farm business than the 'cotton croppers' are to teach Latin and Greek in the classrooms vacated by the college professors." Criticism of this sort came frequently from farm leaders in the Northeast and Far West where farmers believed that, unlike the farmers of the Middle West and South, their interests were not being served by AAA. Criticism of the intellectuals, in other words, was part of a large campaign against the farm program, not necessarily a reflection of anti-intellectualism. [21]

The Farmers Union, a group that received little attention from Triple-A officials during the early years of the New Deal, objected to the power that had been placed in the hands of intellectuals. In the fall of 1933, President Simpson charged in a letter to Roosevelt that the "brain trust" did not speak nor understand "the farmers' language" and suggested that some of its members had "been in the employ of the crooks in the past and may not have severed all of their connections." [22] In speeches at the same time, he referred to Roosevelt's advisers as the " 'brainless trust.' " [23] Another leader of the Farmers Union called upon FDR to appoint business and farm leaders (especially Simpson) as Presidential advisers and suggested that "school teachers, expert economists, and other theorists have never done anything constructive; they don't know how; cannot do it. . . . Established business firms are not composed of such experts." [24] Simpson looked upon production control as a highly undesirable way to raise farm prices, and the Farmers Union believed that "dirt farmers" should administer the farm program. Under the leadership of Simpson's successor, E. H. Everson, the expanding organization continued to criticize this method and the influence of men like Wilson, although a few leaders of the group supported the farm program. [25]

As an urban intellectual, Tugwell came under attack from people who reflected or appealed to the hold of Protestant fundamentalism upon the rural mind. One of his speeches, for example, pictured the "more abundant life" as the goal of the New Deal and seemed to include "wine, women, and song" in the new abundance. Cries of protest came from clergymen, the religious press, and religiously oriented (or at least prohibition-minded) laymen. Furthermore, he and his fellow members of the "brain trust" were denounced by critics of the production control program who based their criticisms upon religious assumptions. Included in the group were leaders of the Grange, a farm organization that lacked the Farm Bureau's enthusiasm for the New Deal. These critics argued that the program violated God's plan for man or at least the virtues of the Protestant ethic, especially industry, thrift, and saving. The severe drought of 1934 seemed evidence of divine disapproval. "What does it say in the Bible about saving up in good years to tide one over the lean years?" Grangers were asked by Republican senator Lester J. Dickinson of Iowa. This former McNary-Haugenite and active prospect for the Presidency wished that "someone would take a Bible and present it to some members of the brain trust."[26]

During the spring of 1934, critics of the farm program frequently denounced Tugwell and his philosophy.[27] In the widely publicized "Wirt affair" of March and April, much attention was paid to him. Wallace quipped before the press at the time that another controversial figure had been brought into the department "to take the fire off of Rex" and that as a consequence of the advertising he was receiving, including the denunciation of his textbook for preaching "communism," he should be able to sell the book in Russia.[28] The affair was part of a large campaign conducted by the Committee for the Nation, an organization of business and farm leaders united by an interest in using monetary policy to raise prices. They hoped to force the Roosevelt Administration to resume its monetary experiment and to drop its other measures, including the farm program. The affair involved charges by Dr. William A. Wirt, the superintendent of schools in Gary, Indiana, that "brain trusters" were using their power in government to "overthrow the established American social order."[29] One left-wing critic of the Administration laughed at Wirt's charges, suggesting to Tugwell that "no one knows better than you, that there is no trend in this Administration to any radicalism, for we have only subsidized State Capitalism with Morgan, Baruch, Swope, and the industrial and financial magnates using the President as a foil."[30]

Wirt and his supporters regarded Tugwell as the dominant figure
in the "brain trust" and threw a spotlight on a paper he had presented
in 1931, a paper that one historian labels Tugwell's "most radical
pronouncement."[31] In it, he had pointed out the changes that would
be involved in the development of a planned economy. They included
the abolition of the business system. By this he had meant, not the
destruction of private ownership, but the destruction of *laissez faire*.
He had defined the system as characterized by the free venture for
profits in an unregulated economy. Much of the paper had dealt with
the costs of planning, especially powerful government controls, and
the consequent need to proceed slowly and democratically toward it.[32]

As the Wirt affair moved along, another controversy developed out
of Wallace's recommendation that Tugwell become Under Secretary
of Agriculture. This was a new post, established as a consequence of
the great increase in the pressure on the secretary's office.[33] Its creation
gave Wallace a chance to bring Wilson back to the department as
assistant secretary. Wilson had a talent that Tugwell made no effort
to develop: an ability to work successfully with the leading people in
farm politics. As the historians of the department have written, Wilson's "method of approach and his background as a farmer, county
agent, college professor, and State extension leader made it possible
for him to experiment with new ideas and new programs without becoming a center of controversy."[34] Tugwell, on the other hand, seldom
concealed his distaste for and distrust of the views of many of the
leading people in farm politics.[35] One of Appleby's friends reported
after Tugwell paid a visit to Iowa that many there regarded him as
"too high brow" and "a snob,"[36] and at least one land-grant college
official wished that "Tugwell had been brought up in an agricultural
college."[37]

Two conservative and powerful Southern Democrats, Senators
Ellison D. ("Cotton Ed") Smith of South Carolina and Harry Byrd
of Virginia, led the opposition to Tugwell's promotion. Smith, the
chairman of the Senate Agricultural Committee, insisted that the position should be filled by "one familiar with the lowly and despised
occupation of farming instead of a professor" and that "the man who
holds that job should be a graduate of God's University, the great
out-doors."[38] The Virginian, although he had assured Tugwell as
late as April 26 that he was "heartily in favor" of the economist's
confirmation by the Senate and that only Republicans would oppose
it,[39] now pictured him as a dangerous centralizer and collectivist who

lacked respect for the Constitution. Pressed by his adversaries in the committee hearings, Tugwell protested that he did not favor the Russian system and labelled himself a conservative. Nevertheless, the two senators picked up support from those who viewed the professor as an extreme radical with an "un-American" philosophy. "The dismissal of Professor Tugwell from the governmental service," a New Yorker advised the President, "would greatly reassure businessmen as to the devotion of your Administration to constitutional principles."[40] The strength of the opposition forced Roosevelt, after some delay, to apply pressure, including the use of patronage, to remove Smith's roadblock and obtain the promotion in June.[41]

In the summer of 1934, Tugwell's denunciations of the processors, distributors, and other business groups that had been criticizing the farm program troubled Chester Davis. The new Under Secretary's rhetoric reflected his distrust of business leaders, his belief that strong government controls were needed, and his tendency to see hostility to the New Deal as a product of selfish economic interests. His speeches also reflected the efforts being made by Jerome Frank and others to reform the agricultural marketing system so as to reduce the prices paid by urban consumers. Tugwell's critics charged that he hoped to arouse class conflict. Davis believed that cooperation between farmers and businessmen was needed to preserve the farm program and to make the marketing agreements workable, and he feared that Tugwell threatened to block the development of good relations between Triple-A and the "middlemen."[42] As Appleby explained to a friend:

The point at issue is a rather fundamental difference of opinion concerning the wisdom of attacking the processors. Chester believes that Earl Smith and Cliff Gregory are the best examples of successful farm leadership and they make it a point always to play with the big boys.[43]

". . . the realistic Davis," Professor Schlesinger has written, "was determined to work for the farmer within the existing structure of agricultural power."[44] Tugwell doubted that such an approach could produce desirable results, but he was losing most of his influence in Triple-A.[45]

Additional difficulties were rising that would reveal the narrow limits on his influence in that agency and would destroy the remnants of it. The farm program was being criticized by reformers and radicals as well as by conservative business leaders and their allies. Soon after Triple-A had gone into operation, various individuals, groups, and journals, including *Harper's* and *The Nation*, began to criticize AAA for its impact upon tenant farmers. The leader of the Socialist party, Norman Thomas, pushed this line in an especially vigorous fashion, arguing over and over again that Triple-A harmed these farmers in a number of ways and that the government should protect their rights, including their right to organize. In 1934, a new organization, the Southern Tenant Farmers Union, joined the battle, contending that Triple-A's cotton contract discriminated against the tenants, that the agency failed to enforce the provisions designed to offer some protection for these people, and that those in charge of the cotton program shared the landlord's point of view. In fact, many of the administrators were landlords![46]

Before the beginning of 1934, leaders in the department grew troubled about the problem and the criticism and sought ways to protect both the tenants and the farm program.[47] "Norman Thomas has been attacking us rather bitterly on this score in the south and the communist brethren are looking toward the field as a rich one to cultivate," Wallace warned. While he worried about "radical agitators," he felt they had a chance of success only where conditions were bad. Thus, recognizing the bias of his department, he encouraged Harry Hopkins to devote some of his attention to the rural poor. "The human rights are even greater than the land problem," the Secretary suggested, "and I am afraid it would be too easy for the representatives from Agriculture and Interior to overlook these rights."[48] Tolley and Ezekiel gave some thought to the impact of Triple-A on the tenants, and a Wisconsin-trained economist, Calvin Hoover, was called from his post at Duke University to take the lead in an investigation of this problem. In the early months of 1934, Hoover found that, although Triple-A was not the basic source of the tenants' difficulties and could not solve them, the landlords who dominated the farm program in the South were not giving their tenants a fair share of the benefit payments and were using the production control program as an excuse to reduce the number of tenants. Following his recommendations, a special committee was established in AAA to handle charges of maltreatment of tenants.[49]

In the months that followed, the administration attacked the problem in a cautious fashion. Most officials lacked confidence in the critics, believing that they presented a highly inaccurate view of the impact of Triple-A on the tenants and that they blamed the New Deal for a situation that had existed for many years. Furthermore, most officials hesitated to take any step that might alienate Southern landowners and cause them to refuse to cooperate in the farm program. Thus the officials frequently expressed faith in the great majority of these people and in the state and local agencies — the extension services and farmer committees — that were chiefly responsible for the administration of the farm program in the South. AAA relied heavily upon these agencies in dealing with landlord-tenant relations,[50] and Davis cautioned his investigators to avoid any suggestion that Washington lacked confidence in the planters, committeemen, and county agents. "The investigations," he explained, "are as much for the protection of committeemen, county agents, landowners, and others who have been unselfish and conscientious in these matters as it is for the protection of tenants or the Agricultural Adjustment Administration."[51]

Urban reformers and radicals in Triple-A, led by the legal counsel Jerome Frank and closely associated with Tugwell,[52] were not satisfied with the steps being taken and found at the beginning of 1935 a chance for a bold move. Davis, most Triple-A officials, and the landowners had interpreted the contract between the government and the landowners in the cotton program to mean that they were required, as far as possible, to keep the same number of tenants as had been on their land in 1933.[53] But now, for the first time, AAA lawyers were called upon for an opinion, and they ruled that the contract required landlords to keep the same people, not just the same number.[54] Here was an attempt to use the farm program to provide greater security for these low-income groups, an attempt the lawyers justified as necessary in order to realize the basic purpose of the legislation. They argued that it sought to promote the economic welfare of all rural groups, not just the landowners, and that the alternative interpretations of the contract did not provide adequate protection for the tenants. Among other things, the new ruling would assist efforts that were being made to organize these people, for it would prevent landlords from dismissing participants in union activities. In fact, the new interpretation had been advocated for some time by the Tenant Farmers Union, and the opinion was given as a consequence of the efforts of that organization. Throughout the South in the late months of 1934, landlord-tenant contracts for the new season had been negotiated in the customary fashion, and some landlords had evicted tenants who had joined the union and recruited substitutes. In December, 1934, the union had taken one of these landlords into court to test his right to make these changes. At this point, Frank's division had been called upon for an opinion on the cotton contract.[55]

Extension leaders in the South quickly protested the new ruling. They argued that it could not be enforced and would produce endless litigation. They argued also that it would create major problems for the extension services and farmer committees that were called upon to enforce it. Finally, they warned that it could seriously hamper and possibly destroy the cotton program.[56]

To Davis, the entire farm program seemed to be threatened by these urban people who had only recently moved into farm politics. Their ruling struck him as a dishonest distortion of the meaning of the cotton contract and but another in a long series of impractical acts by the lawyers that had harmed the Triple-A, preventing it from operating efficiently and effectively and risking the hostility of the leading groups in farm politics. He believed that his agency existed to bring higher prices to commercial farmers, not to reform the Southern social system or the nation's methods of marketing its crops; and he resented the view that the farm program was "entirely worthless so long as it did not result in a social revolution in the South."[57] Triple-A's task was economic recovery, a task that seemed to him to be of fundamental importance and one that had to be completed before progress along other lines could take place. He feared attempts to mix social reform with the recovery program:

To undertake to tie up the solution of the deep-seated social problem with the Agricultural Adjustment programs would probably make it impossible to carry out these emergency programs successfully. Regrettable and undesirable as some of the conditions are, it is not possible or advisable to undertake a definite and complete solution of these underlying economic and social problems as part of an emergency program designed to relieve the existing economic emergency.[58]

In addition, he had doubts about the ability of the federal government to develop a new social order in the South:

. . . the march of social and economic progress of the share croppers cannot be forced by the Federal Government to proceed much faster than the rate that Southern opinion and Southern leadership will heartily support. To try to force a faster pace would merely be to insure violent controversy, lack of local co-operation in administration, evasion and ineffectiveness for the plan.[59]

Influenced by these beliefs, Davis decided that he must either free himself of the Frank group or resign.

Fortunately for Davis, Wallace shared his views of political realities, at least to some extent. As had the Administrator, the Secretary had been working for more than a decade to develop a program capable of raising farm prices and had close ties with the Farm Bureau, commercial farmers, and their representatives in Congress. Although he admired Frank, Wallace had for some time been growing concerned about the political difficulties that the lawyers were generating, and now he believed that they had "allowed their social preconceptions to lead them into something which was not only indefensible from a practical agricultural point of view but also bad law." [60] He denied that the farm legislation gave the department the power "to change the undesirable social system in the South . . . ," [61] and, familiar with the "habits and customs" of Southern farm leaders and congressmen, he feared that if he followed "the extremist city groups there would be such a break with the men on the hill that the agricultural program might be destroyed." [62] The destruction would involve not only the interest in higher farm prices that he shared with the commercial farmers and their representatives but also the hopes for a fundamental reorganization of agriculture that he shared with the social scientists. He had advised Roosevelt late in 1934 that "the active interest and support" of the farm leaders meant "a very great deal to the successful inauguration and execution of a national land planning program." [63]

Two social scientists helped Davis and Wallace reach their decisions. Davis discussed the issue with Wilson; both Wilson and John D. Black, who admired Davis, accepted Davis' view of Triple-A's function, and distrusted the Tugwell-Frank group and their supporters, advised Wallace that for administrative and political reasons he had to support the Administrator. Wilson believed that the tenant problem in the South was an old one that should be attacked but not in a manner that would harm the adjustment program. The urban group, he believed, did not understand the farmer and consequently expected revolutionary changes; it might discredit and destroy the production control program in efforts to promote them. [64]

Tugwell, while sharing the hopes of Wallace and Wilson, did not believe that the salvation of the farm program depended upon firing the people who were unpopular with the major groups in farm politics. He, however, had a different background, a less cautious approach to politics, and a more critical attitude toward the leading figures in farm politics. Furthermore, by early 1935, the Under Secretary did not have enough power to save Jerome Frank. His relations with Wallace had been deteriorating for several months, and his influence in the Roosevelt Administration generally was in decline. Davis' influ-

ence, on the other hand, was growing. He had become part of what
Roosevelt termed his "inner cabinet" and had especially good relations with Congress.[65]

Thus, on February 5, 1935, Davis "purged" the Frank group from
Triple-A. In a press conference the following day, the Administrator
explained that the step had been taken in order "to have in the key
positions in Triple-A men who have some familiarity with farm problems and who have a farm background." Wallace supported the action,
explaining that "we don't like to have a ship that lists stronger to the
left or the right, but one that goes straight ahead." When one reporter
suggested that "you were going to the right when Peek was in and you
got rid of the right, and now you are rid of the left and are going down
the middle course," Wallace agreed. A moment later, however, apparently not fully satisfied with the "purge," he suggested that "we
might have to take on some more left-side ballast so we can go straight
ahead."[66] While his aide, Appleby, defended the move as necessary
in order to unify the department "administratively," he regretted the
action "profoundly," principally because of the way in which it was
done, for he was very fond of Frank.[67]

Involved in the "purge" was a reluctance to challenge power arrangements in farm politics.[68] ". . . all of the more important political pressures are producer pressures," Wallace believed, "and it has
always been my feeling that efforts to advance the consumer point of
view in government . . . will have to be rather quietly made."[69] As
the urbanites had caused trouble on the question of food prices, some
observers in Washington interpreted the event as a triumph of processors and middlemen over consumers and the general public.[70] Concern
about the farm groups, however, had played a much more important
part in the thinking of department officials than this interpretation
implied. Important farm leaders, sharing Davis' doubts about the
desirability of "city men" in "a farmer's department," had been calling for their dismissal, supported the purge when it came, and, at
least for a time, became more enthusiastic about Wallace and Triple-A
as a consequence of the action.[71] Acccording to Raymond Gram Swing,
writing in *The Nation*, the firing revealed that power in agricultural
politics lay with the processors, the distributors, and the big producers.
Roosevelt, the journalist maintained, was unwilling to make the
"frontal attack" needed to take "economic power from the interests
in agriculture who hold it and are increasing it."[72] The President kept

out of the episode, discussing it only briefly with Wallace and allowing him to handle it.[73]

After the purge, the department issued a new ruling on the landlord-tenant section of the cotton contract. The ruling specified that landlords were not required to keep the same tenants. It went on to insist, however, that this did not mean that landlords had no obligation under the section, that the department expected that no landowner would reduce the number of tenants on his farm as a consequence of the cotton program, and that landowners were expected to carry out the provisions of the section in a way that would give the tenants as much security as they would have in the absence of the program. On the other hand, while the department insisted further that the Secretary had a duty to protect the tenants in certain ways, the new ruling announced that no attempt would be made "to supervise the customary arrangements between landowners and tenants."[74]

The officials who promoted the purge hoped to develop and maintain an alliance behind the production control program, composed of the nation's commercial farmers and important urban business groups. Confident that the program would raise farm prices and keep them at a profitable level, the men were convinced that the operations of the program itself could persuade the farmers to support it. Businessmen, department officials believed, should support the program for several reasons. It not only held the businessman before the farmer as a model to be copied, but it promised to improve the businessman's economic and political situation. Promoters of this form of farm relief continued to believe and to argue, as they had in 1932, that it would supply farmers with the purchasing power needed for business prosperity and develop the satisfaction in farm communities that would make the farmer a conservative force in American politics.[75]

Some business groups, especially those that depended very heavily upon farm prosperity, continued to support the farm program. Wilson discovered, for example, "that the businessmen of the Northwest, because of their direct relationship to farm income and to the agricultural life of the community, have a very high degree of loyalty to the AAA. . . ."[76] Rogers of Prudential, Wood of Sears, and Harriman of the Chamber of Commerce remained supporters of the program. "I am just as convinced now as I was then [April, 1932] of the immediate and ultimate success of the [allotment] plan in the solution of the agricultural problem . . . ," Rogers wrote to Wilson in the summer of 1934.[77] "I am one of the businessmen who, selfishly perhaps (because my business is greatly dependent on the welfare of the farmer) but nevertheless, consistently, has supported the Agricultural Adjustment Act," Wood informed Roosevelt later that year.[78] Wood used the pages of the Sears mail-order catalogue to publicize his support of the New Deal farm program.[79] Harriman continued to believe that "for the first time a wise and constructive farm policy has been adopted, one that is both realistic and effective." [80]

In May, 1935, however, Harriman lost his position as president of the chamber, and the change symbolized growing discontent among business leaders with the New Deal, including the farm program.[81] Well-known business leaders and their conservative political allies had formed the Liberty League in 1934 to fight the New Deal, and the Liberty Leaguers had their own *Farm Journal* to battle against the agricultural program that tried to raise farm prices. This publication, which claimed to be the most influential farm magazine, had among its major owners two leaders of the Liberty League, J. Howard Pew and Joseph N. Pew, Jr., officers of the Sun Oil Company. Their publication, which filled its pages with slashing attacks upon the New Deal, its farm program, and the role of the intellectuals, busily devoted itself to the promotion of an anti-New Deal alliance between business and agriculture.[82] Closely related to this was the formation in April, 1935, of the Farmers Independence Council, a pressure group designed to draw the farmers away from Triple-A and composed in large part of leading financiers and manufacturers, including Lammot du Pont, Alfred P. Sloan of General Motors, Winthrop A. Aldrich of the Chase National Bank, and Arthur Beeter of Swift and Company. A historian has characterized the group as "at least a blood cousin" of the Liberty League and "a propaganda organ for industry, the meat packers, and some large cattle interests"; [83] and Ed O'Neal denounced these people and others like them as men who "farm the farmers" and as "Wall Street Hayseeds" masquerading as farmers while trying to defeat legislation real farmers wanted.[84] Among the objects of the council's attacks were the "college-bred crack-pots" and "the theories of the Tugwells." [85]

Thus, by 1935, the task of uniting farmers and urban businessmen behind production control appeared even more difficult than it had three years earlier. While many farm leaders and some businessmen applauded the program, many others bitterly opposed it. The social scientists were encountering additional evidence of the complexities of farm politics. Many opinions prevailed concerning the role that government should play in bringing prosperity to commercial groups on the farms and in the cities. To add to the complexities, other participants in the political process, less interested in enlarging profits, reminded the social scientists that commercial groups were not the only ones affected by farm relief programs. And the social scientists could not agree with one another about the best ways to behave in this complex political situation in order to protect the program that they hoped would lead to a large-scale reorganization of American agriculture.

CHAPTER 7

Planning for the Rural Poor

To Norman Thomas, the most striking feature of the production control program was its harmful impact upon the rural poor. This impact troubled the social scientists in farm politics, for their plans were not limited merely to efforts to improve the lot of commercial farmers and the use of the land. In accepting democratic as well as business and scientific values, the intellectuals hoped to use the land in ways that would make life better for all social groups. Even before the purge of the Frank group, efforts to tackle the problems of tenant farmers, farmers on submarginal land, and farm laborers, including Wilson's subsistence homesteads program and Gray's land purchase activities, got under way; after the purge, those efforts were expanded with the establishment of the Resettlement Administration headed by Rex Tugwell. Tugwell quickly learned, however, that great difficulties faced those who hoped to move down this path, for the most powerful pressures in farm politics favored the rural businessman.

The social scientists made some of the earliest efforts to deal directly with the problems of lower-income groups in rural America. "The simple fact that rural poverty existed in this country was never openly recognized by our government until approximately five years ago," an official noted in 1939. "Public recognition of the fact has come still more slowly. The idea of poverty has been traditionally associated with city slums. . . ."[1] Prior to the New Deal, Wilson's experiments in tenant rehabilitation at Fairway Farms represented an interest that did not exist in many other places. The agricultural economists, agricultural colleges, and extension services paid little attention to what the 1930's found to be an extensive series of problems. As a consequence, basic research had to be done at the same time that programs were getting under way, and administration suffered from inexperience in dealing with a serious situation.[2] Nevertheless, the planners plunged forward, moved by democratic convictions that their plans must consider all the people on the land, not just the commercial farmers and the ways to use the land itself more efficiently.

While Jerome Frank hoped to use Triple-A to improve the lot of the tenant farmers, the social scientists tended to think in terms of developing special programs for the lower ranks in agriculture. Calvin Hoover's report in the spring of 1934 had suggested that a "comprehensive policy for the economic rehabilitation of Southern agriculture" was "plainly required,"[3] and Wilson's and Gray's Land Planning Committee had called later in the year for an investigation of tenancy and for legislation on the subject.[4] In January, 1935, Hoover advised Wallace that the administration must face the fact that its farm program had "been of little net benefit to the tenants, sharecroppers, and laborers in the South" and that alternative programs must be provided for these groups. He believed that "all possible means to encourage and to require cotton producers to keep their accustomed number of tenants and sharecroppers should be made" but suggested that "extremely drastic measures to compel landowners to keep these people would be futile and ill-advised," as the market for cotton was declining and thus there was a "natural tendency . . . to dispose of surplus labor." He suggested a program to help these people "purchase small semi-subsistence farms in which they can produce the greater part of their necessities."[5] Hoover looked ultimately to industrial expansion as the solution to the ills of Southern agriculture. Through growth of this kind, he believed, the problem of agricultural surpluses would be solved by diminishing the supply of labor in agriculture on the one hand and by increasing the demand for agricultural commodities on the other.[6]

Another advocate of industrialization, Ezekiel, also insisted that

Triple-A could not solve the problems of the rural poor. While he believed that reports of a large displacement of tenants under the control program were "greatly exaggerated," he did admit "that the major part of the increased income under the program has gone to landlords rather than tenants." He insisted, however, that "in dealing with the cotton surplus problem the AAA was dealing with an emergency which required immediate action and . . . could not wait to take that action until the whole social system of the South had been remodelled." Alternative ways were needed to deal with the problems of tenant farmers.[7]

Gray and Wilson were already at work on alternatives. In mid-January, 1935, Gray advised Wallace that the tenancy problem in the South was "one of the most serious and complex socio-economic problems in rural America" and that it was "high time that a comprehensive effort be initiated to develop a new social economy for a large proportion of the Southern tenant population."[8] Before the end of the month, Wallace authorized Wilson to work vigorously on a request from Senator John Bankhead, Democrat from Alabama, that a bill be drafted that he could sponsor. Tapping his experience at Fairway Farms and hoping to promote experimentation with "new conceptions of relationships between farm families and the land," Wilson worked on a proposal to establish a government agency to buy land, sell it to farm families, and maintain some control over its use.[9] Gray and his subordinates believed that tenancy was an increasingly serious problem that had to be faced in the "immediate future." Unhappy that the United States was one of the few countries that had "done nothing either to promote a better form of agricultural tenancy than that which has haphazardly developed under our system of competitive and highly speculative land ownership, or to aid competent but landless agriculturists to establish themselves as owners," these social scientists assisted with the development of the proposed legislation.[10] At the same time, Wilson and Gray helped to form the National Committee on Small Farm Ownership. A product of the work of the Julius Rosenwald Fund on behalf of the rural poor in the South, the committee contributed to the drafting of the Bankhead bill and then worked to gain support for it.[11] Support came from department leaders, including Wallace and Davis, for they saw the bill as a solution to problems that Triple-A could not solve.[12]

Although department leaders were moving, they were moving slowly, for they hoped to coordinate any attack upon the problems of the rural poor with other programs, including production control and the retirement of submarginal land. As Sidney Baldwin points out, "in supporting efforts designed to help low-income farmers, the Department was not free to ignore the needs of other farmers." [13] Tugwell, however, moved forward much more boldly. For some time, he had been growing increasingly concerned about rural social problems and more unhappy with the department and Triple-A. The purge increased his unhappiness, prompting him to submit his resignation from the department. Roosevelt was able to keep him in place, but the economist remained bitter about the firings, displeased with Wallace, and convinced that AAA was dominated by the big farmers and that it discriminated against sharecroppers, tenants, and farm laborers. Consequently, he sought alternative ways of improving the lot of the rural poor. At the same time, he sought a means of coordinating the many agencies that dealt with the land. The two aims were closely related, for he believed that rural poverty resulted chiefly from a misuse of the land which in turn encouraged inefficient use of resources. Thus the government should buy the acres that were being used improperly, switch them to better uses, move the people to places where they could make a living, and help these people with loans and supervision. He discussed his ideas with Wilson, Wallace, and Roosevelt; the President by executive order on April 30, 1935, brought various activities together into a new agency, the Resettlement Administration, and supplied it with funds made available by the Emergency Relief Appropriation Act of 1935. It seemed necessary to rely upon an executive order and emergency funds, for congressional approval seemed unlikely. As the chief promoter of the step, Tugwell was chosen as administrator of RA. While he remained Under Secretary of Agriculture, his new agency was independent of the department.[14]

Rather than change the policies of the Department of Agriculture, Roosevelt had established a new agency to deal with the problems of the rural poor. Furthermore, he had placed a critic of Triple-A in charge of RA. Tugwell hired another critic, Dr. Will W. Alexander, as his top assistant. Clergyman, educator, and expert on race relations, Alexander, working with Edwin Embree and Charles S. Johnson and financed by the Rockefeller Foundation and the Rosenwald Fund, had just published a short study, *The Collapse of Cotton Tenancy*, which criticized the crop control program for its impact on the tenants and attempted to publicize their plight and produce action. Along with Embree, George Foster Peabody, and Frank Tannenbaum, Alexander had carried his case to the Administration, discussing it with Roosevelt, Wallace, Tugwell, Wilson, Gray, and Appleby, and had battled for the Bankhead bill. Alexander's appointment as assistant administrator was welcomed by his associates as a great and unusual opportunity to develop a program to help tenant farmers.[15]

The new agency attempted to improve land-use practices and to elevate those who were underprivileged as a result of past mistakes in the use of the land. The people included destitute groups living in once thriving but now exhausted lumbering, mining, and oil regions, sharecroppers in the South, and farmers on poor land in the Great Lakes cut-over region, in the drought area of the Middle West, and in the Appalachians. Gray's Land Policy Section was transferred to RA, and Gray became an assistant administrator of the new organization besides being director of its Division of Land Utilization, which took charge of all land purchase and land-use planning functions. In two years, although Congress failed to provide the kind of authority that Tugwell sought for the purchase of submarginal land, Gray spent over $50,000,000 acquiring approximately 9,000,000 acres of land. "The Federal government had never before undertaken to acquire so large an area in an equally short time," Gray reported to the President.[16] Poor farmland was converted to other uses, and conservation methods were put into practice on it. The planning staff of the Land Policy Section and the regional and state planning consultants of the Resources Board were transferred to RA, staffing the Land-Use Planning Section of Gray's division. A product of BAE's Land Economics Division, E. H. Wiecking, headed this section. It conducted a comprehensive program of national land-use planning that defined the nature of the nation's land-use problems and recommended changes in land-use practices.[17] ". . . the major effort of our land-use planning work at this time should center on planning for adjustments in those 'problem' areas which are characterized by critical maladjustments in the relation of people to land resources." Gray advised his subordinates.[18]

RA provided another illustration of the way in which the New Deal built upon the work of Gray's Division of Land Economics. The research in which that agency had long been engaged supplied a foundation for this action program. Just before RA was created, the division had completed a large study of the Southern Appalachians. It concluded that the basic problems of the region grew out of maladjustments in land use and in the relation of population to land and suggested that changes could not be made unless there was "a planning agency vested with powers and resources sufficient to cope with actual problems." After the establishment of such an agency, the work of Gray's old and new divisions became so closely integrated that the chief of the BAE, Al Black, began to fear that the Division of Land Economics had become merely a service agency of the Resettlement Administration and was not giving enough attention to basic research.[19]

Two striking features of RA were the wide variety of its activities and the broad use that it made of social scientists. In addition to land purchase and resettlement, the agency provided relief for victims of drought, guidance for migrants, loans and supervision to poor farmers to help them improve their operations, and loans to tenants to enable them to buy farms. RA also built communities and tried to develop more secure contracts for tenant farmers.[20] Tugwell called upon a rural sociologist, Carl C. Taylor, to direct the Rural Resettlement Division, a unit that took over tasks formerly handled by the Subsistence Homesteads Division and FERA.[21] Paul Taylor, an economist who had studied labor economics with John R. Commons and who had become a specialist on the problems of agricultural labor, supervised the early development of camps for migratory workers, a pitifully poor group of people.[22]

These programs for the rural poor assumed that rural poverty demanded an attack upon its causes, not just relief. The situation had taken many years to develop, and only long-run programs could correct it. Nor could the solution come entirely from indirect action, such as the expansion of urban employment. Rural poverty had to be dealt with directly through specially devised programs. And these programs needed to be devised because all Americans, not just the rural poor, suffered from poverty in agriculture, for it meant inadequate purchasing power, destruction of land, disease, costly social services, and the like. In other words, the programs assumed that a planned attack needed to be made as a consequence of the interdependent nature of modern society.[23]

Most important, the planned attack needed to be made because worthy human beings suffered directly from rural poverty. The programs rested, for the most part, on democratic rather than business assumptions, looking upon all men, not just those who had demonstrated abilities in business, as worthy of help from government. Involved here was a concept of man that stressed environment rather than innate qualities.[24] Wilson, for example, assumed that "poverty is not so much a matter of innate capacities or of inferior heredity, but rather the result of the interaction of the people, their institutions, and their social environment."[25] Again and again RA's literature testified to a faith that "these farmers are poor, not because they have suddenly become shiftless and lazy, but because their farms simply cannot be farmed at a profit."[26] The men in these poor environments had rights that the government must recognize:

The public has long been made aware of the social costs involved in the city slums, where improper housing, inadequate diet, disease and ignorance retard human development and hamper social progress. We are now becoming aware of similar conditions in rural areas, resulting from a century of unguided land settlement, and unrestricted private exploitation of natural resources. If these conditions of life are to be alleviated, and human life given the hope and opportunity which are its natural right, either some economic opportunity must be brought to these poverty-stricken rural areas, or the people must be offered the chance of moving to a place where opportunity now exists.[27]

This democratic concept of man did not mean that all of the rural poor should be treated in the same way. Not all of them could be made into commercially successful family farmers, for some knew only self-sufficient or plantation agriculture or had physical or mental deficiencies. Nevertheless, the government should take action. It could help them form cooperatives or obtain more secure tenure arrangements. The degenerate should at least be provided with relief. And nearly everyone, some more than others, should be provided with the guidance needed to raise their status. All but a few, in other words, had a capacity for improvement, and all were worthy of help.[28]

The planners disagreed about the best ways of approaching the vast problems that faced them. It appeared to some of the planners that their colleagues seemed more interested in land than people or seemed to think only of physical and economic factors and to ignore sociological ones. Some planners believed that the most desirable goal would be to help the rural poor make the transition to urban life, and thus they constructed three "greenbelt towns." Others stressed the richness of rural life and hoped to find ways to maintain contact with the land for large numbers of people. There were also conflicts between those who emphasized resettlement and those who believed in rehabilitating farmers on the land they occupied by providing financial and technical assistance.[29]

Tugwell emphasized resettlement, technological development, and urbanization. He looked upon subsistence homesteads as archaic and impractical, and he lacked enthusiasm for rehabilitation, believing that more fundamental changes in the use of the land were needed. He was responsible for these homestead and rehabilitation programs simply because he and Roosevelt agreed that all programs developed for the rural poor should be administered by one agency.[30]

The family farm provided a major focal point of controversy. Tugwell did not want it to be the only goal for the programs; he believed that only the most able tenants would benefit from a program designed to convert them into owners and that it would not solve the basic problem of insecurity. He wanted the government to experiment also with long-term leases and large-scale cooperative farms as well as with various other types of cooperatives, and he was highly critical of members of Gray's unit who had strong doubts, based on the study of cooperative experiments in America, that cooperative farming would succeed. The critics of this type of farming also disagreed with one another; some, like Carl and Paul Taylor, embraced a Jeffersonian philosophy that emphasized the virtues of the small, simple family farm, while others, like Wilson's friend Elmer Starch from Montana State College and Fairway Farms, advocated large, mechanized units to be formed by reorganizing existing arrangements in areas where people were unable to make a living from the farms they operated. After Tugwell and Carl Taylor reached a parting of the ways, Tugwell substituted an advocate of cooperative farming, Walter Packard, as head of the Resettlement Division. Cooperative farming became a small but important part of RA's activities.[31]

There were also disagreements concerning the proper organization of this agency. Hoping to avoid the difficulties he had encountered with FERA, Gray proposed that land purchase and resettlement — both of which were to be bigger programs than they had been in 1934 — should be handled by one administrative unit, but Tugwell rejected the proposal and established two divisions headed by Gray and Carl Taylor. Although the two men represented different disciplines — land economics and rural sociology — and had somewhat different points of view, cooperation was easier than it had been in 1934, for the two men were members of the same organization and were closer together intellectually than the representatives of AAA and FERA had been. Gray and Taylor worked in adjoining offices and took advantage of this opportunity to consult with one another and

to coordinate their activities. Gray and his lieutenants, however, remained dissatisfied with the resettlement program.[32]

Beyond the differences of opinion lay agreement that rural America
should be approached as something more than simply the home of
rural businessmen and that government should do more than increase
their profits. The programs, in other words, challenged the dominant
orientation of farm politics. Not surprisingly, therefore, Tugwell and
the Resettlement Administration came under heavy attack. Undoubtedly, internal weaknesses in RA, Tugwell's well-established tendency
to generate controversy, and nonagricultural dimensions of the agency's activities contributed to the attack.[33] Much of it, however, grew
out of the challenge that Tugwell and the Resettlement Administration
offered to the major powers in agriculture.

Critics were inclined to stress apparent administrative shortcomings in the agency and to suggest that they resulted from the selection
of impractical men to handle the programs.[34] "Too much theory and
too many professors," Congressman Clifford Hope complained. "The
Resettlement set-up here in Washington is so highly organized that
apparently no one has jurisdiction over anything, and I have never
seen a finer example of what can be done in the way of government
buck-passing. . . ."[35] "If Tugwell were a real executive," Robert E.
Wood advised Roosevelt, "he would be at his job trying to accomplish
something. There is . . . no evidence to show that he has really
accomplished anything for the millions that have been allotted to
him."[36] Had these critics been more sympathetic with the aims of RA
they might have paid more attention to the difficulties that Tugwell
faced in the development of it. Challenging the notion that he was a
poor administrator, his biographer emphasizes "the overwhelming
obstacles which confronted the RA."

Its basic task was extremely difficult, calling for vast, scattered and diverse
operations. The press was generally hostile. Most of the agency's clients were
poor and ignorant. The community idea encountered a dominating attachment
to the traditional on the part of the clients themselves and the rest of the population, which harbored no deep-felt concern for the plight of the rural poor.
Moreover, the RA had to carry out its functions while going through the process of initial organization — a process complicated by the inheritance of projects from other agencies.[37]

Many critics opposed the fundamental assumptions of the programs. These people disliked the idea of spending money on the poor
and charged that if they "had what it took" they would help them-

selves. "Substantial farmers, bankers and businessmen in rural areas complain bitterly against federal resettlement or rehabilitation of the needy," one commentator noted.

In their hardboiled opinion many of the Tugwell beneficiaries need a dose of energy and ambition rather than cows, ploughs and seed paid for by Uncle Sam. Local burgomasters fear that once government aid is withdrawn, the resettled and rehabilitated will become public charges which the towns and counties must support.[38]

RA's critics included urban property owners near the community projects, businessmen who feared that resettlement would take away their customers, and financiers who preferred government credit agencies that operated according to good "business principles" and without "subsidies";[39] but representatives of the large commercial farmers provided the most effective opposition. Southern cotton planters opposed changes in the sharecropping system, while the corporate farmers of California and their allies in the Chambers of Commerce criticized the camps for migratory workers. As constitutional rights were respected in the camps, they provided a place where efforts could be made to organize the workers; employers could block such efforts in the camps they owned. Many commercial farmers warned that RA must not aggravate the farm surplus problem, and their spokesmen, especially in the Farm Bureau, made their reservations known, decrying aid to the "shiftless." Such powerful men as Byrd and Glass of Virginia, Bailey of North Carolina, and Harrison of Mississippi expressed these views in Congress and subjected the programs to constant pressure and criticism. They had no desire to see the government upset the class structure in agriculture.[40] "I know what's the matter with Harry Byrd," Roosevelt told Tugwell when the Senator was objecting to a resettlement project in Virginia. "He's afraid you'll force him to pay more than ten cents an hour for his apple pickers."[41]

Some members of Triple-A also disliked Tugwell's efforts. There was much talk of conflict between the objectives of the two agencies.[42] When a decision was made at the end of 1936 to place RA in the Department of Agriculture in hopes of reorienting the programs somewhat, solving the appropriations problem, and giving the department the power to deal with all farm people, many of the officials in the department feared the change, believing that Tugwell would antagonize the cotton planters and shatter cooperation between them and AAA.[43] On the other hand, the Southern Tenant Farmers Union also criticized the decision to move RA, for the union regarded the depart-

ment as dominated by the "rich and large land-owning class of farmers and their political-pressure lobbies."[44]

Thus, powerful opponents, many of whom supported other programs developed by the social scientists, fought the programs for
the rural poor. "In a democracy such as ours," Marquis Childs concluded after watching the attacks upon rural poverty,

it is difficult or impossible to confer any benefit unless there exists or can be
created an articulate, organized demand for that benefit. A benefit implies some
change in the *status quo*, perhaps to the disadvantage of those already privileged. Therefore the privileged forces incline to unite in order to preserve what
exists, at the sacrifice of what might be, no matter how intelligent and reasonable the latter.[45]

Tugwell recognized that he could gain effective support more easily
for ideas about raising farm prices than for proposals about elevat-
ing the status of impoverished groups. "The people who are being
worked with do not count greatly in their communities," he observed:

Many of the clients cannot, or at any rate do not vote and so, especially in the
South, the politicians can afford to call them lazy, shiftless, no-account. The
efforts toward farmer aid can more profitably go to the better citizens among
the rural folk who can be expected to suitably repay political efforts made in
their behalf.[46]

In this situation, Tugwell was forced to tackle vast problems with
small sums of money.[47]

The situation did not seem hopeless, however, for Tugwell and the
programs for the rural poor had friends as well as enemies, and thus
some power could be mobilized behind ideas about major social and
economic changes. To many people who advocated a substantial over-
haul of the social and economic systems, Tugwell seemed to be an
intelligent and idealistic promoter of necessary changes who was being
hounded by "reactionaries," representatives of "special interests,"
"monopolists," the "money trust," and enemies of efforts to improve
the lot of lower-income groups.[48] Late in 1935, the *New Republic* referred to Tugwell's work as "one of the few remaining fragments of
what ever was once hopeful in the New Deal,"[49] and a year later an
old reformer, Frederic C. Howe, commended Tugwell for his "vision
. . . of a different kind of America."[50]

Roosevelt and a number of people in and out of Congress supported
the programs for the rural poor. The President regarded RA as "experimental perhaps, but nevertheless probably as important to civilization as the Research Department of the General Electric Company."

After the agency had been in operation for a year, he pointed out that it had made 104,000 farm families practically self-sustaining by supervision and education along practical lines. This seemed to Roosevelt to be "a pretty good record." [51] In Congress, some members of both parties, chiefly from the South, the Midwest, and the Far West, frequently battled for the programs. Outside of Congress, they picked up support from many social workers, educators, philanthropists, religious leaders and planners, and from a few newspapermen. Encouragement and help came also from Eleanor Roosevelt, John Steinbeck, organized labor, and the Farmers Union. Conspicuously absent from the list were the other major farm organizations.[52] "We are the only farm organization supporting his [Tugwell's] activities . . . ," one leader of the Farmers Union announced in 1936. "Resettlement is our friend in court. Let's make it stronger and even more worthwhile." [53]

Although Tugwell advised Norman Thomas that the political situation prevented RA from changing Southern agriculture overnight and thereby caused the Socialist to complain to Roosevelt that the Administrator was afraid of powerful Southern senators,[54] he did try to push his ideas boldly. Some of his lieutenants, in fact, believed that he wanted to move too rapidly, failed to understand people, and did not treat congressmen, farm leaders, and representatives of the land-grant colleges properly. These members of the Resettlement Administration believed that he did not give enough attention to the exploration of the methods needed to accomplish objectives and that he was impatient with and intolerant of those who knew that such explorations were necessary and who disagreed with him. To others in RA, however, their chief seemed both a practical man and a man of courage, ready to battle for his ideas without regard for his personal career, while the more cautious members of the agency were so fearful of losing their jobs that they would not fight for their convictions.[55]

Tugwell concluded that the American party system needed to be reorganized, and he proposed a scheme that challenged the efforts of those seeking an alliance of commercial farmers and urban business groups. Elements of the Democratic party annoyed him, especially the powerful Southern "reactionaries" like Senators Smith, Byrd, Bailey, and Glass. On the other hand, he got along well with progressives in both parties, men like Senators Black, Bankhead, Norris, Wheeler, and La Follette. Roosevelt provided some encouragement, for he, believing that certain groups in the Democratic party stood in the way of needed reform, considered the idea of either re-making that party or creating a new Progressive party.[56]

Tugwell envisioned a new Progressive party, based on an alliance between farmers and workers. In Los Angeles in October, 1935, he made an impassioned plea for such a party and such an alliance. Picturing the period as involving "the death struggle of industrial autocracy and the birth of democratic discipline," he insisted that the progressives had to "lead the way toward this future and to pre-vent another turning backward to the past." They had to make cer-tain that the job was done in a democratic and evolutionary fashion. If the forward motion did not continue and Americans returned to "the job of getting rich at one another's expense," there would soon be a "vast rising of rebellious, exploited people. . . ." To stop the forward motion, "the reactionaries" would try to split the farmers and workers. They, however, were the "natural progressive allies . . . :"

We should succeed at once in establishing a farmer-worker alliance in this country which will carry all before it, which will reduce our dependence on half-way measures and allow us to carry through these reconstructive ones both in agriculture and in industry without which our nation cannot continue either free or prosperous.

Behind the proposal lay assumptions about the movement of his-tory and the behavior of groups. Industrialism pushed history toward a collectivistic society that could not be resisted successfully, for cooperation and "central compulsion" were needed to make an indus-trial economy function without frequent depressions. Powerful busi-ness leaders, however, resisted the movement because so many of them stood "to gain from disorder and disunity rather than from cooperation. . . ." This resistance, if successful in the short run, might lead to revolution when the next depression hit. On the other hand, workers and farmers were most likely to support the movement, for they had the most to gain from it. To function smoothly, a highly productive industrial system required that they be prosperous. The role of the progressive leader, then, was to make these groups fully aware of their common interests and thus to unite them. With such support, he could achieve the change democratically and not be forced to compromise constantly with business groups.[57]

Tugwell had selected a hot spot in which to make such a speech. Many farm and business leaders in southern California regarded radi-calism as a major threat, feared that a farmer-labor alliance would take shape, and worked hard to develop cooperation between agriculture and other lines of business. The Chambers of Commerce and the Farm Bureau in the state had organized the Associated Farmers to resist efforts to organize workers in the canneries, processing sheds, and fields. Hostility toward Paul Taylor's migratory labor camps was related to this.[58]

The speech touched a sensitive nerve and produced more criticism than any other Tugwell pronouncement. Vigorous protests came from the editors of *The New York Times*, Hamilton Fish, Bainbridge Colby, Senator Dickinson, Elizabeth Dilling, the Daughters of the American Revolution, the Liberty League, and others. Republicans made much of the speech in the 1936 campaign. These critics charged that the intellectual was spreading "class hatred," seeking to promote a "class revolution," and hoping to establish "regimentation," "class government," a "communistic state," etc. The critics pointed out that Marxists called for such a political alliance.[59] A number of left-of-center groups were calling for a farmer-labor party at the time,[60] and the reaction to Tugwell's speech suggests that many people on the right wing of American politics feared that such a party might take shape.

Businessmen in farm politics indicated that they would resist any effort to form a farmer-labor alliance. "This is the old I.W.W. appeal which was imported from Europe in the days before the Russian Revolution," George Peek maintained. "It neglects the outstanding fact that most farmers are capitalists and that labor generally has a real stake in the capitalistic system." [61] The *Farm Journal* warned of the dangers of dividing groups as Tugwell proposed and, at the same time, counseled the farmer about the dangers that urban labor posed for him. Russia was put forward as "the outstanding example" of the implications of the professor's proposal. There "the peasant is again a serf as he was a century ago. He is merely laboring for the city populations, instead of the nobility and the Czar." This would happen in America if farmers followed Tugwell's advice. Instead, they should join forces with the urban businessmen:

many industrial leaders are deeply interested in farm prosperity . . . the bigger the manufacturer, the more clearly he understands the identity of interest between industry and agriculture.[62]

Another vigorous promoter of an alliance between the farmer and the businessman, Robert Wood, also was shocked by Tugwell's proposal and told Roosevelt and Wallace so. The Sears company's executive argued that Tugwell's close ties with the President made the professor dangerous, for "his entire size-up of the situation in the United States is absolutely wrong." According to Wood, only "the extreme radicals" liked Tugwell. Business and farm leaders did not, nor did most of the American people, who wanted reform but not the radical changes that he advocated. As to the proposed alliance:

No more vicious speech was ever delivered than the one Mr. Tugwell delivered in Los Angeles when he called on the farmers and the workers of the country to unite, practically urging them to revolution. That speech did more to put doubts in the minds of liberal men who have been friendly to the Administration than any other one thing that has happened in the past three and one-half years.

"As one who has been a friend of the Administration," Wood added, "I hate to see it saddled with such a liability and the Los Angeles speech certainly proves him to be a liability." [63]

Roosevelt's political general, James A. Farley, agreed that Tugwell had become a political liability. On May 9, 1936, Farley advised the Cabinet that "the two main points of greatest attack by the Republicans will be WPA and Tugwell." Farley suggested to FDR that Tugwell should not be used in the campaign, and the President agreed. [64]

The decision, however, did not prevent Republicans and others from attacking the professor and other intellectuals around Roosevelt. Republicans ran full-page advertisements in the national farm magazines containing descriptions of Landon as "a practical man" who came from "a farm state," was "a self-made man" who understood "agriculture without the help of Tugwellism," and had "a sound, workable agricultural program." [65] They circulated a pamphlet attack with such titles as "REX THE FIRST: The Ruler Nobody Elected," [66] a title that reflected the often repeated but absurd charge that Tugwell dominated Roosevelt and the New Deal. [67] The Republican candidate for the Presidency attacked Tugwell, and the Republican National Committee as well as other campaign orators frequently issued statements associating the intellectuals with revolution, radicalism, communism, and the like, all the while insisting that these men on the far left controlled national policies. [68] In addition, Al Smith, who had broken with Roosevelt and was campaigning for Landon, frequently attacked Tugwell, suggesting in Pittsburgh that he should "get one of these raccoon coats that college boys wear at a football game and . . . go to Russia, sit on a cake of ice and plan all he wants" and asking in New York "in the name of all that is good and holy, who is Tugwell and where did he blow from." [69]

Early in October, when asked about the attacks upon him, Tugwell replied that he had "no comment on politics." *The New York Times* reported that "from now on until November he expects to remain at his desk in Washington, attending to Resettlement business, with perhaps an occasional visit to one of his regional offices." He made only one major public statement during the period. Obviously, this most vigorously criticized professor had been placed "under wraps" by the Democratic campaign strategists. [70]

Although Secretary Ickes believed that Tugwell had been "a good deal of a political load for the President to carry," [71] the size of Roosevelt's victory suggests that the load had not been too heavy. [72] In fact, during the campaign the Republicans had taken pains to indicate that their attacks on Tugwell and the "brain trust" did not grow out of anti-intellectualism, as some suggested. [73] The Republican party formed its own "brain trust" to help with the campaign, a development that delighted supporters of the Democratic professors. "Ever since 1933, the practical men who run the Republican party have vibrated between superior ridicule and angry denunciation of the existing administration for calling to its counsels the despised professors," the *New Republic* reminded its readers.

It was assumed that the way to win the voters back to the Republican Party was to persuade them that the management of the country would be safe only in the hands of those practical men who, because they scorned theoretical knowledge, had blessed us with 1929 and 1932.

After rubbing this salt into the fresh wounds, the publication continued with obvious enjoyment: "But it appears to be the fate of the Republicans to make costly blunders. And so now . . . they flatter Mr. Roosevelt by imitating his brain trust." [74] In the House, the Texas progressive Democrat, Maury Maverick, made a speech on this new brain trust and then urged Tugwell to help him turn out a pamphlet with "some damaging stuff" against it. "If we divert the minds of the people off our own brain trust we can take a lot of wind out of the Republican bag." [75] Some Republicans agreed; they opposed their own advisory group because it weakened their case against the New Deal's professors. [76] According to M. L. Wilson, the development was "a great break for F.D.R." [77]

Although the creation of a "Republican brain trust" suggested that many Americans had developed a positive attitude toward certain types of intellectuals, Tugwell recognized that he was not acceptable to many powerful people and that if he remained in government he could look forward to a continuation of the tiresome criticism that had been heaped upon him for nearly four years. His biographer has concluded that "the general pattern of Tugwell's . . . reaction to the attacks was sensitiveness at first and growing insensitiveness as time passed." Roosevelt had "thanked him for the way he stood up under fire" and had remarked to the Secretary of Interior that "no one connected with him or the Administration had been subjected to such criticism as Rex had. Yet Rex had never whimpered or asked for sympathy or run to anyone for help. He has taken it on the chin like a man."[78] He was, however, "still capable of resentment."[79] Furthermore, he recognized that criticism of him complicated RA's tasks and that the agency could more easily secure funds from Congress if he were not in charge. In addition, he resented the fact that in spite of his loyal service to the Administration he had not been allowed to participate in the 1936 campaign.[80] Consequently, just after Roosevelt's big victory, though the President made a well-publicized trip with Tugwell and Alexander to a greenbelt town in order to reaffirm his personal faith and interest in Tugwell and Resettlement,[81] Tugwell resigned.

His friends had interpreted the victory as a vindication of him, and his enemies had feared that it would lead to an increase in his influence, but Tugwell knew that the orientation of the party, with many powerful Democrats regarding him as a dangerous liability, would prevent him from accomplishing what his friends hoped and his enemies feared. Even the particular brand of progressivism that was then exerting such a large influence on the Administration displeased him, for it was the Brandeis type that distrusted his proposals for centralized planning.[82] As Sternsher has written, "[Tugwell's] personal influence at the White House had dwindled."[83]

When Tugwell looked beyond government to the pressure groups, he found little to encourage him. "Management is seeking nothing, apparently, except the enlargement of profits," he wrote, "and labor nothing but an increasing share in them. This is not an atmosphere in which one who is concerned for the nation's welfare can hope for very much." The behavior of the voters provided a base for some optimism. "Perhaps in time the demand for economic statesmanship will sink in."[84]

The social scientist had experienced disillusionment. According to Professor Sternsher, Roosevelt's rise to the Presidency had "raised Tugwell's enthusiasm and expectation in the field of institutional reconstruction." He had soon learned, however, "that there would be no quick change from an individualistic to a more collectivized society, that the New Deal would comprise measures which from his standpoint were essentially superficial." By the end of 1936, developments "brought him to bewilderment, to an inability to span the gap between his basic ideas about planning and the actual New Deal programs." [85]

To the great amusement of the press, this critic of business joined a business firm — the American Molasses Company — after leaving Washington.[86] One critic, reflecting an assumption frequently involved in the criticisms of the intellectuals, applauded Tugwell for the switch, suggesting that "after a little seasoning in private business" he could "return to public life with much more practical ideas." [87] The planner, however, did not remain in business for long but soon accepted positions as chairman of the City Planning Commission and as Commissioner of the Department of City Planning in New York City, hoping to accomplish there what he had been unable to achieve in the nation and revealing once again that he did not have inseparable ties with agriculture.[88]

His spot as Under Secretary of Agriculture was filled by the more rural M. L. Wilson. Wilson had much better relations with the powers in the Democratic party. In 1935, for example, he had worked closely with one of Tugwell's most vigorous critics, Senator Smith of South Carolina, on amendments to the Agricultural Adjustment Act. Wilson was able to do this although he recognized Smith's dislike of the social scientists and believed that Smith was ignorant of modern conditions.[89] Unlike Tugwell, Wilson participated in the 1936 campaign, making wise suggestions about the selection of speakers for the farm belt, using his wide contacts in farm circles to inform himself on voter sentiment and other political realities, and campaigning strenuously in farm areas.[90] "I want you to know how much I appreciate the splendid cooperation you have given me and your real help in making the work of the Women's Division successful," an officer of the Democratic National Committee wrote to Wilson after the victory in November. At the same time other officers of that committee wrote that it felt "a deep debt to you, and it will rely upon you through the next few years to keep the torch of Democracy burning as brightly as it does today." [91]

Wilson's relations with the leaders in farm politics were also much more friendly than Tugwell's. Wilson's "standing in the agricultural world is at the very top," Appleby believed.[92] When the Montanan replaced the New Yorker in January, 1937, congratulations poured in, as they had when Wilson replaced Tugwell as Assistant Secretary nearly three years earlier. Words of praise came from farm leaders like O'Neal and Taber, from presidents of the land-grant colleges, extension directors, deans of the agricultural colleges, editors of farm journals, congressmen from farm areas, and from executives of railroads, farm industries, banks, insurance companies, Montgomery Ward, and Sears, Roebuck.[93] While some of Wilson's supporters called attention to similarities between him and Tugwell and expressed satisfaction with the important roles in farm politics of both social scientists, many of the people shared the view of a railroad official who wrote: "I think you will fit in much better than Rex did. You understand the problems first hand."[94] "Mr. Wilson is a college professor but also a very practical man who has had a great deal of experience in the West," Congressman Hope explained to a group of Kansans.[95]

Obviously, many of the leading figures in farm politics distinguished between different types of intellectuals and preferred the Wilson type. His presence in Washington encouraged many farmers and businessmen, as well as representatives of the agricultural colleges, to cooperate with the New Deal farm programs.

While Tugwell thought of a farmer-labor alliance, Wilson gave top priority to an alliance between the commercial farmers of the South and Middle West. The introduction of the tariff issue into the 1936 campaign had troubled him, for he recognized that industrialists who had an interest in higher tariffs sought an alliance with Middlewestern farmers and that the Republican strategy sought to break the ties among the farmers of the corn, wheat, and cotton regions that had taken shape in the McNary-Haugen fight of the 1920's. "The plan of forcing a wedge between the Southern and Western farmers is the familiar tactic of the G.O.P.," Wilson informed a friend. "Often before it has worked and may work this year." The "intense propaganda" about agricultural imports could "serve its purpose of distracting attention from the main issue: the absolute necessity of maintaining the friendly working relationships between the farmers of the West and South so as to assure a permanent and effective national program."[96] This alliance, it should be noted, was the one

that Ed O'Neal and Earl Smith of the Farm Bureau were busily working to maintain and enlarge.[97]

Wilson, in short, was much closer to the leading figures in farm
politics than Tugwell was. Upon leaving Washington, the latter published his thoughts about the possibilities of a farmer-labor alliance,
recognizing that many obstacles stood in the way of its development
but suggesting that they could be overcome. He challenged the idea
that farmers had a natural affiliation with businessmen, arguing that
the farmers' most serious quarrels were with bankers and merchants
rather than with workers and suggesting that "the La Follette following is enough to prove that farmers and workers will unite when a
coherent program which appeals to both groups is presented and
when the leadership is adequate."

He believed, however, that the major farm organizations and labor
unions could not provide the leadership needed to form the new party.
The farm groups represented the upper classes in agriculture and
often cooperated with "the farmer's natural enemies." The members
of the Farm Bureau and the like were "those farmers who would be
least likely to recognize any common interest with workers." Nor
could the "old unions" provide the leadership, for they spoke for
"the aristocracy of labor." These groups contributed to the "growing
class distinctions in American life."

The Farmers Union and the CIO, dipping lower into society and
criticizing business more vigorously, offered more hope. They "might
in time work out that 'natural' cooperation which many liberals have
talked of," Tugwell believed. "But so far," he added, "the strength of
the Farmers Union is regional rather than national, even though its
interests are broad. So that an alliance of this sort seems a long way
off. . . ." Consequently, Tugwell believed that the alliance had to
be created by progressive leadership. The task would be difficult; it
would take time; Roosevelt could only lay the groundwork during
his second administration. If the groundwork were laid, however, a
later forceful progressive leader could create the alliance.[98]

To Tugwell, this alliance seemed essential to provide the power
necessary to promote the kind of planning that he had in mind, including his plans for the rural poor. Programs for that group did not stop
with his departure from Washington. In fact, he chose his own successor in RA, Will Alexander, and thereby helped to guarantee the
survival of the agency and to prevent men who were hostile to it from
influencing the choice of administrator.[99] The programs for the rural

poor, however, now moved in directions that failed to satisfy Tugwell. His work did not "grow into our national policy," as one of his supporters had predicted it would.[100]

After the election, Roosevelt established the Special Committee on Farm Tenancy to study and publicize the problems of tenancy in hopes of gaining the support needed to set up an effective program.[101] Congress had refused to pass the Bankhead bill in 1935 and 1936; and Roosevelt, trying to avoid a new program that would increase government spending, had stopped pushing the bill during the election year.[102] RA, the Land Planning Committee of the National Resources Board, and the USDA, however, had continued to give attention to the question and had shaped plans for a well-publicized study of it. Wilson, Tugwell, and Gray had played important roles in these developments. In addition, both Republicans and Democrats had promised during the campaign to attack rural poverty.[103]

Roosevelt's instructions to the new committee reflected the Jeffersonian elements in his political faith and his desire that farm programs should not be limited to those that served only the larger and more prosperous farmers. He advised the group to

thoroughly examine and report on the most promising ways of developing a land tenure system which will bring an increased measure of security, opportunity, and well-being to the group of present and prospective farm tenants. The rapid increase of tenant farmers during the past half century is significant evidence that we have fallen far short of achieving the traditional American ideal of owner-operated farms. The growing insecurity of many classes of farm tenants, frequently associated with soil depletion and declining living standards, presents a challenge to national action which I hope we can meet in a thoroughly constructive manner.[104]

Gray, because of his long familiarity with the subject and the availability in his organization of much of the relevant material and technical personnel, became executive secretary of the committee and chairman of its technical committee. His Division of Land Economics had done significant work on tenancy in the early 1920's and had returned to the subject in 1936, working with RA's Land-Use Planning Section. This work had convinced Gray that the land and the commercial farmers as well as the tenants suffered from the existing system and that government action was needed to change it. He was especially critical of the ways tenants were treated by landlords in the South and believed that the system there had been disintegrating for many years and that Triple-A had merely accelerated the process.

He did not advocate the ownership of family-sized farms for more than a small number of the tenants, for he believed that most of them lacked the personal qualities, experience, and capital that were required. He recommended that the government should help "qualified operators" become owners of such farms but should provide assistance of other types for most Southern tenants. The government should improve landlord-tenant relations and develop a "small holdings program" for those who were incapable of operating large farms successfully.[105]

In addition to Gray and his staff, a number of social scientists contributed to the work of the committee. Next to Gray's, Wilson's role was the largest. Tugwell, Ezekiel, John Black, Al Black, E. G. Nourse, Lowry Nelson, Charles S. Johnson, Howard Odum, William I. Myers, and Henry C. Taylor, among others, also contributed.[106] They struggled to develop a report that would be both accurate and effective; they hoped to move the reader to sympathize with the plight of the tenants and to convince him that the report conformed to the standards of scientific dependability that many of the contributors represented.[107]

The technical committee's draft offended some members of the larger committee, especially Ed O'Neal. They regarded the draft as too critical of tenancy, landlords, the South, and race relations and, in spite of objections from some of the social scientists, forced the technicians to alter the draft. Nevertheless, O'Neal remained dissatisfied and finally protested formally against features of the report. He disliked the suggestion that those who purchased farms under the program would be required to wait a substantial period before making final payment, a provision designed to give the purchaser greater security and enable him to devote more of his money to the needs of his family, to check speculation and transfer of land to absentee landlords, and to enable the government to supervise the purchaser's operations. O'Neal believed that the principle of ownership was involved and that a man should be allowed to buy and sell his land quickly if he desired. O'Neal also wanted state and local administration to be controlled by the extension services. ". . . we don't want theorists coming into our areas and . . . putting over things that we know are impracticable and will not succeed," the farm leader insisted. He warned that the report would antagonize the organization and farmers he represented and also many congressmen.[108]

The committee's labors, involving meetings in Washington and five regional centers during December, January, and February as well as research by Gray and his associates,[109] produced a report to the President on February 13 that advocated a continuation and expansion of major RA programs. The report stressed the great increase in tenancy during the preceding half century but recognized that rural poverty and insecurity were not limited to tenant farmers. Aware that abuses associated with tenancy had been developing for two centuries, the report suggested that they could not be corrected overnight but advised that the nation could and should attack them as rapidly as its resources of manpower, money, and experience would permit. "Most civilized nations have set their hands to a similar undertaking, and some of them have been engaged in it for many years. It is high time that the nation begin the task." Concluding with a call for action — "action to enable increasing numbers of farm families to enter into sound relationships with the land they till and the communities in which they live," the report recommended two types of action: measures "to facilitate movement upward from rung to rung by farmers who are prepared to take such steps" and others "to increase security on each of the ladder's various rungs." The proposed list was long and included both federal and state activity; the report contained a warning against restricting action to any one approach. "The Committee offers recommendations on facilitating farm-home ownership, but at the same time it is well aware of the limitations of this approach in solving the whole farm-tenancy problem." The report recognized that the American emphasis on ownership in fee simple was an important cause of the insecure, destructive, and speculative type of agriculture existing in many places, that simple efforts to enable tenants to obtain farms could not solve the problems, that a large proportion of farmers should continue as tenants, and that a major objective of a program should be to improve relationships between landlords and tenants so as to obtain greater security and income for the latter and encourage them to improve their farms.[110] "Taken as a whole," Murray Benedict has written, "the Farm Tenancy Report constituted the most comprehensive analysis of the problems associated with low-income farm groups and the most carefully considered set of proposals relating to them, that had been made up to that time."[111]

The report, along with Roosevelt's enthusiastic endorsement of it, helped produce a new piece of legislation, the Farm Security Act of July, 1937. It did not conform to the committee's recommendations, for they had encountered strong opposition from members of the House Committee on Agriculture as well as from the Farm Bureau. Nevertheless, the new law was significant. It represented a new type of legislation which specifically included the problems of tenancy and poverty within the sphere of agricultural policy.[112] It converted a temporary agency based on executive authority into a permanent, authorized bureau of the Department of Agriculture.[113] The act contained provisions on rural rehabilitation and the retirement of submarginal lands but emphasized loans to tenants to enable them to buy family-sized farms. The loans could extend over a forty-year period, could be made without requiring a down payment, and were available at 3 per cent. The legislation authorized annual appropriations for this purpose of $10,000,000 for fiscal year 1938, $25,000,000 for 1939, and no more than $50,000,000 for each year thereafter.

To administer the program, Wallace established a new agency in September, the Farm Security Administration. It operated inside the department and replaced the Resettlement Administration. The change in name reflected the move away from Tugwell; originally he had emphasized the retirement from agriculture of submarginal land and the resettlement of people on good land, but by late 1937 resettlement was but a minor (although frequently criticized) part of the functions of the agency, and another agency was in charge of the land purchase program. The difficulties of resettlement, including the reluctance of people to move and the difficulty of finding enough good land, had for some time been helping the advocates of rehabilitation in place. The efficient family farm now became the main goal of the agency's policies. The rehabilitation program, the largest FSA activity, dealt chiefly with poor farmers — owners as well as tenants — who needed loans, guidance, and other forms of help to maintain, improve, and enlarge their operations; the tenant purchase program, the second largest activity, helped tenants and laborers acquire and develop farms of their own. Almost every one of the resettlement projects was of the family-farm type. This emphasis on the family farm reflected one of the pressures under which the whole effort for the rural poor operated, for this type of farm was endorsed by agricultural orthodoxy. Tugwell's cooperative farms, on the other hand, struck congressmen and others as communistic and were attacked accordingly. FSA administered only four of these.[114]

Tugwell disliked this emphasis upon the family farm. "It is really too bad that the tenant bill as it passed allowed nothing for communal and cooperative activities," he wrote to Roosevelt. "I am sure they would grow slowly here; and we need to be more cooperative, all of

us, if we need anything in the world."[115] Other critics of the changes
in the programs for the rural poor agreed with him. William L. Blackstone, a representative of the Tenant Farmers Union, besides being
unhappy with proposals for the control of the various programs,
strongly dissented "from the 'small homestead' philosophy as the solution for the majority of the southern agricultural workers" and advocated "cooperative effort under enlightened Federal supervision";
another representative of the union, Gardner Jackson, called upon
the House committee to promote the unionization of tenant farmers
and sharecroppers, large-scale rehabilitation measures, and cooperative farming, not the family farm.[116]

Tugwell, Blackstone, and Jackson, however, were outside the main-
stream of farm politics. Wilson, on the other hand, supported the new
program. Alexander regarded him as one of FSA's best and most
influential friends within the department.[117] When Senator Bankhead
first introduced his bill, Wilson had referred to the proposal as "a bill
to establish a kind of Federal Fairway system . . ."; and when the
tenant purchase program got under way, it adopted the tenant purchase
contract that had been developed at Fairway Farms.[118] The contract
obligated the purchaser to accept supervision in the management of
his farm and finances.[119] Although he believed that there were good
as well as bad forms of tenancy, rejected "the assumption that all
the problems of our agricultural population can be solved by pursuing
the family commercial farm approach," and wanted to experiment
with various tenure arrangements, the "ideal of the family size farm"
occupied a larger place in his schemes for agriculture than in Tugwell's. Wilson was "a deep believer in farm ownership by the family
who operates the farm."[120] As did Roosevelt and Wallace, Wilson
hoped and worked for more adequate legislation but believed that the
Bankhead-Jones Act was a significant accomplishment. "The funds
available for the purchase of farms to be resold to tenants is not very
great," he informed a friend. "It will be a start, however, and it will
serve as a demonstration which I hope will lay the basis for a widespread public interest and a gradually extending plan in connection
with tenancy."[121]

Although this emphasis on the family farm conformed to agrarian
orthodoxy, Congress provided but small support for FSA's efforts to
increase the number of family farmers. By June, 1939, the agency
had received 146,000 applications for loans to purchase farms and
had been able to serve only 6,180 of them. By 1940, tenant farmers

were increasing at the rate of 40,000 per year, while the law allowed FSA to make fewer than 10,000 loans per year. "Obviously," the Director of the Budget informed Roosevelt, "this Bankhead-Jones Act program can be regarded as only an experimental approach to the farm tenancy problem."[122] Triple-A had spent more each year to encourage the commercial farmers of one state to participate in the production control program than FSA was able to loan in the entire nation to help tenant farmers become owner-operators. By the end of February, 1936, AAA had sent $133,000,000 in benefit payments into Texas.[123]

The major pressures of farm politics produced many difficulties for those who hoped to develop large programs for the rural poor. As a leading student of farm politics has observed, "government agricultural policy . . . is largely designed and administered for the benefit of commercial farmers." Low-income farmers lack effective pressure groups and have not been a separate force to be reckoned with in elections. "The bulk of low-income farmers are in the South, where traditional voting behavior, the one-party situation, the poll tax and the racial problem have prevented the emergence of this group as a separate force in the electorate."[124] The realities of farm politics made life difficult even for the planners who were heavily influenced by faith in the family farm and nearly impossible for a person as unorthodox as Tugwell. Frustrated earlier than other planners, he had dreamed of major changes in the party system and had departed from Washington long before Wilson, Tolley, and other social scientists in farm politics.

Nevertheless, in contributing to the establishment of the Farm Security Administration, Tugwell, Wilson, Gray, and other social scientists had promoted significant changes in farm politics and farm policy. For several years after the passage of the legislation of 1937, FSA played an important role in American life. Its rehabilitation program, especially, picked up new supporters and increasingly larger appropriations. The agency became an important part of the Department of Agriculture and a major participant in agricultural politics and had a significant impact upon rural life. "Between 1937 and 1942," a student of the agency has concluded, "the FSA emerged as a major challenge to the economic, social and political *status quo* in American agriculture." "Generally," Baldwin writes, "the agency was a summons to agricultural leaders, to other governmental organizations, and to private groups and individuals to match the FSA in its fight against rural poverty and ignorance, and in its effort to convert the ideals of democracy into democratic reality."[125] Members of the agency encountered many obstacles. In June, 1940, Tugwell's successor resigned, in part because his appearances before the Senate and House appropriations committees were being "made increasingly difficult by the opposition of certain powerful southerners and reactionary northerners who concentrated on FSA their ire against the New Deal and their fear of its threat to white supremacy."[126] Accomplishment as well as frustration, however, characterized the experiences of those who attempted to elevate the lot of the rural poor.

CHAPTER 8

Making Progress and
Repairing Damage

As Tugwell pushed forward with his plans for the rural poor and encountered the frustrations that drove him from Washington, other social scientists, led by Wilson and Tolley, also faced difficulties, but ones that could be remedied. The old enemies of production control, the processors, presented the greatest difficulties, but the agency of production control, Triple-A, provided opportunities to move forward along the lines that had been projected in the Christgau bill. As this progress took place, the damage inflicted by the processors on the price-raising program was repaired.

Despite attempts to convince businessmen that they should support the production control program, the "middlemen" remained troublesome and effective critics of that farm relief effort. Earl Smith of the Farm Bureau saw the handlers and processors of farm products and the speculators in these commodities as the chief sources of opposition.[1] Wilson believed that several groups ignored arguments concerning the importance of farm purchasing power and that they would always oppose any program that tended to ensure equality for agriculture. They included processors whose income depended upon volume because of their fixed overhead and who disliked any increase in the bargaining power of the farmers.[2] Cotton distributors, like Will Clayton of Anderson, Clayton and Company of Houston, were especially vigorous critics, arguing frequently that crop control was destroying the American cotton industry, suggesting that emphasis should be placed on helping cotton regain foreign markets, and developing a good deal of pressure for a change in cotton policy.[3] As Wilson described one of these critics, he was "typical of a certain type of cotton exporter whose income comes from volume sales."[4] Cutting back on the production of cotton obviously did not promote the interests of such businessmen. In speaking of the big processors, Wallace explained that they made their money from volume and they demanded "that the Republican party sacrifice everything in order to stimulate production of farm commodities regardless of price. . . ."[5]

The processors probed the political process in many places in their efforts to stop the program. After failing to prevent Congress from authorizing production control, they tried unsuccessfully to secure the dismissal of the administrators of the program. They also returned to Congress to fight the efforts to amend the act in 1934 and waged a widespread propaganda campaign seeking to exploit any dissatisfaction the farmers had with the program and contending, for example, that they actually paid the processing tax. The campaign included criticism of the intellectuals.

Finally, the Supreme Court provided the business group with a great opportunity. As early as 1932, charges of unconstitutionality had troubled the promoters of the allotment plan, and soon after Triple-A began to function, Ezekiel and other economists prepared defenses of the program to be used in court. They tried to rest the government's case on as broad an economic base as possible. An intense legal battle led by the food industries got under way in 1935, attacking the constitutionality of the processing taxes that seemingly taxed the processors for the benefit of the producers and advocating court injunctions against their collection. Then, on January 6, 1936, in *United States v. Butler*, which grew out of hostility toward Triple-A in the textile industry and the refusal of the receivers of the Hoosoc Mills to pay the tax, the United States Supreme Court declared that the processing tax and the production contracts violated the Constitution.[6]

Tugwell has written that the Court helped AAA by "rallying to its support even its most lukewarm beneficiaries."[7] However, while there is evidence to support this interpretation,[8] other social scientists who were much closer to this farm program in 1936 were somewhat discouraged as well as surprised by the sweeping character of the decision. While the ultimate outcome may have been an improvement over the first farm relief program, before that point was reached Wilson and his colleagues found many "ways in which agriculture was injured when the processors won their court fight."[9] Escape from a tough spot seemed difficult. While the agricultural officials did not give up their belief in production control just because the Court had dealt it a severe blow, they believed that the decision had made control hard to accomplish. They even considered a Farm Bureau proposal that the states, relying upon the colleges and committees of farmers and federal financial support and supervision, administer a farm program with price-raising and soil-conserving goals.

The policy makers did, however, have another plan to propose, one that was based upon work in Tolley's Program Planning Division. Shortly after the Supreme Court's decision, officials in the department met with the farm leaders, who had responded to the decision with unanimous determination to get new price-raising legislation, and in less than two months pushed through Congress a scheme in which payments obtained from general revenue were to be made to farmers who shifted acreage from soil-depleting to soil-conserving crops and employed soil-building practices. The meeting with the farm leaders indicated that not all of them shared the Farm Bureau's enthusiasm for production control, and the new conservation measure appealed to farm leaders like Taber of the Grange who had not liked the earlier program. Department officials, however, looked upon the new one as capable of both complying with the ruling of the Court and achieving the earlier objective. The soil-depleting crops happened also to be the surplus crops, including wheat and cotton, while the soil-conserving ones, such as grasses and legumes, were not surplus commercial commodities.[10]

In a sense, the Court had only pushed the administration into a soil conservation program that had been developing in the Planning Division since late 1934. In fact, Murray Benedict suggests that the division's "major contribution was that of laying the groundwork, and doing the preliminary thinking that made possible a quick shift to a new type of program when the initial one was tossed into the discard by the adverse ruling of the Supreme Court."[11]

For some time before 1936, the division had been seeking ways of making the effort to raise prices work also to promote improvement in land-use practices. In the beginning, the economists had been dis-

mayed to find that administrators were reluctant to insist that farmers
in the different commodity programs must not use their "rented" acres
in ways that would hurt the established producers of other commodities like peanuts and potatoes. A Replacement Crops Section had been
established in the division to consider the use of those acres and had
worked with some success to encourage the administrators to promote
the planting of erosion-preventing and soil-conserving crops on acres
that had been devoted to cotton and other surplus commodities.[12]
According to the head of the section:

The constructive use of the contracted or shifted acreage accompanying a control program in connection with basic surplus crops fits immediately into a
long-term program of desirable land use, not only encouraging the improvement of rotation on individual farms, but forwarding major conservation programs such as erosion control, permanent soil improvement, reforestation, wild
life, etc.[13]

Many features of the original AAA troubled Tolley and his lieutenants. It paid little attention to regional and individual differences
and did not allow the colleges and the farmers to contribute as much
as they could to the planning of the programs. The planners feared
that Triple-A programs would become rigid and would freeze existing
patterns of farming rather than promote conservation and shift the
production of crops into the regions in which they could be grown
most successfully. AAA treated each commodity separately, while
the planners hoped for a regional approach, one that would recognize
that the adjustments needed varied from region to region. Rather than
a series of commodity programs, Tolley wanted regional programs,
and he hoped to use the payments to farmers in a positive rather than
a negative way. He wanted to pay farmers to improve farm management and to conserve the soil, rather than to merely reduce output.

Tolley's greatest fear was that the farm program would serve only
the interests of established commercial farmers. He watched them
organize and press their demands, and he warned against the "frequent tendency" of pressure groups "to think in terms of group monop-
oly rather than the public welfare. . . ." He had confidence that
"thorough education along economic and social lines" could prevent
such a development. This education would teach farmers that a nation
must import if it wished to export, that the public interest required
soil conservation and low-cost farming, that tenants or laborers who
were considered somewhat in the light of undesirable aliens or in-
truders in the industry they served could not be expected to function

as "good citizens" within that industry, and that success of the farm program depended heavily upon increased purchasing power among city laboring people. "If economic democracy is to be anything more than a phrase to cover the selfish desires of any given class which uses the term," he advised, "it must mean that the welfare of each individual and class in the nation is in the long run best served by that type of policy which will best serve all individuals and all classes."[14]

In line with these ideas, the planners developed a regional adjustment project and a county agricultural planning project during 1935. Late in 1934 and early in 1935, Tolley, Elliott, and Wilson had outlined their ideas in meetings with several groups.[15] In February, the Planning Division issued a lengthy statement on "Regional Problems in Agricultural Adjustment." It raised two questions:

What total volume of production would be required to give consumers an adequate supply of food and clothing, and at the same time assure farmers a reasonable income for their work and the use of their land and equipment? What production would result if each farmer followed that system which gave the most efficient use of labor and equipment and best promoted soil conservation?

The statement stressed the importance of regional differences in agriculture, surveyed the various regions and their adjustment problems, and concluded with the suggestion that regional and intraregional planning needed to be developed much further than AAA had carried it and that efforts needed to be made to determine how the work might be divided among the farmers and state and federal agencies.[16]

Tolley, along with Wallace and Wilson, arranged four regional adjustment conferences that were held during the first half of March in order to "gain a better picture of the local and regional problems to which future agricultural policies should be adapted, the needs for research and the possibilities of harmonizing adjustment programs with the principles of conservation and proper land utilization."[17] Department and college officials attended the conferences, with the department represented chiefly by Tolley and Wilson and the colleges by the directors of the extension services and the experiment stations and by agricultural economists.[18] Wilson and Tolley came to the sessions convinced that in order to make the transition from the emergency to the long-run program they needed first to develop a cooperative research project designed to provide a sound basis for coordinating production adjustments that were needed from a price point of view with adjustments that were needed from soil conservation and efficient operation points of view.[19] They discussed with the college representatives the adjustments in production that would be needed in each type-of-farming region if farmers employed conservation practices, adopted the best methods of farm management, and produced the crops that were best for their land.[20] One enthusiastic extension director provided Wallace with a description of the meeting in Salt Lake City:

Our old friends M. L. Wilson and Doctor Tolley showed great skill in bringing out a full and free expression of opinion on the questions involved. They made every form of opinion and every point of view equally welcome. I have attended many meetings through many years but this one was certainly the most democratic and the most successful in bringing a group of men to a right and desired conclusion merely by creating an atmosphere of free expression while retaining good will and the best of feelings. Both leaders are entitled to a lot of praise and thanks from all of us.[21]

The officials agreed to study the questions and meet again late in the summer. For the next six months, the Planning Division, the colleges, and the BAE devoted a great deal of time and energy to the project. At the second series of meetings, with Wallace, Wilson, Tolley, and Elliott, among others, representing the department, findings were compared and discussed. Out of this process came the conclusion that the production of cash crops should be reduced and the production of soil-conserving crops should be increased and that the adoption of soil conservation methods throughout the country would bring production in line with existing markets. In other words, the needs of crop control and soil conservation could be achieved by the same adjustments. These conclusions were presented and discussed at the November meeting of the Land-Grant College Association, and they stimulated interest in reorienting the farm program so as to promote conservation and give fuller consideration to local and regional needs.[22] "The big thing at these meetings," Secretary Wallace suggested, "was the conviction that we were building a sound foundation for long-time agricultural adjustment. We were at last approaching the problem in the way we would have liked to approach it in 1933 had there been time."[23]

The regional adjustment project continued to function for several years. The Planning Division directed the work, and the colleges, the BAE, and occasionally the Soil Conservation Service, the Forest Service, the Farm Credit Administration, the Division of Grazing, and the Resettlement Administration participated in it. The project developed recommendations on systems of farming or ranching designed to check or prevent erosion, to promote efficient farming, and to bring national production in line with demand. Attempts were made to influence the conduct of Triple-A and other "action" agencies so that they would encourage farmers to move in the desired directions. Regional conferences continued to be held, and AAA provided the state agencies with a substantial amount of financial assistance for their efforts.[24]

While most of the work in this project was done by the department and the colleges, at the second series of conferences in 1935 Wilson introduced a proposal for a county agricultural planning project that would draw the farmers into the planning process. One aim would be the education of the farmers. The facts developed in the regional adjustment project would be carried to the farmers in hopes of molding their views. The project assumed that understanding and acceptance of plans by farmers were needed if the plans were to be adopted and continued. But the process of education would move in two directions, not just one, for Wilson and Tolley believed that the best plans and programs could not be developed by experts alone. Farmers possessed the greatest fund of intimate knowledge available on local agricultural problems and situations, and most of those responsible for developing and administering farm programs could not obtain such knowledge. On the other hand, the project assumed, most farmers did not have an adequate understanding of many of the outside forces that affected their welfare. Consequently, farmers, scientists, and administrators had to be drawn together if the best possible agricultural programs were to be developed.[25]

The proposal caught on quickly. It led to another meeting in September with extension leaders who agreed to cooperate in the project. By the first of the year, every state but California was involved. During the next two years, more than 2,400 county committees participated in the project. The planners hoped that eventually the project would grow to include every county in the country.[26]

The committees tackled questions similar to those involved in the regional adjustment project. In response to questions in 1936 about the quantities of the different farm commodities that would be produced if the farming systems were adjusted in order to maintain soil fertility and control erosion and if all land not suited for agriculture were shifted to other uses, the farmers recommended substantial decreases in the production of soil-depleting crops and substantial increases in those that conserved the soil. The farmers, in fact, recommended even larger changes than the experts had in the regional

adjustment project in 1935. During the next two years, the committees
continued to function while efforts were made to improve farm programs in ways that would use the land more intelligently.[27]

Wilson looked upon the formation of the county committees as
"the most significant thing in the field of agriculture" in 1936. "It has
as its objective the preparation of farmers' minds so that they will
grasp eagerly and participate enthusiastically in the formulation of
county soil conservation programs," he explained to another economist. The potentialities seemed "almost unlimited" and included a
revitalization of the democratic process throughout the nation as well
as the effective solution of immediate problems.[28]

At the same time that these projects were taking shape, Wilson
developed two educational programs. For some time he and Wallace
had been interested in organizing a discussion group program for
farmers, and late in 1934, various organizations, including the Association of Land-Grant Colleges, had encouraged these officials to develop such a program. Wallace appointed a committee headed by
Wilson to guide the activities of the department in this area. Early
in 1935, the committee helped the agricultural colleges in ten states
to experiment with discussion. Encouraged by the success of the experiment, Wilson and his associates developed plans for a larger
program which went into operation in more than thirty states during
the winter of 1935–1936. By the end of 1936, although the degree
of enthusiasm varied from state to state, the extension services in
thirty-nine states had discovered enough interest in the project among
farmers to justify the appointment to extension staffs of discussion
leaders.[29]

This program attempted to educate the farmers on the basic social
and economic problems of agriculture and its relations with other
parts of national and international life. The promoters hoped that
the program would enable the farmers to think of more than life on
their individual farms, to gain an understanding of the broad economic
and social problems that faced them, and to play a more active and
intelligent part in planning farm programs. Thus, the groups discussed
such matters as foreign trade, the number of people living on the land,
the farmer's share of the national income, the control of farm production, national land policies, the obligations of farmers and consumers
to one another, the rural life of the future, and the treatment of farm
laborers. While the advocates of discussion assumed that an intelligent
understanding of programs like production control and conservation

would lead to support for them, these leaders sought to avoid propaganda and attempts to bring people to any specific or "right" conclusions. Instead, the aim was to provide people with the means of getting facts, information, and opinions which would assist them in reaching intelligent conclusions.[30] In response to a suggestion that the chief purpose was to give the federal government an opportunity to put over its objectives, Wilson insisted that the program gave a full and fair hearing to all sides of the issues considered.[31]

The program reflected confidence in rural people. Wilson and his associates assumed that these people wanted better opportunities to get information and to think through the basic questions that faced farmers. The promoters also assumed that farmers would usually make sound decisions when they had the facts and a chance to talk things over.[32]

Although one critic of the Farm Bureau welcomed Wilson's discussion program "as a substitute for pressure politics,"[33] the promoters of it attempted to gain the cooperation of that organization and to assure its leaders that it would benefit from the program. When they advised against any step that "might tend to encourage the organization of new rural groups instead of using existing organizations for carrying on the discussion program,"[34] department officials took steps to assure the Farm Bureau of their desire to cooperate with existing farm organizations.[35] "Not only does it furnish another excellent opportunity for bureau cooperation with one of our programs," Wilson's assistant wrote to a Farm Bureau official, "but I believe the bureau stands to gain a great deal by getting solidly behind the discussion project. For instance, the old question of good programs and lively meetings which will bring out attendance and help build up interest in the organization can certainly come as a major by-product of discussion."[36]

Late in 1935, O'Neal sent a letter to all state Farm Bureaus urging them to cooperate. He pointed out that the state units could have confidence in the program, for it had been developed by Wilson and his staff and they had no intention of setting up new organizations of farmers but planned to work through existing ones. He advised further that "the promotion of these discussion groups will do much . . . to bring about a better understanding of our program." And he added revealingly: "If properly utilized, this program . . . should result in increasing the effectiveness of our Farm Bureau units in molding public opinion, as well as stimulating interest and participation in local Farm Bureau meetings."[37] He was alert to every opportunity to increase the size and power of his organization.

This cooperation with the leading farm organization reflected Wilson's basic approach to the problem of power. Unlike Tugwell, Wilson tried very hard to work with the leading individuals and groups in farm politics. He did not simply respond to their pressures, however. He attempted by various methods to alter their patterns of behavior.

In addition to the discussion group program, Wilson also developed "Schools for Extension Workers" or as they were often called "County Agent Schools" or "Schools of Philosophy." Recognizing that most of the people administering the farm programs were products of agricultural colleges and had been trained in science and technology and believing that their outlook needed to be enlarged if democratic planning was to be developed successfully, he decided that the administration should call upon leading academic people to meet with the members of the action agencies and the extension services and discuss philosophy, the social sciences, history, and the techniques of conducting discussions. Encouraged by Wallace and Tolley, Wilson gave a great deal of attention to this project, which took shape in the spring and summer of 1935 with help from nearly three hundred philosophers and social scientists. The first school was held in Washington in October and was attended by members of the federal extension service. In the next four months, nine states sponsored schools for their extension workers. Enthusiasm mounted rapidly; approximately a thousand people attended these early schools, and plans were developed for an expansion of the program. During the next two years, it spread throughout the nation, serving extension workers chiefly but expanding to include other groups, especially the farmer committeemen of Triple-A. The schools, which lasted for five days, focused on the broad implications of the farm programs, and combined lectures and discussions, were held only upon request. Extension service personnel, many of whom disliked the New Deal, accepted the program, for its speakers represented a variety of viewpoints and received the freedom necessary to express them.[38]

One of the important aims of the planners now emerged quite clearly. They hoped to alter the point of view of the people in the extension services. Because they played major roles in the farm programs, the county agents needed to think more than they were accustomed to about social and economic problems and about regional, national, and international relationships if the programs were to move in the directions the social scientists desired. The county agents needed education in economics, sociology, political science, and philosophy, and they needed inspiration so that they would have, in Tolley's words, "a cheerfully creative rather than a wearisomely receptive attitude" toward the "aims and ends in agricultural policy and program making . . . ." The planners hoped to make the county agent "a considerably different sort of public servant than what he was in predepression days and the days before agricultural adjustment."[39]

To supervise these educational efforts, Wilson recruited Carl F. Taeusch, a philosopher who had been one of Wilson's teachers at the University of Chicago. Taeusch had studied philosophy at Harvard and had taught at the University of Chicago, at the University of Iowa, and at the Harvard Business School. His philosophy, which Wilson admired, resembled that of Commons and Tufts. Taeusch had been closely associated with the latter while both were teaching in Chicago. At Harvard, he had developed courses in business ethics and had edited the *Harvard Business Review.* He joined the department in the spring of 1935, soon became the leader of a new section of the Planning Division — the Program Study and Discussion Section — and worked with Wilson on the development of these educational programs.[40]

Taeusch's section had important roles to play in both programs. In discussion, staff members of the section assisted the states and organizations that desired to organize discussion groups, prepared materials for their use, actively promoted their development, and conducted training schools for discussion leaders. Two staff members, assisted in each school by three or four people with temporary appointments, chiefly professors from liberal arts colleges, organized the schools for extension workers, prepared materials for them, lectured and conducted discussions in them, and advised on the improvement of the program.[41]

Early in 1935, Wilson had written to a friend that his thinking kept "moving more and more towards regional agricultural planning along the lines outlined originally in the so-called Christgau Bill of three or four years ago."[42] By the end of the year, Tolley and Wilson had developed programs resembling the program that had been advocated in that bill. Furthermore, as Wilson had expected, Roosevelt supported these developments. On October 25, 1935, he publicly described and supported the Planning Division's ideas concerning a modified and permanent agricultural adjustment program. "As I see it," Roosevelt informed the nation, this program had two principal objectives:

First, to carry out the declared policy of Congress to maintain and increase the gains thus far made, thereby avoiding the danger of a slump back into conditions brought about by our national neglect of Agriculture.

Second, to broaden present adjustment operations so as to give farmers increasing incentives for conservation and efficient use of the nation's soil resources.

He believed that the modified program would serve the advantage of both producers and consumers, and he "[could] think of nothing more important to the permanent welfare of the nation than long-time agricultural adjustment carried out along these lines."[43] Department planners interpreted this statement as additional evidence that the President accepted their ideas and would provide the support needed to put them into practice.[44]

In spite of the many encouraging developments in 1935, however, Tolley grew unhappy with the attitudes of administrators in his department and returned to his post at the University of California in September of that year. Wallace and Davis had allowed him to work as he wanted, without raising questions about the ways in which money was spent and without demanding immediate practical results. During the first year of the division, he had been rather satisfied with its impact upon the operations of Triple-A, but during 1935, AAA seemed to become complacent. Many of its administrators seemed interested only in reducing production, making payments to farmers, and increasing the farmers' income. A group of economists concluded after careful study that "the program seems on the whole to take on more definitely the character of financial aid for everybody and less that of specific implementation for a planned system of efficient farming."[45] These administrators were satisfied with the existing program and did not like Tolley's proposals for change. Furthermore, his superiors were unwilling to put pressure on these officials. When Tolley would suggest changes, Davis would raise questions about the political implications, asking if the changes were practical now and suggesting that leaders could move only as fast as their army, and Wallace would raise doubts about the wisdom of trying to move at the moment. Thus, impatient with the rate of change in Triple-A and doubtful that the attitudes of the officials would enable him to accomplish much more, he returned to academic life. At the same time that he had been allowed to construct instruments for the promotion of change, he had encountered a new resistance to it within the government.[46]

The Supreme Court, however, accomplished what Tolley could not. It forced the officials to make changes in their programs and gave the social scientists a new opportunity to push their ideas successfully. Davis called Tolley back to Washington to help in the emergency created by the decision, and the economist found that the Court had revived the old willingness to experiment among those administering Triple-A and benefiting from it.[47] Thus, he was able to achieve things he had been trying to achieve for more than a year. "The driving personality behind the new 'soil conservation' program," one newsman reported, "is Prof. Howard R. Tolley, forty-six, heavy shouldered, bald, and tough in a good natured way."[48] (". . . as you know he has a very practical head on him," Wilson wrote to a friend.[49]) Even the farm leaders listened to the social scientist. Their meeting with department officials endorsed a set of general principles that had been drafted by a committee headed by Earl Smith "after consultation with some of the economists of Washington in whom we have greatest confidence . . . ."[50] "The specific ideas in regard to method came," Professor Benedict has written, ". . . not from the farm leaders but from the policy makers of the AAA, particularly its Program Planning Division."[51] ". . . the objectives . . . are to be found . . . in the type of agricultural planning work which was carried on by the state experiment stations through the national project last year," Wilson informed one experiment station director. ". . . the summaries of the project . . . indicate that if soil conservation methods were practiced throughout the country the volume of production would be about right to meet the domestic needs and reasonably anticipated exports."[52]

Tolley not only played a major role in developing and drafting the new program; he was called upon to administer it. The choice symbolized the fulfillment of long-held ambitions. Davis encouraged Wallace to select Tolley. Tired, eager to try his hand at something new, and not satisfied with his relations with some of the men in the department, Davis resigned after the new legislation took shape. He understood and believed in the plans that Tolley had in mind but thought that the economist should be the person to carry them out.[53]

The new legislation enabled the administration to compensate farmers for the expenses involved in soil-conserving and soil-building practices. The public expenditures seemed justified by the public benefits that would result. Tolley believed, on the basis of work conducted by the Planning Division, that several benefits would come

out of the program if most farmers participated in it. Soil fertility would be increased; production costs would be lowered; crop
yields would be increased; production would be shifted away from
surplus crops, and supply and demand for commodities would be
brought into balance.[54]

Roosevelt endorsed the switch in the farm program. When the Supreme Court invalidated the Agricultural Adjustment Act, he indicated that he hoped to move along the lines that the Planning Division
had been developing. ". . . we must avoid any national agricultural
policy which will result in shipping our soil fertility to foreign nations," he told the press.[55] When he signed the new Soil Conservation
and Domestic Allotment Act, he referred to the new measure as one
"which helps to safeguard vital public interests not only for today,
but for generations to come," as "an attempt to develop out of the
far-reaching and partly emergency efforts under the Agricultural
Adjustment Act, a long-time program for American agriculture," and
as following "the outlines . . . which I recommended in my statement of October 25, 1935."[56] In short, in the mid-1930's, Roosevelt
justified the confidence Wilson and Tolley had had in him in 1932.

The new legislation enabled AAA to participate more actively in
the large-scale attack upon land problems that was under way by 1936
and to associate itself more closely with the increasingly popular
efforts to conserve the soil. "The states and nation are now unleashing
the greatest broadside attack on land-use problems of our history,"
Tugwell announced enthusiastically. "If this task is completed, our
national heritage will be secure," he prophesied. "If not, we shall go
the way of Mesopotamia, Egypt, and China, and part with our collective birthright for a mess of individualistic pottage."[57]

The Soil Conservation Service was one of the agencies at work promoting an active interest in better use of the land. Its mission was the
battle against soil erosion. Both Tugwell and Wilson assisted in the
development of the agency. In 1933, Tugwell had helped the crusader
for soil conservation, Hugh Bennett, enlarge the work in which he had
been engaged on a small scale in the Department of Agriculture for
several years. Bennett complained to Tugwell that the department
was not sufficiently interested in his work, and Tugwell tried to get
Ickes to establish a special bureau for Bennett within the Public Works
Administration. Ickes instead made him director of the Soil Erosion
Service within the Department of Interior and gave him a chance to
expand his operations. As SES dealt with agricultural lands, Wallace

soon grew concerned about Bennett's work and the possibility that it would add to the tensions between Agriculture and Interior. Thus, Wallace suggested that the work belonged in his department. The Grange, the Farm Bureau, the Land-Grant College Association, and a special committee that investigated SES agreed, and Tugwell arranged the transfer. Despite Ickes' desire to hold on to the work, Roosevelt in March, 1935, moved Bennett back to Agriculture. A month later, Congress directed Wallace to create a Soil Conservation Service as a permanent part of his department.[58]

As chairman of the department's Land Policy Committee, which Wallace had established late in March, Wilson quickly turned his attention to the new agency and looked for ways to expand its work. The great drought of the mid-thirties, which he observed firsthand, did much to move him and others to the conclusion that action was needed immediately to conserve the soil. The report of his Land Planning Committee in 1934 had paid attention to soil erosion and had recommended that the national government should obtain the cooperation of state and local agencies in soil erosion work. The Soil Conservation Act of 1935 provided that the Secretary might require the Soil Conservation Service to confine its work to states that passed laws of their own establishing a suitable soil conservation policy. Wilson consulted with a number of people, including Congressman Marvin Jones of Texas, Governor Alfred M. Landon of Kansas, Wallace, Davis, Tolley, Gray, and others in the department. His top lieutenant on the matter was Philip Glick, a very able young lawyer, who had been helping Wilson since 1933, had the skills needed to translate ideas into law, and had been giving a good deal of attention to the legal aspects of land planning, a field which, according to Tolley, was "essentially unexplored" and "in many respects . . . the key to effective action . . . ."[59]

Working with these people, Wilson developed and promoted a proposal to move beyond the limited number of demonstration projects that SCS was conducting and to establish soil conservation districts that would enable farmers to work together in the battle against soil erosion, a proposal that harmonized with the democratic schemes he had been pushing for a decade. He directed the drafting of a model statute during 1935, hoping that it would be recommended to the states as legislation they should pass in order to work with SCS. The proposed statute authorized the establishment of soil conservation districts to carry on erosion control work throughout the districts, help farmers control erosion on their lands, and enforce needed conservation practices upon lands of uncooperative farmers. A district was to be established only after the majority of farmers endorsed it in a referendum and was to be controlled by the local farmers and their representatives. The proposal assumed that a program to modify land-use practices could be made effective only if farmers cooperated voluntarily. Thus, the suggested statute was drawn in such a way that it provided machinery which could be used by the farmers after they had been educated in the need to act. Little compulsion was to be involved. Wilson viewed a soil conservation district as an efficient institutional agency for the purpose of a land-use program and the embodiment of the principles of economic democracy in agriculture.[60] After Roosevelt had sent letters to all of the governors early in 1937 urging the passage of the legislation, Wilson traveled to various parts of the country to discuss the model statute with state groups. In the next four years, nearly all the states passed soil conservation laws, and 548 districts were established.[61]

Besides soil conservation, the new farm program that Tolley administered harmonized with other ideas that he and other planners had been advocating. Since 1933, they had been calling for a change in AAA's contract system. It allowed a farmer to participate in more than one program, signing contracts to take one tract of land out of the production of cotton, another out of corn, and so on. During 1934 and 1935, the planners proposed a system of one contract per farm in hopes of developing arrangements with farmers that would be consistent with good farm management as well as with the production-control and price-raising aims of the adjustment program. Now under the new program, each farm was treated as a unit and had one plan and one contract governing all its operations. In addition, the organization of Triple-A was changed from commodity to regional divisions, a change that Tolley had tried to get Davis to make earlier. Drawing upon the national type-of-farming map that had been developed under Elliott's direction after the 1930 census, Tolley and Elliott, with help from others, divided the nation into five regions, and Tolley, Wallace, and Wilson decided that AAA should be reorganized in this pattern. Thus, Tolley had the chance he had long been seeking to promote a coordinated system of national, regional, and individual farm planning.[62]

Although the legislation of 1936 harmonized with many of the social scientists' ambitions and effectively promoted better management of the soil, these men came to regard the program as inadequate. It failed to provide an effective system of controlling production and raising prices. The drought of 1936 had kept production down, but 1937 was a good crop year, and the inadequacies of the law became quite obvious. Although farmers reduced the acreage devoted to surplus crops, they produced more by better cultivation and the use of more fertilizer. Acreage went down, but yields went up! Consequently, the development after 1936 of a Supreme Court more tolerant of the New Deal[63] enabled department officials, led by Wallace and Tolley and working with farm leaders, to obtain legislation in February, 1938, that pursued production control more directly. Although the attack upon the processing tax prevented a return to the self-financing feature of the original Wilson program and forced the administration to rely upon general tax revenues, the processors had not permanently destroyed production control.[64]

The new Agricultural Adjustment Act contained many other features of interest to the social scientists, including soil conservation and a crop-storage scheme called the "ever normal granary," designed to guarantee adequate supplies of farm products for consumers as well as adequate prices for farmers. While the new law seemed to the social scientists to be an improvement over earlier legislation, it did not strike them as perfect. They did not expect perfection, however. Wilson referred to the act as "a product of the democratic processes." What he meant was that it had not originated with one group. The Administration, the farm organizations, and the agricultural committees of Congress had made contributions and had been forced to make compromises with one another.[65] He expected to move forward in this fashion.

Thus, by the spring of 1938, social scientists who had promoted the Christgau bill and the Allotment Plan in the early 1930's could find much to satisfy them in the agricultural programs that were in operation. To a great extent, the group had triumphed over their most effective opponents, the processors, and had established a production control program. As expected, that program was leading to the fulfillment of the larger ambitions that Wilson and Tolley had shared eight years earlier. Contributing to their sense of satisfaction was the realization that the President shared their hopes of helping the individual farmer to use his land for the products for which it was best fitted, to maintain and improve its fertility, to prevent overproduction, low farm prices, and crop shortages, and to decrease farm tenancy and increase farm ownership.[66] Scientific, business, and democratic values influenced his thinking as well as theirs about agriculture.

CHAPTER 9

Elevating
the Bureau of
Agricultural Economics

Progress had taken place, yet the goal of a coordinated attack upon land problems, dreamed of in the Christgau bill and in the Land Utilization Conference, remained elusive. In the fall of 1938, a major effort was made to move toward that goal. The Bureau of Agricultural Economics that Henry C. Wallace and Henry C. Taylor had established in 1922 became the central planning agency for the Department of Agriculture. Wallace's son, the Secretary of Agriculture in 1938, made the decision; one of Taylor's economists, Howard Tolley, moved into the chief's office; and the bureau embarked upon the most ambitious and controversial period of its career. Although the motives for the move were mixed, from the point of view of the ambitions of the social scientists the elevation of the BAE seemed desirable, for it provided new opportunities to develop the methods and accomplish the aims of the Christgau bill.

The lack of coordination had created political problems for Wallace. In directing the numerous new farm programs, he had several groups to satisfy, especially Congress, the colleges, and the farmers, and they were quick to criticize any confusion and conflict in the relations among the programs.[1] In addition, he faced competition from Harold Ickes, who was eager to become secretary of a new Department of Conservation that would include agencies now housed in the Department of Agriculture, particularly the Forestry Service. Wallace opposed the proposed changes and countered with a suggestion that all land-use activities with an important relation to agriculture, and these included forestry in his definition, should be in his department. In Ickes, Wallace faced a competitor who paid close attention to any suggestions that the Secretary of Agriculture was a poor administrator, and thus Wallace needed to coordinate the land-use activities of his department in order to defend himself against the ambitions of the Secretary of Interior.[2]

Wallace had begun his search for an effective way of coordinating these activities in 1935. In March of that year, he had established a departmental Land Policy Committee, with Wilson as chairman and the key officials concerned with land use as members, and with authority to try to bring the activities of all departmental land-use agencies into harmony with one another.[3] In December, 1936, the Secretary added the Committee on Departmental Coordination. Again, Wilson served as chairman. Explaining the step, Wallace said:

The Department is coming into a period in which we shall have to strengthen, realign and coordinate much of the work of the Department as we effect a transition from the emergency character of much of what was done during the last Administration. It is a time for tying together, tightening up, smoothing out and improving procedure, and making for better working relationships.[4]

The next major step came in July, 1937, with the establishment of an Office of Land-Use Coordination in the Secretary's office. Earlier in the year, Wallace had called upon a number of people for recommendations on what over-all arrangements should be made. He received advice from a large group, including Wilson, Tolley, E. H. Wiecking, and Al and John Black. As a consequence, the new office was established to devote full time to efforts to coordinate the many types of land-use work in which the department was involved. According to the memorandum establishing the office,

there has been a surprisingly small amount of duplication, working at cross purposes, and confusion in the Department, considering the wholly new, extensive, and varied tasks the organization has undertaken in recent years. But . . . the present situation within the Department is not perfect, . . . we can increase efficiency, and . . . we can give still better service to agriculture and the public generally.[5]

As Land-Use Coordinator, Milton Eisenhower played an important role in the elevation of the BAE. A man with a decade of experience in the department as a public relations officer, he had been giving much thought to the best ways of organizing the administration of a department that had been growing rapidly, adding a multitude of new functions in a short period of time. Distressed by conflict, like the conflict between Triple-A and SCS over the best methods of soil conservation, convinced that coordination was very important, and confident that men would cooperate if given an opportunity, he looked for ways to make Agriculture a more efficient and effective department that could switch each type of land to its best use and thereby reduce substantially the need for government "interference" in farming. He concluded that the USDA needed a central planning agency that could coordinate the activities of the action agencies and the extension services.[6]

One problem facing the department was the deteriorating relations between it and the land-grant colleges. Tolley's conduct of Triple-A contributed to this. He took a cautious approach to the touchy question of landlord-tenant relations in spite of the efforts of his friend Ezekiel to promote changes in the administration of the farm program that would provide more adequate protection for tenants. Ezekiel was convinced "that the farm owners, constituting less than half of those engaged in agriculture, have been the dominant element in the preparation and administration of AAA programs" and that this had resulted, especially in the South, in the owners' "receiving the lion's share of the benefits resulting from the program."[7] Tolley agreed, was increasingly troubled about the plight of the rural poor, and advocated a limit on the size of the payment that a farmer could receive from Triple-A, but he listened to the advice of officials like Cully Cobb, who warned that an unwise decision on landlord-tenant relations could touch off a revolt among the planters against the farm program. As head of the Planning Division, Tolley had insisted that the sharecroppers of the South deserved a fair share of the benefits of that program, but he had antagonized Jerome Frank and his allies by advising them that they could not remake the world overnight and should proceed more slowly in their efforts at reform and by lining up behind Davis in the "purge."[8]

Tolley proceeded more boldly, however, in efforts to promote other kinds of changes in American agriculture and to reduce the role of the extension services in the administration of the farm program.

Many of the extension workers, devoted to the production of particular commodities like cotton, tobacco, or wheat, were critical of his attempts to develop diversified and grassland and livestock farming. C. E. Brehm, the director of the extension service in Tennessee, complained in 1938 that Triple-A had

gotten so technical and complicated, no one can understand it, and it gets more complicated every day. This inevitably is going to defeat the whole AAA program. You can't get people to continuously support something when they don't know how it works, and you can't educate people on procedures in a program that changes daily.[9]

Tolley had great faith in the potentialities of the farmer committee system and believed that the committees had obtained enough experience to enable the farmers to operate more independently of the extension services in the conduct of the farm programs. By 1937, extension still played a role in the administration of Triple-A. While the role was quite small in the North Central region, it was very large in the South. Extension participated in the selection of state committeemen, provided members of state committees, and supplied some of the state executive officers. The county agent, especially in the South, tended to serve as secretary or executive officer of the county committee. In addition, extension participated everywhere in the educational activities connected with the farm program.[10] Critics of the extension services, especially the Farmers Union, disliked their large part in administration, chiefly because they had close ties with the Farm Bureau and helped that organization grow.[11]

Tolley did not seek to divorce extension from Triple-A. He wanted the extension services to continue to perform some administrative services and to devote a great deal of time and energy to educational activities related to the program. He did, however, want the farmers to become more important in planning and administering the program, especially at the county level and in the South, and he wanted the election of county committees to become the universal practice. Finally, in 1938, believing that he was not getting the cooperation he needed from some of the extension services in planning for an expansion of the AAA's conservation program and a shift from surplus crops to grasslands and livestock farming, Tolley suddenly took the state administration of Triple-A away from the state extension services and set up separate state and county offices.[12]

As Tolley pushed for changes, he encountered a mixed reaction. A good many officials in the colleges, chiefly in the Northeast and to some extent in the Middle West, wanted to be free of administrative responsibilities and to devote their full energies once again to research and education. Other officials, however, especially in the South, believed that extension should run the programs, and they regarded Tolley's efforts as a slap at them. Consequently, they attacked him, hoping that he would be removed from his post, and they picked up support from Farm Bureau leaders who feared an independent and powerful farmer committee system, even though Farm Bureau members were heavily represented on the committees, and wanted the extension services to play very large roles in administration.[13]

Unhappiness with Tolley was but part of the broader picture of dissatisfaction in the colleges with New Deal farm programs. As the departmental historians have explained:

Before 1933, the nonregulatory work of the Department was channeled to the individual farmer through the extension services of the land-grant colleges under a 1914 memorandum of agreement. The Agricultural Adjustment Administration and the Soil Conservation Service established direct channels which reached the individual farmers.[14]

Many college officials believed that the national government was trying to play too great a part in the direction of agricultural activities in the states and that the extension services should be relied upon more heavily.[15] A number of officials complained about the "strong tendency on the part of certain bureaus and agencies in the U. S. Department of Agriculture to go direct to the individual farmer, thus overlooking the possibilities of making larger use of state and local agencies. . . ." "How, for example," a number of Midwestern directors asked in April, 1937, "can a Land-Grant College have much to say about the direction of work in the State when a nearby powerful office with abundant funds and large technical personnel is operating at will across state lines?" They suggested that the SCS and RA should organize their work on a state basis through offices established at the colleges which would allow the federal officials to cooperate closely with the schools.[16] At the annual meeting of the Land-Grant College Association later in the year, demands were made that "the Land-Grant College be designated as the sole agency for leadership in research and extension education in all so-called action or other programs dealing with individual farmers. . . ."[17]

Tension prevailed in the relations between the extension services and the federal agencies responsible for the programs for the rural poor. Although the Resettlement Administration and the Farm Security Administration obtained some cooperation from extension, the agencies tended to be quite critical of the services, contending that they lacked sympathy for the rural poor and worked only with the upper-income groups in rural areas. Many of these state and county officials did dislike RA and FSA programs, and the officials resented suggestions from department leaders that extension failed to reach the lower-income groups.[18]

As discontent mounted, the Land-Grant College Association and the department established committees on federal-state relations. Wilson, along with Wallace and other representatives of the department, had discussed the subject with members of the association at its annual meeting in November, 1936, and had agreed to explore the problem with a department committee and to meet with a college committee to reach an understanding on the increasingly complex question of federal-state relations. In December, Wallace designated Wilson and Eisenhower as the department committee. Believing that the problems arose partly "from the many new responsibilities" that had "strained machinery that was originally set up to handle the ordinary research, regulatory and educational activities of the Department," the Secretary regarded the work of the committee as "exceptionally important." After several meetings, Wilson and Eisenhower decided that the committee should be enlarged. Wallace therefore added five people with a great deal of experience in supervising various classes of work carried on by the department in the states. In this committee, Wilson served as chairman and Eisenhower as secretary.[19]

The Program Planning Division devoted a good deal of energy to the work, hoping to find ways of broadening the planning program that was then centered in Triple-A. By the end of 1937, more than 2,400 counties had planning committees consisting of ten to twenty farmers working with the county agents, and some Triple-A administrators were finding the committees' recommendations helpful in making changes in the programs. The committees dealt primarily with the possible effects of an adequate soil conservation program upon the production of major crops but were gradually extending their activities to include land classification and mapping. Thus, it seemed possible to extend this program beyond AAA and connect it in major ways with all the action programs in the department. At the moment, however, this was essentially a Triple-A, not a department-wide, program. It could broaden the point of view of the people involved in the counties and lead them to think in terms of general agricultural planning, but about all that could result under existing arrangements were changes in AAA operations.[20]

Elliott, Tolley's successor as director of the Planning Division, was not fully satisfied with his county planning project. While he believed that in most states there was a sincere and honest effort to get the information requested, he found that in a number of them the work was done in "a perfunctory manner" and that in some he had to battle constantly to get anything done, and he was convinced the program could not succeed until it received more wholehearted support both in the department and in the state colleges.[21]

By early 1938, Wilson's committee had developed a proposal for a planning project that assumed an organization that could conduct agricultural land-use planning could provide a proper adjustment of relations between the department and the colleges and could coordinate the department's action programs. Planning, according to the committee's statement, "Agricultural Planning and Federal-State Relations," was "the key to coordination." The statement suggested that "the principal solution to the present Federal-State relations problem lies in devising a method which will result in the formulation of sound county, State and national land-use plans, on the basis of which all land-use programs may be brought into united action toward common objectives" and specified in some detail the procedures that should be followed.[22] Wilson regarded the document as a major development in the department's relations with the states and believed it should receive very serious thought and consideration on the part of the department's personnel.[23]

The statement circulated widely in the department and among college officials. Department agencies expressed an interest in the proposed program and a willingness to cooperate in it. They were also eager to know who was going to run it.[24] Some college officials, however, were rather fearful of it. One suggested that the program would "get too technical, get too many statistics, charts and wares of the agricultural technicians' stock in trade into program planning, and defeat any real program planning at the outset." He argued that the people should "build these programs from the rural community up and not from the top down" and that they "[could] do it with some guidance and help from the College and the U.S.D.A."[25] Another official complained that Wilson's committee wanted to demote the colleges:

Fundamentally, it means that they do not wish any longer to accept the land-grant institution as the agency in the state with which to deal. They desire to deal with a land-grant institution on an equal basis with the Farm Security Administration, the Federal soil work, the State Planning Board, the State Forestry Commission, the State Veterinarian's office and every other agency in the state which happens to deal with agricultural affairs. The report of this committee . . . shows clearly that the individuals on this committee, at least, think of the land-grant institution as being only one institution among perhaps two or three dozen in the state with which the United States Department of Agriculture should deal.[26]

Nevertheless, the members of the college committee on federal-state relations approved the statement.[27]

The next step took place on July 7 and 8 in a conference at Mount Weather, Virginia, a department outpost in the Blue Ridge Mountains near Washington where refuge could be found from the capital's summer heat. The conference was held to obtain formal approval and wider acceptance of the proposal. Nearly fifty representatives of the department and the colleges participated; Wilson served as one of the presiding officers. The conferees agreed that the Secretary, not the colleges, was responsible for administering the farm programs, that the colleges would cooperate in planning the programs, and that the department would work with the colleges in state, county, and community planning committees composed of directors of extension, county agents, representatives of the department's agencies and bureaus, and farmers. Although there were some doubts about how well the officials would cooperate, a good deal of enthusiasm prevailed at Mount Weather.[28]

While Tolley hoped to use AAA to direct the new program, other department officials had other plans. Many members of Triple-A hoped to see someone other than Tolley placed in charge of its operations even though officials in the North Central Division, especially, applauded his efforts to reduce the role of the extension services in the farm program. These officials disliked the political attitudes of many extension leaders — their fear that the farmer committees would develop into a new farmers' movement, their desire to keep the committees out of political campaigns, and their hostility toward the New Deal. "It is always difficult for me to believe that it is possible to have effective administration of any program when it is not in the hands of its friends," Claude Wickard, the director of the North Central Division, remarked.[29] Triple-A officials discovered, however, that Tolley, as had Davis before him, wanted to keep the farmer committees out of political campaigns and pressure-group activities. One of his closest and most loyal associates, Alfred D. Stedman, had been warning for some time against any effort "to try to use AAA organizations of farmers as if they were parts of a political machine. . . ."[30] Attitudes such as these could block efforts to use the farmer committees to help many in Triple-A to achieve one of their goals: the election of Wallace as President of the United States.[31]

People outside Triple-A also complained about Tolley's approach to politics. After the 1936 election, Senator Joseph Guffey, Democrat of Pennsylvania, had protested to Wallace that while Davis had cooperated splendidly with senators, there had been "a very great lack of cooperation since Mr. Chester Davis retired as Administrator." It appeared to the Senator that Wallace's subordinates were "more interested in working with the opponents of the Administration than in cooperating with me and my colleagues." Guffey concluded that "the farmer does not appreciate what has been done for him as much as he should because too many reactionary Republicans are engaged in administering the program," and he warned Wallace that "continued friendly relations between your Department and men on Capitol Hill depend largely upon a change in the manner in which some of your subordinates are attempting to carry out your program."[32]

Many of Tolley's critics in his organization believed that, as an economist, he was out of touch with the farmers. "Tolley looked more like a genuine dirt farmer and thought less like one than any man in the Department," Wickard's biographer has remarked.[33] Tolley's critics argued that he could not speak effectively to farmers, that he feared them, and that he made proposals they could not understand. According to Tolley's opponents, Triple-A needed a new leader who spoke the farmer's language, could revive the lagging spirits of the organization, would allow it to participate in politics, was satisfied with a program that increased the income of commercial farmers, and would not make frequent proposals for change in the program and in the operations of the farmers.[34]

One top administrator in Triple-A, Cully Cobb, resigned late in the summer of 1937 as a consequence of his unhappiness with Tolley's leadership. A short time later, he criticized the Administrator in a letter to Wallace. The occasion was a "crop limit idea" proposed by Tolley and John Hutson, an economist serving as one of Tolley's assistant administrators. Cobb argued that the farmers did not understand nor want it and that they "thoroughly distrusted it, even going so far as to question the motives behind it." They want "something more definite, less devious; something more direct; something . . . that would place them in a position to defend themselves and the program which . . . was becoming more and more difficult to explain and defend." The Southern rural journalist argued further that almost all of the administrators of the farm program opposed the proposal. "I believe that you have sensed the fact already that you have a pretty serious situation in the Agricultural Adjustment Administration there in Washington," Cobb added. ". . . The first big problem is that of checking . . . the widespread loss of confidence, which loss of confidence made it easier for me to give up my work there than otherwise would have been the case." [35]

Top men in the Secretary's office shared the doubts about Tolley. Here the leading figures were Paul Appleby, one of the most powerful figures in the department and a man with a strong interest in administrative organization, and Rudolph ("Spike") Evans, an Iowa farmer who had worked up through the farmer committee system. They were working for Wallace's nomination as the Democratic presidential candidate in 1940. Appleby was widely regarded as the Secretary's "right hand man and . . . campaign manager," — "as Wallace's 'Louie Howe.'" [36] A militant New Dealer, eager both to improve the administration of the new programs and to maintain the momentum of the reform movement, he hoped to see Wallace unite the farmers with urban labor and the "liberal" businessmen and believed that if Wallace were to obtain the nomination it was necessary to combat the views that he was not a strong administrator and that he was "a special pleader for agriculture." [37] Tolley struck the Secretary's executive assistant as both a poor politician and a poor administrator, insufficiently forceful, too slow in making decisions, and inept in his relations with the power groups in farm politics. Apparently, Appleby also had doubts about Tolley's liberalism and his willingness to promote the liberal orientation in farm policy and politics that seemed desirable and necessary. Clearly, Tolley as Administrator of Triple-A seemed to jeopardize plans for a presidential campaign that were brewing in the department in the late 1930's. [38]

Although Wallace admired Tolley, he had also grown unhappy with the economist's handling of his job. His tendency to push ideas doggedly, even though this alienated important people, disturbed the

Secretary. Wallace liked Tolley's suggestions but believed that he
was trying to move too fast. The Administrator's report for 1937–
1938 troubled Wallace. Tolley and his top assistants, Stedman, Hutson, and Jesse Tapp (a journalist and two economists), had decided
that the annual report of AAA should be an accurate and careful
stock-taking of how much Triple-A had accomplished. They employed Harold B. Rowe, an economist from the Brookings Institution,
to help them. Elliott and others in the Planning Division and several
members of BAE also contributed. The result reflected Tolley's complex attitude toward his work: his sense of accomplishment and his
awareness of shortcomings. While the report stressed "the great worth
of a truly pioneering effort in the development of a national farm
program," it provided cautious estimates of the amount of change
that AAA had promoted and pointed out that, in efforts to promote
soil conservation and efficient farming, "the Administration continues
to face several problems for which a satisfactory solution has not yet
been attained" and that "a great deal remains to be accomplished"
to fully attain the objectives of "establishing agricultural planning
by the farmers themselves — effectively assisted by the Department
of Agriculture, State agricultural colleges, and other agencies — as
a recognized and permanent institution." [39] All of those involved in
the preparation of the report were proud of its frankness. Wallace,
however, feared the ways in which the opposition would use it but
published it when Tolley refused to make changes. Experiences such
as these convinced the Secretary that the farm program could operate more effectively under the leadership of a more "practical"
man. [40]

The Mount Weather Agreement seemed to provide a way out of a
difficult situation. It provided a chance to remove Tolley from his
present position and to give him a job that could both satisfy him
and make use of his well-recognized abilities as a leader of social
scientists. Conferring with Eisenhower, Appleby, and others, Wallace
concluded that Evans should become Administrator of AAA, that the
BAE should be made the central planning agency for the department,
charged with the responsibility of carrying out the terms of the agreement, and that Tolley should become chief of the new BAE. There he
could work closely with other social scientists and perhaps find a
better chance to push his ideas successfully than AAA had provided. [41]

In a memorandum of October 6, 1938, Wallace defined Tolley's
new assignment. The problem, according to the memo, was "to pro-

vide for the formulation of our broad objectives cooperatively, with all agencies agreeing upon basic facts, accepting common standards, deciding upon priorities, formulating acceptable judgments." The assumption was that the problem required "some machinery for bringing the right people together at the right time and for considering the right questions." Departmental machinery was needed that would "enable state and local planning to reach the Secretary in a truly significant and usable form and which will, at the same time, integrate the general planning and program forming activities of the Department; the combined results to guide all action programs of the Department." Thus the Secretary called upon the BAE "to serve as a general agricultural program planning and economic research service for the Secretary and for the Department as a whole." The bureau would not be in charge of "such detailed planning as is inherently a part of administration and operations," but Wallace expected that this type of planning "would remain within the framework of objectives and procedures formulated in the Department's general plans" and would "be performed in accordance with standards and criteria developed by the Bureau." [42]

While Wallace's motives were mixed, one of them was a serious interest in fulfilling the terms of the agreement. He believed that with the passage of the 1938 Adjustment Act the department had the authority it needed and that now the greatest need was to coordinate the various programs and thereby get them to operate more effectively. He regarded Tolley as well qualified to handle the planning job. Overlooking some of Tolley's troubles, the Secretary announced that he knew "few men who could fill this exacting position so acceptably to the trained scientists and economists, to the practical program administrators, to the people in the Land-Grant Colleges and to the farmers." [43] Fortunately for Wallace, he had a loyal friend, Al Black, serving as chief of the BAE, who agreed to take a less important post even though he also would have been a good choice for the new assignment. [44]

Satisfying Tolley proved somewhat more difficult. A few years earlier, he undoubtedly would have welcomed the opportunity to become the chief of an agency with so much prestige in his profession. Now, however, the change seemed a demotion, for the job he lost was looked upon as second in importance only to the secretaryship. Furthermore, Wallace handled the change in the same crude fashion he had employed in the "purge." He did not discuss it with Tolley in advance but simply announced on October 6 that his decision had been made. Then he tried to persuade Tolley to accept it, offering him no explanation for his removal from Triple-A and arguing that he was not being fired but was being moved into a post with great opportunities to pioneer in the field of planning, that he was the most capable man for this, and that the new post would free him of the tasks that had exhausted him in AAA. Tolley was shocked, hurt, and unhappy, especially as he believed he was being treated badly by a man he admired. He thought that Wallace's Presidential ambitions lay behind the move and that his main aim was not to get a unified and integrated program but to get an administrator of Triple-A who would use its committees to assist the drive to place Wallace in the White House.

Nevertheless, after struggling with the decision for several days, Tolley agreed to accept the new assignment. As he had resigned from his position at the University of California in 1936, no alternative was immediately available. Furthermore, the job did provide a chance to work along lines that had long interested him.[45] The change in the status and function of the BAE meant, John Black reported enthusiastically a short time later,

that for the first time there has been provided in the federal government an agency set-up of the form needed to enable the professional economist there to function as the "general staff." . . . Equally vital it provides for the bringing into collaboration with this staff in Washington a sort of general staff in each of the states, to whose functioning the professional agricultural economist should contribute in large measure.[46]

Tolley's good friend Wilson helped him adjust to the change. The Under Secretary suggested to Tolley that the new BAE would provide a valuable opportunity and that he should see what he could make of it. Wilson also suggested that he, Tolley, and a few others should travel to different places in the country to study and observe the operation of some of the programs with which Tolley did not have a firsthand acquaintance. The trip helped him to cool off, get his bearings, and develop ideas on procedure and methods of operation that would help to unify and integrate the programs of the department and the colleges. Upon returning to Washington, Tolley went to work with new enthusiasm, convinced that he had a new opportunity to improve farm programs and to develop more productive working relationships between the bureaucrats of the department and the professors and extension workers in the colleges.[47]

Perhaps Tolley's awareness of Wallace's sincere belief in planning and admiration for economists influenced the decision to accept the change. To Tolley as well as other economists in the department, Wallace seemed the only Cabinet officer in the country's history who understood and sympathized with planning. He had made the department an extremely exciting place for social scientists.[48] The director of research for the President's Committee on Administrative Management had concluded in 1937 that Wallace's department gave greater attention to broad economic problems and made greater use of economists as advisers to the Secretary than any other department.[49] Wilson looked upon Wallace as one of the nation's "greatest thinkers,"[50] and Ezekiel regarded him as "probably the best Secretary of Agriculture we ever had."[51] "As one who in the past had dreamed that some day the government could be run by intelligence and statesmanship instead of hunch, misinformation, and prejudice," Ezekiel wrote in 1940, "the past eight years of working with him have indeed been like a dream come true."[52] Although Wallace had frequently disappointed Tolley, the economist believed that the Secretary had the knowledge, vision, understanding and democratic principles needed to be a worthy successor of FDR.[53]

Wallace was helping economists to play a role that Tolley believed some of them must play. Convinced that many problems could not be met "within the framework of laissez-faire economics" and that inevitably the public would demand action on those problems, Tolley insisted that the technical competence to deal with them could be developed only if a substantial number of economists had "direct contact with the knotty problems of their day and generation."[54] Under Wallace, a large number of economists achieved that contact.

So great were the opportunities for agricultural economists during the Wallace years that many of these men concluded that they must work hard to improve their profession. Some of them feared that the supply of well-trained economists could not meet the great demand, while others worried about the quality of the training that was being provided. Consequently, some, including Al Black, Ezekiel, and Wilson, considered ways of improving the profession so that it could accomplish more.[55]

To Wilson, it seemed obvious that much more was being demanded "than the science of agricultural economics can give. . . . Agricultural economics has more or less had its own way in the field of the social sciences in relation to agriculture, and . . . often the economists have been pretty narrow . . . ," he believed.[56] "They have a highly compartmentalized view of human life," he suggested, and "this highly segmented approach will in time prove itself ineffective." [57] Consequently, he supported the call for the development of schools of social engineering that had been made by Professor Joseph S. Davis of Stanford. Students in such schools would range beyond economics, investigating science, social psychology, cultural anthropology, and social philosophy.[58]

Under Wallace's leadership, in other words, agricultural economists found opportunities to promote changes in farming and felt forced to make changes in their own profession. In 1938 he raised the status of the BAE, an institution of major importance to these people, and early in the following year he declared that "during the next two or three years the Bureau of Agricultural Economics is very definitely in a field where it can, if its imagination is set on fire and it catches a full vision of its possibilities, become an organization of most extraordinary significance." Insisting that he believed "wholeheartedly and enthusiastically" in what BAE was now doing, he suggested that this was part of a large test in a time of crisis of democracy's ability to be efficient.[59]

Thus, by 1939, the social scientists had some basis for optimism. One of them, E. H. Wiecking, while believing that the program would develop slowly, viewed "the Mt. Weather Agreement and the subsequent reorganization of the Department as really epoch-making steps whereby all levels of Government and the officials of all agencies and the local people themselves will really for the first time have a well set up machinery for doing the land-use adjustment job as it needs to be done." [60] Supported by Secretary Wallace and Under Secretary Wilson, Tolley had a new opportunity in 1939 to accomplish what he and Wilson had outlined in 1930.

CHAPTER 10

Building the Planning Program

During 1939 and 1940, Tolley and his lieutenants, with assistance from Wilson, devoted most of their time and energy to the construction of the planning program. They encountered a good many obstacles but found much to encourage them in the progress of the work. Tolley's behavior, and also Wilson's, indicated that their years in office had not changed their ambitions; they remained what they had been in 1930. Now, however, the social scientists seemed to be experiencing the fulfillment of those ambitions.

The new BAE was not itself an "action" agency. In fact, an action program it had conducted briefly — the land purchase program — was removed from its control when the change was made in the bureau's status. Gray had continued to serve in the Resettlement Administration until it was replaced by the Farm Security Administration on September 1, 1937. The Bankhead-Jones Farm Tenant Act of that year had called for the development of a program of land conservation and land utilization, including the retirement of submarginal farm land and the conversion of it to uses for which it was better suited, and authorized the expenditure of $50,000,000 over a three-year period for the purchase of land. For the first time, the department had acquired its own funds to buy land not suitable for farming. This program was placed under the BAE; Gray became Assistant Chief of the bureau in charge of land utilization; RA's Land-Use Planning Section was consolidated with the Division of Land Economics; efforts were made to coordinate the program with the department's other land-use activities; and care was taken to improve the handling of problems connected with the relocation of people. When BAE became the central planner, however, the land acquisition, development, and management functions were transferred to the Soil Conservation Service.[1]

Gray's work was nearly over. The land purchase program had moved forward rapidly under his leadership and had support from both friends and foes of other features of New Deal farm programs. Many of these people, including Secretary Wallace, advocated an enlargement of the program.[2] Although there was some dissatisfaction with Gray as an administrator,[3] and he recognized several "gaps" and a need for "closer integration of the various policies," he was quite satisfied with what had been accomplished. "The task of the immediate future," he believed, "consists mainly in further development along the main lines of advance already established. . . .[4] The future historian of land policy will surely regard this past 5 years as revolutionary," he predicted in 1939.

It marks almost a complete break with the traditional policies of America. It has witnessed the beginning of new policies which will be continued and expanded for generations. . . . the birth pains are over, and the new American land policy, rough hewn as it still is, is ready to face the future.[5]

That future had to be faced without Gray, however. In 1940, he suffered a cerebral hemorrhage that forced him, a man not yet sixty years old, into retirement in 1941. "Your submarginal land program," Tolley wrote to Gray a few years later, "marked a turning point in agricultural policy."[6]

Gray's Division of Land Economics continued to function as the primary research agency in the field of land utilization, servicing other agencies concerned with the department's land programs and carrying out basic research related to them. By 1941, even though some of its members had been transferred to other divisions following the reorganization of 1938, the division was by far the largest in the bureau, having grown from fewer than 50 members in 1932 to 356. The expansion reflected the general expansion under the New Deal of activities in the field of land utilization and the large role that the division had played in those activities. The BAE as a whole had grown from 92 social scientists in 1930 to 768 in 1940.[7]

As a planning rather than an action agency, the BAE's task was to coordinate and direct the work of other agencies. Early in 1939, the bureau and the other agencies in the department drafted a "Memorandum of Understanding" that provided the basis for financing planning within the states and for translating the results of planning into action. According to the memorandum, the BAE was to have primary responsibility for "general planning" involving the analysis and synthesis of information for the shaping of broad plans and programs while the action agencies were to be primarily responsible for "operations planning" to carry out the broad plans and programs.[8]

To implement the memorandum, the Inter-Bureau Coordinating Committee was established, with Tolley as chairman, Elliott as vice-chairman, and representatives of other department agencies as members. Within a short time, a decision was made to rely chiefly upon special coordinating committees and subcommittees rather than upon the general committee. Composed of representatives of the BAE and the other agencies, these committees were usually headed by the BAE representative. At times Tolley played this role; more often, he called upon his lieutenants to serve as "coordinators" or "integrators." Social scientists who had been working with him for several years, including Elliott, Eric Englund, Roy Kimmel, O. V. Wells, and Raymond C. Smith, served in this capacity. The committees dealt with a long list of problems, considered the ideas and recommendations that were made by the farmers, administrators, and researchers involved in the planning program, and developed reports containing recommendations, usually on coordinated approaches to the problems. Some of the committees operated indefinitely, providing a constant check on major departmental programs in hopes of achieving continuing unity in the activities. Usually, however, a committee ceased to exist after its report had been considered and approved first by Tolley and then by the Program Board.[9]

The Program Board had been established by Wallace's memorandum of October 6, 1938. It was composed of the leaders in the department, including Tolley and the heads of the action agencies. Tolley, along with Al Black, Evans, and Eisenhower, served on the executive committee of the board, and Eisenhower was chairman. This agency reviewed and evaluated the plans and programs developed under the leadership of the BAE in the light of the interests of the farmers and the general public, the administrative feasibility and practicability of the proposals, and the over-all needs of the department. After this review and evaluation, the proposals were passed on to the Secretary for his consideration and action.[10]

The elevation of the BAE had not led to the abolition of the Office of Land-Use Coordination. In fact, it had important duties to perform in the new operation. In addition to his role as chairman of the Program Board, the Land-Use Coordinator represented the Secretary in promoting "administrative coordination" of all departmental land-use activities. Eisenhower's task was "operational planning" while Tolley's was "general land-use planning." Drawing the line between these jobs proved difficult at times, and the effort to do so produced some conflicts. Furthermore, Eisenhower was reluctant to apply much pressure on the administrators to get them to put the recommendations of the board into action. Nevertheless, Tolley looked upon Eisenhower as one of his allies.[11]

Conflicts between the BAE and the action agencies appeared more frequently. Wallace had not legally obligated the action agencies to cooperate with the BAE. In fact, on the department's organizational chart, the bureau was on the same level as Triple-A and other action agencies. The BAE had no authority over them and only an opportunity to develop plans and to seek the consent of the agencies to proposals that involved changes in the operations of the agencies. They were to do their own "operational" planning. That is, they were to decide what practical steps, if any, they should take to put the BAE's suggestions into action. Action frequently depended upon the willingness of the Secretary to apply pressure.[12]

At times, officials of the action agencies seemed cooperative. Prior to the Mount Weather Agreement, the Farm Security Administration had strongly endorsed "the whole proposal to make planning the coordinating force in the various Federal and State programs,"[13] and after the new arrangements were made, Evans of Triple-A assured Tolley that he was "very anxious to have this over-all planning work succeed."[14] After Al Black became governor of the Farm Credit Administration late in 1939, it cooperated with the BAE. He believed, for example, that FCA should use credit in ways that would carry out the plans devised by the planning committees.[15]

Tolley enjoyed especially good relations with the Farm Security Administration. They were not perfectly harmonious, especially as the BAE at times criticized FSA operations, but leaders of the latter sympathized with the BAE's intentions, hoped that the planning project would continue to function, and frequently drew upon the recommendations of the planning committees. Tolley struggled to perfect relations between the two agencies. He admired the enthusiasm and liberalism of the organization, finding it quite different than AAA. As time passed, FSA became one of BAE's best friends.[16] Unfortunately for Tolley, his friend was not the most powerful action agency.

Furthermore, most officials in the department's more powerful agencies, the Soil Conservation Service and Triple-A, disliked Tolley, resented the fact that Wallace had given great responsibilities to him, and had no desire to be bossed by him. Many men in AAA did not understand his aims and felt that he was motivated by resentment of his treatment in their agency and by a drive for power. They were convinced that the substitution of Evans for Tolley had improved the administration of the program; they were quite proud of it, resented criticism of it, and were determined to maintain it. They were certainly unwilling to allow a group of social scientists to change it.[17]

The BAE did push many proposals for changes in Triple-A. Believing that the agency had not done nearly enough to improve the lot of lower-income groups in rural America, the social scientists pushed for changes in this area. Recognizing that Triple-A officials were interested chiefly in making payments to farmers and raising farm prices and farm income, the BAE battled for proposals designed to get more conservation from the program. BAE officials also criticized Triple-A and other agencies for not using the facilities of land-use planning more extensively for the development of their programs.[18]

Both Triple-A and SCS were critical of the county planning committees. Officials in these agencies feared that those committees, rather than AAA or SCS committees, might become dominant in the counties. Evans resented proposals for changes in his operations that were coming from the planning committees and tried unsuccessfully to get Tolley to place new restrictions on them. The Administrator maintained that AAA committeemen were the best field people to talk about anything involving their programs and that his committees were more effective and in a better position to understand the wishes of the farmer than any others because they were elected and not appointed, as were the county planning committees.[19] John D. Black discovered, after interviewing several hundred officials in Triple-A and SCS, "that they felt the county committees were proving to be obstacles to the carrying out of their particular programs the way they wanted to do it." In one county, for example, the planning committee had voted against the establishment of a soil conservation district, believing that the methods of SCS were inadequate for the type of land that prevailed there.[20]

Triple-A leaders also disliked the schools of philosophy that the BAE was now promoting. The leaders regarded the schools as agencies of propaganda and doubted that they could make important contributions to the farm program. Thus, these officials were reluctant to authorize participation in the schools by AAA committeemen.[21]

In dealing with the officials of the action agencies and other groups involved in the planning program, Tolley did not always behave as a cautious diplomat. Very interested in his work, he devoted a great deal of energy to it. In Washington and in the field, he applied large amounts of pressure to the various parts of the department and devised bold schemes in order to develop a unified farm program and to discover just how much support Wallace would provide. He was inclined to push his ideas aggressively, to become impatient with those who did not pick up ideas quickly, and to make no effort to conceal his dislike for certain people. As Dean Albertson has described him: "The kindly outlines of his massive face, the slow rumbling tones of his Hoosier accent, and the shy friendliness of his chuckle and smile effectively masked an intense, inquiring mind and a temper which could erupt with startling swiftness."[22] His operations as central planner were influenced to some extent by resentment of the way he had been treated. He was sometimes stubborn in his relations with others in the department and made demands that they regarded as unreasonable. When Appleby advised him to be more cautious in his demands for increases in the bureau's budget, Tolley replied that Appleby had pushed him into the planning job and should support him in it. It seemed to Appleby and others that Tolley was not a good team player and that he was too independent and lacked a proper sense of his responsibilities to the Administration.[23]

Although Tolley's lieutenants often insisted upon the need for a "realistic" approach, they frequently alienated others by failing to behave in a cautious fashion. O. V. Wells, for example, maintained that an economist in his position, in order to be successful, had to develop solutions to problems that would commend themselves "to the common sense of the intelligent layman" and had to have "a wide experience of men and affairs and a strong feel for what, with the

human instruments available, will or will not work." Such an economist had to "evaluate not only what should be done but also what can
be done considering the alternatives that are open and the resources
at hand." Wells recognized that this type of economist would be "an
almost constant source of disappointment to those reformers and aca-
demicians who work chiefly in terms of the ideal solutions, and who
usually underestimate the difficulties of successfully planning and
operating an action program."[24] Theories such as these, however, did
not always control the behavior of the intellectuals. Often, rather than
attempt to employ quiet, persuasive techniques, they approached the
action agencies boldly, determined to show them how to plan and to
insist that the BAE must approve of the plans of the agencies before
they were passed on to the Secretary.[25]

One of the boldest and most important of Tolley's lieutenants was
Bushrod W. Allin. Like so many of the social scientists in these programs, he was a Wisconsin-trained economist who had been heavily
influenced by John R. Commons and had taken from him an awareness
of the importance of organized and often competing groups in the
economic and political processes and a tendency to believe that the
man of ideas must be sensitive to the realities of the situation if he
were to accomplish anything in politics. ". . . the agricultural economist who would wish to improve the well-being of farmers in a
manner consistent with the general welfare must have an understanding of diplomacy as well as economics," Allin believed.[23] By tempera-
ment, Allin was a dynamic, self-confident, outspoken, at times
impulsive Texan with a capacity for forceful expression. He was
not noted for tact and diplomacy and thus antagonized a number
of important people and caused others to feel that he should not be
taken seriously.[27] One member of the BAE complimented him for his
"skill in cutting through entanglements of discussion to draw it all
to focus with a right question, simply and sharply phrased; . . .
power of pungent statement and telling analogy; informality and consistent good humor; . . . clear sense of the ground you want to
cover." This colleague added, however, that along with Allin's "clear
sight and power of forceful statement" was an occasional tendency as
a discussion leader to override viewpoints that differed from his own.[28]

Allin played a major role in the development of the planning project in the states and counties. As a member of the Division of Program
Planning, he had been one of the leaders in the earlier county planning
project, and as a member of Eisenhower's office, he had contributed

to the shaping of the Mount Weather Agreement.[29] Characteristically, he was enthusiastic about the agreement. "The conference was most successful," he informed another social scientist:

I believe there occurred for the first time a meeting of minds between the Department and College people. Planning has been definitely agreed upon as a principal procedure for promoting better coordination between the Colleges and the Department. I think it is entirely correct to say that everyone left the conference well pleased with its results and even enthusiastic concerning the possibilities of planning on the community, county and State levels.[30]

With the reorganization of the department, he became head of the BAE's Division of State and Local Planning, which was formed in March, 1939, and was composed of a small staff in Washington and representatives in the regions and states. Among other functions, this division negotiated memoranda of understanding and project agreements with the colleges and promoted the development of planning organizations in the states and counties. The division also had important parts to play in the planning process itself. Its work kept it in close contact with the colleges and the action agencies in efforts to get them to participate in the shaping of the plans and to translate the plans into action.[31]

Allin had a broad conception of his new responsibilities. While the old county planning project had been limited largely to the efforts of Triple-A, the extension services, and the farmers to promote conservation, the new program added the other action agencies and other aims to this list. He insisted that the term "land-use planning" should not be defined in a narrow way but should be recognized as meaning "agricultural planning." All of the department programs had land-use implications, and good land-use planning would provide "a basis for coordinating and localizing and fitting emergency programs into a long time objective. . . ." Confident that the department's representatives at Mount Weather had had such a broad conception in mind, he was determined to implement it, and he criticized colleagues who had more limited notions of BAE's responsibilities. He also tried hard to prevent planning from "degenerating wholly into a fact-collecting operation."[32]

Obliged to deal with the agricultural colleges, Allin was rather critical of them. He regarded them as timid in the social sciences. Believing that those disciplines were inherently controversial, he insisted that researchers in this area could not have the "cool 'disinterestedness'" that characterizes physical scientists. "The only reason for giving opinions and advice," he suggested,

is to influence the thinking of those who "pass judgement." If you do this, you can't escape becoming identified with the policies adopted upon your advice, and if those should not turn out well in operation — that is, if a considerable body of public opinion should become displeased with the results — you can't escape merely by saying that the policies you recommend were based on objective facts. And you can't give opinions and advice that are merely facts. What legislators have to have is the meaning of facts — not simply facts.

He warned that a college that hesitated to take a stand ran the risk of "developing a reputation for being an 'academic' and over-cautious institution which provides no leadership in dealing with real problems."[33]

Allin also criticized the colleges for failing to recognize that a new situation had developed, involving a significant increase in the importance of federal action. He was enthusiastic about the New Deal, and he suggested that the colleges needed to adjust to it. "Prior to the inauguration of these farm programs," he advised one extension director,

it might have been reasonably correct to assert that "program planning" should be developed only from "the bottom up" by local people, and that technical representatives of Federal agencies should participate in such work only in an advisory capacity. But such an assertion is no longer valid. The work must be done from "the bottom up" and from "the top down." Planning must start at both ends. It must meet at some point so differences can be resolved. This is what is meant in the document "Agricultural Planning and Federal-State Relations" when it is proposed that not only farmers but also representatives of Federal agencies operating in the county participate in county planning to the end that we may bridge the gap between planning and the "action" of public agencies.[34]

One of Allin's most important tasks was the negotiation of the memorandum of understanding with the colleges. It formalized the Mount Weather Agreement and clarified relations between the department and the colleges. According to the memorandum, state committees were to be established composed of the state extension directors as chairmen, the state BAE representatives as secretaries, the directors of the experiment stations, other state officials, the state representatives of departmental agencies, and farmers. Joint land-grant college-BAE committees were also to be formed, consisting of the state BAE representatives and the directors of the extension services and the experiment stations and serving as informal working subcommittees of the state land-use planning committees. County committees were to be organized by the extension services and composed of farmers and state and national officials serving in the counties. On a county committee, farmers were to constitute a substantial majority; one was to serve as chairman, and the county agent was to be the executive officer or secretary. The extension services were also to form community committees composed of farmers. The BAE representatives were to have headquarters in the colleges, represent the department in the project, work closely with college officials, and help plan, organize, and conduct agricultural land-use planning and research in the state, stimulate planning in the counties, and bring the recommendations of the county committees to the state committees and the department. The directors of extension were to appoint project leaders to be actively in charge of the county planning project. The Chief of the BAE and the Federal Director of Extension were to correlate the work of the state project leaders and BAE representatives in order to develop regional and national programs.[35]

Tolley assumed that in every state, college officials would sign the memorandum and join in the planning project, and he and his lieutenants hoped to avoid the application of pressure on the officials to get them to sign.[36] Unfortunately, in several states, college officials refused to sign, and the degree of cooperation between the bureau and the colleges and the extent to which the schools applied themselves to the project varied greatly from state to state. Old antagonisms between Tolley and some of the college people persisted, and new sources of friction between BAE and the colleges developed as the experiment moved forward. Some of the officials were simply skeptical of it or indifferent toward it. They doubted that it would produce much action, believed that it would soon "blow over," and thus preferred not to get their staffs excited about it. They could not believe that the department would be guided by the recommendations of the planning committees, and they forced department officials to make special efforts to generate interest and to demonstrate that "the Department of Agriculture means business."[37] One poetic critic suggested that the purposes of county planning were to safeguard the appropriations of the bureaus and the re-election of the Democrats and portrayed Wallace as saying to his bureau chiefs and the coordinators and integrators:

> Get together with each other,
> Get together with the farmers,

> Make a plan for agriculture,
> Find a balance of adjustment,
> Lest we face annihilation,
> Lest we perish in disaster,
> Lest we not be re-elected
> By the votes in 1940.[38]

The program also suffered from fears about the department's intentions. When the memorandum of understanding was first drafted, Gray complained that it would subordinate the BAE and the department within the states to the extension services. "I recognize that the State Extension Service has an important part to play in setting up county and community committees and encouraging their activity; that such groups can contribute both data and judgment to local planning; and that the acquiescence of such groups in decisions is desirable when possible," he told Tolley, "but it is quite another thing to subordinate the Federal interest, activity and administrative responsibility and particularly its technical and policy aspect to the State Extension Service."[39] Some college officials, however, viewed the program in a quite different way and feared that it would establish federal domination. They wanted a large degree of independence within the states and feared that the department would "steal the show."[40] A few extension directors raised questions about the motives of the department in suggesting state committees, and one suggested that this was just another procedure for developing federal control of the agricultural programs of the state.[41] Another extension director feared that the bureau was going to dominate the program, simply using the extension service and leaving it in a position to be blamed for all that went wrong. He complained that he was being "unduly pressed" to sign the agreement the way the department wanted it, and he expressed the hope that his "misgivings . . . as to the import of certain details which have been under controversy have been imagined rather than real."[42]

The director of the extension service in the state of Washington, F. E. Balmer, was an especially vigorous and consistent foe of the project. He was critical of the emphasis upon land-use planning, seeing it as part of a long-time tendency in the department to overwork one idea at a time.[43] He looked upon the county committees as an invasion of extension's territory, disliked Allin, and believed that he and his lieutenants were trying "to grab all the power and run things from Washington."[44] The director insisted that land-use planning was merely the continuation of the program-building procedures already established by the extension service and that he must control the program, two positions that caused Allin to complain that "land-use planning work is not merely old-line Extension work, nor is the Director of Extension responsible solely for all the land-use planning in the State" and to advise one of his subordinates to "find some way to let Director Balmer know that we cannot cooperate with the College on this project unless the College is willing to make it a truly cooperative activity."[45] Another member of Allin's division suggested after several years of trouble with Balmer that "we will have to have a showdown as to whether we are going to have a democratic approach to agricultural planning in this state or whether we are going to have it dictated by the Director of the Extension Service." The BAE official added that he was "convinced that the Director does not believe in democracy."[46]

California also provided problems, although the state developed an unusually active and successful land-use planning program. The officials refused to sign the memorandum; they believed that doing so would constitute an undesirable departure from custom.[47] They regarded the work as desirable and welcomed the help of the department in furthering the work they had been doing, but they wanted to maintain a good deal of independence and feared "domination of the planning program from the top down."[48] Nevertheless, although the BAE was quite critical of the California officials, the two groups were able to cooperate to some extent.[49]

A major source of difficulty in many places was the provision in the memorandum calling for the assignment of a representative of the BAE to each state. Tolley and Allin hoped that these representatives would play major roles in the program and be treated as the equals of the directors of the extension services and the experiment stations in this work.[50] Some of the leaders in the colleges, however, feared that these officials would run the planning work in the states, possibly going directly to the county agents and county committees without working through the directors. Thus, efforts were made to restrict the activities of the representatives and to subordinate them to college officials. There was some resistance to the proposal that the representative should serve as secretary of the state committee and some attempt to limit his responsibilities as secretary to routine tasks. Other efforts were made to limit him to the collection of facts. Tolley and Allin resisted proposals of this type.[51]

In Illinois, for example, college officials feared the BAE representative and suggested that a representative of the college should be chairman of the state committee and have full discretion in selecting the secretary.[52] The dean of the college contended that making the BAE representative secretary "would be an undue delegation of authority and would jeopardize the stability and continuity of the projects." He insisted that "so far as the citizens of Illinois are concerned, the stability, the continuity, the reliability, and the success or failure of the state's agricultural program is the risk and the responsibility of the College of Agriculture, University of Illinois."[53] Despite the school's great interest in land-use planning, it did not cooperate closely with the BAE.[54]

As the BAE had funds that could be made available to the state extension services, it could apply pressure upon the colleges to obtain the arrangements that it desired.[55] Kentucky provided an example of the use of such pressure. There, according to one member of the BAE, the belief in the right of the state to manage its own affairs was very strong.[56] The dean of the agricultural college tried to define the responsibilities of the BAE representative in a more narrow way than Tolley and Allin would accept.[57] This led to major difficulties in the selection of a representative, especially as the dean had doubts about the BAE's candidate for the position.[58] Finally Allin asked the college official if it would be agreeable to him "to discontinue financial cooperation with the Bureau of Agricultural Economics in land-use planning work until such time as we can find a suitable representative."[59] The official resented the suggestion, but Allin persisted, suggesting that the work in Kentucky was being hampered by the lack of a representative and that the dean's attitude was responsible for the failure to appoint one. The official responded with a defense of his handling of the matter, suggesting that the agreement provided "that the BAE representative shall be approved by the College of Agriculture" and that the college could "take the time to make such investigations and to give such considerations to the appointment as it finds necessary."[60] The bureau then agreed to continue to cooperate for a limited period but suggested that if a "mutually acceptable" person could not be found within that period, financial support would be discontinued "until such time as we are able to agree upon a State BAE representative and, as a consequence, are, in a position to cooperate effectively in the land-use planning program in Kentucky."[61] Agreement was reached before the deadline, but developing good relations with the dean continued to be a problem, for his view of his power in the program conflicted with Allin's.[62]

In Tennessee, the financial inducements failed to work perfectly, for the officials in the extension service there doubted that the money that could be obtained was worth the additional trouble. They did not have a strong desire to cooperate with other agencies in the planning process, and they entered into the work without enthusiasm, found it difficult to reach agreement with the BAE on basic principles, and made little progress. As late as 1941, the state land-use planning committee was not completely organized.[63]

Thus, as the planning project moved forward, there were many problems marring relationships between the BAE and the colleges. There were problems about the use of funds, the allocation of credit for the work, the amount of time that the county agents should devote to planning, and the quality of the men chosen as state and regional BAE representatives.[64] Some extension directors charged that the department was using the planning committees as pressure groups for its programs.[65] Some college people, in short, looked upon the BAE as an unwelcome competitor — even as a dictator, not an ally. "In some few states, we have spent years of futile effort in an attempt to set up and operate a cooperative planning organization . . . ," Allin complained early in 1942. "In spite of our best efforts we have succeeded in arousing but little interest in cooperative planning."[66]

Department leaders recognized the fears in the colleges about federal domination and attempted to overcome them. "The process of planning, as we conceive it, is cooperative — not authoritarian," Wilson assured the Land-Grant College Association soon after the Mount Weather Agreement and the reorganization of the department;[67] a short time later, leaders in the bureau promised college officials that the work would be in line with the letter and spirit of the agreement.[68] On another occasion one of the BAE's land planning specialists explained the objectives of the department in suggesting the state committees and was able to reduce the fears of one extension director.[69] Allin often proceeded cautiously, allowing the schools a good deal of freedom in staffing and operating the program and tolerating, in at least one difficult situation, a state representative who did not represent the bureau "with backbone and farsightedness."[70]

Although their responsibilities kept them in Washington much of the time, Tolley and his lieutenants, such as Elliott and Allin, went into the field whenever they could to promote cooperation and generate interest. They also tapped Wilson's skills in dealing with people. Early in 1940, he resigned his post as Under Secretary of Agriculture to become National Director of the Extension Service. One of the motives for the change was the belief that he could encourage the college and extension people to participate more actively in planning without antagonizing them. With encouragement from Tolley, Wilson spent a good deal of time moving about the country, building support for the program.[71]

Efforts such as these were fairly successful. Despite the attitudes of many college officials, only three states refused to sign the memorandum, and only one refused to join in any way in the planning project. By the end of August, 1939, all states except seven had signed, and before the end of the year, four of those seven were added to the list of signers. Two more states participated without signing the memorandum.[72] By the end of the first year, 70,000 farm men and women were organized into community and county committees in 1,120 counties and 47 states. By June 30, 1941, all but one state (Pennsylvania) and almost two-thirds of the counties (nearly 2,000) were formally organized and active in the planning process. The 47 state committees had 1,371 members, including 678 farm men and women, the county committees had 57,313 members of which 40,002 were farm folk, and more than 82,000 farm men and women served on community committees. The various committees were promoting changes in rural life — conserving and building soil, improving medical facilities, revising tax systems, switching acres from wheat or tobacco to livestock, cover crops, and food for home consumption, developing farm-to-market roads, altering school curricula, closing poor land to farming, changing the size of farms, establishing cooperatives, etc.[73]

Some of the college officials were very active in and enthusiastic about the work. According to the representative of the BAE in the West, Idaho stood out "as one that is doing the best job, all things considered. The Extension Service is for planning one hundred percent."[74] The Dean of the School of Agriculture at Texas A. and M. wrote to Tolley early in 1940 to express his conviction that land-use planning would be "one of the most vital factors for the welfare of agriculture during this coming year and for a number of years ahead. . . ." According to the Dean, had this program "been started and worked out in Texas fifteen or twenty years ago it would have . . .

saved the State millions of dollars." He pledged Tolley "full support" and hoped to see "the work not only continued, but increased in size and scope." [75]

Perhaps a major explanation of the substantial degree of cooperation that developed was the careful way in which the planners in Washington pushed their point of view on questions like the representative character of the county planning committees. The county agents usually selected the farmers who served on the committees, and as those agents tended to associate most closely with the more substantial members of their communities, the committees did not represent all interests, especially those of the rural poor. In many counties, the Farm Bureau dominated the committees. [76]

Washington officials interested in the planning project both recognized that the committees did not represent all interests in their communities and believed that they should. Early in 1940, Allin listed efforts to get a more representative group participating in the land-use planning process as one of the "next steps" that could "improve the planning process." [77] He had long been interested in establishing "truly representative" planning committees and regarded elected committees as preferable to committees appointed by county agents. [78] Wallace, Wilson, and Tolley also preferred elected committees. When Allin informed the Secretary that often the county agents selected the committees, Wallace indicated that he hoped that eventually it would "be practical for the farmers themselves to do this choosing." [79]

Some of the social scientists doubted that even elected committees represented the interests of all rural groups and suggested other ways of developing more representative committees. The sociologists in the BAE suggested that their techniques of "community delineation" could supply the basis for more adequate committees. By investigation, the sociologists could discover the "natural" neighborhoods and communities, provide information on the "representativeness of the committeemen," and supply a basis for the "mobilization of the rural community and rural leadership." These sociologists, housed in BAE's Division of Farm Population and Rural Welfare, suggested that, as a new function of a community, land-use planning could succeed only if it first recognized the way in which rural people were organized and then attempted to fit land-use planning into that social organization. Both the "general interest" organizations — the community and the neighborhood — and the "special interest" organizations — the lodges, clubs, institutions, etc. — should be drawn into the work and represented on the committees. In 1940, the division launched a nation-wide program of community delineation as part of the land-use planning program.[80]

Also in 1940, the BAE developed a study of the planning process designed chiefly to determine to what extent the committees represented all groups and areas in the counties and to secure data upon which to base recommendations for changes in the make-up of the committees. The study assumed that to promote "the greatest amount and most effective local participation possible in County Land-Use Planning, the committees should be representative, the local residents and committee members should participate thoroughly in the deliberation of the committees, and the people should be informed of the activities and recommendations of the committees." According to the participants in the study, chiefly members of the divisions of Farm Population and Rural Welfare and of State and Local Planning, county and community committees should represent "natural" neighborhoods and communities, various income levels, special interest groups, such as tenants, landowners, farm laborers, and rural youth, and various types of farming, including part-time and subsistence farming.[81]

The promoters of the planning program proceeded cautiously in promoting their theory that all rural groups should be represented in the formulation of agricultural programs. The tendency was to try to influence the extension and farm leaders to take the necessary steps. Frequently, however, these leaders resisted. When suggestions were made that sociologists should be employed, extension leaders usually replied that they knew their communities and did not need any outside help.[82] When one Washington official made a strong statement concerning the need to be thoroughly democratic in county planning, a state official replied that, in his area, domination of the committees by the large landowners was perfectly proper and the only way such programs could be carried out.[83] Late in 1940, a special subcommittee of the Land-Grant College Association recommended that "with experience and training, popular election of committee members is advisable, but in initial stages, the county agents should consult representatives of the other agricultural agencies and farm people in securing mutually satisfactory committees."[84]

Although Allin sometimes antagonized colleagues who did not share his interest in making the committees more representative, he tolerated slow progress in this direction. He believed that there were a number of practical reasons why the less advantaged groups could not now be adequately represented. Some of them moved too frequently; many were not interested; social barriers blocked those who were. Consequently, farmer membership on the planning committees was drawn "too largely from the ranks of the more prosperous farmers and landowners, particularly in those areas where small farmers, tenants, sharecroppers, and farm laborers comprise a heavy majority of the agricultural population." Although he denied that this prevented the committees and the department from developing an interest in the rural poor, he believed that "the formulation of plans without participation of part of the people for whose benefit they are made is not all that might be desired in a democratic process." By 1941, however, he believed that the committees were becoming more representative, and he expected "further and more rapid progress in this direction." [85]

The composition of the committees and the tendency to proceed carefully in efforts to promote change were parts of a pattern in the political operations of Wilson and his associates and reflected their assumption about the need to be "realistic." Wilson believed that significant changes could come about only in a slow fashion, and he emphasized the "realities of the situation at a particular moment and the pragmatic problem of doing the best that could be done in terms of all aspects of the present situation." For him, a grasp of "the realities" meant that one could not attempt "too much reform all at once" and involved working with groups like the extension services, the Farm Bureau, and the leading commercial farmers and attempting to push them into new activities. [86] He had worked in this way throughout the 1930's and had made progress. He had hesitated to take steps that might antagonize the Farm Bureau and its allies. The "purge" of 1935 had provided a major illustration of the procedure. Vigorous attempts now to stimulate mass participation in the committees — to recruit people of the sort that the county agents seldom contacted and that did not belong to the Farm Bureau — might only alienate the groups whose cooperation seemed essential.

Surely the program could not succeed if the planners alienated the farmers who had some interest in planning and were willing to give it a try and whose operations were large enough to have a significant impact on their areas. The planners were very interested in gaining the cooperation of these people. Generating interest and action even among the more substantial farmers and their allies — the county agents — was a very big task. The county agents had been trained simply to make farms more productive and were now being called upon to do much more. Most of the farmers had not even begun to plan their own farms and were now being called upon to make plans for an entire county.[87] In addition to limitations on their knowledge, their time was limited. As college officials in Nebraska informed Wallace, "It must be recognized that the type of farmer who should be a member of these committees is a busy man and can be expected to contribute his time only during slack seasons."[88]

The planners proceeded cautiously in their approach to the development of the planning committees, a feature of the program that was tremendously significant to the social scientists. They hoped to expand the role of the farmers in the planning process. The notions about planning and administrative machinery that had developed out of Wilson's conception of democracy and that had already appeared in the Christgau bill, the Allotment Plan, AAA, SCS, and the county planning project were carried further in the county and community land-use planning committees. Wilson, as well as other department leaders, hoped to make their agency "the most democratic spirited department in the Government or any other government. . . ." During the winter of 1937–1938, he had conducted a lecture series in the USDA, designed to stimulate thinking about the meaning of democracy and its operations in the twentieth century. Prominent people from outside the department, including Charles A. Beard, Thurman Arnold, Ruth Benedict, and George H. Gallup, had presented lectures; each lecture had been followed by a seminar in Wilson's office, attended chiefly by the Secretary's staff, the bureau chiefs, and the administrative officers. One result was a book, *Democracy Has Roots*.[89] The planning committee system represented an effort to establish a democratic method of planning and assumed that farmers as well as the experts had valuable ideas to contribute and that ideas could be translated into effective action only when they had broad popular support.[90]

Although the development of the planning committees reflected confidence in the ability of farm people to wrestle with complex social and economic problems when given a chance,[91] the social scientists insisted that the experts must also play effective roles in the planning process. Gray, especially, feared those who depreciated the importance of the role of the technician in land-use planning and those who implied that committees of farmers, operating at the local level, were alone capable of finding the answers to problems of extreme complexity. He insisted that the leadership of technicians was essential.[92] "The advantages of the democratic process . . . can be effectively and continuously realized only if the process is adequately serviced by competent technicians at the State level, and, even more, at the county or district level," he advised as the new program was taking shape. "Lacking the assistance and direction supplied by competent technicians, the county planning process is likely to result in biased, perfunctory, 'half baked' judgments in many of the counties; noncomparable data, lack of continuity of effort, and in some counties, discouragement and abandonment of the undertaking." [93] And, according to one of Gray's lieutenants:

County planning is another mechanism for gathering and interpreting data in the form of farmers' experiences and for securing judgments as to their collective significance for action; but the planning technique — the rendering of integrated judgments, the final synthesis of the facts — still should be directed by, and finally checked by, a trained mind.[94]

In other words, the planning program involved an attempt at cooperation between farmers and experts, including social scientists. Both were needed, and the role of neither group should be given too much emphasis, for each could make contributions and each had shortcomings.[95] An article by Englishman Harold Laski, "The Limitations of the Expert," circulated widely in the bureau in 1939 and 1940. Laski had argued in 1930,

it is one thing to urge the need for expert consultation at every stage in making policy; it is another thing, and a very different thing, to insist that the expert's judgment must be final. For special knowledge and the highly trained mind produce their own limitations which, in the realm of statesmanship, are of decisive importance. . . . We must ceaselessly remember that no body of experts is wise enough, or good enough, to be charged with the destiny of mankind. Just because they are experts, the whole of life is, for them in constant danger of being sacrificed to a part; and they are saved from disaster only by the need of deference to the plain man's common sense.[96]

"It has occurred to me," one state BAE representative wrote to Allin, "that the principles set forth in this article are fundamentally part of the basis for the Land-Use Planning process." [97] Basically, according to Allin, county planning "was a means of integrating the ideas of laymen with those of Federal and State technicians and administrators." [98] The most promising feature of the whole program, according to another leader in the bureau, was the "fusion of practical experience and 'expert knowledge.' " [99]

One implication of the program was that the social sciences should develop a pragmatic orientation. Members of the BAE were very enthusiastic about the book, *Knowledge for What?*, that the sociologist Robert Lynd published in 1939. "Insistent public dilemmas clamor for solution," the explorer of "Middletown" pointed out:

Decisions will be made and public policies established. . . . If the social scientist is too bent upon "waiting until all the data are in," or if university policies warn him off controversial issues, the decisions will be made anyway — without him. They will be made by the "practical" man and the "hardheaded" politician chivvied by interested pressure-blocs.

Lynd hoped that social scientists would play a crucial role in the decision-making process and maintained that this meant that the social sciences must emphasize the analysis of the more critical problems of American culture and the devising of concrete programs of action.[100] "Mr. Tolley has about made *Knowledge for What?* required reading for everybody in the Bureau of Agricultural Economics," Wilson informed Lynd in 1939. "It does not require much administrative compulsion to get them to do this, for it puts on the printed page a great many of the intangible ideas that are floating around the Department."[101]

The experiment in democratic planning demanded that the social scientists, as well as others in the department, attempt to understand the farmers and give them an understanding of and interest in planning. Wilson responded vigorously to this demand, enlarging programs he had been developing since moving back into the department in 1934.[102] He arranged impressive programs to broaden the education of the members of the department in philosophy and the social sciences and to bring those disciplines to bear upon the work of the department. He made special efforts to draw social psychologists and cultural anthropologists into these activities, for he believed that they could make major contributions.[103]

One of Wilson's most notable efforts along this line was his promotion of research into the attitudes of farmers. As soon as he had returned to the department, he had attempted informally to bring its members into closer contact with conditions throughout the country.[104] Then in 1936, he had initiated an opinion study. Operating on a small scale at first, with a study of the attitudes of Iowa farmers toward AAA and their relations with government, and gaining strong support from Wallace and Tolley, Wilson had expanded the program, developing a staff within the Program Planning Division and extending the study throughout the country. In this period, the work was quite informal and impressionistic. Several men simply moved about the country talking with farmers; scientific sampling techniques were not employed. But the head of the Division of Farm Population, Carl Taylor, worked hard to improve the project.[105]

Following the change in the bureau's status, the work became much more systematic and sophisticated. The new Division of Program Surveys was established in 1939, and a highly regarded social scientist, Rensis Likert, was employed to head the new unit. Trained at Columbia University, where he had received the Ph.D. degree in psychology, he was a dynamic and original man with strong research interests who had worked with insurance companies on opinion surveys and had published in this field. Under his leadership, the department's public opinion work drew upon the techniques of market research and the new Gallup Poll, developed a detailed methodology for conducting interview surveys, and played a leading role in shaping new sampling procedures that assumed representative data could be obtained from the use of small samples.[106] According to one student of the growth of social research in the United States, Likert's division "assumed the leadership in introducing the sample interview survey as a basic social science tool and as an instrument of governmental policy" and "prepared the way for the subsequent use of the interview survey in the Office of War Information, War Production Board, Office of Price Administration and other war-time agencies."[107]

These activities were influenced by Wilson's belief that each social group had its own cultural pattern that determined its behavior to a large degree and contained nonrational and irrational as well as rational elements. His contacts with sociologists, cultural anthropologists, and social psychologists had made him an active and influential proponent of the "cultural approach." He insisted that the planner needed to know much more than what appeared rational from an economist's point of view. He had to understand the customs, traditions, and values of the particular people with whom he worked.[108] "If the economists are to cooperate with farmers in the planning process, and if the administrators of vast programs are to administer them wisely and democratically," Tolley maintained, "it is perfectly obvious that we need to know much more about farmer attitudes than we now know."[109] The new disciplines of cultural anthropology and social psychology, Wilson believed, could promote understanding of "the nature of our culture and bring us down into the field of reality as to the way people think and actually perform."[110]

The social scientists viewed these activities as efforts to bring science to the service of democracy. "While it might be possible to put new programs across by administrative decree backed by force," a social psychologist in the BAE suggested, "this is not the American way. We must . . . operate within the framework of the democratic process."[111] If the government employed scientists and their best techniques to gain an understanding of the people, then officials could shape and operate programs that would serve popular needs and desires.[112] According to Likert, recent changes in the relations between Congress and the executive branch made his work essential. So much power had been granted to the executive branch that in order to ensure democratic government, administrators needed a means of ascertaining quickly, accurately, and at very little expense how the people affected by laws wanted them to be administered.[113]

In addition to efforts to understand the farmers, attempts were made to change their ideas and also those of the officials who worked with them. "Our first and mutual duty," Wilson told the college leaders, "is to lead public opinion through understanding, not merely to follow it whither it may drift."[114] Here the schools of philosophy and discussion groups that had begun to function in 1935 figured prominently as these programs were continued and expanded by the new BAE. Carl Taeusch, who now became head of the bureau's new Division of Program Study and Discussion, continued to manage this educational work. By 1941, the schools were being held at the rate of twenty-five per year, with an average of 250 people meeting for four days. By that time, fifty-six schools had been held for nearly 9,000 extension workers; twenty for about 4,500 teachers of vocational agriculture, rural librarians, and clergymen; eighteen for approximately 3,000 members of the department; and fourteen for over 9,000 farm men and women, most of whom were members of Triple-A and land-use planning committees and the national farm organizations. The schools gave special attention to the broad implications of agricultural problems and to their proposed solutions but ranged beyond these matters to questions of foreign relations and basic philosophy. Each school was addressed by five or six noted lecturers, many of whom were critical of the farm programs. Frequent participants included departmental members like Ezekiel and outsiders like John D. Black and the historian Walter Prescott Webb.[115]

With a great deal of help from Wilson, Taeusch continued to push the discussion group program. By 1941, he had held over one thousand leadership training conferences dealing with discussion techniques and encouraging the prospective leaders to form small groups of their farm neighbors to discuss the broader phases of agricultural policy. By that time, more than thirty extension directors had, in response to requests from Taeusch, appointed state discussion group leaders.[116]

Taeusch tried to conduct his work in cooperation with the extension services. They were given preference as sponsors of the schools. The program implied, however, that the type of education offered in the agricultural colleges was inadequate, and some extension directors showed no interest in providing schools of philosophy for their staffs. In those states he felt justified in holding schools in cooperation with other agencies. By the end of 1940, nearly two-thirds of the schools had been sponsored by the extension directors while in the others the directors had been kept informed of the activity. In February, 1941, three schools were held. The first, which met from the eleventh to the fourteenth of the month in Provo, Utah, had been requested by the Provo Junior Chamber of Commerce and was attended by farm and town people and representatives of various state agencies. The second was held in eight places in Arkansas for two weeks, had been requested by the assistant director of extension, and was attended by extension workers and farm people. The third met in New Brunswick, New Jersey, on the twenty-fifth, twenty-sixth, and twenty-seventh of February, had been requested by the extension director, and was attended by extension workers.[117] In the discussion group program, some of the extension services conducted a program that dealt with a much more limited list of problems than BAE leaders desired, and only about twenty states cooperated with the bureau in a large way. In the uncooperative states, Taeusch worked with other interested groups.[118]

As Taeusch defined his work, its purpose was "to strengthen the democratic processes. . . ."[119] Consequently, efforts were made to link the work closely with the land-use planning project in order to provide the planning committees with more effective methods of procedure as well as with a background of informed public opinion.[120] He warned that there was "a serious danger of the BAE getting into the former position of AAA . . . , namely that of a one-directional method of 'telling folks what to do,'" and he suggested that his division "could contribute to the bureau's effectiveness by helping to introduce the discussion method into the regional BAE conferences and the county planning activities." Thus, he and Allin encouraged all state BAE representatives to cooperate with and promote the discussion program, suggesting that "if farm men and women get a better understanding of their problems, they will give better support to planning programs" and "will help in developing these programs and support the committeemen who are trying to carry out the programs."[121]

Taeusch had a great deal of confidence in the discussion method, regarding it as superior to the "one-directional activities" employed elsewhere in the department to educate people. His method could stimulate more participation in program formulation and contribute to a better understanding of the subject matter. " 'You can't teach an old dog new tricks' was unfortunately for a while supported by the educators and psychologists who insisted that the 'intelligence quotients' of human beings remained constant," he remarked. "But more recent experience, and a more intelligent approach, have demonstrated the tremendous possibilities of adult education."[122]

In addition to their confidence in the educational programs, the planners expected that actual participation in planning would give the farmers an understanding of it and an interest in it. John Dewey's concept of "learning by doing" influenced the work as did the theory of change propounded by the sociologist William F. Ogburn. The latter suggested that people developed a greater interest in change after they had experienced the success of an initial change, and the planners promoted experimental and unified county programs in which special efforts were made to push the planning process along rapidly so that the farmers could see the results of planning and thus develop a strong interest in it.[123] Prior to 1939, the Program Planning Division had conducted an experimental county project in which experiments with different types of programs were carried on in a small number of counties. Their aim was to develop new techniques and procedures that could be applied widely by Triple-A. The experiment suggested that the experimental approach might be a useful device for working out and testing alternative ways of coordinating the land-use programs of all governmental agencies.[124] Then in 1939, efforts were made to develop a unified program in at least one county or area in each state, carrying the work beyond the point of recommendations to include the development of a program of action in 1940 which would involve changes in the programs of the agricultural agencies at work in the counties. Here was an attempt to meet the demand that the results of planning be translated quickly into action.[125]

Also in line with the desire to develop interest in planning on the part of farmers, Allin rejected the suggestion that a master plan was a prerequisite to successful local planning. He advocated instead an emphasis upon problems, arguing that if a local planning committee began with the notion that a master plan must be formulated before action could start, members would become discouraged.[126]

In short, the social scientists promoted a two-way educational process. Wilson, for example, insisted that unless plans have a democratic base, are understood, appreciated, and wanted by the rank and file of the farmers they will not serve the best purpose. On the other hand, he believed that if the farmers got the facts they would be able to see their real interests far more clearly. They would then participate in "self-conscious, alert, well-informed and socially inspired groups of rural people" to devise plans to promote their interests.[127]

Wilson believed that the hold that a group's culture had upon it meant change would take place only in a slow fashion, but he was confident that change could be promoted by education and experimentation. "It is true," he believed,

that facts do not dissolve prejudices when there is no will or interest on the part of the individual in giving up his prejudices. But the tenacity with which the farmer or the laborer holds to his delusion or to his preconception is weakened by facts which have been made available to him through a research program and through the technique of open democratic discussion.[128]

"I am a firm believer in the idea of social evolution and social change as well as evolution in the natural world and that this civilization is confronted with the problem of creative and inventive thinking in adjusting itself to the age of science," he explained. This meant that one must not think "wholly in terms of so-called economic soundness of the present" but must engage in "social experimentation." This "experimental approach rather than a dogmatic approach" struck him as "a very important element in New Deal thinking and philosophy."[129]

Thus the planners attempted to educate themselves on the farmer's culture in order not to get too far ahead of him and, at the same time, worked to accelerate the movement of farmers toward acceptance of, participation in, and support for a democratic method of planning and promoting change. "I think that we in Washington are always apt to shoot entirely too high and to assume the mass of farmers are thinking about the same as we are thinking," Wilson observed. "It is for this reason that I think the study of rural attitudes would accurately show us what the attitudes of farmers are on certain questions, how they got those attitudes, and how those people can be reached through the Extension Service and through systems of adult education. . . ."[130] The goal was "economic democracy in action . . . farmers, experts and administrators cooperating in the different phases of policy formation. . . ."[131]

Unfortunately, many of the administrators were reluctant to participate in the program that Wilson and the BAE were promoting. Equally important, after 1939 Wallace stopped providing strong support for the BAE. Early in 1939, Wallace obtained approval of the change in the bureau's role from the President, the Bureau of the Budget, and Congress. The details of the change were discussed with the budget bureau, which gave its approval. Then the President, in his proposed budget for fiscal 1940, informed Congress of the change, and the department supplied a detailed explanation of it. In the hearing on the agricultural appropriations bill before the Agricultural Department Subcommittee of the House Committee on Appropriations, the reorganization of the department was discussed fully, and the committee acted on the budget with full understanding of the situation. The subcommittee's chairman, Clarence Cannon of Missouri, went so far as to compliment Tolley, saying, "I see this is a position requiring much tact and diplomacy; naturally that accounts for your selection as head of the Bureau."[132]

Wallace also informed the department of his strong interest in the bureau's new role and of his determination to support the BAE in its efforts to coordinate the activities of the various action agencies. He knew that the cooperation of the agencies was a great question mark and that backing from the Secretary's office was essential. He had been advised that bureaucratic jealousies would prevent the approach from working, at least after he ceased to be Secretary. He insisted, however, that the concept was "so sound" that it would continue to work, and he warned gently: "As long as I am Secretary of Agriculture and have a certain amount of influence with the chiefs of other bureaus, I shall hope for their continuing, willing cooperation." Throughout the year, he frequently presided over the meetings of the Program Board, participated actively in its deliberations, supported the recommendations that the BAE pushed, and put pressure on the action agencies to follow them. Consequently, Tolley was quite enthusiastic; his new effort seemed to be producing results and influencing programs.[133]

In 1940, however, Wallace's attention turned increasingly to the national political situation and away from the matters that interested the BAE. Tolley now seldom received the kind of support that he needed in order to get cooperation from agencies like AAA. He concluded that he must fight to make the planning effort succeed and that defeat was a strong possibility. Then, he lost completely the assistance of one of the most important supporters of planning. In August, after being nominated for the Vice-Presidency rather than for the Presidency, Wallace resigned from the department to concentrate upon the campaign.[134]

By 1940, hostility among administrators, especially in Triple-A, and the lack of firm support from the Secretary were problems for the social scientists. The attitudes of many college officials and farmers also posed difficulties. Nevertheless, farmer participation was growing, planning committees were taking shape and participating actively in the planning process, and various educational programs were operating and attempting to promote participation in and support for planning. The work of the planning committees, the schools of of philosophy, and the discussion groups might change the ideas of enough farmers, county agents, and administrators and generate enough support for planning to enable it to triumph over hostility and indifference, to play a strategic role in the shaping of farm policy, and to develop an integrated agricultural program. There were bases for optimism. "It may be some time yet before the full significance of this program will be well understood in the majority of counties, but I believe we are making real progress," Tolley wrote to a college official early in 1940.[135] And, he reported later in the year:

Excellent results have been attained in many of the 1,540 counties where the work had been started by July 1, 1940. These results indicate that the method adopted is a sound one, that the program is developing in the right direction, and that farmers are willing to assume the responsibility and local leadership necessary for the work.[136]

Many of his associates shared his optimism.[137]

With some justification, the social scientists could believe that the country was moving forward in the development of a system of planning that they had been promoting for a decade. The pattern of values that had been involved in the Christgau bill was now incorporated into the activities of the BAE, and that agency had apparently been placed near the center of the policy-making process in farm politics.

PART THREE

The Frustration
of the
Planners

CHAPTER 11

Destroying the Planning Committees

The decade of the 1930's, the years of the Great Depression, was a period of progress for Wilson, Tolley, and their close associates. In the half decade that began late in 1940, the years of war, the fortunes of these men experienced a sharp reversal. Years of frustration replaced a decade of accomplishment. A combination of factors produced the change. A powerful supporter of many of the activities of the planners, the American Farm Bureau Federation, had grown opposed to their ideas and now provided leadership in the attack upon the social scientists. When it began, even more important supporters of these men, Roosevelt and Wallace, preoccupied by war and political ambition, were not available to defend the planning program against its enemies. The attempt to make planning democratic in method provided the focal point in the early attack, for the Farm Bureau saw the planning committees as threats that had to be destroyed. In 1942, Congress took the action needed to destroy them.

The Farm Bureau that opposed the social scientists in the 1940's was a larger, more powerful organization than the one that had helped them earlier. Massive membership drives, involving efforts to exploit the Farm Bureau's ties with Triple-A and the Extension Service, had been very successful after 1932, especially in the South. "In all four regions," Christiana Campbell writes, "the increase in membership during the New Deal period was striking, but the percentage increase in the South was by far the greatest." [1] In 1933, the organization had but slightly more than 150,000 members; by 1940, it had nearly 450,000. By then, as Grant McConnell has written, it "had established itself in a position of preeminence among farm organizations." [2] And its growth continued. By 1946, membership exceeded one million, with all but 200,000 members located in the Middle West and South. [3]

As the Farm Bureau grew in size, its leaders grew unhappy with the New Deal. To them, it seemed that the Roosevelt Administration had become dominated by the forces of urban liberalism, especially organized labor, and biased against the farmer. Henry Wallace and his department had drawn away from the Farm Bureau, developed new ties with the Farmers Union, and rejected the idea that their job was to serve the interests of commercial farmers. The officials seemed too interested in the rural poor and the urban consumers. Furthermore, the department's tendency to develop committees of farmers to plan and administer farm programs seemed likely to create groups that would replace the farm organizations in the policy-making process, depriving the Farm Bureau of its status as the leading spokesman for the farmer and providing department officials with the power needed to dominate farm politics and to alter the orientation of farm policy. [4]

For some time, Farm Bureau leaders had been making suggestions for changes in the ways farm programs were planned and administered. [5] Shortly after the Mount Weather Agreement, the farm group announced that planning must be determined by those engaged in the industry and criticized "the present national trend to create agricultural planning agencies composed of other than farmers." The organization regarded such planning as a direct challenge to farm organizations and was determined to recognize only planning that was developed and approved by farmers through their own organizations. [6] One of Tolley's top lieutenants believed it would not be difficult to make "a satisfactory showing that planning as now conceived in the Department is in general consistent with this resolution." This was "certainly . . . true of . . . county planning." [7] In the months that followed, however, Farm Bureau leaders revealed that they were unhappy with the planning as well as with the administrative machinery and that they wanted their own organizations and the extension services to become much more important in planning and carrying out the programs.[8]

In 1940, the farm organization perfected its proposals. Its Washington office supplied President O'Neal with a report charging that the administration of the farm programs was characterized by duplication and overlapping, pointing to the recent tendency of Triple-A to reduce its dependence on the extension services and to develop its own field organization as a major illustration, and denying that land-use planning had removed duplication. The planning project, in fact, according to the report, involved the danger of federal domination of state and county planning and usurped the functions of the farmers' own groups by developing a new organization rather than relying on existing ones to deal with problems normally handled by them. Revealingly, the report charged that the project duplicated objectives for which the Farm Bureau had been created by the department.[9] Finally, in December, the farm group proposed the creation of a five-man nonpartisan board, representative of agriculture, to plan and administer farm programs on the national level and the reliance upon extension services in handling those functions on the state and local levels; and soon, O'Neal carried the proposals to Roosevelt and to Congress.[10]

The farm group was attempting to maintain and expand its power. "The fundamental aim," Mrs. Campbell has demonstrated, "was to take control of agricultural programs away from the Department of Agriculture, which was believed to be no longer the farmers' advocate, and give it to the farmers themselves (i.e. the organized farmers)."[11] As a consequence of the power of the Farm Bureau among farm organizations and its great influence upon the extension services, the recommendations, if put into effect, would inevitably produce an especially large increase in the power of that farm organization.[12]

The Farm Bureau had powerful friends in Congress, eager to promote its interests. Chairing the subcommittee on the USDA of the House Committee on Appropriations was Clarence Cannon, a Democrat from rural northeastern Missouri, a long-time member and, like several of his colleagues, a warm admirer of the Farm Bureau. He believed that every farmer should promptly affiliate himself with the organization because it was "the only hope of uniting the farmers of the country into an effective and aggressive farm organization, the only defense against predatory interests and their attempts to force

down the cost of food and raw materials, and . . . the only hope of
securing a fair price for farm products in the open market." "You
represent and speak for the farmer of the United States," he said
to Farm Bureau leaders, "and for that reason your statements carry
particular weight with this committee." Thus, he gave them an unusually large amount of time to present their proposals and then labeled
their testimony "the most valuable contribution which has been made
by anybody who has appeared before the committee this year." In
line with O'Neal's proposal that "the Extension Service should be
responsible . . . for the State-wide planning program of the Bureau
of Agricultural Economics," the subcommittee cut the budget request
for the BAE by one-half million dollars in order to restrict it "to the
purpose specified at the time of the reorganization of the Bureau, i.e.,
the central program formulating agency of the Department. . . ." [13]

Apparently the Soil Conservation Service assisted the Farm Bureau
at this point. Two Democratic members of the subcommittee who
played important roles in this attack upon land-use planning expressed the SCS point of view. Congressmen David D. Terry of
Arkansas and Ross Collins of Mississippi criticized the planning program for encroaching upon, duplicating, and taking credit for the
work of SCS. [14]

Wilson had been watching these developments carefully. Earlier he
had criticized proposals to rely upon the farm organizations to administer the programs; [15] and when Farm Bureau leaders told him late
in the summer of 1940 that they believed "the various agricultural
programs within a county should be consolidated and should be
administered under the direction of the county agricultural agent," [16]
he suggested to them that they did not understand how the planning
program related to the problem of coordination and "that it would
be unfortunate for them to proceed with their consideration of these
matters until they knew what was taking place in the field of land-use
planning." Thus, they should observe work in one Virginia county. [17]
Then on December 10, speaking before the organization's national
convention, he tried to convince the entire group that the program
had great value. [18]

At the same time that Wilson tried unsuccessfully to restrain the
Farm Bureau, he also tried to prevent college officials from accepting
the proposals. He warned that they contained dangers for the extension services and would interfere with their primary function — education — and he suggested that land-use planning in accord with the

Mount Weather Agreement was the solution to the problem of coordination.[19] O'Neal, however, was also seeking support from these officials; and at an early December meeting of leaders of the Farm Bureau and the Land-Grant College Association, the latter, although rather fearful of the proposals, encouraged the farm group to proceed.[20]

Wilson also alerted Appleby to these developments.[21] A careful student of administration and a critic of both the Farm Bureau and the extension services, Appleby recognized the dangers involved in turning administration over to county agents. "We don't hire these people and can't fire them," the new Under Secretary pointed out to Roosevelt. "To delegate federal responsibility to people who are not responsible to the federal government, I think would be ruinous."[22] Soon he prepared a lengthy critique pointing out that "the outstanding characteristic of the proposal is the thorough manner in which it would split responsibility and authority of Federal administration at the national level, disperse it among Federal and non-Federal organizations at the State level, and remove it from the Federal structure entirely at the county level." The critique suggested that the farm group hoped to "create such confusion in administration by *official* agencies that a *non-official* agency, the Farm Bureau, would become the only possible unifying force" and thus would regain the powerful position it had had before the changes in administration of Triple-A and the development of the land-use planning program.[23]

Top officials were aware of the implications for them of the proposals, and the BAE gained support from the Secretary's office in 1941. Wickard also had a personal reason for battling against the farm group. The return of Midwestern farmers to the Republican party in 1940 after supporting Roosevelt in 1932 and in 1936 had prompted O'Neal to ask the President to substitute Chester Davis for Wickard as Secretary. Convinced of the importance of an alliance between the farmers of the Middle West and South, fearful that the Democratic party would become the party of the South and the great industrial centers, and persuaded that Wallace's behavior had alienated the midwesterners, O'Neal believed that the change from Wickard to Davis was one essential means of restoring the alliance.[24]

Thus, by early 1941 the department and the Farm Bureau were battling vigorously and openly. With encouragement from Congressman Charles H. Leavy of Washington, the third-ranking Democrat on Cannon's subcommittee but a man who did not have the chairman's degree of enthusiasm for the Farm Bureau, Wickard challenged the charge of widespread duplication and conflict among programs and argued that the suggested method of administration would deprive the executive branch of its ability to fulfill the responsibilities placed upon it by Congress and would lead to confusion, duplication, and inefficiency. He suggested that behind the proposal lay the farm organization's dislike of the department's land-use planning procedures. He defended them, suggesting that they should continue so that local people could deal successfully with the problems of soil erosion and surplus production; and he pictured the role that the BAE had been playing since 1938 as the culmination of efforts to eliminate the confusion among agencies in the early years of the New Deal. By means of the land-use planning program, he maintained, the department was moving toward the "goal of adapting national programs to the specific needs of all States, agricultural counties, communities, and individual farms." This, not duplication and conflict among programs, was the really difficult problem in administration at the present time. In its own defense, the BAE challenged the assumption that it duplicated other parts of the department and argued that in its role in program formulation it took "the basic and most constructive step in avoiding overlapping and conflicting functions and duplication of efforts."

In this fashion, the department worked for the restoration of the half million dollars. Tolley explained that the cut would mean that the BAE would be forced to reduce its cooperation with the states and to cease contributing toward the employment of about two hundred cooperative employees. Cooperative planning "would have to be seriously curtailed, especially in the States and counties — where it is most important. . . ."[25]

The BAE gained support at this time from college officials, despite the encouragement they had given the Farm Bureau a few months earlier. There were still disagreements between the BAE and the extension directors, and some of them shared O'Neal's attitude toward the department. Eleven directors, including those from Pennsylvania, Illinois, Washington, California, and Kentucky — states in which the BAE had been encountering especially strenuous opposition — provided no support for it in the battle. Four of them wanted to abolish the program, while the others wanted the funds to be granted directly to the extension services.[26] The farm organization, however, did not get the volume of support that it wanted or expected, perhaps because many of the leaders in the schools now agreed with Wilson about the dangers involved. It appears to one student of the Farm Bureau that

various land-grant college and Extension officials prodded O'Neal and the Farm Bureau into battle with other agencies [in 1936 and 1937], and then when the battle became rough and the Farm Bureau wished to carry it further than the gentlemen of the colleges and the Extension Service wished, the politicians of academe began to run for cover.[27]

The BAE and the schoolmen had just completed a major attempt to clarify and improve their relations. During 1940, a special subcommittee of the Land-Grant College Association, chaired by "an ardent supporter of the work that the Bureau was trying to do," [28] Director John R. Hutcheson of Virginia, had studied the question and had prepared a report that was approved by two major committees of the association.[29] Allin had objected to early drafts, arguing that they defined the program as "almost exclusively an Extension activity" and seemed to reflect the view of those who wanted to prevent "full and effective participation by technicians and administrators. . . ." [30] After revisions were made, Allin became quite satisfied. "I believe that the Committee's understanding of the Bureau's relation to land-use planning is precisely the same as ours," he wrote to Wilson. "If any Directors other than the members of the Committee make any interpretations of the document at variance with ours, I believe we shall have no great difficulty with them in arriving at a common understanding." [31]

A short time later, O'Neal called upon college officials for support. He explained to Director L. R. Simons of New York, the chairman of one of the association's top committees, that many directors had informed him of their opposition to the planning program and that thus he was proposing that the BAE's budget should be cut by one-half million dollars so as to remove the agency from this activity. Simons promised only to seek the views of other directors.

Simons did not produce the response O'Neal was seeking. Although the New Yorker had some disagreements with BAE leaders, he also had reservations about the Farm Bureau proposals. Furthermore, he believed that his state favored continuation of the planning program, and he regarded the Farm Bureau's fears of the planning committees as foolish. In addition, he resented the tendency in Congress to identify the extension services with the Farm Bureau. When he could find no evidence to support the view that extension officials had helped to produce the House's cut in the BAE's budget, he called upon the directors, not to support the Farm Bureau, but to urge their senators to reject the House's recommendation.[32]

The extension directors quickly demonstrated overwhelmingly that they were not mere puppets of the American Farm Bureau Federation. Simons wired his senators that the House action would "seriously curtail cooperative extension work" and that "all farm organizations in New York favor and are helping sponsor this work and are strengthened by the better relationships developed through the contacts their representatives have with each other on the State and County land-use committees."[33] Other representatives of the extension services followed Simons' lead. Then C. W. Creel, the assistant secretary of the association, appeared before the Senate subcommittee to urge the senators to provide the BAE with the funds it needed for "financial cooperation with the land-grant colleges, in land-use planning work." In support of Creel's proposal, Simons supplied the senators with a good deal of material, including the Mount Weather Agreement, the statement by Hutcheson's subcommittee, and evidence that the farm organizations in New York endorsed the project and that thirty-seven directors had wired him of their approval of the work and their opposition to the cut in the BAE's budget. Senator Richard Russell of Georgia, the chairman of the subcommittee, also accepted for the record telegrams submitted by Senator Gerald P. Nye which indicated that the governor of North Dakota, the president of the North Dakota Farmers Union, and the director of the extension service there liked the program and opposed the cut. Nye expressed his own enthusiasm, as did Senator James E. Murray of Wilson's Montana, another state in which the extension director advocated continuation of the program. Obviously, there was much support for it.[34]

As department and college leaders rallied to the defense of the BAE, Tolley and his associates attempted to strengthen it and its planning program, chiefly by demonstrating their usefulness in the new situation created by the outbreak of war in Europe.[35] Wilson advised the extension directors early in 1941 that the planning organization provided the means to bring the thinking of farm people and their representatives in government to bear upon the problems created by the war, and he suggested that the state land-use planning committees were "in a strategic position to take the lead in developing comprehensive and well-considered State programs for agriculture." "The Bureau has an unusual opportunity to assist State Land-Use Planning Committees in facing these problems," Tolley advised, "and it is my belief that we should give this activity a high priority." An inter-bureau coordinating committee headed by Elliott drafted "Suggestions for a Unified State Agricultural Program to Meet the Impacts of War" that were approved by the Program Board and the Secretary. By summer, the state planning committees had prepared programs, and Elliott's committee had prepared a national summary of them which was entitled "Agriculture's Plans to Aid in Defense and Meet the Impacts of War" and was accepted by the Program Board.[36]

Indicative of his hopes of building support was the fact that Tolley sent a copy of this document to the chairman of the Senate Agriculture Committee. Tolley referred to the document as "a national summary of the most recent efforts of State and county agricultural planning committees" and "the outcome of very careful work on the part of thousands of farm people throughout the country, aided by personnel of the Department, the Land-Grant Colleges and other State and Federal agencies." He suggested that the Senator might find it "useful as a reflection of the kind of thinking that is going on in the country" and assured him that it was "proving most helpful to the Department." [37]

With this work moving forward, Tolley made a major effort to improve the planning machinery. He was unhappy with the degree of cooperation being provided by department agencies, the amount of use the department was making of the machinery, and the rate at which matters pertaining to planning were being handled and plans were being translated into action. Thus, he proposed various steps to strengthen the machinery, to extend it into every agricultural county, and to guarantee that the agencies would contribute as much as they could to the undertaking. Without these changes, he feared, planning would "progressively decline and become more or less futile and ineffective." Obviously eager for more support from Wickard, Tolley hoped that if his suggestions were accepted the changes in procedure would be announced by the Office of the Secretary. For that purpose, a memorandum to the bureau chiefs was drafted for Wickard's signature. It expressed satisfaction with the work that the state planning committees were doing in the defense crisis and proposed the changes that Tolley desired.[38]

Late in May, Tolley outlined his suggestions in a memorandum to Appleby, and early in June, they discussed them in the Under Secretary's office with other officials. Everyone present approved "the general idea of improving the effectiveness of, and relying more heavily upon, the cooperative planning process. . . ." A number of questions were raised, however, and each agency agreed to give further consideration to the matter and to submit its views to Appleby.[39]

Leaders in Triple-A were in no mood to accept suggestions from the BAE. They seldom neglected a challenge to their power nor an opportunity to expand it, and they resented Tolley's criticism of their operations in his report for 1940. ("The analysis of this program has shown that a disproportionate share of the funds has been expended for maintenance of established practices," he had reported. At another point: "A study in Arkansas indicated that shifts from tenant to laborer status were due to the A.A.A. program in some instances.") [40]

Within a few days of the meeting in Appleby's office, Triple-A filed a protest. The agency argued that the planning committees had not gotten down to definite practical objectives and were not dealing with practical problems of interest to AAA. The protest suggested also that the planning machinery was being used to implement prejudices and biases of individuals who were opposed to the objectives of the AAA program. Therefore, Evans and his men feared any increase in the power of the planning committees and suggested that Triple-A committeemen should be relied upon for any special service to further the defense program.[41]

Tolley received a more encouraging response from Director Hutcheson's subcommittee when it met with the BAE in mid-June. Wilson and Tolley explained to the directors that the proposals in the memorandum were "purely tentative and . . . made for the purpose of obtaining the careful consideration by all cooperating parties of ways and means of making land-use planning still more effective." [42] Hutcheson believed that if the department would "reorganize things somewhat above the state level, create a little more enthusiasm for the planning process among the leaders of the action agencies, forget the regional office set-up, and give us more money to be spent in the counties and states for promotion of cooperative agricultural planning . . . , we will be in a position to do a very effective job." He also believed it would be fatal to cooperative planning to attempt any radical change in the procedure within the states at this time, for real progress under procedures already developed was just beginning.

Agreeing that if farm people were to make their maximum contribution to the defense effort they had to be fully informed and that the planning committees were the best agency for carrying information to farmers and bringing back suggestions from them, Hutcheson's group recommended to other college officials that steps be taken immediately to organize committees in all counties. The group cautiously advised that the committees "should stick closely to the field of planning and carefully avoid undertaking things which can be more effectively done by action agencies and farm organizations." (Later, the Executive Committee of the Land-Grant College Association, concerned that the committees might take over functions of the extension services, qualified the subcommittee's statement to refer to the planning groups as simply "the best agencies for conducting agricultural planning.")[43] Nevertheless, although fears in the colleges persisted, Tolley believed that the way had been paved for greater cooperation with the directors.[44]

Congress, however, intervened to check this development. Despite the support that the BAE had received, the lawmakers approved the cut of one-half million dollars. This meant that the bureau had to reduce substantially the amount of financial assistance to the colleges for their work on land-use planning. The state BAE representatives could continue to serve, but only by making cuts in other areas could Tolley provide a small sum for the "cooperative employees" who were hired by the extension directors and partly financed by the BAE. Tolley hoped that the colleges would not be forced to stop their efforts, and he received word from a lieutenant attending a regional planning conference that, while the cut was discouraging, it had not destroyed the determination of the cooperative states to go ahead. Director Simons, however, pointed out that now there could be no increase in the number of committees.[45]

After Congress acted, Wickard added to Tolley's disappointments. Although the BAE and its committees had been moving more rapidly than the Secretary in preparing plans for the defense crisis and Tolley had been urging that the planning committees be used to coordinate agricultural programs in the field during the emergency, Wickard, early in July, stepped into the controversy between BAE and AAA, created new state and county defense boards to coordinate the defense activities of the department, and relied heavily upon Triple-A in the new arrangements. He made AAA officials chairmen of the boards and directed the chairmen of the state boards to report directly to him.[46]

In part, Congress had forced Wickard to move in this direction by blocking plans to expand the planning committee system, but the development also reflected the Secretary's ties with AAA. An Indiana farmer, Wickard had served in this agency throughout the 1930's, beginning in the Corn-Hog Section in 1933 and rising to the top of the North Central Division. He had replaced Wilson as Under Secretary and then Wallace as Secretary in 1940. From the BAE's point of view, Wallace's first choice of a successor would have been more satisfactory, but an attack of arthritis prevented Wilson from accepting such a large responsibility.[47] As Secretary, Wickard remained rather close to his old friends in Triple-A; like them, he had a dim view of the planning program. After becoming Secretary, he had shown little inclination to provide the firm pressure needed for the BAE to succeed in its efforts to coordinate the activities of the action agencies.[48]

The new development also reflected Wickard's attitudes toward Tolley and men of his type. The Secretary disliked intellectuals and shared the belief of many that Tolley was not a practical man. Furthermore, for a brief period as a high school senior, Wickard had been a student in Tolley's classes. Lacking confidence in himself as Secretary, he felt especially uncomfortable when his former teacher entered the room.[49]

Although the BAE had failed to establish itself and the planning committees as the key agencies in agriculture's defense efforts, Wickard did place an important responsibility upon the bureau at the same time that he established the new defense boards. Pressed by the President and others to get the farmer to contribute all that was needed in the emergency, the Secretary was forced to turn to the one agency that had been thinking about the expansion of production — the BAE; thus Wickard called upon Tolley in July to establish an Interbureau Production Goals Committee to develop figures on requirements for all major commodities. With O. V. Wells taking the lead, the BAE quickly developed a set of production goals that emphasized expanding the production of certain essential commodities. The committee reported to the Program Board before the end of August, and early the following month Wickard announced his production goals for 1942. Four sectional conferences were then held to consider the report on production goals and the plans to aid defense and to meet the impact of war. The conferees reached conclusions about goals, and then the planning committees translated the conclusions into action programs for the states and counties. Departmental agencies, however, did not readily accept the suggested programs. Officials in Triple-A, still fearful of surpluses and wedded to a program of restricting production, found adjustment to the new situation difficult, lashed out at Tolley for suggesting unreasonable goals, and insisted that they should shape decisions about production. Nevertheless, the production goals program continued to function under the direction of the BAE, to call for increases and shifts in production, and to reflect the influence of the diet studies.[50]

In December, however, Wickard took another slap at Tolley. The Secretary announced the first large-scale reorganization of the department since 1938; included in the changes was a provision that Tolley should no longer report directly to the Secretary. Instead, one of Tolley's lieutenants, Wells, became liaison between Tolley and the front office. For some time, Wickard had been replacing top-level Wallace appointees with men of his own choice. Now it was Tolley's turn. Although not formally replaced nor demoted, he and the BAE had been pushed aside, and he found the change very discouraging. He seldom came to the Secretary's office or talked with Wickard after December. In fact, from March to June, 1942, Tolley worked part time for the Office of Price Administration, believing that it provided more opportunities for accomplishment than he was finding in the Department of Agriculture. The move prompted rumors that he was about to resign from the BAE.[51]

Although the bureau's influence was declining rapidly, the BAE remained in theory the department's planner but in fact was in a state of great confusion about what it was to do. In January, 1942, Tolley tried to get Wickard to clarify matters and proposed the transfer of certain agencies to the BAE so that it would contain "those functions and agencies which ought to be in a staff-agency Bureau charged with the over-all responsibility of economic research and planning."[52] For several months, as Triple-A had struggled to dominate the new boards, he and others had attempted to obtain large roles in them for the planning committees and the BAE representatives.[53] Now Tolley suggested to Wickard that he should "settle the question as to whether the existing field planning structure of the Department should be retained and strengthened so that it can be of maximum service to the War Boards, or liquidated to make way for new planning machinery to be set up by the War Boards."[54]

One matter soon became clear: The Secretary would not back BAE's efforts to expand the planning program. Men in the Secretary's office even suggested that the agency should divert some of its funds from planning to other purposes. Tolley pointed out that this would

force him to abrogate agreements with the colleges, and Allin hoped
that if the Secretary wished to do this he would inform BAE's leaders
so that they could "begin to figure out which ones to break first." [55]
The bureau had hoped for an increase of $400,000 in its appropri-
ation for fiscal 1943, including $44,780 for regional and national
program development, the "apex of the Bureau's work," and $350,000
for cooperative agricultural program planning; [56] but the Bureau of
the Budget slashed this request and submitted to Congress a budget
that forced Tolley and Allin to decide that they could not negotiate
project agreements with the colleges for the coming year. [57] Allin's
Division of State and Local Planning was now replaced by a staff
organization in the Chief's office, the Agricultural Planning Field
Service, [58] and Allin advised the BAE representatives that their function was "likely to be relatively more that of *developing plans and
programs* and relatively less that of *selling a planning procedure* to
others." [59]

The Farm Bureau now made a major effort to redefine the role of
the BAE. On February 6, O'Neal returned to the House Subcommittee on Agricultural Appropriations, praised Congress for its action in
1941 "effecting a substantial saving in the administration of the land-
use planning program," informed the congressmen that no farmer had
complained about the curtailment, and suggested "that this entire appropriation for program-building can be eliminated completely. . . .
We believe that the functions of the Bureau of Agricultural Economics
should be restricted to research and fact-finding," the farm leader
reported. "It is unwise and unnecessary for the Bureau . . . to build
up a large staff reaching out into the States for agricultural planning
purposes." [60]

The subcommittee, however, was not as friendly as it had been
earlier. Clarence Cannon had moved up to the chairmanship of the
Appropriations Committee and had thus been forced to move down
to the second spot on the subcommittee. Congressman Malcolm C.
Tarver of Georgia had taken over the chairmanship, and he had a
somewhat more critical attitude toward Farm Bureau's proposals and
a somewhat higher regard for the BAE than Cannon had. Under Tarver's leadership, the subcommittee recommended only a small cut in
the budget that had been proposed for the BAE. [61]

The congressional friends of the Farm Bureau were forced to carry
their case to the floor of the House. Here leadership was provided by
Everett McKinley Dirksen, the second-ranking Republican on the

subcommittee and a representative of rural Illinois, the state with the largest Farm Bureau organization. The group's leader there, Earl Smith, had deserted Roosevelt in 1940 and was a vigorous advocate of the proposals on reorganization.[62] Dirksen praised Tolley as "one of the headiest, one of the finest, one of the most able men in the United States" who "could make far more money in private business than he does working for the Government," but, he suggested, "we are almost planning some of our farmers out of existence" and should "cut out functions which are only remote to the farmers' interest and which could and should be curtailed." The Illinois Congressman indicated that he was following the suggestions of the Farm Bureau — "one of the largest, oldest and most stable farm organizations" — in proposing that the BAE's budget be reduced by an additional $100,000. "This Bureau was originally established as a fact-finding agency and it should return to those functions," he insisted; thus his proposal plus the subcommittee's would reduce the budget for economic research and program service by $466,000 and wipe out completely the $584,-000 that had been proposed by the Bureau of the Budget for cooperative agricultural program formulation.[63]

Tarver fought Dirksen's proposal, arguing that it would substantially destroy the BAE and prevent it from functioning with any considerable degree of efficiency. Attempting to use Dirksen's praise of Tolley, Tarver suggested that "we ought not to assume that a man of the public spirit manifested by Dr. Tolley . . . would undertake to deceive the Congress as to the necessities for the efficient carrying on of the work under his jurisdiction." When Dirksen replied that he also regarded Tugwell as an able man (the Congressman often heaped scorn upon this economist), Tarver replied that he "would not want to mention Dr. Tolley in the same breath with Dr. Tugwell."[64]

The battling congressmen had quite different relations with the Farm Bureau. Dirksen reminded one supporter of the BAE that his proposal was endorsed by that organization and it spoke "for the dirt farmers of America" — "for the farmers that plow the soil and not the paved streets in Washington. . . ." Tarver replied that the subcommittee had adopted only part of the farm group's suggestions and Congress would not be "justified in writing an appropriation bill based solely on the opinions of representatives of the Farm Bureau Federation."[65]

Clarence Cannon now provided strong support for his Republican neighbor from Illinois rather than for his fellow Democrat from

Georgia. Regarding Cannon as the leader of the House farm bloc, Farm Bureau leaders had been pleased with his decision to remain on the vital subcommittee on Agricultural Appropriations. They had given him a medal for distinguished service to American agriculture at their annual meeting in December, 1941, praising him as "a crusader for farm parity" and "one of the House's outstanding authorities on agricultural matters." They were pleased that he was "a life-long and successful farmer, a member of his local Farm Bureau, and an outspoken advocate of farm organization as an essential to the attainment of economic justice for agriculture and a sound national economy." [66]

At first, Cannon had opposed Dirksen's proposal, but on March 6 the Missourian announced to the House that he had changed his mind. Rumors quickly circulated that O'Neal had put pressure on his friend, and Cannon's subsequent behavior seemed to confirm them, for he made a large effort to demonstrate his loyalty to the farm leader and his organization. Challenging the charge that they represented only large landowners, he insisted that the group was composed "exclusively of average farmers" and not only represented the small farmer but represented him effectively; and he praised O'Neal for rendering greater service to agriculture and to the country as a whole than many Senators, Governors, Cabinet officers, and Congressmen by the score who object to the Farm Bureau because it has secured legislation under which the farmer cannot be exploited by those who want to take his products away from him at less than the cost of production.

"God bless him," Cannon exclaimed, referring to the farm leader.[67]

Picking up support from the "economy bloc," the friends of the Farm Bureau defeated Tarver.[68] The farm organization then publicized and praised their work and pressed for acceptance of it by the Senate. Arguing that it was supporting adequate appropriations for the BAE's research and fact-finding program but insisting that the agency stay in its proper field, the organization charged that the BAE had been building up a nationwide field organization with the apparent objective of developing a super-planning agency and maintained that necessary planning in agriculture could be carried out best by the Extension Service and other established agencies, along with the farmers' own organizations.[69] In recommending to the senators that the BAE should be restored to its original purpose, O'Neal explained that the proposed reduction in its budget was "intended to eliminate the so-called regional and local planning activities of the Bureau . . .

and the regional and State offices which are maintained by the Bureau for this purpose." [70]

Tolley and his lieutenants battled to preserve their planning program. They supplied the Secretary with a statement criticizing the Farm Bureau's demands and the House action, arguing that the cuts would "not only eliminate the little that remains of the planning work, but would very seriously hamper that very activity for which Mr. O'Neal urges adequate appropriations, namely, the function of research, fact-finding, study of agricultural problems." They tried to persuade both Wickard and the senators that the BAE could not "do its work efficiently without a field force." [71]

Wickard, however, refused to provide the BAE with the support it needed.[72] He and his budget officer had supplied a small amount of support in their appearances before the House subcommittee; Wickard, in his prepared statement for the Senate, did defend the bureau's role in the formulation of programs as well as in economic research. His oral remarks, however, dealt only with the BAE as a fact-finding agency. "That is what I regard as the primary work of the Bureau of Agricultural Economics," he told the senators, "and I am sure this million-dollar cut . . . would seriously impair the usefulness of the Bureau in this work of fact-finding." [73]

The Secretary was not bowing before the Farm Bureau. He was battling it on other issues, including the appropriations for the Farm Security Administration. He simply did not regard the BAE's planning program as worth another fight. A year earlier, the battle for it had helped him withstand the Farm Bureau's challenge to his position and authority. Since then, he had turned away from the BAE and had found other ways of defending his department against the Farm Bureau's charges. Large appropriations for FSA, on the other hand, now seemed essential, for its loans and guidance to small farmers could help him achieve his major goal: a substantial increase in agricultural production. Roosevelt also stayed out of the fight over the BAE while he battled the Farm Bureau on other issues.[74]

College officials also disappointed the BAE. Late in 1941, Milton Eisenhower had advised the Secretary that efforts should be made to improve relations between the colleges and the department, for, if they "sincerely came to an agreement, the criticism of a farm organization would be pretty ineffective." [75] But now only one extension director — E. J. Haselrud of North Dakota — provided support for the BAE in Congress.[76]

The bureau's support had declined drastically since 1941. The change in the behavior of the college officials is not easy to explain, especially as most directors disliked the war boards because of Triple-A's power in them and the planning committees provided an alternative way of coordinating war-time programs. Yet the directors did not battle for the alternative. Perhaps, as Charles Hardin suggested, the action of the directors was controlled by fears stimulated by a rumor that AAA circulated, a rumor that Tolley was trying to build a farm organization to replace the Farm Bureau.[77] Perhaps that group itself had brought pressure to bear upon officials who had supported the BAE.[78] Certainly their interest in planning had not evaporated. At their association's annual meeting in November, 1941, Hutcheson's subcommittee had recommended that "planning committees . . . should be maintained in every agricultural county," for "land-use planning committees are the best agencies for the development of sound agricultural programs on State and county levels." [79] After Congress had cut off all funds for state and local planning, many — perhaps most — extension directors regretted the development, and many of them informed the BAE that they regarded the work as very useful, they were unhappy that the bureau could no longer cooperate with them in land-use planning, and they hoped to maintain the committees. Six months later, planning committees were still at work in about half of the states.[80] Perhaps extension leaders had merely concluded that they would be foolish to fight for an agency that did not have strong support from its superior officer, especially after the fight of 1941 had accomplished nothing.

Of the farm organizations, only the Farmers Union provided support for the planning program. "It has seemed to us," Glenn J. Talbott, the president of the North Dakota Farmers Union told the senators, "that the participation of these farmers, as an example of democratic duties and responsibilities, as well as rights and privileges, is extremely important." Talbott also defended the discussion group program as "tremendously important for revitalizing democratic processes right down among the citizens of our country." "How would that improve agriculture?" one skeptical senator inquired.[81]

Talbott's testimony suggested that Tolley's defense of the Farm Security Administration had helped to draw the Farmers Union to the defense of the BAE. This farm group was battling vigorously against the Farm Bureau in defense of FSA and cooperating in this battle with other liberal groups, including the CIO;[82] Talbott indicated that he liked the work the BAE had been doing on the contribution that low-income groups could make to agricultural production in the war period.[83] In February, Tolley had defended FSA before Senator Byrd's Joint Committee on Reduction of Non-Essential Federal Expenditures, arguing that abolition of the agency would lead to an increase in poverty on the farms and in problems for the "Food for Victory" program, which could not succeed "unless the low-income groups have credit, guidance, skills and more security of tenure." FSA and its friends were using this argument to defend the agency against its enemies.[84]

Another important critic of the Farm Bureau spoke out in defense of the BAE. Soon after the House action, Donald Murphy wrote an editorial in *Wallaces' Farmer* that indicated that this farm journal had remained loyal to an agency that the first Secretary Wallace had established and the second had placed in a key position. Murphy called attention to the importance of the fact-gathering activities of the BAE and the action of the House in "knocking out four-fifths of the work" and urged farmers to demand that their farm organizations and congressmen "keep this powerhouse of farm progress in operation." In response to a request from Tolley, Senator Russell entered this in the record of his subcommittee.[85]

This was the sum of support for the BAE: weak efforts by the Secretary and somewhat more vigorous efforts by one extension director and two agrarian liberals. Together, they accomplished very little. The only senator to defend the planning activities of the BAE and its committees was Nye of North Dakota, a prominent agrarian liberal but also a leading isolationist whose influence had been shattered by the attack upon Pearl Harbor.[86] Other senators were worried that the economic and statistical work would be harmed by the House action. Thus the Senate subcommittee recommended that Congress should give the BAE $500,000 more than the House had proposed but that a proviso should be added that no part of the funds should "be used for cooperative agricultural program formulation."[87] Not fully satisfied, O'Neal advised members of the House once again that the BAE should be returned to its status as a research, fact-finding agency.[88] In conference, representatives of the two committees compromised on the size of the appropriation and changed the proviso to read "that no part of the funds . . . shall be used for State and county land-use planning," a change designed to indicate that the prohibition was limited "to work at the State and county levels." In this form the bill was accepted by both houses of Congress.[89] Congressman Tarver, who had been defeated by zealous friends of the Farm Bureau, felt that the legislation would be "satisfactory to the most ardent advocates of economy" but feared that the amount would be "insufficient to provide for the adequate carrying on of the work of this very important Bureau. . . . "[90]

Although the Farm Bureau feared the planning committees, in the crisis of 1942 they had not demonstrated an ability to behave as a farm organization. Farmer members of the committees had not risen to the defense of land-use planning. Obviously, the social scientists had failed to develop the power and interest needed to protect planning from its enemies. This did not demonstrate, however, that, as some have suggested, the attempt to establish "grass roots democracy" was foolish[91] and that the planning experiment failed because it lacked vitality.[92] As Grant McConnell has suggested, "the fact that the entire structure of the committees came under attack is important evidence that the committees had become potential centers of power" and "the failure of the committees lay in the fact that their power could not be developed quickly enough for their own preservation."[93] The entire episode indicates that the planning needed some means of defending itself. The planners had not had enough time to develop committees that represented rural America more adequately than the Farm Bureau did and that were willing and able to battle against that representative of the commercial farmers of the corn-hog and cotton sections. The Farm Bureau, scenting danger in the air at an early stage in the development of the committees, had begun an attack upon them when the social scientists were just beginning to grapple with the problem of the representative character of the committees, and the farm organization possessed enough power to destroy them or at least to sever their ties with the BAE. The social scientists had attempted to work with the Farm Bureau in the shaping of farm policy and, at the same time, to develop a more democratic method; but the Farm Bureau was unwilling to tolerate the growth of a farmers' movement with a democratic base that might change the nature of farm politics.

One observer of the experiment, John D. Black, believed that the first reason for the failure of the program was that

it was too audacious, and undertook to do too much all at once. The proposal for a two-way planning process all the way from Washington to the county and community and back to Washington, however noble in conception, was too revolutionary to succeed all at once. It needed years to work itself out.[94]

Black believed, nevertheless, that, had the program been allowed to continue, "our agricultural people and institutions would be doing a much better job than they are doing now. . . ."[95] Another observer, however, has suggested that "if the Land-Use Planning Program . . . had not been destroyed by unfriendly interests it would surely have exploded from the fatal flaw of its own pretensions." One of the false propositions upon which it rested, according to Professor Hardin, was "that local citizens will clearly recognize local political issues and readily accept the burden of deciding them."[96] Perhaps internal weaknesses would eventually have destroyed the program, but the historian must note that external forces did in fact destroy it.

Allin denied that planning had failed as a consequence of internal weaknesses in the experiment. "County planning did not die because there was too little emphasis upon inspiring local people toward self-help," he insisted. "It was killed by Claude Wickard and the Farm Bureau. . . . It had no chance from the start, except as it received the unqualified support of the Secretary of Agriculture."[97] Certainly Wickard's role was crucial. "It was this lack of solid secretarial support after 1940 which contributed significantly to the failure of the Land-Use Planning Program," one well-informed student of farm politics has remarked.[98] And John D. Black suggested, "it is possible that if Wallace had remained Secretary of Agriculture and had continued such support as he gave in 1939 and 1940, and the war had not intervened, the role assigned to the Bureau would have been increasingly realized over the next ten years."[99] In other words, changes in the Department of Agriculture had contributed to the success of the Farm Bureau's attack upon the planning committees, and Wallace's presidential ambitions had contributed to the destruction of one part of the BAE's program just as in 1938 they had played a part in the elevation of the BAE.

As dreams were shattered, a wave of bitterness and anger swept over the BAE, and Wickard was the object of much of the strong feeling. Allin believed that the least the Secretary could do was send the extension directors an expression of sympathy over what had happened in order to "avoid encouraging them to consider with strong reservations any future proposals that might be made to them by the Department." [100] So the economist drafted a letter for Wickard's signature:

I want you to know that the Department still believes firmly in the basic objectives of this work which was started in 1938, appreciates the fine contribution it has made, and hopes that the States somehow will be able to carry on even in the absence of financial support from the Department. It may be that after the war, when conditions are somewhat different from the present, the Department will be able again to give direct help.[101]

Another economist suggested that the Secretary should sign the letter "since the Department, rather than the Bureau, encouraged the States to undertake land-use planning work." [102] But Wickard did not sign.

BAE men were also bitterly critical of the Farm Bureau.[103] They did not believe that O'Neal's great interest in their activities reflected any opposition to cooperative planning as such. They were convinced that "if he could control the various State Extension Services and if they, in turn, could control the land-use planning work, Mr. O'Neal would be positively in favor of it." The social scientists believed that the farm leader's aim was to require "that farmer participation in cooperative planning with public agencies should be dominated by Farm Bureau members" even though "millions of farmers" were not members of the organization. "The surest way to kill democracy," the agency suggested, "is to have the privileges of pressure groups monopolized by one such group. . . . Nothing could lead us more certainly to Fascism." The action of the House subcommittee suggested to the BAE that its mistake lay in "insisting that cooperative land-use planning should not be dominated by either the American Farm Bureau Federation or those few State Extension Directors who blindly do its bidding." [104]

Although bitter and angry, BAE men were not without hope. Clinging to their belief in the great value of the work, they hoped that the department would return to it in the future and that, in the meantime, the extension services would continue to operate the planning committees.[105] Democratic planning had to be kept alive "in spite of all subversive efforts to the contrary," one BAE representative wrote.[106] "We know," Allin wrote to his men, "that we have already given vital stimulus to cooperative planning in many States and that agencies outside the Department of Agriculture are increasingly interested in the planning procedure we have fostered." He expressed confidence "that the democratic process will continue in many States and eventually rise again to a new high." [107]

Although Tolley hoped that some remnants of the planning machinery would continue to function, his mood was not optimistic. He believed that land-use planning had been killed because it had been making progress. That progress had alarmed two powerful groups — the Farm Bureau and Triple-A — and then Wickard had refused to provide support. Now Tolley undertook the unhappy task of dismantling the Agricultural Planning Field Service with its system of state offices throughout the nation. He had tried to obtain the funds needed to maintain those offices but had failed. He was able to find places for Allin and a few others, but most of the hundred or so who had been selected to provide leadership in the development of state and local planning had to find jobs outside the bureau. There was uncertainty in his agency about its place in the department's wartime program and confusion about the amount of attention it should continue to give to planning. To him, it seemed that his program "was pretty well down the drain" and that the BAE had become once again "a fact-finding and semi-ivory tower research organization." He felt "pretty much frustrated." [108]

CHAPTER 12

Demoting
the Bureau of
Agricultural Economics

Although Tolley believed that the events of the early 1940's had in effect restored the old BAE, in theory the agency remained the department's central planner. Consequently, the bureau continued to devote some of its energies to planning. In this work, as in other activities, the BAE became identified with the liberalism of the period, both agrarian liberalism with its emphasis upon government action on behalf of the small family farmer and also the urban variety that stressed the welfare of the city working classes and civil rights. As a consequence, the bureau strengthened itself with the leading liberal in farm politics, James Patton of the Farmers Union, but created new troubles for itself with the Farm Bureau and its allies. The appointment of a new Secretary eager to change the department added to the BAE's difficulties. Thus it found itself first in new battles and then stripped of even its theoretical claim to the role of central planner for the USDA.

The pattern of identification with liberalism had begun to emerge in 1942. In the appropriations battle, most of the bureau's support had come from agrarian liberals. After the battle, an urban journal that was fighting against the "powerful groups within America" who were "attempting to use the war in order to destroy the New Deal"[1] rose to the defense of the BAE. In August, the *New Republic*, which had published an enthusiastic article on the planning program a year earlier,[2] criticized the Farm Bureau for crippling one of the BAE's most useful enterprises and offered two explanations for this action: resentment of BAE's refusal to support the farm organization's position on high price supports and fears about the planning committees.[3] Although little else was said at this time about conflict between the economists and the farm organization on price policy, that conflict would grow larger in the years ahead.

Late in 1942 and in 1943, the BAE participated again in another controversy involving the Farm Bureau on one side and various liberal groups on the other. Here the focal point was the Farm Security Administration. C. B. ("Beanie") Baldwin, Will Alexander's successor, was very pleased with the support that his agency was receiving from the BAE. "We are now at a point where BAE material is becoming increasingly useful to us," he had informed Tolley during the fight over FSA early in 1942. "Our present war efforts accentuate the importance of your research on low-income farmers. I hope that we can continue to receive the valuable contributions of your staff."[4] As the controversy grew hot again at the end of the year, Tolley drew upon BAE statistics to show that while medium- and large-sized farms were producing close to their capacity, production could be increased nearly 10 per cent if small farmers were granted FSA loans. FSA now drew heavily upon this evidence, for it provided a defense against the Farm Bureau's attacks and a challenge to O'Neal's arguments that FSA clients could not produce large quantities of food and that price policy was the key to greater production.[5] Here the BAE was associated with the Farmers Union, Roosevelt, and a number of important senators in a losing battle against the Farm Bureau and its allies, including an anti-New Deal, bipartisan coalition in Congress that subjected FSA to vigorous criticism, slashed its appropriation, added to the list of restrictions on its activities that Congress had been building for several years, and, in September, 1943, caused Baldwin's resignation.[6] To a man who had been involved in the attacks upon rural poverty since the days of Rex Tugwell, "Baldwin's resignation marked the end of the big Resettlement-Farm Security adventure." The dominant groups in farm politics "wanted to be rid of people who had come into the Department under Tugwell."[7] Roosevelt, following advice from Patton of the Farmers Union and Jonathan Daniels, a White House adviser, sent a letter to Baldwin designed to assure FSA's friends that the President still believed in the programs of assistance to the small farmer and hoped to maintain and expand them.[8] Clearly the BAE had become associated with those who hoped to maintain and enlarge the reform features of the New Deal but not with the dominant groups in farm politics.

Also in 1943, Tolley publicly criticized one of the most important alliances in farm politics: the ties that existed in many states between the Farm Bureau and the Extension Service. Here again, the BAE cooperated with the Farmers Union and its allies.[9] Tolley's criticism appeared in *The Farmer Citizen at War*, a book that he and others in the bureau had written on their philosophy, their attitudes toward agriculture and farm people, and their proposals for improvement in rural life. The book expressed the BAE's enthusiasm for the program killed by the Farm Bureau and Congress and suggested, on the ties between the farm organization and the extension services:

it is a very real danger to democracy and good government if any private organization actually does assume a possessive attitude to a public agency, if it does seek to influence unduly the actions of a public agency. Never has this danger taken more ominous shapes than now. This country has plain before it the terrible experience of other countries. It is just such a confusion of relationships that creates "corporate states"; in just such crossing of private and public lines is the breeding-ground of totalitarianism. America cannot be too careful in seeing to it that it does not "happen here."[10]

The BAE's role in these battles of 1943 produced no immediate difficulties for it; the agency's sociological work, however, led to a major attack upon it the following year. That work was directed by Carl C. Taylor, another product of the rural Middle West. Born in Iowa, he had been educated at Drake University, the University of Texas, and the University of Missouri, receiving a Ph.D. from Missouri in 1918. There Thorstein Veblen had contributed to his development. After a career of teaching, research, and administration, chiefly at North Carolina State College, he had entered government service in 1933 and worked in the Subsistence Homesteads Division, the Land Policy Section, and the Resettlement Administration. Late in 1935, he had been placed in charge of the BAE's Division of Farm Population and Rural Welfare.[11]

Taylor's government service reflected the pragmatic orientation of rural sociology and his own strong conviction that the sociologist must play a large role in any attempts to plan.[12] He insisted that sociological knowledge was needed in the farm programs and that the need would not be met "if the sociologists are not in the council of planners or if sociologists refuse to place themselves on the hot spots which planning and action agencies necessarily occupy."[13] He and his men criticized the assumptions of economists, arguing, for example, that raising farm income was not enough, that more attention must be paid to such matters as health, education, recreation, and morale in rural life, and that the economists too often looked upon man as merely economic in nature, moved along by economic considerations, and did not pay enough attention to noneconomic factors like the impact of customs upon agricultural production.[14] "The outstanding aspect of the immediate situation," Taylor argued, "is that the attempts of the various action agencies to 'do something' for or with farm people have made us realize as never before that the success of such attempts depends upon the farm people themselves — what they are, their conditions and social status, and patterns of behavior and thinking."[15] When economists attempted to pay attention to such factors, they handled them badly.[16]

Convinced of the great importance of the role of the sociologist, Taylor and his lieutenants worked hard trying to "sell sociology" to others involved in the farm programs.[17] "We have an opportunity to demonstrate the value of Rural Sociology and we must find the way of doing that," the Taylor group believed.[18] The task was not easy, however, for they had to combat, as Taylor put it, "the widely prevalent belief that sociologists know theory but not phenomena and processes and that the theory they do know is seldom applicable or is difficult of application in the field of concrete programs."[19] He tried to persuade Alexander that social research was "just as fundamental for the guidance and projection of the Resettlement or Tenancy program as is Land Planning Research" and criticized Gray for failing to use sociologists in land-use planning.[20] ". . . the practical sociologist's greatest contribution to the problem of readjusting people to the land," Taylor argued, "is on the one hand to assist the land economist in arriving at judgements on areas for evacuation, and on the other hand, to keep the engineers, architects and other 'paper planners' from assuming that cultural processes and human habits can be disregarded in making economic and social adjustments."[21] When Allin sought men to represent the BAE in the states and regions, Taylor suggested several sociologists. "I do not name any of these men as Sociologists," he remarked, "but as the type of personalities who could do Regional and State jobs, and who in these jobs would pour sociological hormones into the blood stream of the whole planning process." [22]

Although economists headed the bureau during Taylor's years of service, they provided strong support for his work. Al Black more than tripled the division's budget, and Tolley maintained it at a high level, for he believed that his agency should include all of the social sciences. Wallace and Wilson shared this belief, and not even Wickard, who lacked Wallace's appreciation of the social sciences, cut the division's budget. Other agencies also called upon the division for help and supplied it with additional funds. Consequently, Taylor was able to expand the work, recruit top-flight members of his profession, and produce publications that were highly regarded by sociologists outside the USDA. Taylor himself became president of the Rural Sociological Society in 1939 and of the American Sociological Society in 1946. [23]

Taylor tried to make the work contribute to the development of his discipline as well as to the operations of the planning and action agencies. He sought ways to take advantage of the demands stimulated by depression and war that sociology become more useful and to employ these demands to develop research programs that would also make it more scientific. Critics suggested that rural sociology gave too much attention to the immediately practical and not enough to the development of a science; Taylor believed that sociologists could and should be concerned with both the solution of pressing problems and the development of a science and that well-financed work in the first area (and the association of sociologists with other people) could contribute to the realization of the second goal. [24]

Guided by a broad conception of its responsibilities, Taylor's work took the BAE into some of the most controversial areas of farm politics. It both reflected and promoted the rise in the USDA of an interest in the rural poor. [25] The sociologists criticized agricultural economists for their "preoccupation with commercial farmers to the exclusion of those large groups which may be designated as non-commercial" and insisted that the BAE should give a good deal of attention to the lower third in agriculture and to "what the various agricultural programs could and should do for low-income farm families." [26] Taylor believed that sociology could make greater contributions than any other discipline to the study of the disadvantaged classes in American agriculture, and he devoted much of his attention to them and turned out an important publication on the subject, designed, among other things, to promote concern about these people.[27] Triple-A felt the barbs of the sociologists, who called attention to the poor treatment of low-income groups by the agency and to the inadequacies of its farmer committees.[28] Taylor also criticized other action agencies, the extension services and the farm organizations for inadequate contact with the whole of rural America.[29] On the other hand, he regarded FSA's program as "the finest in the country. . . ."[30]

FSA and the Farmers Union applauded this attention to lower-income groups,[31] but some members of the department criticized the work of the sociologists. There were doubts about its value and fears that it would provide ammunition for opponents of the Administration.[32] Tolley insisted that BAE researchers should be free to reach and report their conclusions,[33] but pressure from Triple-A led to the deletion of material critical of that agency from Taylor's work on a group of American communities.[34]

Long a leader in the development of community studies, a major aspect of rural sociology, Taylor gained a chance in Washington to carry that work much further and to produce results that received a good deal of attention and were highly regarded by anthropologists and sociologists.[35] By 1944, he looked upon these community studies as the best things that had been done during his period as head of the division. "None of them have been perfect but we were on the trail of findings which would reveal a great deal to farm people on the one hand and to sociologists on the other," he believed.[36]

A study of two communities in California's Central Valley took the BAE into the center of a hot controversy and created a great deal of trouble for it.[37] In 1942, the Bureau of Reclamation had called upon the BAE for help in determining whether or not the acreage limitation principle of federal reclamation law should be applied to the giant reclamation project in the Central Valley. The principle specified that no landowner should receive for an unlimited period more of the subsidized water from a federal reclamation project than was needed to irrigate 160 acres. Marion Clawson, an economist with years of experience in the BAE, was placed in charge of the investigation; and he, Paul Taylor of the University of California, and the Division of Farm Population soon designed a study of two communities to test the assumption that family-sized farms produce more

desirable communities than large farms do. Clawson placed chief
responsibility for the study in the hands of Walter R. Goldschmidt,
a young anthropologist who had been trained at the University of
California, working chiefly with A. L. Kroeber and Paul Taylor, and
who had already made a study of one California town that resembled
the famous "expeditions" to "Middletown" and "Yankee City" in the
1920's and 1930's.

Goldschmidt concluded in the spring of 1944 that conditions in
the two towns justified the acreage limitation principle. Dinuba, the
town surrounded by small family-sized farms, was superior to Arvin,
a town based on large farms, especially from a democratic point of
view. Inequalities in landholdings promoted inequalities in economic
security and social stability which in turn led to a host of other inequalities, including political ones.

Before the anthropologist reached his Jeffersonian conclusions, an
attack upon him and his work got under way. Democratic Congressman Alfred J. Elliott of the Arvin and Dinuba area initiated the
attack; and a news commentator sponsored by the Associated Farmers, the owners of Arvin's largest fruit farm, and a farm journal that
was highly regarded by many leaders in California agriculture — the
Pacific Rural Press — quickly joined the fray. These Californians
soon picked up support from people in and out of the state, including two prominent opponents of the New Deal, Fulton Lewis, Jr., and
George Sokolsky. The critics portrayed Goldschmidt as a "silly professor" unacquainted with the realities of farm life and guilty of
behaving in a dangerously unpatriotic fashion.

Behind the attack lay the desire of the large landowners in the
valley that the acreage limitation principle should not be applied
to the project. Elliott was promoting legislation with this end in view
at the same time that he was criticizing the study. A piece of research
needed to be discredited because it threatened plans to obtain water
from a government project without being forced to reduce the size
of farms.

The attack produced demands that restrictions be placed upon research by the BAE. In April and again in June, 1944, Elliott brought
these demands to the floor of the House, and in July, the directors
of the California Farm Bureau called upon the BAE to stop such
wasteful work and turn to more useful activities. For the moment,
nothing came of these demands. The study had defenders, including
the National Farmers Union, who hoped that the acreage limitation

principle would be applied to the Central Valley Project. Once again, the BAE had placed itself on the Farmers Union side of a battle that involved the Farm Bureau.

It is ironical that work supporting the position of the Bureau of Reclamation should produce trouble for the BAE. Since the early 1920's, the two agencies had been quarreling, but in the early 1940's, efforts were made to substitute cooperation for conflict. With Clawson in charge of this aspect of BAE's work, the agency participated in the Columbia Basin Joint Investigation as well as the Central Valley Project Studies and tried to influence the reclamation projects.[38] One reward was an unusually large amount of criticism for the BAE because a community study challenged the position of powerful groups in California agriculture.

Although the Arvin-Dinuba study contributed to the growth of distrust of the BAE among powerful groups and to the increase in demands that restrictions be placed upon it, work on cotton prices and race relations played even larger roles in those developments. This work grew, in part, out of the agency's efforts to plan for the postwar world.

In 1941, Wickard had called upon the BAE to provide general leadership for the department's postwar planning; and as the war moved along and Congress pushed the BAE out of state and local planning, the agency devoted more and more of its time to this. The work was carried on by an interbureau committee in Washington and nine regional committees composed of representatives of the agricultural colleges as well as the department and attempted to accomplish what they could without the help of the machinery that had been destroyed.[39] Talk persisted about the possibility of re-establishing the state and county planning committees,[40] and efforts were made to work closely with the colleges, although this was sometimes difficult; some college officials did not want to be drawn by the BAE into controversial areas.[41]

Agricultural planning for the postwar world was influenced heavily by fears both about the loss of markets and about a great depression that peace might bring. The BAE, however, rejected the notion that a depression was inevitable and even insisted that farmers could continue to produce at the wartime level. Avoidance of depression and of restrictions upon production depended upon wise government policies designed to maintain and expand markets, chiefly in the cities. Some of the policies should promote international economic cooperation; even more important from the point of view of the farmer's economic interests were policies aimed at full employment in American cities. Thus, in their speeches, discussions, and publications, members of the BAE tried to convince farmers that their economic welfare depended first of all upon policies designed to promote the interests of urban workers. Clearly, the planners had rejected agricultural fundamentalism.[42]

The department's leading critic of agricultural fundamentalism, Mordecai Ezekiel, played a large role in these attempts to plan. Throughout the 1930's and early 1940's, he had stressed the importance of expanding industrial production, industrial employment, and purchasing power. He had become enthusiastic about the ideas of John Maynard Keynes and his leading American disciple, Alvin Hansen, and, like them, saw government spending and taxing policies as major tools for the accomplishment of these goals. But Ezekiel believed that these tools were not sufficient. Production planning, involving a Bureau of Industrial Economics to complement the BAE and cooperation among government, business, labor, and agriculture in planning committees, was also necessary.[43] And so, he had worked with a group of liberal businessmen interested in planning, hoping to enlist their active support for the steps that seemed necessary, and had helped to draft legislation designed to plan the expansion of production.[44] Because he believed that the welfare of farmers and workers depended upon the simultaneous progress of both groups and that the liberal control of American politics depended upon a coalition between the workers of the East and the farmers of the South and Middle West, he had criticized "shortsighted conflicts" between the groups and had urged Wallace in his speeches to call attention to the "fundamental unity of interest between farmers and workers," a theme that became very prominent in Wallace's statements.[45] In the 1930's, Ezekiel had criticized the political practices of the conservative wing of the Democratic party and the pricing policies of the giant corporations, seeing them as frustrating efforts to achieve an economy of abundance, and in the early 1940's he also concluded that farm groups were pushing farm prices up too rapidly.[46]

In postwar planning, Ezekiel, who returned to the BAE in 1944 after an absence of fourteen years, did more than any other member of the agency to push the theme that agricultural prosperity after the war depended chiefly upon industrial expansion.[47] Working mainly on the problem of maintaining demand for farm products, he pre-

pared a widely circulated pamphlet on the subject, headed an inter-
agency planning group that provided aid to communities wishing to
promote industrial development, studied the international dimensions of farm problems, and represented the department at the Bret-
ton Woods Monetary Conference.[48] He also worked with Wallace once
again, helping the new Secretary of Commerce prepare his well-
publicized book *Sixty Million Jobs*. This was an important contribution to the public debate on the full-employment issue that raged
throughout 1945 and led to the Employment Act of the following
year. Ezekiel, as well as other present and former members of the
BAE, especially Louis Bean, Russell Smith, and James Maddox,
made several important contributions to that development.[49]

In their planning for the postwar world, BAE leaders were involved
in the liberal movement of the period and in the attempts to develop
cooperation among nations. Bushrod Allin, now a special assistant to
Tolley, supplied leadership for much of the postwar planning.[50] In
response to one of his literary efforts on the subject, a colleague suggested: "You will do well as a writer so long as the present administration is in power! I would hate to see you put out such stuff, however, if Governor Bricker took over."[51]

The BAE's point of view emerged in challenging fashion in its
plans for the cotton South, a subject to which the agency turned in
the late stages of the war. Recognizing that government efforts to
maintain cotton prices at high levels were driving American cotton
out of the world market by encouraging buyers to turn to synthetics
and cheaper foreign cotton, Stine, Elliott, Wells, Ezekiel, and others
in the BAE in late 1944 and early 1945 developed a plan to let cotton
prices drop to a level at which American cotton could meet the competition and to use government payments in ways that at first would
pay farmers the difference between prices received in the market and
"parity" prices and ultimately would encourage many farmers to
move out of cotton production and to make other changes. The plan
also recognized that the number of people seeking a livelihood from
southern farms was greater per acre and per unit of resources than
in other parts of the country and that cotton could be produced only
at a high cost in some of the areas in which it was being produced.
The plan proposed to restrict cotton production to the lands best
suited for it, switch other land to other uses, reduce the number of
people and the amount of land involved in farming in the South,
diversify southern agriculture, enlarge the average southern farm,

and develop farms that were owned and operated by farm families. Heavy emphasis was placed upon the industrialization of the South and upon government promotion of these changes. Its activities would include training programs for those who chose to leave agriculture. Once the necessary shifts in cotton production had taken place, however, the government would not need to make payments to the farmers, for the market would supply them with a satisfactory income.[52]

As this "Conversion Program for the Cotton South" harmonized with the kind of thinking that planners in the bureau had been doing for a long time, they were enthusiastic about it and began to prepare similar plans for other parts of the country.[53] "The distinctive feature of this approach," the BAE announced,

is its assumption that no lasting solution to the problems of cotton can be developed in terms of cotton alone; but that the whole pattern of agriculture and, in fact, of the entire economy of the region, should be considered.

The agency was so bold as to suggest that "alone of all possible approaches, the conversion program offers a way towards curing, and not merely palliating, the ills that have beset the agriculture of the South."[54] At times, BAE men were more cautious and insisted upon the tentative and preliminary character of their proposal and the need for more research upon it, and they did pay some attention to alternative policies.[55] Yet they supplied, as John Black suggested, "an analysis *which appeared to leave the country with only one feasible or sensible course of action.*"[56] One BAE leader referred to it as "probably the best suggestion on the southern problem we have ever had."[57]

Recognizing that "our people will not tolerate for very long any program superimposed on them which they do not thoroughly understand and approve,"[58] Tolley encouraged wide and critical discussion of the plan. As early as December, 1944, and again two months later, Wickard discussed it in a general way before House committees concerned with agriculture; shortly thereafter, the BAE provided congressmen with a fuller explanation. Special efforts were also made to bring the plan to the attention of Southern newspaper editors and college and government officials. In mid-June, the BAE organized three two-day meetings of the regional planning committees in the South; Elliott, Ezekiel, Sherman Johnson, and Henry Jarrett of the BAE led the discussion. Efforts such as these produced a large amount of publicity for and generated a great deal of interest in the plan.[59]

Interest appeared in a number of places: various parts of the national government, the land-grant colleges, the American Farm Economics Association, congressional committees concerned with agriculture, *The New York Times*, and the Department of State. In the last, a major critic of the established cotton program—Will Clayton—had just become Assistant Secretary in charge of foreign economic policy, and officials were concerned that the existing program might wreck efforts at international cooperation.[60] An economist applauded the plan as one of the best government documents and the first step in the direction of abandoning the policy of preserving the southern *status quo* and substituting a policy designed to reconstruct southern agriculture "to a point where it is on a sound economic structure and fully able to compete." [61]

No one was more enthusiastic than James Patton. He congratulated Tolley on the excellent piece of work and assured him that the Farmers Union intended "to support it in the coming months and years in the South." [62] As Patton interpreted the plan, it not only met the fundamental economic problems of cotton but also endorsed the Farmers Union point of view on the shortcomings of the USDA. The plan "recognized that the interests of two-thirds of the farmers in this country have never been adequately represented in the Department of Agriculture" and that the emphasis in the department "has been placed on service to the upper one-third, economically speaking, of the farm families in this country and upon the commodities they produced." [63]

Criticism of the plan developed at least as rapidly as support for it. Some of its admirers, recognizing the power of the cotton interests, praised the BAE for its courage.[64] One of these predicted, however, that no action would be taken until southerners were "absolutely cornered, backs against the wall," and he called attention to "the efforts at various cotton conferences to gloss over these hard facts." [65] The ranks of the critics included many important southern groups—journalists, commissioners of agriculture, directors of experiment stations and extension services, congressmen, cotton planters, and Farm Bureau leaders. Throughout the war, the Farm Bureau had pressed for government guarantees of high prices and against administration efforts to restrain inflationary pressures on farm prices and to substitute subsidies for price increases. These efforts had been supported by the Farmers Union and by organized labor and had been interpreted by their rural opponents as subsidies to consumers and a reflection of the pro-labor bias of the Roosevelt Administration. Now, the farm group battled against all proposals to let prices drop in the postwar period and demanded that the new Truman Administration maintain the price support program.[66] Critics of the conversion plan had doubts about the rate at which the South could industrialize and fears about low cotton prices. New opportunities would not develop as rapidly as workers were pushed out of cotton, and cotton farmers would be forced into bankruptcy once again by low prices in a world market while industrialists continued to benefit from the protective tariff. Doubts were raised about the willingness of Congress to appropriate enough money to provide the cotton farms with compensatory payments, and some critics suggested that change in the cotton country should be promoted by education, not federal action.[67]

As the controversy mounted, a change took place in the top command of the Department of Agriculture. The new President pulled Clinton Anderson of New Mexico out of the House of Representatives and substituted him for Wickard. The change was announced on May 23, was quickly approved by the Senate — Anderson was popular in Congress — and took place on July 1. Anderson had battled against Wallace and for Truman's nomination for the Vice-Presidency at the Democratic national convention in 1944; and, like Truman, Anderson had made his reputation as a congressional investigator, serving as chairman of the House Special Committee to Investigate Food Shortages in the early months of 1945. He had criticized many government food programs and made a number of recommendations to remedy shortages.[68]

One of Anderson's first tasks was the reorganization of the department, for Truman had returned to it the functions that Roosevelt had transferred to the War Food Administration in 1943; Anderson's experiences as investigator had given him ideas about changes that were needed.[69] He was unhappy with much that had taken place in the department in recent years and eager to follow the advice of a friend who, hoping that Anderson's administration would rise "beyond the idealism of Wallace's and the mediocrity of Claude Wickard's," had counseled him to "build an *Anderson regime*."[70] To help with reorganization, Anderson called upon a man who not only had experience in this area but also shared the new Secretary's unhappiness with recent developments in the department. This was Milton Eisenhower, who had left the USDA in 1942 and was now president of Kansas State College. Unhappy with the way the department had been broken apart, Eisenhower was delighted that it was to be unified again and was eager to help Anderson accomplish his objectives. He believed that at one time it had been the best administrative organization in Washington and that the executive task was not "too onerous" if the department was properly organized and authority and responsibility were wisely delegated. The policy and legislative phases of Anderson's job, however, struck the educator as staggering, for he did not regard some of the action programs as "either necessary or compatible with our democratic philosophy." [71]

At first, prospects for the BAE seemed to have brightened. Surely, Eisenhower was a friend. He called Anderson's attention to Tolley as one of the "extremely able USDA officers willing to help you . . . ," [72] and when Eisenhower's Committee on Organization first went to work, it dealt with other parts of the department, suggesting to the men of the BAE that their agency would not be affected by the reorganization. [73]

Anderson seemed likely to be a much better Secretary from the BAE point of view than Wickard had been. One leader in the agency remarked that Wickard's years had been characterized by "vacillation, indecision, compromise" and believed that now the department was "finally getting some first rate leadership" and that the work of the BAE would be recognized and utilized. "The results obtained by the BAE in its general research and planning functions have been given too little attention . . . ," Likert wrote to Tolley. "With the new leadership in the Department, I feel confident BAE will be given an adequate opportunity to play the important role of which it is capable. . . ." [74]

The new Secretary did appear quite receptive of BAE suggestions. Coming to his job as "the apostle of abundant production," he spoke and wrote, as did the BAE, of the importance of the urban worker and the desirability of developing the economy of abundance; and on a number of occasions during his early months in office he seemed to endorse the conversion plan. [75] In November, for example, he addressed a meeting of farm officials in Memphis, Tennessee, and warned of the dangers of high cotton prices and the need for a parity formula that would improve land-use and production methods so that American cotton could compete successfully. [76] He recognized that many congressmen and farm leaders opposed these ideas, but he seemed determined to teach southerners that "the cost of production must come down, if we expect to compete with other nations in the world market or if cotton expects to compete at home against the synthetics."[77] Patton applauded the speeches that suggested Anderson endorsed the conversion plan.[78]

Anderson, however, was already planning to demote the BAE. Perhaps from the first, he had had no intention of using it as a central planning agency. He believed that nobody was interested in its postwar planning activities; he heard that a mistake had been made in 1938, that the BAE's obligations to plan were interfering with its responsibilities in research, that it was losing its reputation as an objective research agency, and that it should become once again exclusively a research institution. Hostile congressmen and farm leaders made these suggestions, but so did friends of the BAE like John D. Black and Paul Appleby.[79] Although Eisenhower believed that in general the BAE had been successful in its program-planning activities, he too now doubted the wisdom of placing that responsibility upon the agency responsible for objective economic and statistical research. He personally discovered no evidence that the BAE's planning function interfered with or influenced the other assignment, but he observed that a good many people felt that such influence was inescapable and that a change was needed to restore the prestige of the BAE. Therefore, his committee recommended early in the fall that the program-planning function be transferred to the Secretary's office and that the economic and research work of the bureau be strengthened.[80]

Only Patton and the Farmers Union defended the BAE. In his appearance before the Eisenhower committee, this farm leader even defended the defunct planning committees, saying that they had served a most useful function, that he very much regretted their discontinuance, and that they should be re-established. He believed it was "essential that some way be found to link the best brains of the Department with the experiences and needs of farmers," and he advocated the establishment of a channel between the BAE and committees of farmers.[81] His organization attacked the Farm Bureau and others for their efforts to cut the BAE off from policy making, arguing that this was "clearly the result of its failure to knuckle under to those interests which do not like the facts that its research brings forth nor the vigor with which it has sought to get the Department to do a little program planning in advance." As to the Eisenhower report, the farm group insisted that "the recommendations to hamper BAE work probably would end any kind of program planning within the department and leave it without its own studied plans, more subject to pressure from the colleges and other outside groups."[82]

Anderson, however, had received advice that he wanted. The friend who had urged him to build his own regime had not included Tolley in the list of career men who were exceptionally capable and trustworthy and had advised Anderson to set up his own policy committee.[83] Now Anderson had similar advice from highly regarded men like Eisenhower that would enable him to say that he acted on the advice of "outstanding men, all of whom had experience both in and out of the Department" and of "very fine, high-grade people" who had done "a fine job for me."[84] He had obtained strong support, in other words, for a decision to demote an agency that had been elevated by Henry Wallace (and still had some ties with him) and to transfer program planning to his own office.

When Patton learned of the Secretary's attitude, he protested once again. He suggested that the BAE was the world's foremost social research agency and that "its fundamental purpose of untrammeled, imaginative, courageous social science research" should be preserved and strengthened. Further, he advised that the agency was "the most dependable of all the guides" available to the Secretary and thus he should "lean more rather than less heavily upon it." "I know," Patton informed Anderson, "that if Claude Wickard had paid more attention to Howard Tolley and BAE, his path would have been far, far smoother than it turned out to be."[85]

Patton did not change Anderson's mind, however.[86] Obviously, this farm leader was not a source of great strength for the BAE. Although it was growing rapidly, his organization was much smaller than the Farm Bureau and was concentrated in the sparsely populated wheat country of the Great Plains rather than in the politically significant corn and cotton areas where the Farm Bureau had most of its membership.[87] Furthermore, he represented a liberal philosophy that had little support elsewhere in farm politics. In 1940, as a young man of thirty-eight, he had become president of his organization, and since then, believing that farmers and industrial workers shared interests and a common significance, he had worked hard and successfully to improve relations between his group and the Administration, organized labor, and other liberal groups. Working with them, he had battled against the Farm Bureau and had attempted to maintain and expand the New Deal, which he defined as a movement to improve the lot of lower-income groups. He was a vigorous critic of farm leaders like O'Neal, maintaining "that those who assume to speak for agriculture while representing only the interests of the top one-fourth of American farmers are not entitled to be taken seriously."[88] These leaders, on the other hand, regarded him as a radical and as a representative of labor, not as a farm leader; and they resented and feared the alignment of organized labor with the Farmers Union and the Administration.[89]

Patton was battling against the farm leaders and other groups with whom Anderson was eager to develop good relations. Anderson had had no ties with the farm groups prior to his appointment as Secretary of Agriculture; now he needed to develop ties with the ones that could help him accomplish one of his major objectives: the return of the farmer to the Democratic party. The most significant desertions had taken place in the Farm Bureau country of the Middle West. One of the things that troubled him about his department was its apparent alienation of the farmers of that region since 1936. He was determined to remedy this.[90] His rejection of R. W. ("Pete") Hudgens, the candidate of the enthusiasts of FSA for Administrator of that agency and his reappointment of I. W. Duggan as Governor of the Farm Credit Administration, although liberals like "Beanie" Baldwin, now an official of the CIO-Political Action Committee, protested that "Duggan's point of view is that of Ed O'Neal, Earl Smith, and other so-called farm leaders," illustrated his efforts to re-establish close, working relations between the department and the Farm Bureau.[91] Accepting Patton's advice on the BAE and rejecting O'Neal's would accomplish little, while demoting the agency might improve the relations of his department and his party with the Farm Bureau besides strengthening his own position within the USDA.

Any doubts that Anderson had about the wisdom of demoting the BAE were erased by the criticism of its sociological work that erupted late in 1945. Two years earlier, Taylor had initiated a large cultural survey project involving the study over an extended period of time of seventy-one rural counties that were selected with care so as to get a good sample of the seven type-of-farming areas that had been delineated by the Division of Farm Management and Costs. The work reflected his division's assumptions about the importance of cultural and psychological factors, the significance of interregional differences in the attitudes, customs, and traditions of farm people, and the need to understand these factors and differences in order to develop successful farm programs. The project illustrated the division's tendency to explore controversial subjects like race relations and class structure. By late 1945, only the initial investigations had been completed, and reports on each area were being prepared for publication in 1946.[92]

Taylor was very enthusiastic about this project. He looked upon it as a very important part of his efforts to make the division a research agency of major significance that would make a contribution to knowledge and would supply part of the background needed for agricultural planning in the postwar period.[93] "By the time we have the 71 counties done I don't think any of us or anyone else will question the fact that we have something," he suggested to his regional leaders.[94]

In the South, the project explored matters of the sort that most southern universities and land-grant colleges carefully avoided.[95] One county selected for study was Coahoma in northwestern Mississippi. There the work was done by a sociologist from the South, Dr. Frank D. Alexander, a native of Tennessee and a graduate of Peabody and Vanderbilt. He had worked for the Tennessee Valley Authority and the National Resources Planning Board and had taught at Clemson before joining the division in 1943 as its leader in the southeastern region. As the county's population had been predominantly Negro since the 1850's, Alexander's thirty-four-page "cultural reconnaissance" contained many references to race relations and was very critical of them. He concluded:

There are two dominant features of the culture of the people of Coahoma County — one is Negro-white relations, the other is the plantation system of farming. Almost every phase of the people's thoughts and behavior is influenced by these two complexes. Schools, churches, families, law enforcement, public welfare, earning a living are all under the domination of the plantation economy. Similarly all of these institutions and activities are carried on within the definitions of white supremacy and racial segregation.

Alexander's report found its way into unfriendly hands. In its present form it was not intended for wide circulation and was marked "For Administrative Use," with the intention that it would be given a more permanent but summary form of publication later as part of a report on the area. Thirty-five dittoed copies were produced, and several of them were sent, chiefly for criticism, to social scientists outside the bureau, including a staff member of the Extension Service in Mississippi.[96] The extension director there, L. I. Jones, obtained a copy. For several years he had been very critical of both the planning and the research activities of the BAE.[97] Now, the copy moved from him to the Mississippi congressmen. Infuriated, they reproduced sev-

eral paragraphs and circulated them among other Southern congressmen.[98]

The offensive paragraphs dealt with race relations. They emphasized the great "gap between the dominant white planter group and
their Negro sharecroppers," the "fairly absolute" white control of
the sharecroppers, the constant attention given by the planters to the
defense of "the institutions (particularly the established race relations) which underlie the plantation system," the tendency of Negroes
to turn more and more to the federal government rather than to the
planter in their quest for security, and the attitudes of the whites
toward the Negroes as a necessary group but "an inferior group which
must be kept in its low caste position." "A peculiar ambivalent attitude to the Negro exists among the whites," Alexander had written.
"They will complain of the inefficiency of Negro labor, condemn them
violently for their shiftlessness, and even wish they had fewer of them;
yet at the same time they constantly display their dependence on
them, revealing beyond a shadow of doubt they are unwilling to give
up their Negroes without considerable protest." [99] He had also offended
by writing of the challenge to the system, reporting that "the militant
Negro leadership in urban centers of the North is making its opinions
felt on the rural Negroes in Coahoma County, for a number of them
subscribe to northern newspapers which do not hesitate to emphasize
injustices done Negroes." [100]

"Ninety percent of the stuff in this proposed bulletin is nothing but
ball-faced damned lies," Congressman Dan R. McGehee of Mississippi
informed his friend Secretary Anderson in November. "The negroes
and whites are getting along a damned sight better in the South than
they are in the North, and if permitted to work out their problem, the
negro will continue to advance to his proper station just as it has taken
thousands of years for the white man to reach his present state." The
Congressman believed that Anderson should be informed because he
"did not know what the many long haired, cracked brained, Un-
American birds are doing that were placed in good positions in the
Department of Agriculture prior to your going in" and because he
"would not approve of such bulletins." McGehee suggested that "the
bird that concocted all this rot should be kicked into Kingdom Come,
and it should be in the lower region of purgatory" and that the department "had more important work to do in behalf of the farmers . . .
than to spend the tax payers' money by hiring a caste of people to
prepare such damned insulting articles. . . ." [101]

After Anderson had heard from his friends in Congress,[102] he provided no support for the BAE. The Mississippians were very important to the Administration. One of them, Congressman William M. Whittington, had recently led a successful fight in the House for legislation giving Truman power to reorganize the executive branch and had received a note of thanks for his "superb effort" from the President.[103] The Secretary believed that Wickard had made a mistake in allowing the department to engage in activities of the sort that had offended these people[104] and he assured McGehee that he could understand his feelings about the excerpts from the report: "I hit the ceiling myself when I read them." Anderson also assured the Congressman that there had been and was now no intention of publishing the report.[105] Regarding Alexander's work as biased, the Cabinet officer reprimanded the social scientist and ordered that no further studies of this type should be made, even though Tolley believed that they provided the BAE with information it needed to keep in touch with farm people.[106]

The BAE was forced to retreat. Taylor provided Congressman Thomas G. Abernethy of Mississippi with a detailed explanation of the project but failed to satisfy him. The Congressman concluded that "the Bureau had gone very, very far afield in some of its activities."[107] Some time earlier, Taylor had suggested that a social scientist in government had two roles to play, "one as a scientist and the other as a member of a policy-making group." As a scientist, "he should stand by his findings without the slightest equivocation to compromise, not allow anyone to disbelieve his findings and insist upon their being given consideration." As a member of a policy-making group, on the other hand, he had to compromise.[108] Now Taylor had to compromise. He and Tolley decided that plans to distribute condensed versions of the initial studies had to be scrapped.[109] One member of the BAE suggested that it should retreat still further in order to protect its economic work. If it continued to infuriate the lawmakers with its sociological work, they were likely to trim appropriations so sharply that in a few years the agency "would have little left for economic investigations of any kind."[110]

Immediately after the Coahoma County affair, Anderson announced his decision to demote the BAE. Included in his decision were reductions in appropriations and restrictions on many of its activities, transfer of the discussion program to the Extension Service, and increases in appropriations for research on the economics of production,

prices, income, and marketing and for the collection of crop and livestock statistics. Most important, he transferred responsibility for leadership in program planning to his office and established a Policy and
Program Committee headed by himself. Quite obviously, by the beginning of 1946, the BAE could no longer function as Tolley hoped.
It was now limited to economic research and the collection of statistics.
In theory as well as in fact, it had ceased to be the department's
planner.[111]

Many participants in farm politics applauded the change.[112] Only
Patton seemed fearful for the future. He provided Anderson with
advice on what must be done to promote the success of the new planning committee and expressed a hope that the new scheme would
work, for he believed that the land-use planning program "left a very
large vacuum when it died."[113]

During its years as central planner for the Department of Agriculture, the BAE had gained the support of an exponent of a liberal
philosophy that was not popular in the part of the American political
process that the agency inhabited. Like Patton, these social scientists
had embraced a philosophy that emphasized government action on
behalf of lower-income groups in both urban and rural areas and
had alienated most of the powerful participants in farm politics. As
the social scientists suffered the successful attack upon them in the
second half of 1945, they might well have asked why their segment
of American politics was usually so very small. They thought in terms
of the common interests of rural and urban groups, and at times urban
groups did participate in farm politics, although seldom when the
fate of the BAE was being debated. That fate was controlled by a small
group composed of farm leaders, rural congressmen, land-grant college officials, and the Secretary of Agriculture.

CHAPTER 13

Restricting the Bureau of Agricultural Economics

Although the American Farm Bureau Federation and its allies had called for the step that Anderson had taken in December, 1945, they remained dissatisfied and demanded new restrictions on the work of the BAE. Their demands during the first half of 1946 demonstrated that they disliked the philosophy of the agency and did not want men with the social scientist's outlook to play a significant role in farm politics. Farm Bureau leaders and key congressmen had concluded that these social scientists no longer sympathized sufficiently with the aspirations of commercial farmers nor respected adequately the customs of the world they inhabited. Once again, only Patton and the Farmers Union offered significant resistance to these men of great power in farm politics. Secretary Anderson tried only to preserve the bureau as a useful instrument for his own purposes. Finally, Congress accepted the demands of the BAE's opponents, and Howard Tolley sought refuge in the United Nations from the hazards and frustrations of the politics of agriculture.

Early in 1946, O'Neal resumed his attack upon the BAE. He wrote to Anderson on the matter, and when the Secretary replied that he had taken planning out of the agency's hands, the farm leader told Anderson that he had not gone far enough.[1] Then the Farm Bureau's president appeared before the Agricultural Subcommittee of the House Appropriations Committee and demanded that the BAE's appropriations should be slashed drastically, that none of the remaining funds should be used for agricultural planning, for the maintenance of regional offices (like the ones in which Goldschmidt worked in Berkeley and Alexander worked in Atlanta), or for the conduct of "social surveys" (like the Coahoma study). The BAE, he argued, should be confined to statistical and fact-finding research, and funds for this purpose should be increased substantially so as to provide farmers and their organizations with basic economic information.[2] In May, the Farm Bureau repeated before the Senate subcommittee the demands for restrictions on the BAE while advocating increases in funds for statistical and fact-finding research, particularly to improve the accuracy of crop and livestock reports.[3]

O'Neal called attention to some of the particular work that troubled him. He included the conversion plan. "Farmers are bitterly opposed to that policy," he told Congressman Tarver of Georgia, who was still chairman of the House subcommittee. The farm leader said that the BAE was "fine" as long as it was a statistical agency,[4] and Charles Hardin has suggested that research on crop and livestock estimates is supposed to be objective:

men can count the number of sheep in a field and get the same results, be they Democrats, Republicans, Socialists, Marxists or whatever. Moreover, this sort of "research" yields tangible results that appeal to "practical men" as something worthwhile. But "economic investigations" especially when used as the basis for formulation of controversial policy are quite another matter.[5]

O'Neal's testimony, however, revealed that even the BAE's statistical work could get the agency into trouble with the farm organization. He insisted that the economists had misbehaved when they supplied the Office of Price Administration with the factual data upon which it based its plan to place a price ceiling on the 1946 crop of raw cotton.[6]

Farm Bureau proposals and testimony indicated quite clearly just how the social scientists must behave in order to satisfy this farm group. The combination of proposed restrictions and expansions in the BAE's activities and the standards for good and bad statistical work demonstrated that the farm group believed the agency existed simply to serve the business interests of the farmers, not to attempt to reform the system or to function as an independent scientific institution.

Once again, the Farm Bureau found a friendly reception in the House Subcommittee on Agricultural Appropriations. Tarver now treated the group as Cannon and Dirksen had earlier. The Georgian applauded O'Neal's testimony on the BAE and his suggestion that its activities should be confined to statistical and factual research work and expressed his general view of the value of the pressure group. "The Farm Bureau, in its evidence before the committee, especially in recent years, has, in my judgement, been very helpful to the committee. . . ."[7]

The Farm Bureau, however, was not the only force at work. Other pressures were also moving the congressmen to act. The farm organization was just a very large and very active part of the situation in which the congressional opponents of the social scientists operated.

Even before O'Neal appeared before the House subcommittee, its members badgered Tolley for three days. (One of his lieutenants congratulated him "for not having exploded before those three days were over."[8]) Tarver tried to force Tolley to say that he advocated the conversion plan, but the economist attempted to make the Congressman understand the difference between a conclusion reached from an economic analysis and a recommendation as to what should be done and that, while his personal philosophy resembled that plan, the BAE had only "suggested that consideration be given to that possibility."[9] Congressman Jamie L. Whitten charged that Tolley was "a pretty adroit witness" who could "talk more and say less than most anybody I have seen since I quite practicing law and left the courtroom."[10] After Tolley left the committee room, Tarver attacked him for his support for the plan. "I do not know that he made an unequivocal admission of that type, because the doctor does not make unequivocal admissions of any type," Tarver remarked acidly. "But that . . . was the substance of his testimony."[11]

The congressmen believed that the plan would have dangerous consequences: low farm prices, regimented production, and the forced resettlement of farmers. Tolley argued that production controls would be needed only if the purchasing power of urban and foreign groups fell to the levels reached during the depression, but congressmen continued to talk of the plan as regimenting farmers and forcing them to depend upon government checks.[12] Senator Bankhead of Alabama, now the leading BAE critic in the Senate and one who referred to the plan with contempt as "Dr. Tolley's big scheme," warned that it involved a forced resettlement and regrouping of the farmers in the South and dictation to them about their use of the land and charged that Tolley wanted to drive the income of American cotton farmers down to Egyptian and Indian levels.[13]

Related to the criticism of the conversion plan was criticism of the BAE's relations with OPA. Tarver charged that the bureau was responsible "for the perfectly senseless and ridiculous proposal recently announced by the OPA to place a ceiling on the 1946 crop of raw cotton. . . ." The bureau had not only supplied the statistical data on which the price control agency based its action, but Tolley had justified the ceiling in the hearings.[14]

The anti-BAE congressmen also paid some attention to the Coahoma County study. Abernethy of Mississippi referred to it as one that the bureau "had no right to make" and that aroused "those of us coming from those areas."[15] Whitten, also of Mississippi, charged that the study slandered "a fine people and . . . a splendid section of this country" and strayed far from the facts and from the intended work of the BAE; he suggested that the farmer might benefit if Congress put Tolley's agency "back to agricultural statistics" and took it "out of the socialization field and the accumulation of claimed data and the printing of such vicious attacks on a county and its people. . . ." Whitten and Tarver insisted that the treatment of Negroes in Coahoma County was "probably better than the Negroes would receive if located in some of the industrial sections of the North . . . ," and the Chairman indicated that the BAE must not be allowed to engage in any other activities of this sort.[16] The entire committee suggested that the report on Coahoma County should not be given further distribution.[17]

In the eyes of the aroused congressmen, the BAE had become identified with some of the main developments of the period, including efforts to elevate the status of the Negro. ". . . if the FEPC or the CIO had made this investigation, I would not be surprised," Whitten remarked, "but I am surprised at the Department of Agriculture doing this. . . ." Money that should have been used to benefit farmers was "being used by the Department of Agriculture for this sort of thing which is nothing in the world but something which we may politely call socialization." The BAE had become dangerous as the Fair Employment Practices Committee and Northern "agitators" were dangerous. Tarver criticized "so-called militant northern Negro leadership," which he regarded "as a most unfortunate thing and which is doing a greater injury to the Negroes of the South than anything else when it comes to the handling of racial problems which exist in the South, problems which in the main are stirred up by these northern agitators . . . ," and Whitten suggested that the BAE was trying to stimulate trouble and to rework "the social set-up of my section of the Nation or the rest of it with racial intermingling."[18]

The reference to the CIO was also significant, for the congressmen as well as the Farm Bureau obviously feared that new giant[19] and associated the BAE with it. Tarver, for one, faced strong opposition in his own district from the labor organization.[20] Republican Congressman Marion T. Bennett of Missouri argued that the conversion plan, while harming farmers, would benefit the consumers in the big cities who would "be able to buy their groceries at the world price level." "It is very important to keep those big city consumers happy," he suggested, "because they have the votes which win presidential elections. And the CIO-PAC has shown that it can deliver those city votes."[21] Presumably, the plan had been "cleared with Sidney," the Congressman added, employing a slogan that Republicans had been using since 1944 to call attention to the apparent power of the CIO leader, Sidney Hillman, in the Democratic party. Another Republican, H. Carl Andersen of Minnesota, attacked the plan along similar lines and suggested that the CIO and the left-wing elements of America would force Secretary Anderson to accept the plan and then would prevent it from providing the farmers with adequate income. Consequently, given the existing power situation, farmers must depend on the market place, not the Treasury if they were to obtain real parity.[22]

The BAE had also tapped fears of the internationalist tendencies of the Roosevelt-Truman Administration. Bennett charged that the conversion plan would benefit foreigners who could dump their farm products here or buy American production at their prices, and Bankhead argued that the bureau wanted the United States to stop producing cotton and buy it from foreigners. "It is a very good tariff argument or international trade argument," he suggested, "but I do not see what the Bureau of Agricultural Economics has got to do with it."[23] Whitten even blamed the State Department, arguing that it had put pressure on the USDA and had sold the plan to Tolley. He condemned Tolley's "internationalized viewpoint" and charged that he and others in Agriculture and State wanted to "reorganize agriculture on an international basis . . . at the expense of the American farmer."[24]

Republican hostility to the New Deal and the Democratic Administration also figured in the attacks upon the BAE. Congressman Andersen charged that the advocates of the plan wanted to establish a regimented economy and to maintain "domination of the political set-up in the country" by "the particular party in power," and Bennett warned that after the 1946 elections "the revolutionary planners may not be around Washington." [25] Obviously, more than the interests of the Farm Bureau were at stake in the controversy.

A major argument of the congressmen indicated that they were determined to prevent the social scientists in the BAE from operating freely. That agency existed for one purpose: to be helpful to the American farmer — to serve the interests of American agriculture.[26] To quote Professor Hardin again, Tarver appeared "to believe in the peculiar worthiness of farmers; hence the *valuation* that farmers ought to get more money." He also believed "that the BAE ought to conceive its role as providing an economic rationale on the basis of which further claims of agriculture may be supported." [27] "Tarver, like many congressmen, was a lawyer," Hardin explained:

Lawyers believe in advocacy. Everyone is entitled to his day in court and to the benefit of counsel. The common law is hammered out by judges case by case in adversary proceedings of "right and wrong, between whose endless jar justice resides." This belief in the way justice emerges in the legal field is projected to the political field, where the farmer too, is seeking collective "justice." The value that a lawyer ought to be an advocate is in turn projected to the economist and others; the economists in the Department of Agriculture, "the farmer's department," ought to present "the farmer's side" of the "case." [28]

As the BAE had developed an association with urban liberalism, Tarver had moved from his role of defender of the agency against the attacks of Dirksen and Cannon to a position in the forefront of the attack. "I resisted efforts to decrease an appropriation some years ago, and have always thought that sufficient funds ought to be provided for you," he said, "but during the last year or two a suspicion has grown up in my mind that you may not be working for the farmer; you may be working more for the consumer of agricultural products. . . ." [29] Tarver's growing unhappiness with the BAE had appeared in 1944 and 1945.[30] In 1945, his subcommittee had suggested that Tolley might have misconceived the objectives of his agency and had used it more in behalf of the consumer than of the farmer-producer. Believing that the farmer was being discriminated against in the handling of the war programs, Tarver had advised that the BAE should do more than report the facts indicating discrimination against agriculture; it should provide information on the causes and suggest remedies. But when Tolley had recommended that the best remedy would be subsidies to the farmer rather than increases in his prices because the former would not promote a dangerous inflation, Tarver and Andersen had insisted that the farmer, as "a very independent individual," did not want a "bounty from the Public Treasury when he feels justified in asking a fair return for his products from the people who consume them."[31] Now, in 1946, Tarver charged that "in fostering the promulgation" of the conversion plan the bureau was "doing a disservice for agriculture."[32]

Over and over, Tarver indicated that he did not believe that Tolley was performing his proper function. "I want to know," Tarver asked, "whether you are working for the American farmer or not, and whether you are active and alive in his behalf; whether you are fighting for him, or whether you are more interested in either looking after the consumer or in maintaining the salary levels of the organization which you represent."[33] When Wells pointed out that the BAE was collecting information on the income farmers received from off-farm work, this seemed additional proof to Tarver that the bureau was not helping the farmer, for the purpose seemed to be "to show that the farmer's income is not so deplorably low as has heretofore been represented. . . ." Tolley's argument that his people were trying "to get the facts as well as possible and to present those facts to you and all the other people in as accurate and unbiased a form as possible," did not satisfy the Congressman. He argued that the economist seemed much more interested in presenting data that harmed the farmer than material that would help him. "I am surprised by that attitude on the part of officials of this Bureau, which . . . ought to be working for the interests of agriculture."[34]

Other congressmen who were involved in a large way in farm politics agreed with Tarver. "The appropriation for this agency is desired by the American people for the benefit of people engaged in agriculture," Whitten asserted confidently. The USDA should look out for the American farmer rather than try "to help out the producers of agricultural products throughout the world at the expense of the farmers of the United States, and particularly the cotton farmers." When Tolley rather desperately tried to assure the Mississippian that he was interested in the welfare of the farmers, Whitten suggested that the economist was "a little late" in expressing this view and that he seemed to share the prevailing bias of his agency against farmers and in favor of industrial workers. Committee members were troubled, according to the southern Democrat, as to "whether the Department is really working for the farmer or against him." The bureau seemed to be trying to refute "any indication that is made that the situation is not too good for the farmer. . . . It just looked," he said, "that those analyses are made for the purpose of serving the interests of those whose interests may conflict with those of agriculture." [35]

A Republican from Minnesota agreed with the southern Democrat. Andersen announced that the longer he listened to the discussion the more he wondered why "we should spend a nickel for this particular bureau if you cannot figure out some better way or better hope for agriculture than this defeatist attitude that you express here today." The Congressman explained that he listened to the discussion with Tolley of the conversion plan "purely from the viewpoint of a man who has earned his living at farming and who farms today." [36]

Andersen's explanation highlighted the contrast in the experiences and background of the congressmen and the social scientists, and the controversy revealed that the congressmen endorsed a philosophy that the economists had rejected. Although he tried, Tolley could not convince the lawmakers that the work of the social scientists could promote the interests of agriculture.[37] He faced men who were involved in and represented the business of farming and who endorsed agricultural fundamentalism. As they saw him, Tolley had an obligation to serve that business; and as they defined its interests, higher prices were the overriding need. They could not nor would not understand a man who had commitments growing out of his responsibilities as a scientist and whose work as an economist had led him away from their agrarian philosophy.[38]

Consequently, the congressmen attempted to impose restrictions upon the BAE's freedom that would guarantee that the agency would serve the interests of the farm business as these men defined those interests. Since, by being too ambitious and engaging in "unnecessary and improper activities," the BAE had failed to carry out its responsibilities, Congress had to place limits on the agency that would return it "to the purpose for which we conceive it to have been originally created, the collection and distribution of statistical and factual data relating to agriculture." These functions were "of the utmost importance to American agriculture" and had to be maintained.[39] To one observer it seemed that the congressmen did not want the agency even to think about such things as the conversion plan, and to one member of the BAE it appeared "that some folks think that BAE should campaign for policies irrespective of their effect upon the general economy."[40]

Also involved in a basic way in the case against the BAE was a denial that social scientists were proper people to play a major role in shaping farm policy. Only people "identified with agriculture" should play such a role, and they included farm organizations, their leaders, rural congressmen, state commissioners of agriculture, and the like. Tarver insisted that the conversion plan "did not originate with the farmers or with those who have been considered as their spokesmen in presenting their problems to the Congress" and that the plan had "not been advocated by any farm organization, by any individual who ever undertook to speak for American agriculture, or by any Member of Congress who comes from an agricultural area or any other responsible authority other than the Bureau of Agricultural Economics and certain college professors who have given some type of study to the theory which is involved." (Apparently Tarver accepted the Farm Bureau's point of view on Patton and the Farmers Union!) Tarver's observation prompted a Wisconsin congressman to take a crack at "the dreamers and schemers who happen for a moment to occupy high positions in the Department."[41]

The House of Representatives followed the advice of the Farm Bureau and Tarver's subcommittee and passed an appropriations bill designed to confine the BAE "to the gathering and dissemination of statistical data related to agriculture."[42] After this congressional action, the department attempted to block some of the proposed changes in the bureau's activities. In his appearance before Tarver's group, Secretary Anderson had not defended the agency and had retreated from his earlier stand on the conversion plan. The congressmen were willing to concede that he had been led astray by his advisers and did not personally want to impose the program on the American farmers, while he seemed willing to use the BAE as a scapegoat.[43] He also agreed with the congressmen in their high regard for O'Neal and the Farm Bureau and in their opinions on the proper people to shape farm policy. Proposals for change in parity "and the actual work of trying to pass on it," he agreed, "should be coming from the farmers themselves and from the farm organizations . . . and should be carefully considered by the agricultural committees of the Congress. . . ."[44]

This may have been designed to satisfy his critics in the Farm Bureau.[45] After this he apparently grew fearful that the opposition to the BAE might go too far and deprive him of a useful instrument.

The department's defense of the BAE, however, was far from bold. No effort was made to argue that social scientists should play large roles in the planning process. No arguments were offered about the importance of freedom for the social sciences. Anderson, in fact, assured the senators that the sociological work that had aroused opposition had never had his approval and had been discontinued. Tolley agreed that the work had been stopped and would not be resumed.

The defense emphasized the argument that the BAE must be maintained as a useful servant. As Anderson expressed the defense, the House bill needed to be changed in ways that would enable the agency "to render appropriate and adequate service to the farmer and to that vast segment of the population of this country that is interested in the production, marketing, and utilization of agricultural commodities." The proposed ban on regional offices was resisted on the grounds that it would severely hamper the bureau's work in the field, while the proposal concerning social surveys was criticized as capable of stopping all or most of the bureau's program. The department suggested that "cultural" be substituted for "social," arguing that "the term 'cultural surveys' more accurately describes the type of study to which there was objection, while at the same time it does not have the wide and uncertain connotation that would be associated with the term 'social surveys.' "[46]

The BAE picked up some support outside of the department. Congressman Harry R. Sheppard, a California Democrat and a member of Tarver's subcommittee, worried about the influx of people to his state, tried to make sure that hostility to the "unfortunate social report" would not prevent the bureau from collecting essential information on population movements.[47] A western farm group, the Hop Growers Association, sent letters to Western senators and congressmen informing them that the group considered the BAE "one of the most important functions of the Department" and that "the mass of public sentiment favors the expansion rather than the curtailment of the old line research and general service activities of the Department . . . ;"[48] and a southern organization, the National Cotton Council, advocated some restoration of funds so that the BAE could continue essential work with the colleges on the problems facing the cotton South. Like the Congressman and the western group, the council indicated that it was not "defending all of the work that the BAE had done in the past." [49]

The Department of Agricultural Economics at the Mississippi Agricultural Experiment Station had helped the National Cotton Council prepare its statement. The chairman of that department, Frank J. Welch, had a friendly attitude toward the BAE, but Director Jones and other leaders in the Extension Service in the state were so hostile to Alexander that they blocked a plan for him to return to Mississippi and help Welch on a research project. Given the situation, Alexander suggested that he should be withdrawn from the South and assigned to another region. [50]

Two other economists — George H. Aull of Clemson College and Theodore Schultz of the University of Chicago — also rose to the defense of aspects of the bureau's work that were under fire. Congress, Schultz argued, was gradually forcing the agency to work on the less important problems and reducing its prestige so that it was no longer attracting the outstanding young men in the profession. [51] The Chicago economist had only recently moved from Iowa State College, where he had experienced the "profound unfriendliness" that the organized political forces in farm politics felt "for agricultural economics research that does not provide the 'right' answers." [52]

Leaders of the land-grant colleges also attempted to apply pressure, but without confidence in their power. ". . . if the farm organizations were united in the plan to make the BAE nothing more than a sort of agricultural census agency," then, according to one college leader, there was "little likelihood that anything private individuals or the Land-Grant College Executive Committee might say would be sufficient to prevent the Appropriations Committee from accomplishing its objective." [53] One official doubted that the BAE could survive under present leadership because O'Neal no longer had "any use for Tolley." [54] Nevertheless, the officers of the Land-Grant Colleges Association informed the Senate of their fears that the language of the House committee "could mean that the Department must not in the future make studies intended to throw light on the fundamental economic problems of agriculture and to estimate the probable effects of specific policies or programs being considered for the aid of agriculture and farm people" and urged changes in the language that would "avoid any possibility of leaving the Department hamstrung in carrying on essential economic research on problems related to public policies affecting agriculture and farm people."

The college officials indicated that they were not defending the BAE's activities as planner. They simply insisted "that it is not sound public policy to liquidate all agricultural economics research because an error was made in one project" and suggested that "no one has claimed that farmers will be benefited by killing agricultural economics research in the Federal Department." [55]

Milton Eisenhower, still eager to help Anderson, also defended the BAE as a research institution. He informed the Senate that the criticism of the agency had been directed against its program-planning activities, not against its economic research and statistical work, that the Secretary's reorganization had remedied this, that the colleges believed that "economic research work in all the States would be weakened at a critical time if such activity were curtailed" in the BAE, and that its work in this area "should be greatly strengthened and expanded with as much of this work as possible being cooperative with the agricultural experiment stations." [56] Although Eisenhower supplied but a limited defense of the BAE, Tolley as well as Anderson thanked the college president for his attempt to be helpful. [57]

A bolder defense came from Farmers Union country. In North Dakota, where that organization had one of its largest units and unusually good relations with the Extension Service, the planning project had been very vigorous. [58] Now the Agricultural Advisory Council called upon Republican Senator William Langer, Nye's successor, to support the BAE "with sufficient funds to operate to the best interest of our farmers. . . ." The planning group informed him that a very effective and popular land-use program had been in operation until Congress had cut off federal funds in 1942 and that a number of county planning committees as well as the state council had continued to function after that date. The council warned that the proposed further cut in the BAE's appropriations "would be injurious to the best interests of the farmers of North Dakota. . . ." [59] Obviously, the agency's planning activities had won for it a few friends who were willing to criticize the entire movement against it, not just the latest phases of that movement.

While the North Dakota group defended the social scientists as planners and not only as researchers, the Farmers Union made a plea for the intellectual freedom of these social scientists. When the House committee ruled that the BAE could not undertake any more social surveys, the farm organization criticized the ruling as "a savage attack on academic freedom of government scientists. . . ." [60]

Although this defense of intellectual freedom amounted to a defense of the BAE's right to do the work that had associated it with the civil rights movement, urban allies of the Farmers Union did not help it in this battle. Their reluctance to do so did not reflect a belief that they should stay out of farm politics, for they had entered this arena when the FSA had been threatened. Nor did their reluctance reflect a negative attitude toward social scientists, for these liberals had accepted a provision in the Employment Act of February, 1946, calling for the establishment of a Council of Economic Advisers. Apparently, they did not believe that they should expend their energy on behalf of this particular group of social scientists even though they embraced the philosophy that urban liberals and the Farmers Union had endorsed in their battle for legislation designed to promote full employment.[61] Whatever the explanation, the consequence was that the agrarian ally of these urban groups had to battle nearly alone on this issue against the powerful Farm Bureau and a small but well-placed group of congressmen.

Consequently, the defense of the BAE accomplished almost nothing. The Senate Subcommittee on Agricultural Appropriations changed the terminology from "social" to "cultural" surveys and suggested that the agency should be allowed to maintain one professional worker in each regional office. All work done by the BAE in the states, however, was to be done in cooperation with or by approval of the land-grant colleges.[62] When final action was taken in June, after the Department of Agriculture and Acting Director of the Budget Paul Appleby had recommended that the bill be approved, the regional offices were abolished completely. This plus the ban on "cultural surveys" virtually guaranteed the Farm Bureau and its allies in the extension services and Congress that they would not be plagued by studies of Arvin and Dinuba or of Coahoma County.[63] The farm organization was pleased with the outcome and, characteristically, took much of the credit for it.[64]

Prior to final congressional action, Tolley resigned as chief of the BAE, convinced that he could not accomplish his ambitions in that position. His troubles with the Farm Bureau, Secretary Anderson, and Congress had convinced him that his days of usefulness in the BAE had come to an end. "I assume he is resigning in protest over the action of the Congress in reducing BAE's appropriations," Eisenhower wrote to Anderson,[65] but Eisenhower and Anderson as well as Congress had contributed to Tolley's frustrations. Frustrated in Washington, he accepted an assignment as chief economist and director of the Division of Economics and Marketing in the United Nations Food and Agriculture Organization, an agency he had helped to establish. In fact, since his troubles of 1942, he had spent much of his time making plans for it, in part because he believed that international economic cooperation provided one way of avoiding the necessity of cutting back on agricultural production once again. FAO seemed to provide a way of raising standards of living throughout the world as the New Deal had once offered him a chance to try to accomplish this at home, and higher standards of living at home and abroad implied full production for American agriculture. His turn to international affairs had been influenced also by a desire to accomplish more than he could in the BAE. Now with opportunities for accomplishment there reduced still further he turned all of his attention to an international activity that was supported by the Truman Administration, hoping to find opportunities of the scope that Roosevelt's New Deal had once provided.[66] "My main reason for deciding to go with FAO," Tolley explained to his staff, "is my belief that my services will probably be more valuable there than anywhere else during the next few years."[67]

Anderson chose O. V. Wells as Tolley's successor. A year earlier, Wells had been recommended to the Secretary as "exceptionally capable and trustworthy," and in a recent Triple-A conference, he had demonstrated his abilities by defending the Secretary against his critics. According to the report of one of Anderson's representatives, the economist had spoken in language that Triple-A men could understand, had handled himself admirably, and had made a very good impression.[68] Although Wells had long been one of Tolley's lieutenants, he was willing to accept the changes that had been made in the BAE's role and was eager to operate the agency cautiously and to keep it out of controversy.[69]

Only Jim Patton seemed willing to defend Tolley's conception of what the BAE should be. This farm leader called upon President Truman to fire his Secretary of Agriculture and listed Anderson's treatment of the BAE as one of the reasons for this suggestion. Patton criticized Anderson for failing to exert real efforts to continue "the formerly successful and useful local or regional planning functions of the Department," for limiting the BAE "to the routine duties of a statistics-gathering agency," for replacing it with a planning board "that has done nothing since it was established," and for showing "no concern over the effort of the House Appropriations Committee to wreck

BAE by ending its social science work and eliminating its field offices." The farm leader went on to charge that Anderson's handling of his office created an atmosphere in which "the highest type of public servant, such as Howard Tolley" could not function.[70] Although many individuals and groups, especially from the cities, joined in this demand for Anderson's ouster, only Patton listed the handling of the BAE as a reason.[71]

All that Patton produced was resentment of his action by Truman as well as by Anderson.[72] The President backed his Secretary, suggesting that Patton was "entirely misinformed" and that Anderson was "as able a Secretary of Agriculture as the Country has ever had" and adding, in characteristic fashion, that Cabinet positions "belong to the President" and that "as long as Secretary Anderson is satisfactory to me, I'll keep him."[73] Truman's action indicated that the story of the BAE as central planner and bold researcher had reached the end.

Although the Farm Bureau had played the leading role in promoting these changes in the life of the BAE, the farm group had not acted without help. Help had come from people interested in protecting the research function of the BAE, anti-New Deal Republicans, and a Democratic Secretary of Agriculture who disliked much that had gone on in his department during the preceding decade. Most important, the BAE, by concerning itself with race relations and cotton prices, had infuriated powerful Southern Democrats who opposed many of the recent tendencies in national politics and policy. Rather strangely, a branch of the Department of Agriculture had become identified in the minds of many — and especially rural groups — with the urban liberalism that had been rising to prominence in recent years.[74] By doing this, the BAE had gained large-scale support only from the Farmers Union, a group that had close ties with representatives of urban liberalism like the CIO but poor relations with other leading farm groups and the influential rural congressmen.

Tolley's resignation symbolized the frustrations that a number of the social scientists felt. In time, many of them, including Wilson, Ezekiel, and Carl Taylor, would also turn their attention to the international programs that were creating new opportunities at the same time that old ones were being destroyed.[75] Although Taylor recognized that sociology was unpopular and that the government could not use many of its findings, he was unhappy that "vested interests" had dashed his hopes and had forced him to cut back sharply on the sociological work in the USDA.[76] Back in the days when Tolley's influence was rising, he had referred to the Farm Bureau as "a very constructive organization which has accomplished much for the farmers." [77] By the summer of 1946, that organization — along with its allies — could list the frustration of Tolley and other social scientists among its accomplishments.

CONCLUSION

Social Scientists in Farm Politics

By the 1930's, social scientists had become one of the influential groups in farm politics. Battling to promote change and to give farm policy a somewhat different shape than the rural pressure groups would give it, they altered American life. Yet, the ideas and experiences of this group of men had roots deep in American history; traditions as well as visions of the future affected their behavior. And one element that came out of the past — the great power of business in American life — had an especially significant impact upon their experiences. It both affected their thinking and offered resistance to their innovating tendencies. Although not free of traditions, the social scientists' hopes for change exceeded substantially those of most major groups in farm politics; the other groups demonstrated in the 1930's and 1940's that the social scientists were not the only men of influence. The social scientists altered America but did not create a radically new America. The nation that existed after their rise, as well as after the coming of the New Deal in general, had many significant similarities with the Old Order.

As critics of *laissez faire*, the social scientists helped to enlarge the role of government in the lives of the farmer. In this aspect of their career, they had links with the past — with the pioneering work of an earlier generation of social scientists, with the progressives of the early twentieth century, and with the farm movement of the 1920's. Even their participation in politics did not represent a radically new development. It represented only an enlargement of the practice of employing social scientists for some of the tasks of modern government.

The enlargement of government was but a means to other ends, and the increase in size did not guarantee that government would be used for the purposes of the social scientists. Using government, they promoted higher incomes for commercial farmers, the retirement of submarginal land, and soil conservation. They were less successful in efforts to check reclamation, to promote large-scale adjustments in agricultural production, such as the reduction of land and labor devoted to cotton in the South, to elevate the economic status of the rural poor, and to increase their political power.

As scientists, these men had roots in the growth of the new universities, the development of scientific agriculture, and the conservation movement as well as in the rise of the social sciences. Their work, however, was also influenced by nonscientific traditions, especially the traditions of American business and American democracy. These men attempted to make the farm business profitable; they even encouraged farmers to imitate the practices of urban businessmen in hopes of accomplishing this goal. Rejecting elitist theories, they promoted the growth of farmer committee systems designed to encourage popular participation in planning and administering farm policy.

Although they promoted popular participation in planning and administration, the social scientists did not accept the theory that they were merely to supply the people with analyses of the consequences of alternative courses of action. This was one role that needed to be played. "The technician's function is to assemble facts and reliable estimates of the consequences of alternative uses that may be made of them," Elliott wrote in 1939. "Decision as to what is to be done in the light of this evidence is the function of the citizen and those he elects to represent him, whose tenure, unlike the tenure of the bureaucrat, is subject to his will."[1] Elliott and his associates, however, did not limit themselves to the technician's role. At times, they committed themselves to particular proposals and battled for them. This characteristic, coupled with the inevitable tendency of a social scientist's philosophy to appear in his work, encouraged attacks upon them.

Defining their roles broadly, these social scientists refused to be mere "servants of power." They did not see themselves as obligated to serve only the established power groups in farm politics but functioned as intellectuals, constantly criticizing the world in which they were involved and attempting to change it. Lacking commitments to any one power group, they attempted to educate business leaders about the importance of farm purchasing power and farm leaders on the significance of urban purchasing power. Influenced by science and democracy, these intellectuals in politics tried to reorganize rural America, including its power arrangements. They even refused to serve slavishly their superior officers in the executive branch, criticized the Presidents and especially their Cabinet officers in charge of farm matters, and on occasion deprived them of aid by resigning and finding other employment.

The degree of success that the social scientists enjoyed, however, depended heavily upon their relations with these political men. The years of accomplishment from 1933 to 1940 were years of substantial support from the President and the Secretary of Agriculture; the years of frustration after 1940 were marked by little support for the social scientists from these political leaders.

The social scientists varied in their approaches to the power groups in farm politics. Several basic approaches can be discerned. Wilson attempted to work with groups like the Farm Bureau and with businessmen who had a strong interest in the farmer. At the same time, he tried to alter their point of view and behavior and to draw additional groups into farm politics. Because he distrusted men like Ed O'Neal much more than Wilson did, Tugwell rejected this approach and called upon political leaders like Roosevelt to go over the heads of the farm leaders, to appeal directly to rural people and attempt to draw them into an alliance with the urban workers. Tolley tended to accept Wilson's method but with less patience than Wilson had. An unhappy Tolley left the Department of Agriculture in 1930, in 1935, and again in 1946, while Wilson remained there until driven from the place by Ezra Taft Benson in 1953. Wells was even more flexible than Wilson and perhaps should be recognized as a representative of still another approach. Determined that social scientists should provide services, he was quite willing to adjust to changes in the situation.

Neither Wilson's nor Tugwell's approach accomplished what the social scientists hoped to accomplish. Both led to frustrations, but Tugwell's produced them more quickly. His challenge to the major power groups was more obvious. Before 1937, he left farm politics, never to return, while Tolley remained nearly a decade longer.

The ultimate frustration of Howard Tolley did not mean that social scientists had ceased to be important in American politics. The BAE survived as a part of the Department of Agriculture. More significant, as the bureau was demoted and restricted, a new agency staffed by economists — the Council of Economic Advisers — was established. The Employment Act of 1946 obligated the President and the Congress to receive advice from economists appointed by the President and approved by the Senate. This legislation left open the questions of which economists should participate in the political process and how much influence they should have but insisted that some of them must participate. In fact, those responsible for the provision in the law calling for the CEA seemed to assume that economists would participate significantly as advisers to the President and thus wanted those economists to be clearly identified, rather than to operate in the shadows.[2] By 1946, in other words, social scientists (at least economists) were very well established in American politics.[3]

Tolley's frustration meant that the most powerful figures in farm politics at the time were determined that the social scientists there must be mere servants of power. They were subjected to overwhelming pressures to demonstrate their utility to the power groups and were faced with men of power who were confident of their ability to determine what would serve the interests of the people they represented. The leading rural pressure group, especially, had grown fearful of the tendencies of these social scientists, believing that, despite their rural backgrounds and their jobs in the USDA, they had become too interested in urban workers, just as critics earlier, especially John Simpson, had charged that men like Wilson were too close to Big Business. The American Farm Bureau Federation insisted that it must dictate the terms of service by the service intellectual. He was not to be an independent force in farm politics but was to accept the dictates of the "farmers" and serve them in the way their "representative" demanded, leaving policy making largely to the farm organizations, a position that powerful congressmen endorsed. When Simpson had led the Farmers Union, he had talked in somewhat similar terms, although he had apparently believed that the farm organizations needed no help whatever from social scientists in solving farmers' problems. Others, like Hirth of the Missouri Farmers Association, agreed.

Tolley's frustration suggested that farm politics could not accept the pattern of values that had been involved in the Christgau bill of the early 1930's. Farming in America was primarily a business enterprise, and farm politics was dominated by men interested first of all in higher prices for the rural businessman. Although science played an important part in his life, scant interest existed in the large-scale reorganization of rural life and the expansion of urban purchasing power that social science suggested to the planners. While farm spokesmen frequently employed democratic rhetoric, most of them had little interest in the attacks upon the problems of rural poverty or in the efforts to promote mass participation in the political process that democracy implied to the social scientists. Each set of values involved in the Christgau bill, in other words, played a part in farm politics, but the parts were not equally significant. Business values were more important to the most powerful men and groups than they were to the social scientists.

Groups like the Farm Bureau were not anti-intellectual if anti-intellectualism is defined as hostility to the participation of economists and the like in public affairs. Even though men like Wilson demonstrated their practical abilities by participating in politics and getting their farm relief scheme accepted by politicians and by farm and business leaders, there was much talk during the New Deal period about the inherent impracticality of such people and the consequent need to drive them out and keep them out of government and to rely instead upon men of experience in business and farming. The Farm Bureau, however, became hostile only when the intellectuals appeared to threaten the economic and political interests of this organization and its members; even then the Farm Bureau did not try to drive the social scientists out of government but tried only to redefine their role so as to eliminate them as a threat but keep them as a servant. Clearly, the Farm Bureau believed that social scientists could be practical men even though the heads of some of them were filled with "impractical theories." The relations between such a power group and the social scientists were determined chiefly by the relations between the group's definition of its interests and the social scientists' ideas.

If anti-intellectualism is defined differently, however, then power groups like the Farm Bureau must be interpreted differently. If anti-intellectualism means hostility toward the free play of intellect, then that organization clearly proved itself to be anti-intellectual in the New Deal era. The Farmers Union, after the rise of Jim Patton, defended intellectual freedom but did not demonstrate much power in its relations with these social scientists. During their period of rising influence, they had rather poor relations with that farm group. Their years of good relations with it were years of frustration for them. The opposite pattern characterized their relations with the Farm Bureau. In the second sense of the term, then, anti-intellectualism dominated farm politics during the period. At least, this type of anti-intellectualism ultimately overwhelmed Tolley and some of his associates.

This is not to say that American politics in general was dominated by anti-intellectualism in the Roosevelt period. A study of farm politics does not allow one to speak with confidence about the whole of the American political process as that time, for it was compartmentalized. At least at times, some of the parts had little contact with some of the other parts. Perhaps Jim Patton's urban allies agreed with him about the importance of intellectual freedom, but they did not join with him in the defense of the BAE. Although it was identified in the eyes of its critics with urban liberalism and internationalism, few urban representatives of those points of view came to the aid of the economists. Neither the CIO nor the NAACP recognized the BAE as a friend worth defending; these groups did not participate in farm politics on this issue. Their representatives in Congress also stayed out of this arena when the fate of the BAE was being debated. On this issue, at least, the Farm Bureau and a small number of southern and midwestern congressmen dominated farm politics and revealed their fears of the intellectuals.

Obviously, the most powerful groups in farm politics in the Age of Roosevelt did not want the social scientists to play as large a role as they believed they should play. The elevation of the BAE had been in line with their ambitions; it represented an attempt to enlarge the role of social scientists in farm politics. It was not, however, an effort to establish them as the dominant group. These social scientists rejected the theory of the business elite that had dominated American politics during the 1920's,[4] but they did not wish to substitute a scientific elite, although Tugwell and Gray placed especially heavy emphasis upon the virtues of those social scientists who rejected *laissez faire*.

The group of economists, sociologists, psychologists, and anthropologists in farm politics endorsed Roosevelt's conviction that the American political process should be a multigroup affair. The New Deal that they helped to shape was produced by many groups and opposed by many others, no one of which could legitimately nor realistically expect that national policies would conform to the group's desires. The social scientists were but one of many groups involved. They had to share influence with others and somehow promote change without alienating too many of these other people. As democrats, men like Wilson and Tolley did not believe that they had a right to dictate farm policy; they simply believed that, as social scientists, they should be encouraged to participate significantly in the operations of government. In the Age of Roosevelt, they received encouragement, promoted changes, but eventually alienated too many powerful men.

Although farm politics remained a dynamic, changing thing after the Age of Roosevelt, the experiences of social scientists in farm politics did not change fundamentally. They remained one — but only one — of the influential groups. "The role of economists in farm policy in the period ahead is . . . likely to continue to be frustrating," a student of government and agriculture concluded recently. ". . . farm policy must be a pluralistic policy designed to achieve a number of values, and, therefore, it will always be diverse, diffuse, and involve much more than economics. Like it or not, so is the real world."[5]

NOTES

ABBREVIATIONS USED IN NOTES

AH	*Agricultural History*
CR	*Congressional Record*
FRC	Federal Records Center, South San Francisco, California
HF	Historical Files, Economic and Statistical Analysis Division, Economic Research Service, United States Department of Agriculture, Washington, D.C.
JFE	*Journal of Farm Economics*
MVHR	*Mississippi Valley Historical Review*
NA	The National Archives, Washington, D.C.
NYT	*The New York Times*
OF	Official File
OHC	Oral History Collection, Columbia University, New York
PPF	President's Personal File
RG	Records Group
	16 Secretary of Agriculture
	83 Bureau of Agricultural Economics
	96 Resettlement Administration and Farm Security Administration
	145 Agricultural Adjustment Administration
RL	Franklin D. Roosevelt Library, Hyde Park, New York
TL	Harry S Truman Library, Independence, Missouri

NOTES TO INTRODUCTION

1. Merle Curti, *American Paradox: The Conflict of Thought and Action*, Chap. 1.

2. Frederick Rudolph, *The American College and University: A History*, Chaps. 6, 10–16.
3. Joseph Ratner, ed., *Intelligence in the Modern World: John Dewey's Philosophy*, 462; Merle Curti, "Intellectuals and Other People," *American Historical Review*, LX (January, 1955), 279; Lewis S. Feuer, "John Dewey and the Back to the People Movement," *Journal of the History of Ideas*, XX (October–December, 1959), 545–68.
4. Richard Hofstadter, *Social Darwinism in American Thought*, Chaps. 4, 8; Henry Steele Commager, *The American Mind: An Interpretation of American Thought and Character since the 1880's*, Chaps. 10, 11, 14, 15; Ralph Henry Gabriel, *The Course of American Democratic Thought*, 215–20, Chaps. 19, 23; Sidney Fine, *Laissez Faire and the General Welfare State: A Study of Conflict in American Thought, 1865–1901*, Chaps. 7–8.
5. Louis Wirth, "The Social Sciences," in *American Scholarship in the Twentieth Century*, ed. Merle Curti, 50.
6. Richard Hofstadter, *Anti-intellectualism in American Life*, 197.
7. Robert S. Maxwell, *La Follette and the Rise of the Progressives in Wisconsin*, 139.
8. For discussion of this aspect of Wisconsin history, see *ibid.*, 128–52; Lawrence A. Cremin, *The Transformation of the School: Progressivism in American Education, 1876–1957*, 161–68; Hofstadter, *Anti-intellectualism*, 199–204; Merle Curti and Vernon Carstensen, *The University of Wisconsin: A History, 1848–1925*, II, Chaps. 1, 2; Maurice M. Vance, *Charles Richard Van Hise: Scientist Progressive*, 112–15.
9. John R. Commons, *Myself*, 76.
10. John R. Commons, *Labor and Administration*, vi.
11. *Ibid.*, 374, 406–7.
12. Commons, *Myself*, 88; see also 110.
13. *Ibid.*, 76–77.
14. Curti and Carstensen, *University of Wisconsin*, I, 288; Robert M. La Follette, *La Follette's Autobiography: A Personal Narrative of Political Experiences*, 26–33.
15. David A. Shannon, "Was McCarthy a Political Heir of La Follette?" *Wisconsin Magazine of History*, XLV (Autumn, 1961), 4.
16. Hofstadter, *Anti-intellectualism*, 199.
17. Curti and Carstensen, *University of Wisconsin*, II, 19–23; Vance, *Van Hise*, 148–64.
18. M. Nelson McGeary, *Gifford Pinchot: Forester-Politician*, Part One.
19. Samuel P. Hays, *Conservation and the Gospel of Efficiency: The Progressive Conservation Movement, 1890–1920*. See also Donald Swain, *Federal Conservation Policy, 1921–1933*, 167–69.
20. Loren Baritz, *Servants of Power: A History of the Use of Social Science in American Industry*, 194.
21. Hofstadter, *Anti-intellectualism*, 429.
22. *Ibid.*, 430.

NOTES TO CHAPTER 1

1. On farm policy, see Gilbert C. Fite, Bushrod W. Allin, Richard S. Kirkendall, and Ross B. Talbott, "The United States Department of Agriculture as an Instrument of Public Policy," *Journal of Farm Economics*, XLII (December, 1960), 1084–1113. On land planning, see the controversy between Samuel P. Hays and J. Leonard Bates: Bates, "Fulfilling American Democracy: The Conservation Movement, 1907–1921," *Mississippi Valley Historical Review*, XLIV (June, 1957), 29–57; Hays, *The Progressive Conservation Movement*; and Bates's review of Hays, *American Historical Review*, LXV (July, 1960), 930–31.

2. M. L. Wilson, Oral History Collection (Columbia University); Louis Finkelstein, *American Spiritual Autobiographies: Fifteen Self-Portraits*, 1–15, 19; Russell Lord, *The Wallaces of Iowa*, 252, 296, 298–301; Roy E. Huffman, "Montana's Contributions to New Deal Farm Policy," *Agricultural History*, XXXIII (October, 1959), 164–65; Mary Wilma M. Hargreaves, *Dry Farming in the Northern Great Plains, 1900–1925*, 114, 133, 147–52, 159, 279–80, 284, 514, 543.

3. Wilson, "The Fairway Farms Project," *Journal of Land and Public Utility Economics*, II (April, 1926), 156–71; Wilson, OHC; Advisory Committee on Economic and Social Research of the Social Science Research Council, *Research Method and Procedure in Agricultural Economics*, II, 319–20; Wilson, "Experimental Method in Economic Research," *JFE*, XI (October, 1929), 578–83; John D. Black, ed., *Research in Farm Management — Scope and Method*, 169–79; Wilson, "Research Studies in Economics of Large-scale Farming in Montana," *Agricultural Engineering*, X (January, 1929), 3–12; R. L. Adams, "The Management of Large Farms," *ibid.*, XII (September, 1931), 353.

4. Malcolm Cutting, "Farm Relief by Factory Methods," *Nation's Business*, XVIII (February, 1930), 47.

5. Finkelstein, *Spiritual Autobiographies*, 16.

6. Wilson to Dwight Sanderson, January 17, 1940, National Archives, Records Group 16.

7. Wilson, "The Source Material of Economic Research and Points of View in its Organization," *JFE*, VIII (January, 1926), 14–15.

8. *An Agricultural Program for Montana*, Montana State College Extension Service, Bulletin 84; L. C. Gray, "Evolution of the Land Program of the USDA," March 22, 1939, National Archives, Records Group 83.

9. Wilson, Howard Ross Tolley, and John Hutson, OHC.

10. Black, *Farm Management*, 11.

11. Tolley, OHC; M. R. Benedict and M. L. Wilson, "Howard Ross Tolley, 1889–1958," *JFE*, XLI (February, 1959), 1; William G. Reed and Tolley, "Weather as a Risk in Farming," *Geographical Review*, II (July, 1916), 48.

12. John D. Black, *Agricultural Reform in the United States*, 334.

13. Wilson, Tolley, Hutson, and O. C. Stine, OHC; interview with Wilson; James Shideler, *Farm Crisis, 1919–1923*, 123–41; James P. Cavin, ed.,

Economics for Agriculture: Selected Writings of John D. Black, 29–30, 68, 72, 307–11, 654–55; H. C. M. Case and D. B. Williams, *Fifty Years of Farm Management*, 82–83, 105, 165–66, 186–88, 195, 200, 205; Henry C. and Anne Dewees Taylor, *The Story of Agricultural Economics in the United States, 1840–1932*, 138–42, 373, 410–11, 428–32, 446, 455–56, 459; "Outlook Work: the First 20 Years," NA, RG 83; Mordecai Ezekiel to C. C. Teague, April 23, 1930, Teague Papers (Bancroft Library, University of California).

14. Wilson, OHC; Eric Englund to Thomas J. Walsh, February 25, 1932, in U.S., *Congressional Record*, 72d Cong., 1st Sess., 5180 (March 3, 1932); Huffman, "Montana's Contributions," *AH*, 1959, 165.

15. Wilson, Tolley, and Stine, OHC; Benedict and Wilson, "Tolley," *JFE*, 1959, 1; *CR*, 71st Cong., 2d Sess., 4102 (February 5, 1931); John Black to Nils Olsen, January 24, 1930, NA, RG 83.

16. *CR*, 71st Cong., 2d Sess., 12119–22 (June 30, 1930); Tolley, "Recent Developments in Research Methods and Procedure in Agricultural Economics," *JFE*, XII (April, 1930), 217–19; C. L. Holmes to Nils Olsen, August 24, 1932, November 24, 1930, NA, RG 83.

17. Elliott quoted in "Outlook Work," 10 ff., NA, RG 83.

18. Tolley, "Research in Local and National Outlook Work," *JFE*, XII (October, 1930), 594.

19. Theodore Saloutos and John D. Hicks, *Agricultural Discontent in the Middle West, 1900–1939*, 419–21; Victor Christgau, "Legislation Needed to Bring About Readjustments in Agriculture," *Proceedings of the Association of the Land-Grant Colleges and Universities*, XLIV (November, 1930), 124–28; Tolley in *CR*, 71st Cong., 3d Sess., 4101 (February 5, 1931); John D. Black, "Doctrines Relating to the Agricultural Policy of the United States," *Proceedings of the Second International Conference of Agricultural Economists* (August, 1930), 226, 232–33; Black, *Farm Management*, 87, 150; Wilson, "Research in the Field of Agricultural Adjustments," *Proceedings of the Western Farm Economics Association*, V (June, 1931), 93–96.

20. *Ibid.*, 100; Wilson, OHC; interviews with Wilson; *CR*, 71st Cong., 2d Sess., 8285–86 (May 3, 1930); 8950–52 (May 14, 1930); 10240–42 (June 6, 1930); 11413–17 (June 21, 1930); 3d Sess., 5323–24 (February 18, 1931); 72d Cong., 1st Sess., 1562–64 (January 9, 1932); *The New York Times*, January 20, May 22, 1931.

21. Evidence available to me does not support Dean Huffman's suggestion that the bill itself "was largely the work of Elmer Starch. . . ." Huffman, "Montana's Contributions," *AH*, 1959, 166. Wilson, OHC; interviews with Wilson, F. F. Elliott, Christgau, and Black; Chris Christensen to C. C. Teague, October 6, 1930, Teague Papers; Black, "Doctrines," *Second International Conference*, 232; Christgau, "A Plan to Control Agricultural Production," *American Cooperation*, 1931, 55.

22. Christgau, "Adjustment of Production in Agriculture," *JFE*, XIII (January, 1931), 1–8.

23. On the bill see Christgau, *CR*, 71st Cong., 2d Sess., 12119–22 (June 30,

1930) ; C. L. Holmes to Nils Olsen, August 24, 1932, NA, RG 83; Christgau, "Legislation Needed to Bring About Readjustments in Agriculture," *Proceedings of the Association of the Land-Grant Colleges and Universities*, 1930, 123–30; Wilson, *Farm Relief and the Domestic Allotment Plan*, 43–45, 52; Wilson, "Agricultural Adjustments," *Western Farm Economics Association*, 1931, 100–101, 107–8; Lord, *Wallaces*, 305; Black, "Doctrines," *Second International Conference*, 232.

24. Black, "Public Participation in Planning Adjustments," *American Cooperation*, 1932, 490.

25. Huffman, "Montana's Contributions," *AH*, 1959, 166.

26. Wilson, "Economic Planning as Applied to Agriculture," *Proceedings of the Western Farm Economics Association*, VI (August, 1932), 76, 79.

27. Lord, *Wallaces*, 305.

28. Black, "Public Participation," *American Cooperation*, 1932, 491.

29. Christgau, "Agricultural Production," *American Cooperation*, 1931, 60.

30. Black, "Public Participation," *American Cooperation*, 1932, 491; L. H. Bean to Eric Englund, October 5, 1932, NA, RG 83.

31. Black, "Doctrines," *Second International Conference*, 76, 79, 85, 232, 235.

32. Richard S. Kirkendall, "L. C. Gray and the Supply of Agricultural Land," *AH*, XXXVII (October, 1963), 206–9.

33. Wilson, "A Land-Use Program for the Federal Government," *JFE*, XV (April, 1933), 220-35.

34. Gray, "Objectives of the Land-Use Planning Program of the United States Government," June 18, 1934, NA, RG 145; Gray, "Farm Ownership and Tenancy," *Proceedings of the Academy of Political Science in the City of New York*, XI (April, 1925), 369–78.

35. Interview with Wilson; *NYT*, December 9, 1934; NBC Radio Speech from Chicago, April, 1932, Wilson Papers (Montana State College); Wilson, "The Place of Subsistence Homesteads in our National Economy," *JFE*, XVI (January, 1934), 73–84; Wilson, "The Problems of Poverty in Agriculture," *JFE*, XXII (February, 1940), 18, 19, 27–29; Wilson to L. H. Goddard, July 1, Wilson to Otto Hoereth, October 17, 1933; Wilson to E. A. Starch, July 3, Wilson to D. C. White, July 17, 1934; Wilson to W. E. Zuech, May 15, 23, 1936; Wilson to Fred Howe, February 14, 1938; Wilson to Erich Kraemer, January 10, 1939, NA, RG 16.

36. John Kenneth Galbraith, *American Capitalism: The Concept of Countervailing Power*, Chap. 11.

37. Wilson and Tolley, OHC; interviews with Wilson; Wilson to Chester Davis, November 2, 1929, Peek Papers (Western Historical Manuscripts Collection, University of Missouri); Wilson to J. W. Wilson, May 20, 1932, Wilson Papers; Wilson to Ezekiel, April 9, Wilson to James Stone, April 9, 1932, Wilson to Tugwell, October 20, 1939, Historical Files, Economic and Statistical Analysis Division, Economic Research Service, USDA.

38. Wilson, OHC; interviews with Wilson; Wilson, *Farm Relief*, 28–36;

Henry Wallace, "The Farmer and Social Discipline," *JFE*, XVI (January, 1934), 5–6.

39. Interview with Wilson; Wilson to A. H. Benton, April 11, 1932, Wilson to W. R. Ronald, January 11, Wilson to R. D. Lusk, January 20, 1933, Wilson Papers; Wilson, "Validity of the Fundamental Assumptions underlying the Agricultural Adjustment Act," *JFE*, XVIII (February, 1936), 17, 25; Wilson, "The Place of the Department of Agriculture in the Evolution of Agricultural Policy," NA, RG 83.

40. Wilson, *Farm Relief*, 9–18, 24, 25, 44.

41. Wilson to Ezekiel, October 25, 1932, HF.

42. Hyde to M. J. Hart, May 2, 1930, NA, RG 16; Robert P. Friedman, "The Public Speaking of Arthur M. Hyde," unpublished Ph.D. dissertation, University of Missouri, 1954, 226–33, 551–55.

43. Hyde to E. N. Puckett, February 11, 1931, NA, RG 83; Friedman, "Hyde," 235–36.

44. Hyde to Sen. Arthur H. Vandenberg, October 17, 1931, Hyde to J. S. Wanamaker, January 3, 1933, NA, RG 16.

45. Wilson, *Farm Relief*, 27–29.

46. Eric Englund to C. W. Warburton, June 15, 1932, NA, RG 16.

47. Wilson to A. H. Benton, April 11, 1932, Wilson Papers.

48. Wilson, *Farm Relief*, 44–45.

49. J. S. Davis, "The Voluntary Domestic Allotment Plan for Wheat," *Wheat Studies of the Food Research Institute*, IX (November, 1932), 28.

50. George Soule, "Planning for Agriculture," *New Republic*, LXVIII (October 7, 1931), 204–6.

51. Wilson to A. H. Benton, April 11, 1932, Wilson Papers.

52. Wilson to E. A. Duddy, March 11, 1932, *ibid.*

53. Wilson to W. L. Grimes, April 2, 1932, *ibid.*

54. Wilson to Ezekiel, April 9, 1932, HF; see also Wilson to James Stone, April 9, 1932, *ibid.*

55. See especially Saloutos and Hicks, *Agricultural Discontent*, 454–58, and Gilbert C. Fite, *George N. Peek and the Fight for Farm Parity*, 230–33.

56. Lord, *Wallaces*, 305.

NOTES TO CHAPTER 2

1. Wilson, "Agricultural Adjustments," *Western Farm Economics Association*, V (1931), 93–108; Wilson, "Economic Planning as Applied to Agriculture," *ibid.*, VI (August, 1932), 73–79, 106.

2. Alexander Legge Press Conference, March 5, 1931, Teague Papers; Wilson, "Agricultural Adjustments," *Western Farm Economics Association*, 1931, 101–5.

3. Wilson to Beardsley Ruml, May 18, 1932; see also Hope, Ronald, and Stockton files for 1932, Wilson Papers.

4. Wilson to Henry A. Wallace, March 25, 1932; see also Wilson to De Los L. James, Wilson to Joseph S. Davis, March 25, Wilson to W. L. Grimes, April 2, 1932, and Stockton file, *ibid.*

5. Wilson to J. W. Wilson, May 20, Wilson to Tolley, March 10, 1932, *ibid.*

6. Wilson to H. I. Harriman, March 11, Wilson to H. A. Wallace, March 25, 1932, Stockton file, *ibid.*; R. W. Brown to Stockton, March 22, Wilson to James Stone, April 9, 1932, HF; Wilson, OHC.

7. Wilson to M. S. Winder, Louis J. Taber, and Albert Goss (3 letters), April 11, 1932, Wilson Papers.

8. Wilson to J. S. Davis, May 18, 1932, *ibid.*

9. Smith to George Peek, April 21, 30, 1932, Peek Papers; interview with Wilson; Wilson, OHC.

10. Fite, *Peek*, 232–36; Wilson, OHC.

11. *Ibid.*; interview with Wilson; Wilson to W. R. Ronald, September 21, 1932, Wilson Papers.

12. W. R. Ronald Memoir (Gilbert C. Fite Copy).

13. Arthur Hyde to Alexander Legge, June 4, Louis Clarke to Hyde, June 22, 1932, NA, RG 16.

14. Wilson to J. S. Davis, November 20, Wilson to Chester Davis, September 7, 1932, Wilson Papers.

15. John P. Gleason, "The Attitude of the Business Community toward Agriculture during the McNary-Haugen Period," *AH*, XXXII (April, 1958), 127–38.

16. Friedman, "Hyde," 533–61; interview with De Los James.

17. Grant McConnell, *The Decline of Agrarian Democracy*, Chap. 1.

18. Interview with De Los James; Wilson, OHC.

19. Wilson to J. S. Davis, March 25, 1932, Wilson Papers.

20. Wilson to J. S. Crutchfield, January 15, Wilson to McCarthy, September 7, 1932, *ibid.*; J. S. Davis memo, March 25, 1930, Teague Papers; Ben C. McCabe to customers of International Elevator Co., March 17, Nils Olsen to Arthur Hyde, April 23, 1930, NA, RG 16.

21. Minutes of the Chicago Meeting, Wilson to J. S. Davis, May 18, Wilson to W. R. Ronald, August 28, Wilson to Henry A. Wallace, September 15, 1932, Wilson to Rexford G. Tugwell, January 25, Wilson to Dr. Ramsey Spillman, February 27, 1933, Wilson Papers; Wilson to Stone, April 9, 1932, HF; Chester Davis to George Peek, April 18, Wilson to Charles McNary, April 20, 1932, Peek Papers; Wilson, OHC; Ronald Memoir.

22. Wilson to Clifford R. Hope, July 22, 1932, Wilson Papers.

23. Wilson to Wallace, March 25, Wilson to Hope, October 10, Wilson to Tugwell, July 25, Wilson to P. P. Gourrich, August 2, Wilson to J. D. Black, August 29, Wilson to McCarthy, September 7, Wilson to Ronald, September 21, 1932, *ibid.*; C. C. Webber to Peek, Peek Papers; *NYT*, October 13, 1932; Wilson, OHC.

24. Interview with Wilson; Wilson, OHC.

25. *Ibid.*; Wilson to Harriman, October 21, Harriman folder, Wilson to Ronald, July 27, Wilson to Crutchfield, October 22, 1932, Wilson Papers; Wilson to James Stone, April 9, 1932, HF; Harriman, "The Farm Problem," (mimeo, copy available in library of Wesleyan University, Middletown, Conn.), 1, 5, 16.

26. Wilson to E. A. Duddy, March 11, 1932, Wilson Papers; Arthur M.

Schlesinger, Jr., *The Age of Roosevelt: The Crisis of the Old Order, 1919–1933*, 182–83.

27. Harriman to I. M. Brandjord, Harriman to Wilson, November 8, 1932, Wilson Papers; Harriman, "The Farm Problem," 2–3, 17, 20, 34–35, 39.

28. Lord, *Wallaces*, 308; see also Earl Smith to Henry T. Rainey, November 11, 1932, Rainey Papers (Library of Congress); Wilson to Ezekiel, October 25, 1932, Chamber of Commerce, *The Dotted Line*, May 31, 1932, HF; *Minneapolis Tribune*, July 15, 1932; *St. Paul Dispatch*, July 16, 1932; *NYT*, December 4, 1932.

29. Wilson to Wood, July 13, 1934, NA, RG 16; Wilson to Tugwell, October 20, 1939, HF; Harriman to Wilson, May 19, June 9, August 4, October 10, Wilson to Tugwell, July 25, October 8, J. D. Black to Wilson, October 20, Wilson to Charles Brand, November 29, Wilson to J. S. Davis, November 30, 1932, Chamber of Commerce folder, Wilson Papers; Wilson, OHC; interview with De Los James; Boris Emmet and John E. Jeuck, *Catalogues and Counters: A History of Sears, Roebuck and Company*, 615–16.

30. Wilson to Rogers, July 22, August 3, 1932, and other correspondence in Rogers folder, Wilson to Harriman, May 4, 17, Wilson to Beardsley Ruml, May 18, Wilson to Chester Davis, September 7, Wilson to Ronald, August 29, September 14, October 29, Rogers to Alexander Legge, October 17, 1932, Wilson Papers; Wilson to Ezekiel, October 25, 1932, HF; Wilson, OHC.

31. Interview with Wilson; Archibald M. Woodruff, Jr., *Farm Mortgage Loans of Life Insurance Companies*, 1, 16, 30, 159–60.

32. Wilson to J. S. Davis, May 18, 1932, Wilson Papers.

33. O. J. Lacy to Wilson, September 28, 1938, NA, RG 16.

34. Robert M. Green, "Farm Mortgage Delinquencies and Foreclosures," *JFE*, XV (January, 1933), 22.

35. Wilson to Rogers, July 22, 1932, Wilson Papers.

36. Wilson to Lacy, January 24, 1933, *ibid*.

37. Wilson to Rogers, August 3, October 25, 1932, January 27, 1933, Wilson to Raymond Moley, August 22, September 6, Wilson to M. S. Winder, October 21, Wilson's speech to Mortgage Bankers Association, October 12, 1932, *ibid*.

38. Wilson to Clifford R. Hope, October 10, Rogers to Alexander Legge, October 17, Rogers to Wilson, October 29, Wilson to Ronald, November 30, 1932, *ibid*.

39. Wilson to Guy Bush, November 29, 1932, *ibid*.

40. Wilson to Hickman Price, October 28, Wilson to Ronald, September 21, 1932, *ibid*.

41. Wilson to J. D. Black, October 7, 1932, *ibid*.

42. Peek to Chester Davis, May 20, 1932, Peek Papers.

43. Saloutos and Hicks, *Agricultural Discontent*, 386, 394, 398, 410.

44. Simpson to Ronald, Wilson Papers, S. D. Gleason to Franklin Roose-

velt, December 27, 1932, Roosevelt Library, Group 27, Box 358; Saloutos and Hicks, *Agricultural Discontent*, 219, 229–31; Wilson, OHC.

45. Gilbert C. Fite, "John A. Simpson: The Southwest's Militant Farm
Leader," *MVHR*, XXXV (March, 1949), 576.

46. There is much evidence on this in the Wilson Papers.

47. Frank Hutchinson to Harriman, August 30, "Report of the 22nd Annual
Meeting of the Stockholders of the Montana Flour Mills," October 14,
C. R. McClave to Harriman, September 13, 1932; HF; "Minority Report
of Special Committee on Agricultural Policy Presented to the Board of
Directors, US Chamber of Commerce, January 13–14," Export Trade
Committee of Millers National Federation to Frank Hutchinson, Febru-
ary 2, 1933, Wilson Papers; Ronald Memoir; Rexford G. Tugwell, *The
Democratic Roosevelt: A Biography of Franklin D. Roosevelt*, 276.

48. McClave to Harriman, September 13, 1932, HF.

49. Hutchinson to Harriman, August 30, 1932, HF. On the basic ideas involved, see James Warren Prothro, *The Dollar Decade: Business Ideas
in the 1920's*.

50. "Minority Report of Special Committee on Agricultural Policy Presented
to the Board of Directors, US Chamber of Commerce, January 13–14,
1933," Wilson Papers.

51. There is much evidence in the Wilson Papers on his relations with the
processors during 1932 and early 1933. See also *The Domestic Allotment
Plan* (Chicago: The Millers National Federation, December 27, 1932),
McClave to Harriman, September 13, Wilson to Ezekiel, September 9,
S. A. Gallier memorandum for Rogers, October 14, O. D. Fisher to Fred
J. Lingham, September 22, 1932, HF; Wilson, OHC; Ronald to Franklin
Roosevelt, November 2, 1932, RL, PPF 74; Peek Diary, December, 1932,
January 23, March 9, 1933, Peek Papers.

52. Kirkendall, "L. C. Gray and the Supply of Agricultural Land," *AH*,
XXXVII (October, 1963), 210–14.

53. Tolley, "The Outlook as a Basis for Adjustment in the Better Farming
Areas," *Proceedings of the National Conference on Land Utilization*,
165–67.

54. Black to Nils Olsen, November 7, 1931, NA, RG 83; Black, *Farm Management*, 147–51.

55. *CR*, 72d Cong., 1st Sess., 2752 (January 26, 1932); *Wallaces' Farmer
and Iowa Homestead*, January 9, 1932.

56. Tolley and Stine, OHC; Charles M. Hardin, *Freedom in Agricultural
Education*, 159.

57. Louis S. Clarke to Hyde, April 15, 23, June 22, Hyde to Clarke, April 20,
Alexander Legge to Hyde, June 1, Hyde to Legge, June 4, Legge to Stone,
June 1, 1932, Wilson to J. S. Davis, January 14, 1935, NA, RG 16; Wilson
to Ezekiel, April 9, May 18, June 18, October 8, Ezekiel to Stone, April 15,
May 17, 18, 24, June 10, Wilson to Stone, April 9, 1932, HF; Wilson to
J. S. Davis, May 18, Wilson to Walter McCarthy, September 7, 1932,
Wilson Papers; Wilson, OHC; interview with Wilson.

58. Clarke to Peek, April 11, Wilson to Peek, May 29, June 1, Peek to Wilson, June 4, Peek to Frederic P. Lee, June 4, Peek to Chester Davis, June 8, 1932, Peek Papers; Wilson to Ezekiel, May 18, n.d. ("Tuesday"), Ezekiel to Stone, May 18, 1932, Wilson to Tugwell, October 20, 1939, HF; Wilson to A. H. Benton, May 18, Wilson to Wallace, May 19, Wilson to John R. Commons, September 21, Wilson to Hickman Price, October 28, 1932, Hope folder, Wilson Papers; Wilson, OHC; interview with John D. Black; Fite, *Peter Norbeck: Prairie Statesman*, 164, 167.

59. *CR*, 72d Cong., 1st Sess., 15393–98 (July 14, 1932), 15641–43 (July 16, 1932).

60. Wilson to Beardsley Ruml, May 18, 1932, Wilson to Walter McCarthy, September 7, 1932, Wilson Papers; Wilson, *Farm Relief*, 36–37; Wilson to Ezekiel, June 18, 1932, HF.

61. Edwin G. Nourse, Joseph S. Davis, and John D. Black, *Three Years of the Agricultural Adjustment Administration*, 13; William Starr Myers, ed., *The State Papers and Other Public Writings of Herbert Hoover*, I, 40, 70; *ibid.*, II, 259; *Wallaces' Farmer and Iowa Homestead*, October 1, 1932.

62. Lyman Wilbur and Arthur M. Hyde, *The Hoover Policies*, 156–57.

63. Daniel R. Fusfeld, *The Economic Thought of Franklin D. Roosevelt and the Origins of the New Deal*, 198.

64. Wilson, OHC; Wilson, "Agricultural Adjustments," *Western Farm Economics Association*, 1931, 105–6.

65. Edgar B. Nixon, comp. and ed., *Franklin D. Roosevelt and Conservation*, I, 109–10.

66. Wilson, NBC Radio Speech from Chicago, April, 1932. Wilson Papers.

67. Wilson to Moley, May 20, 1939, NA, RG 16; Eric Goldman, *Rendezvous with Destiny: A History of Modern American Reform*, 337; Lord, *Wallaces*, 318; Moley, *After Seven Years*, 15, 18–19; Bernard Sternsher, *Rexford Tugwell and the New Deal*, 39–41.

68. Gertrude Almy Slichter, "Franklin D. Roosevelt and the Farm Problem, 1929–1932," *MVHR*, XLIII (September, 1956), 243–49.

69. Tugwell, Notes for a New Deal Diary, December 31, 1932, RL, Group 21.

70. Lord, *Wallaces*, 381–82.

71. Tugwell, "Human Nature and Social Economy," *Journal of Philosophy*, XXVII (August 28, 1930), 481; Tugwell and Leon Keyserling, eds., *Redirecting Education*, I, 75; Tugwell, "A Planner's View of Agriculture's Future," *JFE*, XXXI (February, 1949), 45.

72. Tugwell, "The Place of Government in a National Land Program," *JFE*, XVI (January, 1934), 65.

73. Tugwell, *Industry's Coming of Age*, 26.

74. Tugwell, "Experimental Economics," in Tugwell, ed., *The Trend of Economics*, 422; Tugwell, "Chameleon Words," *New Republic*, XLVIII (August 27, 1926), 17; Tugwell, *Industry's Coming of Age*, 266–67.

75. Tugwell, ed., *The Trend of Economics*, 384; see Sternsher, *Tugwell*, 332.

76. Tugwell: "The Principle of Planning and the Institution of Laissez Faire,"

American Economic Review, XXII (sup.) (March, 1932), 75–92; "Needed Social and Political Adjustment," *Vital Speeches*, I (November 19, 1934), 98; "After the New Deal," *New Republic*, XCIX (July 26, 1939), 325; *The Trend of Economics*, viii, x, 382, 391, 394; "Economic Theory and Practice," *American Economic Review*, XIII (sup.) (March, 1923), 107–9; "Economics," in William Allan Neilson, ed., *Roads to Knowledge*; "Human Nature and Social Economy," *Journal of Philosophy*, XXVII (August 28, 1930), 490; *Industry's Coming of Age*; *The Industrial Discipline and the Governmental Arts*.

77. Tugwell: "Notes on the Life and Work of Simon Nelson Patten," *Journal of Political Economy*, XXXI (April, 1923), 154–208; "Experimental Economics," in *The Trend of Economics*; *Industry's Coming of Age*, 266–67; "Platforms and Candidates," *New Republic*, LV (May 30, 1928), 44–45; "Experimental Control in Russian Industry," *Political Science Quarterly*, XLIII (June, 1928), 161–87; "The Theory of Occupational Obsolescence," *ibid.*, XLVI (June, 1931), 171–227; and "Social Directives in Education," in Tugwell and Keyserling, *Redirecting Education*.

78. Tugwell, "The Preparation of a President," *Western Political Quarterly*, I (June, 1948), 143–45.

79. Tugwell: "Problem of Agriculture," *Political Science Quarterly*, XXXIX December, 1924), 549–91; "What Will Become of the Farmer?" *The Nation*, CXXIV (June 15, 1927), 664–66; "Reflections on Farm Relief," *Political Science Quarterly*, XLIII (December, 1928), 481–97; "Farm Relief and a Permanent Agriculture," *Annals of the American Academy*, CXLII (March, 1929), 271–82; "Agricultural Policy of France," *Political Science Quarterly*, XLV (June–December, 1930), 214–30, 405–28, 524–47; "The Place of Government in a National Land Program," *JFE*, 1934, 59–60, 64–65.

80. Tugwell, "Reflections on Farm Relief," *Political Science Quarterly*, 1928, 490; Tugwell, Diary, December 31, 1932; Moley, *After Seven Years*, 22; Wilson to Clifford Hope, October 10, 1932, Wilson Papers.

81. Sternsher, *Tugwell*, 178.

82. Tugwell, *The Democratic Roosevelt*, 232; Tugwell, Diary, December 31, 1932; Wilson to Ralph Budd, July 22, 1932, Wilson Papers; Wilson and Ezekiel, OHC; interview with John D. Black; Black, Review of Lord, *Wallaces*, in *JFE*, XXIX (August, 1947), 775.

83. Tugwell, "A Planner's View of Agriculture's Future," *JFE*, 1949, 33.

84. *NYT*, August 16, 1934.

85. Tugwell, "The Place of Government in a National Land Program," *JFE*, 1934, 59–60.

86. Tugwell, *The Democratic Roosevelt*, 233.

87. Samuel I. Rosenman, ed., *The Public Papers and Addresses of Franklin D. Roosevelt*, I, 654–55; Tugwell, Diary, December 31, 1932; *Wallaces' Farmer and Iowa Homestead*, August 20, 1932; Peek to S. P. Bush, August 3, 1932, Peek Papers; Wilson, OHC.

88. Wilson to Budd, July 22, Wilson to Hope, October 10, 1932, Wilson

Papers; Louis S. Clarke to Peek, July 18, 1932, Peek Papers; Wilson, OHC; interview with Wilson; Wilson to Herman Kahn, January 17, 1956, RL, Group 31; Wilson to Moley, May 20, 1939, NA, RG 16; Tugwell, Diary, December 31, 1932; Moley, *After Seven Years*, 41.

89. Wilson memo, RL, Group 31; Wilson to Henry Morgenthau, July 28, August 22, Wilson to Moley, August 22, 1932, Wilson Papers; Moley to Wilson, May 18, 1939, NA, RG 16; Wilson to Ezekiel, September 9, 1932, HF.

90. Wilson to Stockton, September 15, 1932, Wilson Papers; Wallace to William Hirth, August 20, 1932, Hirth Papers (Western Historical Manuscripts Collection, University of Missouri); Wilson to Herman Kahn, January 17, 1956, RL, Group 31; Moley to Wilson, May 18, 1939, NA, RG 16; Wilson, OHC.

91. Rosenman, *Public Papers and Addresses of Roosevelt*, I, 693, 703–4.

92. Wilson to Raymond Moley, August 22, Wilson to John D. Black, October 7, 1932, Wilson Papers.

93. Rosenman, *Public Papers and Addresses of Roosevelt*, I, 699–701.

94. Wilson to Christgau, October 6, Wilson to Black, October 7, 25, Wilson to Tugwell, October 24, 1932, Wilson Papers.

95. Wilson to Hickman Price, October 28, Wilson to J. W. Wilson, September 21, 1932, *ibid.*

96. Wilson to A. H. Benton, September 20, Wilson to J. W. Wilson, September 21, Wilson to Moley, September 28, Wilson to Ronald, September, 1932, *ibid.*; Wilson to Ezekiel, October 8, 1932, HF.

97. *Wallaces' Farmer and Iowa Homestead*, October 1, 1932.

98. Wilson to Moley, September 28, Wilson to Black, October 7, Wilson to Hope, October 10, Wilson to J. S. Davis, October 26, Ronald to Verne Brady, November 7, 1932, Wilson Papers; Wilson to Ezekiel, October 8, 1932, HF; Clifford V. Gregory, "The American Farm Bureau Federation and the A.A.A.," in Harwood L. Childs, ed., *Pressure Groups and Propaganda, Annals of the American Academy of Political and Social Science*, CLXXIX (May, 1935), 152.

99. Wilson to Black, October 7, 25, Wilson to Moley, September 28, October 6, Wilson to Tugwell, October 24, Wilson to Harriman, October 21, Wilson to J. S. Davis, October 26, Ronald to Verne Brady, November 7, 1932, Wilson Papers.

100. November 2, 1932, RL, PPF 74; Wilson to E. J. MacMillan, May 18, 1936, NA, RG 16.

101. Slichter, "Roosevelt and the Farm Problem," *MVHR*, 1956, 250–51, 255–58; Frank Freidel, *Franklin D. Roosevelt: The Triumph*, 344–48; Sternsher, *Tugwell*, 185.

102. Ronald Memoir.

103. Wilson, "A Land-Use Program for the Federal Government," *JFE*, XV (April, 1933), 219.

104. Tolley, OHC.

NOTES TO CHAPTER 3

1. *NYT*, November 24, 27, 1932.
2. William R. Johnson, "National Farm Organizations and the Reshaping of Agricultural Policy in 1932," *AH*, XXXVII (January, 1963), 41; *Bureau Farmer*, VIII (January, 1933), 6, 16; *ibid.* (February, 1933), 24; *ibid.* (March, 1933), 6, 23; Orville M. Kile, *The Farm Bureau Through Three Decades*, 191–92.
3. Ezekiel to Wilson, October 17, James Stone to Marvin Jones, December 20, 1932, HF; Wilson to Walter McCarthy, September 7, 1932, Wilson Papers.
4. Wilson to Ezekiel, October 25, 1932, HF.
5. Ezekiel, "The Need for Production Control in the Allotment Plan," November 17, 1932, HF.
6. *NYT*, December 8, 1932; Lord, *Wallaces*, 310, 313; Henry T. Rainey to Earl Smith, November 23, 1932, Rainey Papers; Wilson to Tugwell, October 20, 1939, HF; Ezekiel, OHC; interview with Ezekiel.
7. Wilson to W. R. Ronald, November 25, 30, December 22, 1932, January 11, 25, 1933, Ronald to Wilson, November 28, 30, Moley to Wilson, November 28, 29, Wilson to Moley, November 28, Wilson to J. S. Davis, November 30, December 23, 1932, January 28, 1933, M. S. Winder to Wilson, December 22, Wilson to Rogers, December 23, 1932, Wilson to Lacy, January 13, Wilson to R. D. Lusk, January 20, Wilson to Stanton D. Wicks, January 25, 1933, Wilson Papers; Tugwell, Diary, December 25, 26, 31, 1932, January 11, 12, 14, 21, 29, 31, February 27, 1933, RL, Group 21; Fred Lee to Earl Smith, December 5, Peek Diary, December 16, 23, 1932, Peek Papers; Ezekiel to Stone *et al.*, January 20, 1933, Ezekiel to Wilson, June 23, 1936, Ezekiel to Tugwell, October 20, 1939, HF; *NYT*, December 13, 14, 15, 16, 29, 1932, January 2, 4, 5, 1933; Ronald Memoir; Wilson and Ezekiel, OHC; Edward A. O'Neal memorandum to all State Farm Bureau Federations, March 2, 1933, HF.
8. Peek Diary, December 2, 6, 10, 12, 15, 16, 1932, January 11, February 1, 1933, Peek Papers; Peek, *Why Quit Our Own?* 63–65, 71, 73, 75.
9. *NYT*, January 4, 8, 12, 1933.
10. *NYT*, December 18, 29, 1932, January 19, 26, February 7, 11, 12, 16, 1933.
11. *NYT*, January 26, 1933; Fite, "Simpson," *MVHR*, XXXV (March, 1949), 578.
12. *NYT*, January 4, 8, 14, 15, 17, 18, 19, 20, 21, 1933; Ezekiel to Tugwell, June 20, 1932, HF; John Blum, *From the Morgenthau Diaries*, 29, 38–40, 42.
13. Pamphlets Issued by Institute of American Meat Packers, Rainey Papers; *NYT*, December 11, 15, 16, 17, 18, 20, 22, 1932, January 2, 3, 9, 12, 17, 20, 28, 30, 31, February 7, 27, 1933.
14. *NYT*, December 11, 15, 24, 25, 1932; January 4, 5, 7, 9, 11, 13, 15, 16, 25, February 14, 1933.

15. *NYT*, January 3, 5, 9, 12, 31, 1933; Ezekiel to Arthur D. Gayer, February 3, 1933, HF.
16. Wilson, *Farm Relief*, 38; Ezekiel, Summary of Comments on H.R. 133991 as passed by the House, January 14, 1933, HF.
17. *NYT*, January 10, 20, 28, February 2, 8, 12, 16, 17, March 9, 1933; O'Neal to all State Farm Bureau Federations, March 2, 1933, HF.
18. Ezekiel to Tolley, February 15, 1933, HF; *NYT*, December 29, 31, 1932, January 2, 17, 20, February 2, 21, 1933.
19. Tugwell, Diary, December 31, 1932, January 5, 7, 11, 12, 14, 16, 17, 21, 24, 29, February 27, 1933; Wilson to J. S. Davis, January 28, Wilson to O. J. Lacy, January 13, 24, Wilson to Stanton D. Wicks, January 25, Wilson to Ronald, January 11, Wilson to Rogers, January 13, Wilson to J. W. Wilson, January 16, 1933, Wilson Papers; Tugwell, *The Democratic Roosevelt*, 266.
20. Wilson, *Farm Relief*, 37–39; Wilson to Lacy, January 13, Wilson to Lusk, January 20, 1933, Wilson Papers.
21. Wilson, *Farm Relief*, 6; Wilson to J. W. Wilson, February 3, 1933, Wilson Papers.
22. *Wallaces' Farmer and Iowa Homestead*, 1930–1932; Malcolm O. Sillars, "Henry A. Wallace's Editorials on Agricultural Discontent, 1921–1928," *AH*, XXVI (October, 1952), 132–40; Wallace speech, March 22, 1932, Donald Murphy to Wilson, April 4, 1932, HF; Wilson, Ezekiel, and Stine, OHC; interviews with Wilson, Christgau, and Wallace; Tugwell, Diary, December 25, 31, 1932, January 7, 10, 14, 18, 1933; Tugwell, *The Democratic Roosevelt*, 267–78; Schlesinger, *Crisis of the Old Order*, 108–10, 469; Christiana M. Campbell, *The Farm Bureau and the New Deal*, 62; Gladys L. Baker, *et al.*, *Century of Service: the first 100 years of The United States Department of Agriculture*, 163–64.
23. Shideler, *Farm Crisis*, 123–41.
24. Wallace, "Farm Economists and Agricultural Planning," *JFE*, XVIII (February, 1936), 1, 11.
25. Ezekiel to E. G. Nourse, January 20, 1932, HF; Ezekiel and Wilson, OHC; interview with Ezekiel.
26. Wilson, OHC; Secretary of Agriculture file, Wilson Papers.
27. Tugwell, Diary, December 30, 1932, January 13, 14, February 10, 12, 13, 15, 18, 1933; Paul Appleby to W. W. Waymack, March 1, 1935, NA, RG 16; Schlesinger, *Crisis of the Old Order*, 473; Wallace to William Hirth, August 20, 1932, Hirth Papers.
28. Sternsher, *Tugwell*, 88.
29. Baker, *Century of Service*, 247.
30. Wallace to Roosevelt, May 16, 1933, RL, PPF 471; Report of Special Committee of Farm Organization Leaders, RL, OF, 227xyz; Wallace to Wilson, March 8, 9, Wilson to J. W. Wilson, April 7, 1933, Wilson Papers; Ezekiel to O'Neal and Gregory, March 7, 1933, NA, RG 16; Peek Diary, March 11, 16, 1933; Tugwell, Diary, March 31, April 2, 14, 1933; Ezekiel to Wilson, June 22, 1936, Ezekiel to Tugwell, Octo-

ber 20, 1939, HF; Wilson and Ezekiel, OHC; interview with Wallace; Ronald Memoir; *NYT*, March 9, 10, 11, 12, 1933; Tugwell, *The Democratic Roosevelt*, 274–77; Schlesinger, *The Age of Roosevelt: The Coming of the New Deal*, 38–41; Campbell, *Farm Bureau*, 53, 55; Gregory, "The American Farm Bureau Federation and the A.A.A.," in Childs, ed., *Pressure Groups and Propaganda*, 155–56.

31. *NYT*, March 15, 18, 19, 20, 22, 23, 25, 26, 28, 31, April 1, 4, 8, 9, 12, 13, 16, 29, May 6, 7, 9, 10, 11, 13, 1933; Sydney Anderson to Wallace, March 10, 1933, Simpson to Roosevelt, May 6, Roosevelt to Simpson, May 16, 1933, NA, RG 16; Anderson, Clayton and Co., Circular, March 20, 1933, Rainey Papers; Wallace to Roosevelt, April 22, 1933, RL, OF 1; Ronald Memoir; Campbell, *Farm Bureau*, 55–56; Fite, "Simpson," *MVHR*, 1949, 579–81; Fite, "Farmer Opinion and the Agricultural Adjustment Act," *ibid.*, XLVIII (March, 1962), 660–69. Contradicting the story in the *New York Times*, Wilson and Ezekiel maintain that they were not present for the signing. Gladys L. Baker to author, October 28, 1965.

32. Wilson to Paul Gourrich, June 27, 1932, Wilson Papers; Tugwell, *Diary*, December 31, 1932; Peek to Chester Davis, May 20, 1932; Peek Papers; Ronald Memoir; Henry A. Wallace, *New Frontiers*, 163; Schlesinger, *Crisis of the Old Order*, 106; Campbell, *Farm Bureau*, 41–42, 55; Robert L. Tontz, "Origin of the Base Period Concept of Parity — A Significant Value Judgement in Agricultural Policy," *AH*, XXXII (January, 1958), 3–13; Tontz, "Legal Parity: Implementations of the Policy of Equality for Agriculture, 1929–1954," *AH*, XXIX (October, 1954), 174–81.

33. Ezekiel to Wallace, April 13, 1933, HF.

34. Murray Benedict, *Farm Policies of the United States, 1790–1950: A Study of Their Origins and Development*, 304–5; Fite, *Peek*, 247–49, 252.

35. Peek Diary, April 2, 1933; Peek, *Why Quit Our Own?* 80–91, 93.

36. O'Neal radio speech, March 10, 1934, RL, PPF 1820, Agriculture; McConnell, *Agrarian Democracy*, 71; Campbell, *Farm Bureau*, 56–57, 63; Benedict, *Farm Policies*, 339, 346.

37. Saloutos, *Farmer Movements in the South, 1865–1933*, 281.

38. S. D. Gleason to Roosevelt and Simpson, December 27, 1932, RL, Group 27, Box 358.

39. *Rural New Yorker*, XCII (January 28, 1933), 63.

40. Victor Knauth memo, March 6, 1933, RL, OF 396.

41. Fite, "Farmer Opinion," *MVHR*, 1962, 672–73; compare Orris Dorman to Henry Rainey, December 5, 1932, Rainey Papers; Burke H. Critchfield to Wilson, January 13, 1933, HF; and *NYT*, February 12, 1933.

42. John D. Black, "Planning, Control and Research in Agriculture after Recovery," *JFE*, XVII (February, 1935), 22–24; Harold B. Rowe, *Tobacco under the AAA*, 21–22; Ezekiel to Wallace, December 4, 1934, NA, RG 16.

43. Wilson to Tugwell, October 24, 1932, Wilson Papers.

44. Tugwell, Diary, January 11, 1933.

NOTES TO CHAPTER 4

1. Farm Leaders to Wallace and Peek, May 18, 1933, NA, RG 83; Wallace to E. R. Kindler, July 25, 1933, NA, RG 145; Wilson to J. P. Fabrick, July 17, 1934, NA, RG 16; *NYT*, May 27, 1933; Joseph S. Davis, *Wheat and the AAA*, 50–51; Rowe, *Tobacco under the AAA*, 94–95, 105–6, 273, 280–81; Peek, *Why Quit Our Own?* 106–7, 140; Benedict, *Farm Policies*, 311; Wilson, OHC.

2. Tolley, OHC; Peek to R. G. Sproul, October 7, 1933, NA, RG 145; USDA Press Release, June 22, 1933, NA, RG 16; interview with Tolley; *NYT*, October 15, 1933; *Wisconsin Agriculturist and Farmer*, LX (June 10, 1933), 6; *Pacific Rural Press*, July 8, 1933; Benedict, *Farm Policies*, 304–6.

3. Schlesinger, *Coming of the New Deal*, 61–64; Baker, *Century of Service*, 148–53; Ezekiel, "Plowing the Farm Facts Under," HF; Executive Secretary of the Executive Council to the President, October 24, 1933, Executive Secretary to Members of the Executive Council, November 7, 1933, RL, OF 570; Benedict, *Farm Policies*, 306–8, 311–13; Saloutos and Hicks, *Agricultural Discontent*, 474–77.

4. Wallace to Roosevelt, September 7, 1933, RL, OF 1; Executive Secretary to Executive Council, October 23, 1933, Report of the Executive Secretary of the Executive Council, August 21, 1934, RL, OF 570; Benedict, *Farm Policies*, 332, 333, 335, 380–81, 386; Schlesinger, *Coming of the New Deal*, 64–67; Baker, *Century of Service*, 152, 156; Blum, *From the Morgenthau Diaries*, 52–54, 65–66.

5. Ezekiel to Wallace, August 15, 1933, Ezekiel to Tugwell, October 20, 1939, HF; Ezekiel to Wallace, August 17, November 7, Ezekiel to Stanton Wicks, December 20, 1933, Ezekiel to Christgau, January 11, 1934, NA, RG 16; Wilson and Bean, OHC; interview with Ezekiel.

6. Ezekiel to H. Clemens Horst, September 23, 1935, NA, RG 16.

7. I. G. Davis, "The Social Science Fellowships in Agricultural Economics and Rural Sociology," *JFE*, XVI (July, 1934), 501.

8. W. F. Callandar to Nils Olsen, November 27, 1933, NA, RG 83.

9. Peek to W. L. Westervelt, December 29, 1933, NA, RG 145.

10. Peek Diary, March 11, 18, 22, 25, 29, April 1, 5, 6, May 3, 1933, Mrs. Peek's Diary, Peek Papers; Peek, *Why Quit Our Own?* 92, 98–102, 155; Fite, *Peek*, 243, 252–54; Wallace to Roosevelt, May 15, 1933, RL, OF 1; Tugwell, Diary, February 13, 26, April 3, 1933, RL, Group 21; Tugwell, *The Democratic Roosevelt*, 239, 286, 371; Schlesinger, *Coming of the New Deal*, 46–49; Wilson, OHC; Sternsher, *Tugwell*, 189–94, 199.

11. Peek, *Why Quit Our Own?* 140–46; Fite, *Peek*, 244–51; *NYT*, December 17, 1933; Wallace, *New Frontiers*, 168–69; Ernest K. Lindley and Jay Franklin (The Unofficial Observer), *The New Dealers*, 146–50; Rowe, *Tobacco under the AAA*, 18–20, 105–6, 280–81.

12. Frank to Wallace, December 7, 1933, NA, RG 16.

13. See NA, RG 16, General Correspondence under headings, "Criticisms,"

"Politics," and "Correspondence of the General Counsel of the AAA"; *NYT*, December 7, 8, 12, 14, 1933, June 15, 1936; Lindley and Franklin, *New Dealers*, 98–99, 322; Schlesinger, *Coming of the New Deal*, 49–59; Fite, *Peek*, 256, 259–62, 264–65; Sternsher, *Tugwell*, 195–200; Stine and Bean, OHC; Frank to Peek, October 5, Frank to Wayne Taylor, October 20, Peek to Wallace, November 15, 25, 1933, Peek Papers; Brand to Roosevelt, December 14, 1933, RL, OF 1-K; Frank to Moley, July 1, 11, 1938, Frank Papers (Yale University); Frank, *Save America First: How to Make Our Democracy Work*, 260–63.

14. *NYT*, May 5, December 9, 10, 12, 1933, January 4, March 1, 1934, December 1, 1935; Roosevelt Press Conferences, May 19, December 8, 1933, November 23, 1934, RL, PPF 1-P; Peek to Roosevelt, December 15, Roosevelt to Peek, December 18, 1933, RL, OF 1-K; Davis to Peek, February 5, 1932, Clyde King to Peek, December 4, Peek to King, December 15, Peek to Chester Davis, December 16, 1933, Peek Papers; Executive Secretary to Members of Executive Council, November 11, 1933, RL, OF 570; Wilson to James Stone, April 9, 1932, Ezekiel to Tugwell, October 20, 1939, HF; interviews with Appleby and Tugwell; Fite, *Peek*, 256–58, 262–66; Sternsher, *Tugwell*, 200–202; Saloutos and Hicks, *Agricultural Discontent*, 471–72, 487–88; Schlesinger, *Crisis of the Old Order*, 109–10; Schlesinger, *Coming of the New Deal*, 48–59.

15. Baker, *Century of Service*, 248.

16. Donald R. Murphy to Appleby, December 8, Appleby to Murphy, December 16, Wallace to Murphy, December 19, 1933, Appleby to F. W. Loring, March 2, 1934, NA, RG 16.

17. Benedict, *Farm Policies*, 284.

18. Tugwell, *The Democratic Roosevelt*, 267–68; see also 313.

NOTES TO CHAPTER 5

1. Wilson to W. A. Lloyd, February 20, 1933, Wilson to Tugwell, October 24, 1932, Wilson Papers; Tugwell, Diary, December 31, 1932, January 6, February 27, March 31, April 3, 14, 21, May 3, 1933, RL, Group 21; Lord, *Wallaces*, 322.

2. Paul K. Conkin, *Tomorrow a New World: The New Deal Community Program*, 86–89, 130; Wilson, OHC; Wilson to J. W. Wilson, July 6, Wilson to Eric Gugler, September 1, 1934, NA, RG 16; W. Howard Bishop to Roosevelt, May 6, 1933, RL, OF 503; Schlesinger, *Coming of the New Deal*, 362–63.

3. "Explanation of Subsistence Homesteads and Cooperatives among the Unemployed," "Information on Subsistence Homesteads," NA, RG 96; Report of the Executive Secretary of the Executive Council, August 21, 1934, RL, OF 570; Conkin, *Tomorrow a New World*, 104 ff.

4. Wilson, OHC; Ezekiel, "Plowing the Farm Facts Under," 9–10, HF.

5. Schlesinger, *Coming of the New Deal*, 367–68; Conkin, *Tomorrow a New World*, 100–102, 118.

6. Ely to Wilson, October 25, 1934, NA, RG 16.

7. Baker to Wilson and Tugwell, August 11, Baker to W. F. Willcox, September 7, 1933, *ibid.*

8. Wilson, OHC; Schlesinger, *Coming of the New Deal*, 367; Conkin, *Tomorrow a New World*, 113, 116–17, 123–24, 250; Sternsher, *Tugwell*, 266–67; W. C. Coffey to O. E. Baker, October 2, 1933, NA, RG 16; Executive Secretary to Members of the Executive Council, April 25, 1934, RL, OF 788.

9. Wilson to Ralph Barsodi, September 18, 1934, NA, RG 16.

10. Wilson to Bernarr Macfadden, August 29, 1934, *ibid.*

11. *The Secret Diary of Harold L. Ickes*, I, 129–30, 154, 159–60, 162, 217, 218, 241, 253, 272–73, 288; *ibid.*, II, 669; Wilson, OHC; interviews with Ernst H. Wiecking and Carl C. Taylor; Conkin, *Tomorrow a New World*, 107, 119–24.

12. *Ibid.*, 122 and Chap. 10; Schlesinger, *Coming of the New Deal*, 364–66; Alfred B. Rollins, Jr., *Roosevelt and Howe*, 406–13; Nixon, *Roosevelt and Conservation*, I, 273; Wilson, OHC.

13. Wilson to John Nolen, July 14, 1934, NA, RG 16; Wilson, OHC; interview with Wilson.

14. Conkin, *Tomorrow a New World*, 113, 115–16, 125.

15. Report of the Executive Secretary of the Executive Council, August 21, 1934, RL, OF 570.

16. "Consideration of Decentralization of Industry," November 15, 1934, RL, OF 3-Q.

17. Conkin, *Tomorrow a New World*, 125, 129.

18. Wilson to Everett C. Hughes, January 18, Wilson to Henry Harriman, January 24, 1940, Wilson to L. J. Taber, August 17, 1939, NA, RG 16.

19. Conkin, *Tomorrow a New World*, 94–103, 127; G. E. Pynchon to Richard T. Ely, October 30, 1934, NA, RG 16.

20. Wallace to Roosevelt, July 27, Gray to Olsen, July 26, 1933, Wallace to Ickes, June 16, 1934, *ibid.*; Ezekiel, OHC; Ezekiel to J. S. Lansill, September 21, 1934, HF; Conference with Farm Paper Editors, February 23, 1934, NA, RG 145.

21. Wallace to Ickes, July 27, 1933, NA, RG 16. Mead was the chief of the Bureau of Reclamation.

22. Nixon, *Roosevelt and Conservation*, I, 166–67; "Removal of Poor Farm Lands from Cultivation as an Offset to the Development of Arable Acreage through Reclamation," October 12, 1933, NA, RG 16.

23. Ezekiel to J. S. Lansill, September 21, 1934, Ickes to Secretary of Agriculture, July 23, 1935, Wallace to Wilson, n.d., Charles Eliot, II, to Secretary of Interior, HF; Meeting of the Executive Council, August 1, Wallace Report on the Progress of the Department of Agriculture, December 22, 1933, RL, OF 570; Ickes to Wallace, July 28, Roosevelt to Secretary of Agriculture, August 15, Ickes to Wallace, August 24, Wallace to Attorney General, September 21, Wilson *et al.* to Ickes, August 31, Ezekiel to Tugwell, November 22, 1933, Ezekiel to Wallace, January 6, 1934, NA, RG 16; Conference with Farm Paper Editors, February 23, 1934, NA, RG 145; interview with Tugwell.

24. Wallace to Attorney General, October 5, Cummings to Ickes, October 5, Ickes to Wallace, October 11, 1933, Grover B. Hill to Mrs. A. B. Curry, September 4, 1940, NA, RG 16; Ezekiel to Lansill, September 21, 1934, HF; Phil Hooker, "Chronology of the Land Utilization Program," 1941, NA, RG 96.

25. W. W. Robertson to Wallace, October 2, Clarence D. Martin to Roosevelt, October 2, Wallace to Marshall N. Dana, October 28, 1933, Dana to Wallace, October 23, 1933, NA, RG 16; Dana to Louis Howe, February 25, 1933, RL, OF 402; Conference with Farm Paper Editors, February 23, 1934, NA, RG 145; Edward H. Foley, Jr., Memorandum, September 19, Ezekiel to Tugwell, November 22, 1933, HF.

26. Ezekiel to Wallace, September 1, Eliot to Wallace, October 24, 1933, NA, RG 16; Eliot to Secretary of Interior, October 24, Wallace to Secretary of Interior, November 1, Ickes to Secretary of Agriculture, November 3, 1933, "Planning Land Planning," HF; Wilson, "The Report on Land of the National Resources Board," *JFE*, XVII (February, 1935), 41–42.

27. Gray to Milton Eisenhower, April 8, USDA Press Release, May 9, 1933, NA, RG 83; National Resources Board, "National Land Planning Activities," July, 1934, NA, RG 16; Ezekiel to Seth Thomas, January 27, Wallace to Roosevelt, January 27, 1934, HF; Nixon, *Roosevelt and Conservation*, I, 258, 272–73, 280, 293–94, 296–302, 306–7, 313–14; Roy M. Robbins, *Our Landed Heritage: The Public Domain, 1776–1936*, 417, 423.

28. Tugwell, "The Place of Government in a National Land Program," *JFE*, XVI (January, 1934), 55–69; Ezekiel to Lansill, February 15, Ezekiel to Chris L. Christensen, January 11, 1934, "Report on Uneconomic Farming," October 17, 1933, NA, RG 16; Gray to Ezekiel, December 2, 1933, NA, RG 83.

29. Gray to F. D. Farrell, September 21, 1933, *ibid.*

30. Gray to Farrell, September 21, Gray to Ezekiel, August 31, 1933, *ibid.*

31. National Resources Committee, "Progress Report," June 15, 1936, National Resources Board, "National Land Planning Activities," July, 1934, NA, RG 16.

32. Davis to Nils Olsen, November 9, 1933, NA, RG 83; USDA Press Release, September 27, 1933, June 5, 1936, NA, RG 16; Tolley, Wilson, and Hutson, OHC; Chester Davis, "The Program of Agricultural Adjustment," *JFE*, XVI (January, 1934), 95; Davis, "The Place of Farmers, Economists and Administrators in Developing Agricultural Policy," *JFE*, XXII (February, 1940), 1–9; Edward C. Banfield, "Organization for Policy Planning in the U.S. Department of Agriculture," *JFE*, XXXIV (February, 1952), 18.

33. There is much evidence on this story in NA, RG 16 and RG 83. See also Tolley, Stine, Bean, Wilson, and Hutson, OHC; Henry C. Taylor to Olsen, December 5, 1933, Stine to Taylor, April 25, Taylor to Stine, May 8, J. D. Black to Taylor, July 12, 1934, Taylor to A. G. Black, April 20, Wallace to Taylor, April 30, 1935, Taylor Papers (The State Historical Society of Wisconsin); Wallace, first draft of memorandum from Secre-

tary to Mr. Olsen, HF; A. G. Black, "Agricultural Policy and the Economist," *JFE*, XVIII (May, 1936), 311–19; A. G. Black, "The Need for Generalists," *JFE*, XVIII (November, 1936), 657–61, and J. D. Black, "The Bureau of Agricultural Economics — the Years in Between," *JFE*, XXIX (November, 1947), 1033. This discussion also draws upon interviews with Wilson, Appleby, and Englund.

34. Tolley, OHC; Gray to J. D. Black, June 20, 1933, NA, RG 83; Lord, *Wallaces*, 384–85.

35. Tolley, "The Program Planning Division of the Agricultural Adjustment Administration," *JFE*, XVI (April, 1934), 583, 584; Gray, Report to Assistant Secretary Wilson, August 29, 1934, NA, RG 16; Wells to Englund, February 27, 1940, Holmes to Englund, August 4, 1934, NA, RG 83; Margaret R. Purcell, "A Quarter Century of Land Economics in the Department of Agriculture — 1919–44," October, 1945, HF; Case and Williams, *Fifty Years of Farm Management*, 239–40.

36. Elliott, "Progress and Problems in Regional Agricultural Planning from the National Point of View," *JFE*, XVIII (February, 1936), 96; Tolley, "Program Planning Division," *JFE*, 1934, 582.

37. *Ibid.*, 586, 588–89; Bean, OHC; Report of the Executive Secretary of the Executive Council, August 21, 1934, RL, OF 570; Wilson to Orris Dorman, October 9, Wilson to Dr. Raymond L. Buell, August 7, Wallace to Roosevelt, c. November 27, Ezekiel to Karl M. Mitchell, June 4, 1934, NA, RG 16.

38. Ezekiel to Tolley, September 14, 1934, NA, RG 145; Olsen to Holmes, September 18, Olsen to Smith Brookhart, October 31, 1934, "Statement with Respect to Land-Use Planning Research or Related Work with the AAA," December 1, 1937, Wells to Englund, February 27, 1940, Elliott, "Consumption Habits and Production Programs," October 30, 1934, Steibeling to Ernest Kelley, February 25, Stine to Wilson, May 23, 1941, NA, RG 83; L. J. Fletcher to E. G. Nourse, December 18, 1934, NA, RG 16; Wilson, "Nutritional Science and Agricultural Policy," *JFE*, XXIV (February, 1942), 197–200; Tugwell, "A Planner's View of Agriculture's Future," *JFE*, XXXI (February, 1949), 33–37, 44; Lord, *Wallaces*, 385–87; Benedict, *Farm Policies*, 278, 385–86.

39. Tugwell to Roosevelt, September 28, 1934, RL, OF 1; Agriculture Department report to Executive Council, October 2, 1934, RL, OF 570; Tolley, OHC; interviews with Wilson, Elliott, and Bushrod Allin; Clifford B. Anderson, "The Metamorphosis of American Agrarian Idealism in the 1920's and 1930's," *AH*, XXXV (October, 1961), 182–87.

40. Joseph S. Davis, "Agricultural Fundamentalism," reprinted in O. B. Jesness, ed., *Readings in Agricultural Policy*, 5.

41. Ezekiel to Jennie Levitake, December 2, 1939, NA, RG 16.

42. Ezekiel, "The Shift in Agricultural Policy toward Human Welfare," *JFE*, XXIV (May, 1942), 475.

43. Ezekiel to Wallace, October 20, 1933, RL, OF 1; Ezekiel to Miss Lacy, August 5, 1933, Ezekiel to G. A. Dole, March 10, 1934, Ezekiel to Wilson, December 2, 1935, Ezekiel to Persia Campbell, March 11, 1937, Ezekiel

to D. P. Trent, July 14, Ezekiel to Robert Sher, September 22, Ezekiel to Wallace, December 4, 1938, NA, RG 16; Ezekiel to Secretary, December 4, 1934, HF; *NYT*, November 28, 1933, July 14, December 9, 1934, February 26, March 9, 1936; April 25, 1937; Lord, *Wallaces*, 355; Schlesinger, *Coming of the New Deal*, 215–18.

44. Roy M. Pike memorandum, October 19, 1933, NA, RG 16.
45. Ezekiel to Bean, August 15, 1940, in Bean, OHC; Wilson, OHC; interview with Ezekiel.
46. Executive Secretary to Members of Executive Council, April 25, 1934, RL, OF 788.
47. "Discussion by H. R. Tolley," *JFE*, XVII (February, 1935), 37.
48. Karl Brandt, "The Orientation of Agricultural Economics," *JFE*, XXXVII (December, 1955), 794; Lauren K. Soth, "Making Economics Understandable," *JFE*, XXVIII (August, 1946), 852, Leonard A. Salter, Jr., *A Critical Review of Research in Land Economics*, 51.
49. Ezekiel to Wallace, January 6, 1934, NA, RG 16.
50. Wallace to Bureau Chiefs, March 2, Ezekiel to Jacob Baker, March 19, 1934, ibid.; Wallace to Baker, March 28, "Submarginal Land Program, Circular of Instructions, No. 1, June 7, 1934," NA, RG 145.
51. "Tentative Statement as to Policies in the Expenditure of the $25,000,000 allotted by the PWA for the Purchase of Submarginal Land," March 9, 1934, FERA, "The Land Program," HF; C. F. Clayton to John Dreier, January 10, 1935, NA, RG 145; Gray, "National Land Planning," "Functions of the Division of Land Economics in Relation to the Federal Program of Land Planning," February 9, 1934, NA, RG 16.
52. Gray to A. R. Mann, April 12, Gray to H. L. Price, May 25, 1934, NA, RG 145.
53. "Comments by Paul W. Gates," *AH*, XXXVII (October, 1963), 214.
54. Gray to Mann, April 12, 1934, NA, RG 145; Gray, "National Land Planning," March 5, 1934, NA, RG 16.
55. Amendment to Act of May 12, 1933, Explanation of Attached Amendment, Proposed Amendments, Wallace to Senator Joseph T. Robinson, March 2, 1934, HF; Nixon, *Roosevelt and Conservation*, I, 262–63, 268–71, 325; Ezekiel to Tugwell, March 5, 1934, NA, RG 16.
56. Nixon, *Roosevelt and Conservation*, I, 291.
57. *Ibid.*, 298–99; *NYT*, June 21, 1934.
58. Nixon, *Roosevelt and Conservation*, I, 290.
59. *Ibid.*, 317–18, 332.
60. Wilson, OHC; J. D. Black to H. C. Taylor, July 12, September 18, 1934, Jesse Tapp to Taylor, July 19, 1934, Taylor Papers; "Planning Land Planning," HF; Wilson to John Dexter, August 2, Wilson to Elmer Starch, July 3, Wilson to J. M. Hamilton, July 27, Wilson to J. P. Fabrick, July 17, 1934, NA, RG 16.
61. Wilson to Harold P. Fabian, July 14, 1934, *ibid.*
62. Wilson to Ronald, September 24, 1934, *ibid.*
63. NRB, *A Report on National Planning and Public Works in Relation to Natural Resources and Including Land Use and Water Resources with*

Findings and Recommendations, December 1, 1934, Part II; Wilson, "The Report on Land of the National Resources Board," *JFE,* XVII (February, 1935), 42–44; Purcell, "Land Economics," 12–13, HF; "Relations between the Department of Agriculture and the National Resources Committee," NRB, "National Land Planning Activities," July, Land Planning Committee Minutes, September 24, October 1, 12, Gray, "A Brief Outline of Some of the Policies Suggested for the Report on Land," Gray Report to Assistant Secretary Wilson, August 29, Wilson to Ely, November 27, 1934, NA, RG 16.

64. Nixon, *Roosevelt and Conservation,* I, 341–44.
65. NRC Progress Reports, June 15, 1936, December, 1938, NA, RG 16; "Land Planning," NA, RG 83; Salter, *Land Economics,* 29.
66. Nixon, *Roosevelt and Conservation,* I, 330, 332–33; Stanton D. Wicks to Secretary, December 6, C. F. Holsinger to Wallace, December 19, 1933, U. S. Chamber of Commerce, "Resolution on Land Policies," May 2, 1935, "Land Policy Report, A Summary," November 16–17, 1934, NA, RG 16; Robert E. Wood to Roosevelt, October 24, 1934, RL, PPF 1365; Benedict, *Farm Policies,* 342–46; Campbell, *Farm Bureau,* 72; Saloutos and Hicks, *Agricultural Discontent,* 490, 492–93; Ezekiel, OHC.
67. PWA Press Release No. 406, "Relation between Submarginal Land Withdrawal Work and the Work Concerned with the Replacement and Rehabilitation of Stranded Rural Population," "The Land Withdrawal Program Must be Kept Separate from the Rural Relief Program," Lawrence Westbrook to Emergency Relief Administrators, September 27, 1934, "Report of Conference of Delegates from Certain Drought States," March 1, Westbrook to Regional Advisers, March 9, 1935, HF; Tugwell to Roosevelt, March 3, 1934, RL, OF 1; Conference with Farm Paper Editors, February 23, Wallace to Hopkins, March 21, 1934, W. C. Henderson to Appleby, November 10, Will Alexander to Appleby, December 21, A. G. Black to Appleby, December 1, 1936, Chief, Bureau of Biological Survey to Appleby, January 1, 1937, E. H. Wiecking to C. B. Baldwin, December 30, 1938, E. A. Starch to Wilson, October 2, 1934, Ezekiel to Corrington Gill, January 10, Wilson to Robert Clarkson, February 21, 1935, NA, RG 16; interviews with Tugwell and Wiecking; Carl Taylor to Henry Taylor, January 15, 1935, Taylor Papers; Gray, "The Social and Economic Implications of the National Land Program," *JFE,* XVIII (May, 1936), 263–64.
68. Wilson to Westbrook, n.d., Wilson to Tolley, February 20, 1935, NA, RG 16.
69. Tugwell to D. A. Wallace, December 21, 1934, Wilson to Starch, February 21, 1935, *ibid.*
70. "Objectives in the Land-Use Planning Program of the United States Government," June 18, 1934, NA, RG 145.
71. Gray *et al.* to Wallace, March 23, 1934, NA, RG 16; see also Wallace to Joseph C. O. Mahoney, May 13, 1935, Donald Murphy to Wilson, January 4, 1936, NA, RG 16, and Nixon, *Roosevelt and Conservation,* I, 352–54.

72. *Ibid.*, 327.
73. "Memorandum Concerning PWA Funds Made Available or Allotted for Irrigation in Relation to a Program of Land Retirement," June 24, 1935, HF; Wallace to O'Mahoney, May 13, 1935, NA, RG 16.
74. Gates, "Comments," *AH*, 1963, 214–15; Gray to M. S. Eisenhower, May 25, 1938, NA, RG 83.
75. Ladd to Wallace, July 9, 1935, RL, OF 1-C.
76. Wilson, "We Move Toward a National Land Policy," NA, RG 16.
77. Wilson to Ely, November 27, 1934, *ibid.*
78. Lewis C. Gray, "Land Planning," reprinted in Findlay MacKenzie, ed., *Planned Society: Yesterday, Today, Tomorrow*, 170.

NOTES TO CHAPTER 6

1. U.S., Congress, Senate, *Industrial Prices and their Relative Inflexibility*, 74th Cong., 1st Sess., 1935, Report 13. Gardiner Means, "National Combinations and Agriculture," *JFE*, XX (February, 1938), 53–57; Means, "NRA and AAA and the Reorganization of Industrial Policy Making," RL, OF 1-K, *NYT*, October 29, 1934, January 9, 1935; Schlesinger, *Coming of the New Deal*, 218–19.
2. Wilson, "Validity of the Fundamental Assumptions underlying Agricultural Adjustment," *JFE*, XVIII (February, 1936), 24–26; *NYT*, October 29, 1934, April 12, 1935, April 25, 1937; Executive Secretary to Members of Executive Council, April 25, 1934, RL, OF 788; Means to Eugene McGuire, February 26, 1935, Wilson to the Secretary, February 24, Paul Appleby to John Dixon, October 6, 1936, NA, RG 16; Paul R. Preston to H. N. Tiemann, Jr., April 12, 1935, NA, RG 145.
3. J. D. Le Cron to Judson Q. Owen, January 4, 1936, NA, RG 16.
4. *NYT*, August 1, 1934.
5. Ezekiel to Moley, June 18, 1935, HF.
6. O'Neal, Radio speech, March 10, 1934, RL, PPF 1820, Agriculture; see also Campbell, *Farm Bureau*, 63.
7. Wilson to Ronald, September 28, 1935, NA, RG 16.
8. Wilson and Ezekiel, OHC; O'Neal, "Progress in the New Deal for Agriculture," April 8, 1933, NA, RG 16; Kile, *Farm Bureau*, 203; Schlesinger, *Coming of the New Deal*, 60; Lord, *Agrarian Revival: A Study of Agricultural Extension*, 162–63.
9. C. W. Warburton to J. S. Davis, November 1, 1932, Warburton to M. D. Amburgey, April 18, B. H. Crocheron to Warburton, February 4, Warburton to Crocheron, February 18, Warburton to D. P. Trent, March 16, April 3, Tom Leadley to Warburton, March 24, Wallace to Leadley, March 25, Wallace to Clarence Poe, March 28, J. Phil Campbell to Warburton, March 28, April 1, Warburton to Campbell, April 3, Warburton to Earl Smith, April 7, O'Neal, "Progress in the New Deal for Agriculture," April 8, Extension Committee, Land-Grant College Association to Presidents of Land-Grant Institutions, April 12, 1933, NA, RG

16; Lord, *Agrarian Revival*, 162–63; Gladys Baker, *The County Agent*, 70–71.

10. Senate, Subcommittee on Administration of Farm Programs of the Committee on Agriculture and Forestry, *Report, Abuses and Disruptions of the Elected Farmer Committee System*, 84th Cong., 2d Sess., 1956, 56, see also 2, 54–55. Interview with Alfred D. Stedman; Saloutos and Hicks, *Agricultural Discontent*, 472–73.

11. McConnell, *Agrarian Democracy*, 74.

12. Wilson, "Fundamental Assumptions," *JFE*, 1936, 17, 25; Wallace, "The Farmer and Social Discipline," *JFE*, XVI (January, 1935), 5–6, 10; Tolley, "Objectives in National Agricultural Policy," *JFE*, XX (February, 1938), 35–36; O. V. Wells, "Agricultural Planning and the Agricultural Economist," *JFE*, XX (August, 1938), 753; Ezekiel, "The Shift in Agricultural Policy toward Human Welfare," *JFE*, XXIV (May, 1942), 466; *Wisconsin Agriculturist and Farmer*, LXIII (November 7, 1936), 4; Tolley to Senator Arthur Vandenberg, May 21, 1937, in *NYT*, May 22, 1937; Schlesinger, *Coming of the New Deal*, 72–73; Nourse, *AAA*, 62–63, 257–58.

13. *Ibid.*, 72–74; Baker, *The County Agent*, 71–75, 79–83; Baker, *Century of Service*, 160; McConnell, *Agrarian Democracy*, 74–75.

14. Appleby to George Dillon, March 22, Wallace to Warburton, March 26, Wallace to Warburton, September 22, "A Friend" to Black and Wallace, December 31, Warburton to State Extension Directors, March 29, Black to Christgau, July 5, Warburton to Appleby, July 12, Donald R. Murphy to Appleby, August 13, 1934, January 3, 1935, Appleby to Murphy, August 28, December 24, Appleby to Black, December 24, 1934, Press Conference, February 6, Black to Chester Davis, January 21, 1935, NA, RG 16; Campbell, *Farm Bureau*, 161.

15. *Ibid.*, 172; "A Friend" to Black and Wallace, December 31, 1934, NA, RG 16.

16. Campbell, *Farm Bureau*, 63–67, Chap. 6; McConnell, *Agrarian Democracy*, 73, 75, 82; Kile, *Farm Bureau*, 205; Baker, *The County Agent*, 210–12; Charles M. Hardin, *The Politics of Agriculture: Soil Conservation and the Struggle for Power in Rural America*, 135.

17. O'Neal, Radio speech, March 10, 1934, RL, PPF 1820, Agriculture.

18. *Missouri Farmer*, XXV (August 1, 1933), 8; William Hirth to Roosevelt, December 3, 1934, Wallace to Roosevelt, January 11, 1935, RL, PPF 69; Wilson, OHC.

19. Hirth to James M. Thompson, November 9, 1932, Hirth Papers.

20. *Missouri Farmer*, XXV (April 15, 1933), 9, 25; (July 1, 1933), 8; (September 15, 1933), 8; (December 15, 1933), 14; XXVI (March 15, 1934), 4; (April 15, 1934), 1. Hirth to George Peek, August 25, 1936, Peek Papers.

21. D. C. Dobbins to Roosevelt, September 14, 1933, RL, OF 1-K; *Rural New Yorker*, XCIV (April 20, 1935), 335; (December 21, 1935), 795; XCVII (January 15, 1938), 46. *Pacific Rural Press*, CXXVII (January 20,

1934), 46; (February 3, 1934), 84, 107; (April 21, 1934), 367; (May 19, 1934), 460. Roy M. Pike to Congress, February 23, 1934, Cooperative Dairy Defense Committee to Congress, April 7, 1934, Peek Papers; Campbell, *Farm Bureau*, 67, Chap. 5; Richard S. Kirkendall, "Franklin D. Roosevelt and the Service Intellectual," *MVHR*, XLIX (December, 1962), 469.

22. October 24, 1933, RL, PPF 471; Saloutos and Hicks, *Agricultural Discontent*, 436–37.

23. C. B. Steward to Wallace, August 30, 1933, NA, RG 16.

24. R. D. Bowen to Roosevelt, October 21, 1933, RL, OF 227-misc.

25. Fite, "Simpson," *MVHR*, XXXV (March, 1949), 580–82; William P. Tucker, "Populism Up-to-Date: The Story of the Farmer's Union," *AH*, XXI (October, 1947), 205, 207; W. R. Ronald statement, December 6, John Dexter to Wilson, July 11, Wilson to Dexter, August 2, 1934, Wilson to Ronald, October 27, 1937, NA, RG 16.

26. *National Grange Monthly*, XXXI (September, 1934), 10; (October, 1934), 13; RL, OF 1, Box 1 and OF 1-misc.; NA, RG 16, General Correspondence, Criticisms-Tugwell; *Rural New Yorker*, XCIII (August 18, 1934), 537; Samuel B. Bledsoe confidential memorandum, October 9, 1941, RL, PPF 736.

27. Sternsher argues that "Tugwell's connection with a food and drug bill, introduced in June, 1933, was the most significant single reason for his becoming a prime target of the opposition press." Sternsher, *Tugwell*, 223.

28. Press Conference and news item, April 4, 1934, NA, RG 16.

29. Richard S. Kirkendall, "The New Deal Professors and the Politics of Agriculture," unpublished Ph.D. dissertation, University of Wisconsin, 1958, 332–43; Schlesinger, *Coming of the New Deal*, 457–60; Sternsher, *Tugwell*, 352–53.

30. Benjamin Marsh to Tugwell, April 11, 1934, NA, RG 16.

31. Schlesinger, *Crisis of the Old Order*, 196.

32. Tugwell, "Principle of Planning and the Institution of Laissez Faire," *American Economic Review*, XXII (sup.) (March, 1932), 75–92; Sternsher, *Tugwell*, 99–100.

33. Baker, *Century of Service*, 248–49.

34. *Ibid.*, 250.

35. Wilson, Louis Taber, and Hutson, OHC; Lord, *Wallaces*, 381–82; Campbell, *Farm Bureau*, 173–74; Appleby to Charles Mitchell, August 10, 1934, NA, RG 16.

36. James Le Cron to Appleby, July 9, 1934, *ibid.*

37. Quoted in Sidney G. Baldwin, "The Farm Security Administration: A Study in Politics and Administration," unpublished Ph.D. dissertation, Syracuse University, 1955, 55.

38. *NYT*, April 25, May 29, 1934.

39. Byrd to Tugwell, April 26, 1934, NA, RG 16.

40. Edward M. Crane to Roosevelt, May 21, 1934, RL, OF 1-misc.

41. Wallace to Roosevelt, March 26, May 14, 1934, undated White House

memorandum, RL, OF 1; Roosevelt Press Conference, June 13, 1934, RL PPF 1-P; T. Ralph Jones to Norman R. Hamilton, June 13, 1934, NA, RG 16; Ickes, *Diary*, I, 164; *NYT*, January 8, April 25, May 2, 15, 22, 29, June 8, 9, 10, 12, 13, 14, 15, 1934, April 4, 1935; Sternsher, *Tugwell*, Chap. 20.

42. *NYT*, July 23, 24, August 1, 2, 5, 9, 12, 22, September 13, 29, October 26, November 15, 16, 17, 1934; *New York Herald-Tribune*, November 11, 1934; L. W. Childress to Tugwell, August 14, 1934, Appleby to W. W. Waymack, March 1, 1935, NA, RG 16; Lord, *Wallaces*, 402–3; Sternsher, *Tugwell*, 235–36; interviews with Tugwell and Wallace; J. D. Black to H. C. Taylor, September 28, 1934, Taylor Papers.

43. Appleby to J. D. Le Cron, July 20, 1934, NA, RG 16.

44. Schlesinger, *Coming of the New Deal*, 74.

45. *Ibid.*, 77; Press Conference, February 6, Appleby to Robert L. Webb, March 2, 1935, NA, RG 16.

46. M. S. Venkataramani, "Norman Thomas, Arkansas Sharecroppers, and the Roosevelt Agricultural Policies, 1933–1937," *MVHR*, XLVII (September, 1960), 229–33; Schlesinger, *Coming of the New Deal*, 367–68; Wilma Dykeman and James Stokely, *The Seeds of Southern Change: The Life of Will Alexander*, 207–10; Baker, *The County Agent*, 75–76.

47. D. P. Trent to Extension Directors in Southern States, April 12, 1934, NA, RG 145; Wallace to De Priest, October 19, 1933, Tugwell to C. B. Hampton, February 6, 1934, NA, RG 16.

48. Wallace to Marvin H. McIntyre, March 6, 1934, RL, OF 1; Press Conference, February 20, 1935, NA, RG 16.

49. Jesse Tapp to H. C. Taylor, November 21, 1933, Taylor Papers; USDA Press Release, September 27, 1933, Ezekiel to Cully Cobb, January 26, Ezekiel to Wallace, March 5, December 4, 1934, NA, RG 16; Hoover, "Human Problems in Acreage Reduction in the South," A. D. Stedman to Trent *et al.*, April 18, 1934, NA, RG 145; Ezekiel, Notes on Chapter X of Dr. Nourse's Manuscript, HF.

50. Press Conferences, March 15, May 2, Cully Cobb to John J. Miller, March 26, Le Cron to S. F. Duckworth, April 28, Wallace to Hattie Caraway, May 8, D. P. Trent to Secretary, May 18, C. B. Baldwin to W. J. Greenwood, July 7, Wallace to Morris Sheppard, December 19, 1934, NA, RG 16; E. A. Miller to Cobb, March 24, 26, Cobb, "Procedure in Case Relating to Tenant-Landlord Relations in Arkansas," March 26, "Report of Adjustment Committee on Investigation of Landlord-Tenant Complaints," September 1, Trent to Davis, June 28, December 28, 1934, Cobb to Davis, February 13, 14, 1935, NA, RG 145.

51. "Statement of Policy in Connection with Landlord-Tenant Relations under the Cotton Adjustment Contract," *ibid.*

52. Lee Pressman was involved in these controversies, as were non-Communist reformers such as Frank, Tugwell, Gardner Jackson, and Frederic C. Howe. See Murray Kempton, *Part of our Time; Some Ruins and Monuments of the Thirties*, 54–77.

53. Davis to Secretary, February 4, Cobb to Amberson, March 13, 1934,

Hoover to Secretary, February 5, 1935, NA, RG 145; Press Conference, May 9, W. J. Green to Secretary, December 14, Wilson to B. F. Allen, December 26, 1934, NA, RG 16; Davis Memorandum for President, March 19, 1935, RL, OF 1-K.

54. Frank to W. E. Byrd, Jr., January 14, 1935, NA RG 145.
55. Amberson to Cobb, March 5, Amberson to Appleby, November 21, 27, Amberson to Eva L. Sims, December 9, 1934, Hiram Norcross to Appleby, January 5, W. C. Hudson *et al.* to Secretary, January 10, Frank to Secretary, January 12, Margaret B. Bennett to Secretary, January 12, Hiss to Frank, January 26, Francis M. Shea to McConnaughey, February 4, W. J. Green to Cobb, February 12, Mary Connor Myers to Davis, February 13, 1935, *ibid.*; C. T. Carpenter to Wallace, December 12, 1934, NA, RG 16.
56. I. O. Schaub *et al.* to Cobb, January 16, Arkansas County Agents to Davis, January 26, 1935, NA, RG 145.
57. Davis to Wallace, February 25, 1936, NA, RG 16; Cobb to Davis, February 6, 1935, NA, RG 145; Ezekiel and Hutson, OHC; interview with Stedman; Dykeman and Stokely, *Seeds of Southern Change,* 209–10.
58. "Statement of Policy in Connection with Landlord-Tenant Relations under Cotton Adjustment Contract," NA, RG 145.
59. Davis to Wallace, February 25, 1936, NA, RG 16.
60. Schlesinger, *Coming of the New Deal,* 79; Appleby to Frank, August 13, 1934, Appleby to J. S. Russell, February 15, 1935, NA, RG 16; Stine, OHC; interview with Wallace.
61. Press Conference, February 8, 1934, NA, RG 16.
62. "Interview with Henry A. Wallace," *United States News and World Report,* January 8, 1954, 42.
63. Wallace to Roosevelt, November 10, 1934, RL, PPF 1953.
64. Wilson, OHC; interview with Black; Wilson to Donald R. Murphy, January 31, 1935, NA, RG 16; Black to H. C. Taylor, July 12, September 18, 28, 1934, November 7, 1945, Taylor Papers; Black to Davis, November 15, 1935, NA, RG 145; Nourse, *AAA,* 253–54, 340–49, 391–99.
65. Interviews with Tugwell and Stedman; Sternsher, *Tugwell,* 204, 206–9; Schlesinger, *Coming of the New Deal,* 80, 549–50; Ickes, *Diary,* I, 201; Appleby to Donald R. Murphy, June 19, 1934, NA, RG 16.
66. Press Conference, February 6, 1935, *ibid.*
67. Appleby to Luther Harr, October 17, 1938, Appleby to J. S. Russell, February 15, 1935, *ibid.*
68. Francis P. Miller to Appleby, March 5, 1936, Gardner Jackson to Wallace, September 30, 1937, *ibid.*
69. Wallace to Roosevelt, March 18, 1940, *ibid.*
70. Senator Costigan to Roosevelt, February 7, 1935, RL, PPF 1971; Rio, Wis., *Journal,* February 28, 1935.
71. Charles Holman to Wallace, March 21, 1935, Frank to Arthur Holt, May 3, C. A. Locke to Frank, June 12, "Dairy Section Progress and Problems — Confidential Report," August 10, 1934, NA, RG 16; Wesley

McCune, *The Farm Bloc*, 268–73; Project No. 18, 32–33, 97–99, NA, RG 83; Wilson, OHC.

72. Raymond Gram Swing, "The Purge of the AAA," *The Nation*, CXL (February 20, 1935), 216–17.

73. Press Conference, February 6, 1935, NA, RG 16; Press Conference, February 6, 1935, RL, PPF 1–P; Roosevelt reply to Costigan, RL, PPF 1971.

74. Wallace to W. M. Garrard, March 21, 1935, NA, RG 16.

75. Chester C. Davis, "The Agricultural Adjustment Act and National Recovery," *JFE*, XVIII (May, 1936), 229; Tolley, "Agricultural Stability and Business Stability," April 28, 1937, NA, RG 83; Nourse, *AAA*, 420–28, 431–32.

76. Wilson to Ray Bowden, December 17, 1935, NA, RG 16.

77. Rogers to Wilson, July 16, 1934, *ibid*.

78. Wood to Roosevelt, October 24, 1934, RL, PPF 1365.

79. Emmet and Jeuck, *History of Sears, Roebuck and Company*, 615–16.

80. Harriman to Roosevelt, October 17, 1940, RL, PPF 3572; Harriman to Wilson, January 7, 1936, NA, RG 16.

81. William H. Wilson, "How the Chamber of Commerce Viewed the NRA: A Re-examination," *Mid-America*, XLIV (April, 1962), 107.

82. *Farm Journal*, LIX (October, 1935), 16; (November, 1935), 8; LX (February, 1936), 18; (March, 1936), 15, 68; McCune, *Farm Bloc*, 11.

83. James C. Carey, "The Farmers' Independence Council of America," *AH*, XXXV (April, 1961), 70, 77.

84. Wesley McCune, *Who's Behind Our Farm Policy?* 12, 15, 30, 32, 346.

85. Carey, "Farmers' Independence Council," *AH*, 1961, 72.

NOTES TO CHAPTER 7

1. James G. Maddox, "Suggestions for a National Program of Rural Rehabilitation," *JFE*, XXI (November, 1939), 881; see also Benedict, *Farm Policies*, 356–57.

2. Wilson to A. R. Mann, April 12, 1935, Ezekiel to C. C. Randall, May 27, 1938, NA, RG 16; Carl Taylor, "Conference of the Regional Directors of the Land Program, RA," June 19, 1935, NA, RG 96; Tugwell to Roosevelt, November 5, 1936, RL, OF 1650; Carl C. Taylor, "Research Needed as a Guidance to the Subsistence Homesteads Program," *JFE*, XVI (April, 1934), 314; W. E. Zeuch, "The Subsistence Homesteads Program from the Viewpoint of a Economist," *JFE*, XVII (November, 1935), 710–19; G. S. Wehrwein, "An Appraisal of Resettlement," *JFE*, XIX (February, 1937), 191; Gray, "Disadvantaged Rural Classes," *JFE*, XX (February, 1938), 71–72; Wilson, "Poverty in Agriculture," *JFE*, 1940, 10, 13; Baker, *The County Agent*, 211–12; Lord, *Wallaces*, 300–302; Laurence Hewes, *Boxcar in the Sand*, 96–97, 112–13, 120–21.

3. Calvin Hoover, "Human Problems in Acreage Reduction in the South," NA, RG 145.

4. NRC, "Progress Report," June 15, 1936, December, 1938, NA, RG 16.
5. Hoover to Wallace, January 8, 1935, *ibid.*
6. Hoover, "What Changes in National Policy Does the South Need?" *JFE*, XXII (February, 1940), 206–12; Hoover, "Agrarian Reorganization in the South," *JFE*, XX (May, 1938), 474–81.
7. Ezekiel to William L. Slate, March 7, 1935, NA, RG 16.
8. Gray to Wallace, January 15, 1935, NA, RG 83.
9. Wilson to Donald R. Murphy, January 31, 1935, NA, RG 16.
10. Division of Land Economics, "The Tenant Problem," NA, RG 83; James G. Maddox, "The Farm Security Administration," unpublished Ph.D. dissertation, Harvard University, 1950, 42.
11. A. R. Mann to Wilson, April 9, Wilson to Mann, April 12, 1935, NA, RG 16; Dykeman and Stokely, *Seeds of Southern Change*, 213; Baldwin, "FSA," 130–35, 146–47, 157–59.
12. *Ibid.*, 137–38; Press Conference, February 20, Wallace to Joseph O'Mahoney, May 13, 1935, NA, RG 16; Davis to President, March 19, 1935, Paul A. Porter to Secretary, March 25, 1936, NA, RG 145; Tugwell to Marvin McIntyre, n.d., RL, OF 503; Venkataramani, "Thomas," *MVHR*, 1960, 239–40.
13. Baldwin, "FSA," 147–49; Wilson to Lawrence Veiller, February 20, 1935, NA, RG 16.
14. Wilson, OHC; interviews with Wallace and Tugwell; Ickes, *Diary*, I, 194–95, 241, 292–93, 302–3, 309–10; *ibid.*, III, 281–82; Sternsher, *Tugwell*, 204–5, 262–65; Dykeman and Stokely, *Seeds of Southern Change*, 212; Schlesinger, *Coming of the New Deal*, 373; Tugwell, "The Resettlement Idea," *AH*, XXXIII (October, 1959), 160.
15. Dykeman and Stokely, *Seeds of Southern Change*, 200–16; Baldwin, "FSA," 120–30, 151–52.
16. Gray to Roosevelt, September 5, 1936, NA, RG 96.
17. RA Statement of Purpose, RL, OF 1568; Tugwell to President, April 6, Wilson to Harriman, July 6, 1935, NA, RG 16; "Land Planning," "The Land Use Planning Program, April 30," NA, RG 83; Project Planning Section, "History of Land-Use Policies and Acquisition Activities of the Land Utilization Division," RA, June 30, 1937, NA, RG 96; Purcell, "Land Economics," October, 1945, HF; Tugwell, "The Resettlement Idea," *AH*, 1959, 161; Benedict, *Farm Policies*, 325; Sternsher, *Tugwell*, 273–74.
18. Gray to Regional Directors *et al.*, July 10, 1936, NA, RG 96.
19. USDA Press Release, March 25, 1935; Englund to Black, April 27, Statement to Accompany Dr. Gray's Memorandum of June 3 to Dr. A. G. Black; Black to Englund, April 23, 1936, NA, RG 83.
20. Sternsher, *Tugwell*, 269–78; Baker, *Century of Service*, 206–11.
21. C. W. Warburton, "Circular Letter, Rural Resettlement, No. 1," NA, RG 16; Sternsher, *Tugwell*, 274–77; interview with Taylor.
22. Interview by Anne Dewees with Paul Taylor, February 17, 1941, NA, RG 83; Benedict, *Farm Policies*, 364; Paul Taylor, "Perspective on

Housing Migratory Agricultural Laborers," *Land Economics*, XXVII (August, 1951), 198–200.

23. Carl C. Taylor, "Social and Economic Significance of the Subsistence Homesteads Program — From the Point of View of a Sociologist," *JFE*, XVII (November, 1935), 720–31; Gray, "Federal Purchase and Administration of Submarginal Land in the Great Plains," *JFE*, XXI (February, 1939), 123–31; Tugwell, "Down to Earth," *Current History*, XLIV (July, 1936), 32–38; Tugwell, "Cooperation and Resettlement," *ibid.*, XLV (February, 1937), 71–76; Tugwell, "Changing Acres," *ibid.*, XLIV (September, 1936), 57–63; Tugwell, "National Significance of Recent Trends in Farm Population," *Social Forces*, XIV (October, 1935), 1–7; Hewes, *Boxcar*, 61–62, 64, 69, 72–74; Tugwell, *The Democratic Roosevelt*, 423.

24. On the development of this theory of poverty, see the excellent study by Robert H. Bremner, *From the Depths: The Discovery of Poverty in the United States*. On the "Unorthodoxy of the New Programs," see Baldwin, "FSA," 57–60.

25. Wilson, "Poverty in Agriculture," *JFE*, 1940, 14.

26. "Resettlement Administration," RL, PPF 1830, Resettlement; see other material in this file, Tugwell statement, Conference of the Regional Directors of the Land Program, RA, June 18, 1935, NA, RG 96, and Tugwell, "Relief and Reconstruction," *National Conference of Social Work*, 1934, 32–48.

27. "Land Utilization, Explanation of the Program," RL, PPF 1820, Resettlement.

28. "RA Policy and Procedure: Suggestions, Preliminary Report of the Committee, Land-Use Planning Section, Land Utilization Division," August, 1935, NA, RG 96; Tugwell to Wilson, December 27, 1935, Wallace to H. C. Taylor, April 6, 1937, NA, RG 16; Carl C. Taylor, "Subsistence Homesteads Program," *JFE*, 1935, 730–31; R. I. Nowell, "Experience of the Resettlement Administration Program in the Lake States," *JFE*, XIX (February, 1937), 206–20; Gray, "Disadvantaged Rural Classes," *JFE*, 1938, 82–85; *NYT*, November 15, 1936, January 1, 10, 1937; Lord, *Wallaces*, 459–60; Maddox to E. H. Wiecking, December 13, 1936, NA, RG 83.

29. Interviews with J. D. Black and C. C. Taylor; Taylor, presidential address, American Country Life Association, September 19, 1935, RL, OF 1568; Taylor, "Human Relations in Land-Use Planning," NA, RG 83; Gray, "The Social and Economic Implications of the National Land Program," *JFE*, 1936, 257–73; Taylor, "Land Utilization: The Social Aspects of Land Adjustment Problems," *JFE*, XIX (May, 1937), 588–94; Hewes, *Boxcar*, 81, 96; Conkin, *Tomorrow a New World*, 166–67 and Chap. 14; Sternsher, *Tugwell*, 266–71.

30. *Ibid.*, 265–68, 271–73; Schlesinger, *Coming of the New Deal*, 370–71.

31. Interviews with Wiecking, Walter Packard, C. C. Taylor, and Tugwell; Wilson to Charles Brand, December 31, Wilson to Hugh MacRae, Decem-

ber 24, 1936, Howe to Appleby, January 14, Ezekiel to Gray, January 30, Wilson to W. C. Lee, December 22, 1937, NA, RG 16; "RA Policy and Procedure: Suggestions, Preliminary Report of Committee, Land-Use Planning Section, Land Utilization Division," August, 1935, "Regional Directors Conference, Meeting on Tenure Arrangements and Contracts," January 28, 1936, Wilson, "Community Farms," NA, RG 96; Schlesinger, *Coming of the New Deal*, 370–72, 380; Conkin, *Tomorrow a New World*, 158, 160, 165–66, 169–70, 202–11, Wilson, OHC.

32. Interviews with Wiecking and Taylor; Wilson, OHC; Gray, "Social and Economic Implications," *JFE*, 1936, 264; Gray and Taylor, "Conference of the Regional Directors of the Land Program, RA," June 17–18, 1935, Phil Hooker, "Chronology of the Land Utilization Program," NA, RG 96; "Land Planning," Rex Willard *et al.*, "Land Use Planning — Rural Rehabilitation Coordination," June 30, 1937, NA, RG 83; Wiecking to C. B. Baldwin, November 30, 1938, NA, RG 16.

33. Sternsher, *Tugwell*, 247, 250, 289–90, 292; Schlesinger, *Coming of the New Deal*, 373; Conkin, *Tomorrow a New World*, 176–79, 211–13, 319–20.

34. Acting Director, National Emergency Council to President, September 25, October 19, November 16, 1936, January 5, 16, March 22, April 19, 1937, RL, OF 788; S. K. Stephenson to Roosevelt, December 11, 1935, RL, OF 1-misc.; B. F. Irvine and Marshall N. Dana to Roosevelt, July 12, 1935, Dan Bell to Roosevelt, January 8, 1936, RL, OF 1568; Herb B. Sewell to Roosevelt, February 15, 1936, RL, OF 1586-misc.; Tugwell to Roosevelt, n.d., RL, President's Secretary File, Tugwell folder; Roger A. Derby to Roosevelt, April 7, 1938, RL, PPF 758; *Farm Journal*, LIX (December, 1935), 56; Blair Bolles, "The Sweetheart of the Regimenters," *American Mercury*, XXXIX (September, 1936), 84–86; Wehrwein, "Appraisal of Resettlement," *JFE*, 1937, 190–202; *NYT*, November 17, 20, 1935, February 13, March 31, August 30, October 26, 1936.

35. Hope to Mrs. Plumb Carl, January 31, 1936, Hope Papers (Kansas State Historical Society).

36. Wood to Roosevelt, November 25, 1935, RL, PPF 1365.

37. Sternsher, *Tugwell*, 279–302; see also Conkin, *Tomorrow a New World*, 154 ff. and 319–20.

38. Ray Tucker, in Hagerstown, Maryland, *Herald*, November 29, 1935; see also Tugwell, "Resettlement Idea," *AH*, 1959, 162.

39. Tugwell to Roosevelt, December 1, 1935, March, 1936, RL, President's Secretary File, Tugwell folder; *NYT*, January 4, 10, February 5, 27, March 3, 4, 12, April 27, 28, May 9, 14, 19, 20, 24, July 28, September 1, 1936; Nowell, "Experience of Resettlement," *JFE*, 1937, 214; Nowell, "Discussion," *JFE*, XXIX (November, 1947), 1505–7; Conkin, *Tomorrow a New World*, 173–75, 310; Acting Executive Director, National Emergency Council to President, November 16, 1936, RL, OF 788.

40. John B. Bennett to John J. Riggle, July 15, 1938, NA, RG 83; interview with Paul Taylor; Taylor, "Housing Agricultural Migrants," *Land Economics*, 1951, 199–201; *NYT*, April 22, 1935, May 29, August 2, Novem-

ber 15, 1936; *Bureau Farmer*, IX (April, 1934), 26; Basil Rauch, *The History of the New Deal*, 34; W. J. Cash, *The Mind of the South*, 420–22; Lord, *Wallaces*, 411–12; Hewes, *Boxcar*, 75, 82–83; Tugwell, "Resettlement Idea," *AH*, 1959, 162; Kile, *Farm Bureau*, 255–56, 266–67; Baldwin, "FSA," 167–68.

41. Tugwell, *The Democratic Roosevelt*, 444 n.; see also 444, 472–73, Conkin, *Tomorrow a New World*, 163–64, and Sidney Baldwin's discussion of "Agrarian Orthodoxy" in "FSA," 37–48.

42. Ezekiel to Tugwell, May 3, 1935, NA, RG 16; *NYT*, April 30, 1935.

43. *NYT*, November 12, 14, 1936; Appleby to Carl Taylor, November 2, 1936, Appleby to Wallace, August 17, 1937, NA RG 16; *Kiplinger Agricultural Letter*, November 14, 1936; Lord, *Wallaces*, 428–30; Hardin, *The Politics of Agriculture*, 131–32; McConnell, *Agrarian Democracy*, 86–89; Hewes, *Boxcar*, 79–80; Sternsher, *Tugwell*, 303; Baker, *Century of Service*, 204–5; Conkin, *Tomorrow a New World*, 180–81; Baldwin, "FSA," 109–11; Wilson, OHC; interview with Wallace.

44. National Resources Committee, *Farm Tenancy: Report of the President's Committee*, 20–21.

45. Marquis Childs, *I Write from Washington*, 13–14.

46. *NYT*, January 10, 1937.

47. Sternsher, *Tugwell*, 278; Conkin, *Tomorrow a New World*, 161.

48. See NA, RG 16, General Correspondence for 1934–1936, under such headings as "Criticism," "Congratulations (Tugwell)," "Criticism-Commendations," and "Farm Relief," Subject File, Immediate Office of the Secretary, Wirt Charges, NA, RG 96, General Correspondence for late 1936 and early 1937, and RL, OF 1-misc. for spring of 1934.

49. "Tugwell to the Wolves," *New Republic*, LXXXV (December 25, 1935), 186–87.

50. Howe to Tugwell, November 17, 1936, NA, RG 96.

51. Elliott Roosevelt, ed., *F.D.R.: His Personal Letters, 1928–1945*, I, 554; Sternsher, *Tugwell*, 242; Baker, *Century of Service*, 203–4; Hewes, *Boxcar*, 57, 83.

52. *NYT*, January 6, 28, July 1, 8, August 24, 1935, March 29, May 14, 29, June 24, 1936; Cash, *Mind of the South*, 421; Lord, *Wallaces*, 368, 410; Hewes, *Boxcar*, 68, 72–74, 78–79, 82–83, 96, 201–2; Walter J. Heacock, "William B. Bankhead and the New Deal," *Journal of Southern History*, XXI (August, 1955), 354–55; Conkin, *Tomorrow a New World*, 179, 321; Baldwin, "FSA," 140–43, 156–70; Eleanor Roosevelt, *This I Remember*, 174; McConnell, *Agrarian Democracy*, 88–89; Sternsher, *Tugwell*, 296; and much correspondence in NA, RG 16, 83, and 96, and RL, OF 1568, 1568-misc., and 1650, and PPF 660 and 1362.

53. *Farmers Equity Union News*, II (April, 1936), 2, 3; (March, 1936), 1.

54. Sternsher, *Tugwell*, 295; Schlesinger, *Coming of the New Deal*, 378; Venkataramani, "Thomas," *MVHR*, 1960, 236–37.

55. Interviews with Wiecking, C. C. Taylor, and Packard; Dykeman and Stokely, *Seeds of Southern Change*, 218–19; Sternsher, *Tugwell*, 300–302.

56. Tugwell, *The Democratic Roosevelt*, 227, 247, 358, 409–21, 449.

57. Tugwell, "The Progressive Task Today and Tomorrow," *Vital Speeches,* II (December 2, 1935), 130–35.

58. Clarke A. Chambers, *California Farm Organizations,* 4–6, 42, 46–47, 59, 199; *NYT,* August 2, 1936; Teague Papers, *e.g.,* "California Chamber of Commerce Project on Cooperation of Agriculture and other Major Lines of Business, 1939."

59. There is much evidence on the reaction in RL, OF 1-misc. See also Robert Ramsay to Roosevelt, November 27, 1935, RL, OF 3; NEA Service, January 7, 1936, NA, RG 96; Elmer R. Murphy to Tugwell, February 3, P. G. Nicholson to Tugwell, August 13, 1936, A. D. More to Wallace, August 27, 1937, G. R. Killer to Wallace, November 18, 1935, NA, RG 16; P. M. Abbott to Peek, October, 1936, Peek Papers; Ickes, *Diary,* I, 474; *NYT,* October 31, November 21, December 2, 1935, March 7, 13, September 21, 24, October 5, 7, 1936, January 19, 1937; Sternsher, *Tugwell,* 347–48, 352.

60. Donald R. McCoy, *Angry Voices: Left-of-Center Politics in the New Deal Era,* 62, 70–75, 82, 127, 159, Chap. 4; Irving Howe and Lewis Coser, *The American Communist Party: A Critical History,* Chap. 8.

61. Peek, *Why Quit Our Own?* 121.

62. *Farm Journal,* LX (January, 1936), 18; (February, 1936), 21; see also (August, 1936), 15; (November, 1936), 18, 22–23; LXII (September, 1938), 15.

63. Wood to Roosevelt, November 25, 1935, Wood to McIntyre, October 21, 1936, RL, PPF 1365; Wood to Wallace, October 16, 23, 1936, NA, RG 16. As the New Deal moved left in 1935 and 1936, Wood became increasingly unhappy with it, as File 1365 reveals. Ezekiel came to regard him as "well intentioned" but "exceedingly conservative." Ezekiel to Floyd Reeves, November 16, 1936, *ibid.*

64. Ickes, *Diary,* I, 580; Farley to Roosevelt, May 9, 1935, RL, OF 1-misc.; Farley, *Jim Farley's Story: The Roosevelt Years,* 57.

65. *National Grange Monthly,* XXII (November, 1936), 14.

66. The Peek Papers contain a collection of these pamphlets.

67. Kirkendall, "Roosevelt and the Service Intellectual," *MVHR,* 1962, 459–63; Sternsher, *Tugwell,* 340–47, 355–56.

68. *NYT,* March 4, April 4, September 22, October 1, 2, 4, 27, 1936.

69. *NYT,* October 2, 23, 25, November 1, 1936.

70. *NYT,* October 4, 29, 1936; Harold F. Gosnell, *Champion Campaigner: Franklin D. Roosevelt,* 160; Tugwell, "Grass Did Not Grow," *Fortune,* XIV (October, 1936), 114 ff.

71. Ickes, *Diary,* II, 9.

72. See *NYT* editorial, November 22, 1936.

73. *Ibid.,* June 24, 1934, September 6, 1936.

74. "The Republican Brain Trust," *New Republic,* LXXXVI (April 22, 1936), 299–300.

75. Maverick to Tugwell, May 1, 1936, NA, RG 96.

76. *NYT,* June 16, 1936.

77. Wilson to Selig Perlman, May 4, 1936, NA RG 16.

78. Ickes, *Diary*, I, 692; *ibid.*, II, 9.

79. Sternsher, *Tugwell*, 240, 243.

80. *Ibid.*, 324–26; Brice Martin to Tugwell, November 24, 1936, NA, RG 96; interview with Appleby; Tugwell to Roosevelt, December 21, 1936, RL, President's Secretary File, Tugwell folder; Hewes, *Boxcar*, 91–92, 96; McConnell, *Agrarian Democracy*, 88.

81. Dykeman and Stokely, *Seeds of Southern Change*, 221.

82. Tugwell, *The Democratic Roosevelt*, 414–16, 420–21, 426; Schlesinger, *The Age of Roosevelt: The Politics of Upheaval*, Chap. 21; W. S. Hayes to Roosevelt, August 1, Enrico Micucci to Roosevelt, November 19, 1936, RL, OF 1-misc.; Eugene Agger to Tugwell, November 4, Roy J. Carver to Tugwell, November 20, 1936, NA, RG 96; *NYT*, January 19, 1937; Hewes, *Boxcar*, 91–92, 96; Sternsher, *Tugwell*, 321.

83. *Ibid.*, 324; see also 325, 327.

84. Tugwell, "The Future of National Planning," *New Republic*, LXXXIX (December 6, 1936), 164.

85. Sternsher, *Tugwell*, 328.

86. See for examples "Tugwell: New Deal's Leading 'Red' Gets Job in Wall Street," *News Week*, VIII (November 28, 1936), 16–17, and *NYT*, January 19, 1937. Some were not amused, however, and looked upon Tugwell's move as desertion. Sternsher, *Tugwell*, 323–24.

87. W. R. Gentry to Tugwell, November 19, 1936, NA, RG 96.

88. Lord, "Profiles—Rural New Yorker," *New Yorker*, XI (March 30, 1934), 25–26; Bolles, "Sweetheart of the Regimenters," *American Mercury*, 1936, 82; Cleveland Rodgers, *Robert Moses, builder for democracy*, 132.

89. Wilson to Smith, July 27, 1935, NA, RG 16; Wilson, OHC. See also Wilson to Senator Burton K. Wheeler, July 17, 1934, *ibid.*, for an illustration of Wilson's political sense, his cultivation of important politicians, and his efforts to inform himself on political matters. See Wilson to Senator James Murray, August 20, 1936, *ibid.*: "Please do not hesitate to call upon me if there is anything I can do to assist you in your campaign. It would be unthinkable to have an anti-administration senator elected from Montana this year."

90. E. J. MacMillan to Wilson, April 29, May 21, Wilson to MacMillan, May 18, Wilson to W. R. Ronald, August 13, October 4, Donald Blaisdell to Sam Rayburn, October 27, Blaisdell to Victor E. Anderson, October 9, Wilson to J. L. Humphrey, June 27, Wilson to R. J. Laubengayer, May 14, Wilson to Grover B. Hill, August 15, Wilson to Jay Whitson, November 2, 1936, Wilson confidential memorandum, NA, RG 16.

91. Mrs. James H. Wolfe to Wilson, November 24, Sam Rayburn and Paul C. Aiken to Wilson, November 13, 1936, *ibid.*

92. Appleby to M. H. Alexander, October 30, 1936, *ibid.*

93. See especially NA, RG 16, General Correspondence, Under Secretary, and Congratulations (Wilson) Assistant Secretary. See also John Dexter to Wilson, July 11, J. W. Wilson to Wilson, July 1, 1934, Wilson to L. S. Clarke, November 23, 1935, NA, RG 16; Wilson to Charles E.

Peterson, July 22, 1933, A. D. Stedman to Tolley, November 18, 1937, NA, RG 145; *Progressive Farmer and Southern Ruralist*, XLVIII (June, 1933), 17; *Bureau Farmer*, VIII (June, 1933), 3, 5; *National Grange Monthly*, XXXII (January, 1935), 6; *ibid.* (September, 1935), 16; *Agricultural Leaders Digest*, XV (May, 1934), 9–10.

94. T. A. Hoverstad to Wilson, January 2, 1937, NA, RG 16.
95. Hope to C. L. Hayward *et al.*, April 17, 1935, Hope Papers.
96. Wilson to W. R. Ronald, June 17, 1936, NA, RG 16.
97. Campbell, *Farm Bureau*, 57–58, 122–25.
98. Tugwell, "Is a Farmer-Labor Alliance Possible?" *Harper's Magazine*, CLXXIV (May, 1937), 651–61.
99. Dykeman and Stokely, *Seeds of Southern Change*, 222–23.
100. J. H. Jenkins to Tugwell, November 18, 1936, NA, RG 96.
101. Wilson to Bushrod Grimes, May 28, 1937, NA, RG 16; interview with Appleby; Baldwin, "FSA," 189–91; NRC, *Farm Tenancy*, 27.
102. Wilson to Hugh MacRae, January 29, February 12, 1936, NA, RG 16; Maddox, "FSA," 42–44, 411–12; Baldwin, "FSA," 132–47, 153–56, 164–81.
103. Tugwell to Roosevelt, November 21, Roosevelt to Tugwell, November 25, 1935, RL, OF 1568; Wilson to H. C. Taylor, January 20, Charles W. Eliot, II, to Charles E. Merriam, December 11, Wilson to Eliot, March 19, 1936, NA, RG 16; Wilson to H. C. Taylor, January 20, 1936, Taylor Papers; Tugwell to Roosevelt, November 5, 1936, RL, OF 1650; Paul Appleby to C. C. Taylor, November 2, 1936, NA, RG 83; Dykeman and Stokely, *Seeds of Southern Change*, 224–25; Baldwin, "FSA," 182–89.
104. Roosevelt to Wallace, November 16, 1936, RL, OF 1650.
105. Tugwell to Roosevelt, November 5, 1936, *ibid.*; Gray, radio speech on "Farm and Home Hour," August 30, 1935, RL, OF 1568; Gray to Eric Englund, March 21, 1936, NA, RG 83; Gray to Wallace, January 14, 1935, NA, RG 16; Salter, *Land Economics*, 25, 214, 229.
106. Eliot to Advisory Committee, December 11, 1936, Meeting of President's Committee on Farm Tenancy, December 17, 1936, February 11, 1937, NA, RG 83; Frederic A. Delano to Ickes, February 1, 1937, RL, OF 1650; Gray to Members of President's Committee, December 22, 1936, Ezekiel to Gray, February 25, 1937, NA, RG 16; NRC, *Farm Tenancy*, 28–30.
107. John D. Black to Gray, January 12, Black, January 21, 1937, NA, RG 83.
108. Alexander to D. P. Trent, October 18, 1936, NA, RG 96; Meetings of President's Committee on Farm Tenancy, December 17, 1936, February 10, 11, 1937, NA, RG 83; Baldwin, "FSA," 199–200, 203–4; NRC, *Farm Tenancy*, 22–24.
109. Gray to President, February 13, 1937, NA, RG 83; Wilson to Xenephon Caverno, February 5, 1937, NA, RG 16; Baldwin, "FSA," 193–94.
110. NRC, *Farm Tenancy*, iv, 3–20.
111. Benedict, *Farm Policies*, 362.
112. Maddox, "FSA," 48–50, 410–12.
113. Baldwin, "FSA," 194–98, 202–25, 228.

114. Wallace Memorandum #732, September 1, 1937, HF; Benedict, *Farm Policies*, 326; James G. Maddox to I. W. Duggan, March 13, 1940, C. B. Baldwin statement, May 11, 1943, NA, RG 16; Edward C. Banfield, "Ten Years of the Farm Tenant Purchase Program," *JFE*, XXXI (August, 1949), 484; A. Whitney Griswold, *Farming and Democracy*, 164–67; McConnell, *Agrarian Democracy*, 89–92, 94, 98; Clifford Hope to J. C. Berryman, March 16, 1942, Hope Papers; interview with Packard; Baker, *Century of Service*, 210–12; Maddox, "FSA," 9–19, 36–39, 50, 77–105, and Part II; Baldwin, "FSA," 84–101, 107, 225–28, 244–77, 339.

115. August 26, 137, RL, PPF 564.

116. NRC, *Farm Tenancy*, 22; Baldwin, "FSA," 209–10.

117. Dykeman and Stokely, *Seeds of Southern Change*, 227–28.

118. Wilson to Starch, February 21, 1935, NA, RG 16; Wilson, OHC.

119. Wilson to J. D. Rockefeller, Jr., January 30, 1940, NA, RG 16.

120. Wilson to Hugh MacRae, December 24, Wilson to Charles Brand, December 31, 1936, Wilson to Xenephon Caverno, February 5, Wilson to W. C. Lee, December 12, 1937, Wilson to F. C. Howe, February 14, 1938, *ibid.*; Wilson, "Poverty in Agriculture," *JFE*, 1940, 12; Meetings of Committee on Farm Tenancy, December 16, 17, 1936, NA, RG 83.

121. Wilson to F. C. Howe, February 14, 1938, NA, RG 16; Baldwin, "FSA," 232–34.

122. Harold Smith memorandum for the President, March 29, 1940, RL, OF 1650.

123. USDA, "Summary Statement of Rental and Benefit Payments," NA, RG 16.

124. Hardin, "The Politics of Agriculture in the United States," *JFE*, XXXII (November, 1950), 573.

125. Baldwin, "FSA," 404, 406, and all of Part III.

126. Dykeman and Stokely, *Seeds of Southern Change*, 248.

NOTES TO CHAPTER 8

1. Wallace to Roosevelt, September 17, 1935, RL, OF 1.

2. Wilson to W. R. Ronald, November 28, 1935, NA, RG 16.

3. Walter Parker to Ezekiel, March 13, 1936, RL, OF 258; W. Scholl to Ezekiel, January 15, Wallace to Roosevelt, February 12, 1935, NA, RG 16; Ellen Clayton Garwood, *Will Clayton: A Short Biography*, 102–3, 108–9.

4. Wilson to L. A. Wheeler, February 17, 1934, NA, RG 16.

5. Press Release, October 12, 1936, RL, OF 1.

6. Wilson to Hickman Price, October 28, 1932, Wilson Papers; Ronald to Roosevelt, November 2, 1932, RL, PPF 74; Tugwell, Diary, January 6, 1933, RL, Group 21; Ezekiel to Frank, August 12, Ezekiel to Lacy, August 5, Olcott to Ezekiel, August 6, Ezekiel to Tolley, August 5, 1933, Ezekiel to Peek, August 13, Wallace to Olcott, August 30, Ronald, "Is it Time for a Permanent AAA?" Wilson to Harlan Sumner, July 24, Ezekiel to Wilson, December 2, 1935, NA, RG 16; *NYT*, April 26, May 26,

1934, December 2, 3, 1935; Ezekiel to A. G. Black, May 17, 1935, NA, RG 83; Ezekiel and Louis Bean, OHC; Ezekiel and Bean, *The Economic Bases of the Agricultural Adjustment Act*; Saloutos and Hicks, *Agricultural Discontent*, 500–503; Schlesinger, *Politics of Upheaval*, 470–74; Tugwell, *The Democratic Roosevelt*, 371.

7. *Ibid.*, 372.
8. Saloutos and Hicks, *Agricultural Discontent*, 501–5.
9. Wilson to Ronald, June 17, 1936, Wilson to Harriet Elliott, January 22, 1936, NA, RG 16.
10. NA, RG 145, General Correspondence, AAA, Tolley, 1936–37; USDA Press Release, January 10, Meeting of Representatives of Farm Organizations, January 10, 11, Wilson to F. B. Linfield, January 14, Wilson to E. A. Starch, January 23, Wilson to Alfred Atkinson, January 23, Wallace to Samuel Guard, February 29, Wilson to E. A. Duddy, May 28, 1936, NA, RG 16; Wallace to Stephen Early, June 4, Press Release, October 12, 1936, RL, OF 1; E. A. O'Neal to J. H. Bankhead, January 20, 1936, RL, PPF 1820; Benedict, *Farm Policies*, 349; Baker, *Century of Service*, 165–70; Tolley, OHC; Charles M. Gardner, *The Grange — Friend of the Farmer*, 84, 139–40.
11. Benedict, *Farm Policies*, 348.
12. Jesse Tapp to Henry C. Taylor, November 21, 1933, Taylor Papers; Tolley, "The Program Planning Division of the Agricultural Adjustment Administration," *JFE*, XVI (April, 1934), 588; Elliott, "Progress and Problems in Regional Agricultural Planning from the National Point of View," *JFE*, 1936, 101.
13. J. F. Cox to Tolley, June 11, 1935, NA, RG 145.
14. Tolley, "The Philosophy of Agricultural Adjustment," December 11–12, 1935, Wilson Papers; Tapp to Taylor, June 24, 1935, Taylor Papers; Wilson, OHC; Bushrod W. Allin, "Migration Required for Best Land Use," *JFE*, XVIII (August, 1936), 498–99; Elliott, "Progress and Problems," *JFE*, 1936, 95–102.
15. Tolley and Wilson, "Some Future Problems of Agricultural Adjustment," November 19, 1934, Tolley, "A Land-Use Program for the Cotton Belt," February 1, Elliott, "Some Problems Relating to a Continuing Agricultural Adjustment Program," January 17, 1935, NA, RG 16.
16. NA, RG 16.
17. Wallace to L. N. Duncan, February 20, 1935, *ibid.*
18. Roy F. Hendrickson to Wilson *et al.*, February 20, Hendrickson to F. A. Flood, March 22, Wilson to H. H. Bennett, August 9, Ezekiel to W. E. Grimes, March 18, Wilson to E. A. Starch, February 21, 1935, *ibid.*; Tolley, "Philosophy of Agricultural Adjustment," Wilson Papers; Wilson, OHC.
19. "A Tentative Draft of a Cooperative Research Project for Use in Regional Agricultural Planning," February 27, 1935, NA, RG 16.
20. Wilson, OHC; Tolley, "Philosophy of Agricultural Adjustment," Wilson Papers; Wilson to Ronald, December 17, 1935, NA, RG 16; Wallace at School for Extension Workers, October 19, 1935, NA, RG 83.

21. S. B. Dotsen to Wallace, March 11, 1935, NA, RG 16.

22. Wilson to F. B. Linfield, February 12, 1936, *ibid.*; Englund to Grimes, April 16, 1935, "Report of Some Research Studies Completed by the Division of Farm Management and Costs, BAE, during the Last 10 Years," February 7, Wells to Englund, February 27, 1940, NA, RG 83; *Proceedings of the Forty-ninth Annual Convention of the Association of Land-Grant Colleges and Universities*, November 18–20, 1935, 39–41, 106–8, 110–14, 118–38.

23. *Ibid.*, 39.

24. "Statement with Respect to Land-Use Planning Research or Related Work with the Agricultural Adjustment Administration," December 1, 1937, NA, RG 83.

25. Extension Service, USDA, "Resumé of Experience in County Agricultural Planning," *ibid.*; Wilson to J. W. Haw, September 27, Wilson to Charles W. Eliot, II, November 27, 1935, Memorandum to State Extension Directors, September 25, 1936, NA, RG 16.

26. Wallace to A. M. Eberle, October 14, C. W. Warburton, October 18, 1935, "Resumé of Experience in County Agricultural Planning," Division of Economic Information, Staff Meeting, January 6, 1941, NA, RG 83; Bushrod Allin to Wilson, January 21, 1936, NA, RG 16; Elliott, "Progress and Problems," *JFE*, 1936, 95–102; Wilson, OHC; Tolley, "Philosophy of Agricultural Adjustment," Wilson Papers.

27. "Agricultural Adjustment Planning in Selected Counties for 1937," H. M. Dixon to State Leaders of the County Agricultural Adjustment Project, February 15, Tolley and Warburton to State Directors of Extension, November 17, 1936, "The County Planning Project: A Statistical Summary of Results Obtained in 1935–36," NA, RG 83.

28. Wilson to J. S. Davis, July 2, 1936, NA, RG 16.

29. Hendrickson to A. F. Wileden, May 15, 1935, Discussion Group Materials, Hendrickson to Paul Porter, February 15, Report of the Forum and Discussion Group Project, USDA, 1934–35, June, Wilson to Benson Landis, July 10, Wilson to A. R. Mann, September 23, 1935, Discussion Group Project, March, Hendrickson to Harrison S. Elliott, May 18, Wilson to J. C. Farmer, November 2, 1936, Organization of Discussion Groups in Connection with Program Planning, 1935–36, Donald Blaisdell to W. R. Ogg, January 14, 1937, Blaisdell, "Contributions of the Department to the Discussion Group Program, 1936–1937," NA, RG 16; Hendrickson to Lacy, September 3, 1935, NA, RG 83; Baker, *The County Agent*, 85.

30. Wilson, OHC; Conference on Plans and Programs for Department Activities in Group Discussion, June 16, 1936, National Conference on Discussion Group Problem, May 10–12, Taeusch to Tolley, July 13, 1937, NA, RG 83; Wilson to Raymond L. Buell, July 2, M. S. Eisenhower to Hendrickson, July 3, Hendrickson to Donald R. Murphy, September 30, Hendrickson to W. R. Ogg, October 15, 1935, National Project Discussion Groups and County Forums on National Agricultural Policy, NA, RG 16; Baker, *The County Agent*, 84–85.

31. E. R. Eastman to Wilson, January 23, Wilson to Eastman, February 27, 1937, NA, RG 16.
32. "Organization of Discussion Groups in Connection with Program Planning, 1935–36," *ibid.*
33. Donald R. Murphy to Wilson, January 4, 1936, *ibid.*
34. W. R. Ogg to Hendrickson, September 21, 1935, *ibid.*
35. Hendrickson to Ogg, September 30, 1935, *ibid.*
36. Hendrickson to Ogg, December 3, 1935, *ibid.*
37. O'Neal to all Farm Bureaus, December 18, 1935, *ibid.*
38. Wilson, OHC; interview with Taeusch; Wilson to George W. Russell, May 10, 1935, A Proposed School for Extension Workers, Memorandum for Elliott, February 24, 1936, Taeusch to Tolley, October 18, 1937, NA, RG 16; "Report on Schools of Philosophy for Agricultural Leaders," NA, RG 83; Carl F. Taeusch, "Adequate Perspectives," *Journal of Adult Education,* IX (October, 1937), 410–13.
39. Tolley, "Philosophy of Agricultural Adjustment," Wilson Papers; J. D. Black to Taeusch, August 3, 1937, NA, RG 83; Wilson to O'Neal, October 14, 1935, NA, RG 16.
40. Wilson, OHC; Wilson to T. W. Schultz, May 28, 1935, "Discussion Group Project, 1936–37," October 10, Donald C. Blaisdell, October 13, 1936, Wilson Misc. Memorandum Regarding Discussion Group Project for Fiscal Year 1936–37, NA, RG 16.
41. "Memorandum to the State Extension Directors Regarding Progress of the Discussion Group Project," September 25, 1936, *ibid.*; Program Study and Discussion Section, Statement of Functions, NA, RG 83.
42. Wilson to Donald R. Murphy, January 31, 1935, NA, RG 16.
43. Nixon, *Roosevelt and Conservation,* I, 444–46.
44. Notes from Memorandum to Mr. M. L. Wilson from Mr. Allin, for Sec. Statement, C. W. Warburton to Directors of Extension, October 31, A. G. Black at Conference of State Representatives on the Cooperative Project, Washington, November 7–10, 1935, NA, RG 83; Wilson to Ronald, December 3, 1935, NA, RG 16; Wallace, "Farm Economists and Agricultural Planning," *JFE,* XVIII (February, 1936), 6–7; Wilson, "Fundamental Assumptions," *ibid.,* 26; *Proceedings of the Forty-ninth Annual Convention of the Association of Land-Grant Colleges,* 39–40, 114.
45. Nourse, *AAA,* 385.
46. Tolley and Hutson, OHC; J. D. Black to H. C. Taylor, September 28, 1934, Taylor Papers; Tolley, "Philosophy of Agricultural Adjustment," Wilson Papers; *NYT,* September 5, 1935; C. C. Davis, "Plans, Programs and Public Opinion," *Proceedings of the Forty-ninth Annual Convention of the Association of Land-Grant Colleges,* 136–38.
47. Tolley, OHC; USDA Press Release, June 5, 1936, NA, RG 16.
48. Raymond Clapper in " 'AAA' Family Row?" *Literary Digest,* CXXI (March 21, 1936), 9; see also Hutson and Ezekiel, OHC, and *NYT,* January 13, June 6, 1936.
49. Wilson to Ronald, December 3, 1935, NA, RG 16.

50. Meeting of Representatives of Farm Organizations, January 11, 1936, *ibid.*
51. Benedict, *Farm Policies*, 349.
52. Wilson to F. B. Linfield, February 13, 1936, NA, RG 16.
53. Tolley, Wilson, and Samuel B. Bledsoe, OHC; interviews with Wallace, Stedman, and Paul Appleby.
54. *NYT*, January 5, 1937.
55. Nixon, *Roosevelt and Conservation*, I, 469; see also 470, 472–75, 477.
56. *Ibid.*, 490–91.
57. Tugwell, "Our New National Domain," *Scribner's Magazine*, XCIX (March, 1936), 167–78.
58. Wilson, OHC; "The National Soil Conservation Program Today — A Summary," NA, RG 16; Sternsher, *Tugwell*, 217–18; Nixon, *Roosevelt and Conservation*, I, 361–63, 371–72; Ickes, *Diary*, I, 325–26, 339, 343–44; *ibid.*, II, 669; Benedict, *Farm Policies*, 317–19; Baker, *Century of Service*, 190–94; Schlesinger, *Coming of the New Deal*, 341–43.
59. Tolley to Jerome Frank, October 2, 1934, NA, RG 16.
60. Wilson, "Agricultural Conservation — An Aspect of Land Utilization," *JFE*, XIX (February, 1937), 11.
61. Wilson, OHC; Nixon, *Roosevelt and Conservation*, II, 21–22, 26–27, 37; Wilson to Bean, June 12, 1935, NA, RG 145; Wilson to White, March 5, Wilson to Charles W. Eliot, II, October 2, 1935, December 5, 1936, Wilson to R. W. Blackburn, May 8, 1937, "Memorandum Summarizing Attached Copy of Proposed Standard Soil Conservation Districts Law for Adoption by State Legislatures," "History, Objectives and Progress of the Soil Conservation Service," NRC, "Progress Report," December, 1938, NA, RG 16; Wallace to Roosevelt, February 16, 1937, RL, OF 732; Benedict, *Farm Policies*, 396; Baker, *Century of Service*, 196–97, 251–52.
62. Tolley, Wilson, and Hutson, OHC; Proposed Amendments, n.d., Ezekiel to Secretary of Agriculture, December 4, 1934, HF; Benedict, *Farm Policies*, 350–51; Nourse, *AAA*, 365.
63. See Paul L. Murphy, "The New Deal Agricultural Program and the Constitution," *AH*, XXIX (October, 1955), 160–69.
64. NA, RG 145, General Correspondence, AAA, Tolley; Tolley, OHC; Wilson to R. J. Laubengayer, May 14, 1936, Wilson to James Humphrey, February 12, J. D. Le Cron to N. B. Munson, December 8, Le Cron to W. J. Durbohn, December 6, 1938, NA, RG 16; "Explanation of Main Provisions of the Agricultural Adjustment Act of 1938," RL, OF 1; Nixon, *Roosevelt and Conservation*, I, 496–98; Campbell, *Farm Bureau*, 111–15; Kile, *Farm Bureau*, 234–43; Benedict, *Farm Policies*, 333, 351, 375–84, 388; Baker, *Century of Service*, 170–75.
65. Wilson to F. C. Howe, February 14, 1938, Wilson to Ronald, May 26, 1937, NA, RG 16; Wilson address, November 16, 1938, NA, RG 83.
66. Nixon, *Roosevelt and Conservation*, II, 248.

NOTES TO CHAPTER 9

1. Baker, *Century of Service*, 254; Wallace, "The Importance of Planning in the Development of Agricultural Programs," March 20, 1939, M. M. Kelso to Joseph T. Elove, August 15, 1938, NA, RG 83.
2. Roosevelt Memorandum for Louis Brownlow, December 28, 1936, RL, OF 1; Wallace to Harold D. Smith, n.d., RL, OF 1-C; Jay Darling to Milton Eisenhower, September 21, 1937, Eisenhower to Appleby, July 25, 1938, "A Summary of Relationships between the Department of Agriculture and the Department of Interior," NA, RG 16; Ickes, *Diary*, I, 250, 259, 364–65, 388, 417–19, 523, 527, 534–35, 553, 568, 574, 583–84, 598–99, 601, 604–6, 609; *ibid.*, II, 18, 20–21, 23, 39–45, 86–87, 151–52, 157, 159, 247, 254, 257, 264–65, 268, 278, 282, 291, 294, 305, 307–14, 316–20, 332, 338–39, 345–46, 359, 366, 412, 471, 517; *ibid.*, III, 34, 263, 281–82.
3. Baker, *Century of Service*, 251–52; Elliott, "Significant Trends in Planning in American Agriculture," NA, RG 83; Wilson to E. A. Starch, November 28, 1935, NA, RG 16.
4. Wallace Memorandum, December 3, 1936, NA, RG 83.
5. Wilson Memorandum, July 12, J. D. Black to Wilson *et al.*, July 3, 1937, "Organization and Activities of the Division of State and Local Planning, 1939–40," *ibid.*; "Report of Committee on Coordination, Land Policy and Land Planning Activities of the Department of Agriculture," July 9, 1937, "Report of the Office of Land-Use Coordinator," July 1, 1941, NA, RG 16; Benedict, *Farm Policies*, 394–96; Baker, *Century of Service*, 255–57; John D. Black and George William Westcott, *Rural Planning in One County: Worcester County, Massachusetts*, 127–32.
6. Interviews with Wiecking, Allin, Benedict, and Stedman; Wilson and Stine, OHC; Banfield, "Organization for Policy Planning," *JFE*, 1952, 21; Eisenhower to L. E. Call, September 7, 1937, NA, RG 16; Eisenhower and Roy I. Kimmel, "Old and New in Agricultural Organization," *Farmers in a Changing World: The Yearbook of Agriculture, 1940*, 1125–37.
7. Ezekiel to Wallace, February 5, 1936; see also Ezekiel to Tolley and Gray, October 22, 1936, Gray to Ezekiel, April 1, 1937, NA, RG 16; Ezekiel to Davis, January 31, 1935, NA, RG 145.
8. Ezekiel and Tolley, OHC; for an illustration of Cobb's point of view, see Cobb to Davis, February 6, 1935, NA, RG 145.
9. Brehm to Reuben Bingham, June 10, 1938, Allin to Tolley, October 2, 1937, NA, RG 83; Wilson, OHC; interview with John D. Black; Black and Westcott, *Rural Planning*, 133–34.
10. "Summary of Method of Selection, Tenure, and Duties of Various State and County Officers and Committees Assisting in the Administration of the Agricultural Conservation Programs," NA, RG 16; Gladys Baker, *The County Agent*, 77–79; McConnell, *Agrarian Democracy*, 77–78; interview with Wayne Darrow and Porter Hedge.
11. "Report of the Committee on Ways and Means for Improving the Devel-

opment and Administration of Agricultural Adjustment Programs in the North Central and Western Regions," John J. Miller to Wallace, December 19, 1936, B. F. Abmeyer and M. F. Colter to George E. Farrell, January 20, Resolution of Montana Farmers Union, June 3, A. R. Anderson *et al.* to J. C. Taylor, July 13, Jerry O'Connell to Wallace, July 21, 1937, NA, RG 16.

12. "Report of the Committee on Ways and Means for Improving the Development and Administration of Agricultural Adjustment Programs in the North Central and Western Regions," Wallace to Burton K. Wheeler, July 6, Rudolph Evans to Abe Crouch, July 12, Harry L. Brown, July 19, Ed Hadley clipping, February 19, 1937, NA, RG 16; Tolley and Warburton to State Extension Directors, February 17, Report to Dr. H. R. Tolley on the Referenda, May 4, 1938, NA, RG 83; Tolley and Wilson, OHC; interviews with Stedman and J. D. Black; AAA, *Agricultural Adjustment 1937–38: A Report of the Activities Carried on By the Agricultural Adjustment Administration,* 213–26, 243–46; Black and Westcott, *Rural Planning,* 133.

13. Wilson, OHC; interviews with Black and Allin; Murphy to Wilson, February 17, 1936, Joseph P. Harris, "A Study of Decentralization of Administration in the Department of Agriculture," April 9, Stedman to R. M. Evans, March 19, 1937, "A Report on Sentiment Toward AAA Programs in the Western Region," NA, RG 16; Taeusch to Tolley, July 11, 1938, NA, RG 83; Benedict, *Farm Policies,* 394; McConnell, *Agrarian Democracy,* 78, 82; Campbell, *Farm Bureau,* 161–65, 167–68.

14. Baker, *Century of Service,* 254.

15. Reuben Bingham, Memorandum on Attitude of State Extension Directors, November 2, 1936, John Dexter, Confidential Report, January 4, Murphy to Appleby, February 19, 1937, NA, RG 16.

16. Campbell, *Farm Bureau,* 167–68.

17. Baker, *Century of Service,* 258.

18. "Warburton Circular Letter, Rural Resettlement, No. 1," "Memorandum of Understanding," July 7, Dorothy M. Beck to Tugwell, December 17, GEF to Appleby, December 19, 1935, Harris, Study of Decentralization, Raymond A. Pearson to Wilson, June 25, 1937, NA, RG 16; Baker, *The County Agent,* 91–92, 212–13; Conkin, *Tomorrow a New World,* 160; Sternsher, *Tugwell,* 277.

19. Wallace, Memoranda, December 3, 31, 1936, Division of Economic Information, Staff Meeting, January 6, 1941, NA, RG 83; Wilson, OHC; Baker, *Century of Service,* 254–55.

20. "Summary of Possible Participation of Various Departmental Agencies in County Agricultural Planning," Division of Economic Information, Staff Meeting, January 27, 1941, NA, RG 83; How Can Agricultural Planning be Made a Department-Wide Activity, NA, RG 16; Wilson, OHC.

21. Elliott to Tolley, October 2, 1937, NA, RG 83.

22. "Agricultural Planning and Federal-State Relations," Warburton to all State Extension Directors, July 12, 1938, *ibid.*

23. Wilson to A. G. Black, April 26, 1938, *ibid.*
24. Allin memorandum for Tolley, April 6, 1938, *ibid.*
25. C. E. Brehm to Reuben Bingham, June 10, 1938, *ibid.*
26. Dan T. Gray to J. C. Futrall, April 12, 1938, *ibid.*
27. Wilson to A. G. Black, April 26, 1938, *ibid.*
28. Wilson, OHC; E. H. Wiecking to George J. Baker, July 6, 1938, NA, RG 16; Joint Statement, July 8, 1938, NA, RG 83; Benedict, *Farm Policies*, 394–95.
29. Wickard, "The Future of Agricultural Adjustment," December 12, 1936, NA, RG 16.
30. Stedman to Marvin H. McIntyre, December 23, 1935, RL, OF 1-K.
31. Wilson, Tolley, and Hutson, OHC; interviews with Hedge, Darrow, Allin, Wilson, Tolley, and Stedman; Davis to E. B. Weatherly, July 12, Davis to G. B. Thorne *et al.*, October 1, USDA Press Release, October 14, 1935, NA, RG 145; Tolley, *The Farmer Citizen at War*, 121, 124–26; Nourse, *AAA*, 271–73.
32. November 17, 1936, NA, RG 16.
33. Dean Albertson, *Roosevelt's Farmer: Claude R. Wickard in the New Deal*, 118.
34. "Report of the Committee on Ways and Means for Improving the Development and Administration of Agricultural Adjustment Programs in the North Central and Western Regions," NA, RG 16; Ezekiel, Hutson, Tolley, and Wilson, OHC; interviews with Darrow, Hedge, and Allin.
35. Cobb to Wallace, September 13, 1937, NA, RG 16. A short time later an investigator reported to Wallace: "We have the seeming paradox of criticism and fault-finding almost everywhere, and at the same time a strong, broad undercurrent of farmer support and approval of the conservation program." John Dexter, "A Report on Sentiment toward AAA Programs in the Western Regions, Requested in Letter of December 10, 1937," *ibid.*; Tolley, OHC.
36. Ickes, *Diary*, II, 313, 543; Appleby to Evans, December 28, 1936, Appleby to John M. Goldsmith, April 22, Appleby to James E. Laurence, August 4, Appleby to J. D. Le Cron, August 6, 1938, NA, RG 16.
37. Appleby to Luther Harr, October 17, 1938, Appleby to F. W. Loring, March 3, 1934, Appleby to Wallace, July 9, Appleby to Le Cron, July 20, 1936, Appleby to Mrs. Irving Davis, December 29, 1938, *ibid.*
38. Appleby to Le Cron, July 20, 1934, Appleby to R. L. Burgess, October 20, 1937, Appleby to Willis Mahoney, June 4, 1938, *ibid.*; *Farm Journal*, LXII (December, 1938), 15; Hutson, Bledsoe, and Tolley, OHC; interviews with Appleby, Darrow, and Hedge; Albertson, *Roosevelt's Farmer*, 118–22.
39. AAA, *Agricultural Adjustment 1937–38*, 247, 169, 244.
40. Tolley, Stine, Wilson, and Hutson, OHC; interview with Appleby.
41. Wilson and Hutson, OHC; interviews with Appleby, Stedman, and J. D. Black. Triple-A, despite the large role of economists in its operations, had not produced the adjustments that many economists had hoped and ex-

pected. See "Discussion by W. W. Wilcox," *JFE*, XXI (February, 1939), 44–45.

42. Wallace, Memorandum, October 6, 1938, NA, RG 83.
43. *Ibid.*; Henry C. Taylor to Jesse Tapp, January 31, 1939, Taylor Papers; Wilson, OHC; interview with Wallace.
44. Hutson, OHC.
45. Tolley, Wilson, Stine, and Hutson, OHC; interviews with J. D. Black, Darrow, Hedge, and Stedman.
46. "Discussion by John D. Black," *JFE*, XXI (February, 1939), 26.
47. Tolley and Wilson, OHC.
48. Interviews with Tolley, Wilson, Allin, Elliott, and Wiecking.
49. Joseph P. Harris, "A Study of Decentralization of Administration in the Department of Agriculture," April 9, 1937, NA, RG 16.
50. Albertson, *Roosevelt's Farmer*, 4.
51. Ezekiel, OHC.
52. Ezekiel to Bean, August 15, 1940, in Bean, OHC.
53. Tolley, OHC.
54. Tolley, "Contributions of Agricultural Economics to the General Welfare," *JFE*, XXI (February, 1939), 11–12.
55. See *JFE*, 1936–1944, and Theodore W. Schultz, *Training and Recruiting of Personnel in the Rural Social Studies.*
56. Wilson to Donald R. Murphy, June 2, 1939, NA, RG 16.
57. Wilson to Scudder Mekeel, September 12, 1938, *ibid.*
58. Wilson, "New Horizons in Agricultural Economics," *JFE*, XX (February, 1938), 1–7. One change in the profession that took place under the pressures of the period was in line with advice that Wilson had long been giving. The scope of farm management expanded, moving "from individual farm problems to those of the interrelationships between the individual farm and its own economic environment." Case and Williams, *Fifty Years of Farm Management*, 272–73.
59. Wallace, "The Importance of Planning in the Development of Agricultural Programs," March 20, 1939, NA, RG 83; see also Wallace to Chris L. Christensen, November 29, 1938, NA, RG 16.
60. Wiecking to S. H. Rutford, February 27, 1939, *ibid.*

NOTES TO CHAPTER 10

1. Wallace Memoranda, September 1, 25, 1937, October 6, 1938, "Legislative History of Land Utilization Provisions in the Farm Tenancy Bill," NA, RG 83; Ezekiel to Eisenhower, September 13, 1937, Purcell, "Land Economics," October, 1945, HF; Phil Hooker, "Chronology of the Land Utilization Program, 1941," NA, RG 96.
2. Wallace to Roosevelt, December 21, 1938, RL, OF 1; "Some Suggestions Relative to Conservation," NA, RG 83; National Cooperative Council's Special Legislative Committee, "An Agricultural Policy for the United

States," 1940, Teague Papers; Wallace to Roosevelt, June 11, 1940, NA, RG 16; Benedict, *Farm Policies*, 386.

3. Anne Dewees' interview with Rex E. Willard, February 21, 1941, NA, RG 83.

4. Gray, "Our Major Agricultural Land Use Problems and Suggested Lines of Action," in *Farmers in a Changing World: The Yearbook of Agriculture, 1940*, 414–15.

5. Gray, "Evolution of the Land Program of the USDA," March 22, 1939, NA, RG 83.

6. Tolley to Gray, December 4, 1945, *ibid.*; Wiecking to Henry C. Taylor, February 25, 1946, Taylor Papers; Taylor, "L. C. Gray, Agricultural Historian and Land Economist," *AH*, XXVI (October, 1952), 165.

7. Purcell, "Land Economics," Division of Organization and Personnel Management, "Report on Organization of the Division of Land Economics," April 22, 1941, HF; Millard Peck to Marvin Jones, December 7, 1939, NA, RG 83; Schultz, *Training and Recruiting of Personnel in the Rural Social Studies*, 179.

8. "Memorandum of Understanding," March 11, 1939, NA, RG 83.

9. Wilson and Stine, OHC; NA, RG 83, Tolley File, Inter-Bureau Coordinating Committee; Tolley to Elliott, May 23, 1939, Elliott, "Significant Trends in Planning for American Agriculture," May 5, 1941, NA, RG 83.

10. Wallace Memorandum, October 6, 1938, *ibid.*; Memorandum for the Files, November 10, 1938, NA, RG 16; Baker, *Century of Service*, 261–62.

11. *Ibid.*, 262; "Functions of the Office of Land-Use Coordination with Special Reference to the Bureau of Agricultural Economics," January, Eisenhower to Wilson *et al.*, February 21, Tolley to Eisenhower, March 20, Wallace Memorandum No. 814, April 6, 1939, NA, RG 83; Notes on Minutes of Special Committee on Organization of Administrative Council, June 16, 1941, HF; Tolley, OHC.

12. Elliott in Wilson, OHC; interview with Elliott.

13. "Summary of Possible Participation of Various Departmental Agencies in County Agricultural Planning," NA, RG 83.

14. Evans to Tolley, March 23, 1939, *ibid.*

15. A. G. Black, "Some Current Problems in Agricultural Credit," *JFE*, XXIII (February, 1941), 49–50; Wilson, OHC; Black radio address, April 1, 1940, "Farm Credit and Land Use Planning," NA, RG 16.

16. Tolley and Wilson, OHC; interview with Allin; Tolley to Carl Taylor, August 15, Marion Clawson to Carl Taylor, May 5, Dover Trent to Allin, May 12, 1941, "The Family-Type Farm — How Much Should It Cost," Wilson Cowen to Raymond C. Smith, June 20, 1940, C. B. Baldwin to Tolley, July 24, 1941, Louis S. Drake to Allin, May 25, 1939, NA, RG 83; D. A. FitzGerald to P. E. Miller, March 2, 1940, NA, RG 96.

17. Tolley, Wilson, Hutson, and Ezekiel, OHC; interviews with Elliott, Hedge, Darrow, Wiecking, Benedict, Allin, and Wilson; Claude R. Wickard to Lee M. Gentry, September 18, R. L. Burgess to Tolley, May 22, 1939, February 10, Robert Clarkson to Allin, February 15, March 2, 1940,

"Report of Committee on Relationship of Land Use Planning to the Annual Program of the Action Agencies," Joseph T. Elove to Hugo Schwartz, July 16, 1941, J. D. Black, speech before Graduate School of Public Administration, Harvard University, November 17, Black to Tolley, February 25, 1942, NA, RG 83; John B. Wilson, Jr., to Appleby, July 17, 1941, NA, RG 16; Hardin, *The Politics of Agriculture*, 86–88.

18. Tolley, OHC; interview with Elliott; Dover Trent to Allin, November 28, 1938, "Unified Counties, Culpepper, Va., Lee, Ala.," January 29, Elliott to James G. Maddox *et al.*, July 8, 1940, John R. Fleming to Morse Salisbury, June 17, 1941, William T. Ham to Carl Taylor, June 21, Taylor to David Meeker, June 22, Meeker to W. A. Minor, July 2, 1940; Carl Taeusch to Rudolph Evans, April 5, D. A. FitzGerald to W. Bassett Orr, May 19, Conrad Taeuber to Russell S. Kifer, May 23, Sherman E. Johnson to Kifer, May 24, 1941, "Suggestions of the Bureau of Agricultural Economics in Connection with the Development of the Agricultural Conservation Program for 1942," "Summary of a Report by a Subcommittee of the Inter-Bureau Coordination Committee on the AA Program for 1940 and Subsequent Years," "Some Suggestions Relative to Conservation," "Recommendations Made to Bureaus of the Department of Agriculture in Inter-Bureau Coordinating Committee Reports of 1939 and 1940," "Brief Resumé of the Program Board Report of March 28, 1940," NA, RG 83.

19. Evans to Tolley, January 19, Tolley to Evans, February 3, Meeting of the Inter-Bureau Coordinating Committee, February 5, "Brief Resumé of the Program Board Report of April 10, 1940," NA, RG 83; Tolley and Wilson, OHC; interviews with Wilson and Allin.

20. Black and Westcott, *Rural Planning*, 144.

21. Taeusch to Wilson, August 24, 1939, NA, RG 83.

22. Albertson, *Roosevelt's Farmer*, 118.

23. Tolley, Hutson, Stine, and Bledsoe, OHC; interviews with Elliott, Wiecking, Appleby, J. D. Black, Gladys L. Baker; Black, "BAE," *JFE*, 1947, 1034–35; Meeting of Field Men, March 28, 1939, NA, RG 83.

24. Wells, "Agricultural Planning and the Agricultural Economist," *JFE*, 1938, 764.

25. Stine, OHC; interview with Wiecking.

26. Allin, "The Objectives and Methods of Agricultural Economics," *JFE*, XXX (August, 1948), 546.

27. Interviews with Allin, Wilson, Elliott, Taeusch, and Benedict; Tolley, OHC; Allin, "Is Planning Compatible with Democracy?" August 22, 1936, NA, RG 145; Allin, "Is Group Choice a Part of Economics?" *Quarterly Journal of Economics*, LXVII (August, 1953), 362–79; (November, 1953), 613–14.

28. Morris B. Storrer to Allin, January 27, 1942, NA, RG 83.

29. C. W. Warburton to State Directors of Extension, November 1, 1935, Eisenhower to Wilson, March 30, Allin to Tolley, April 6, Allin to Eisenhower, May 28, 1938, *ibid*.

30. Allin to E. A. Starch, July 14, 1938, *ibid.*
31. Division of State and Local Planning, July 25, 1939, Division of Economic Information, Staff Meeting, January 27, 1941, *ibid.*
32. Meeting of Field Men, March 28, 1939, Allin, Special Memorandum, February 5, D. A. FitzGerald to Rex Willard, May 6, 1941, *ibid.*
33. Allin to Wallace, July 18, 1939, *ibid.*
34. Allin to C. E. Brehm, June 18, 1938, *ibid.*; Allin, "Is Planning Compatible with Democracy?" August 22, 1936, NA, RG 145.
35. "Memorandum of Understanding," February 18, Wallace to Edward O. Elliott, February 27, 1939, NA, RG 83.
36. Meeting of Field Men, March 28, 1939, "Objectives, Procedure and Estimated Cost of Agricultural Planning Project," *ibid.*
37. Eisenhower to F. J. Keilholz, March 20, 1939, NA, RG 16; Carl Taylor to Henry Taylor, June 12, W. Aubrey Gates, November 12, 1939, Kenneth J. Nicholson to Rex Willard, February 21, Willard to Allin, March 17, 1942, NA, RG 83; interview with Allin; Stine, OHC.
38. "The Birth of County Planning," NA, RG 83.
39. Gray to Tolley, January 19, 1939, *ibid.*
40. USDA Conference on Post-War Planning, January 19–20, 1942, Gladwin E. Young to Allin, April 26, Willard to Allin, September 1, Ralph Charles to Allin, October 31, 1939, *ibid.*; interview with Englund.
41. L. E. Sawyer to M. M. Kelso, September 13, 1938, *ibid.*
42. I. O. Schaub to C. W. Warburton, May 12, June 28, 1939, *ibid.*
43. F. E. Balmer to Reuben Bingham, July 7, 1938, see also Willard to Allin, May 9, 1939, *ibid.*
44. Willard to Allin, August 7, 1941, *ibid.*
45. Allin to Willard, September 2, Allin to Harold A. Vogel, September 16, 1939, see also Edwin F. Landerholm to Willard, November 19, 1941, *ibid.*
46. Landerholm to Allin, December 24, 1941, *ibid.*
47. Robert G. Sproul to Wallace, March 23, Willard to Allin, May 9, 1939, *ibid.*
48. Willard to Tolley, May 31, June 5, Bert Smith to Willard, June 4, 1941, Willard to Allin, September 18, 1940, Tolley to Englund, August 9, Tolley to Allin, August 12, 1939, *ibid.*
49. Wilson to B. H. Crocheron, January 23, D. A. FitzGerald to Willard, January 24, Willard to Tolley, March 10, June 5, Bert L. Smith to Willard, June 4, 1941, Willard to Allin, March 17, C. B. Hutchinson to Roscoe E. Bell, July 23, Willard to Tolley, August 1, 1942, *ibid.*
50. Tolley to Thomas Cooper, December 26, 1939, Tolley to Rainer Schickele, February 15, 1939, *ibid.*
51. Tolley to H. J. Reed, May 31, W. W. Clark to Gladwin E. Young, June 7, C. E. Brehm to Tolley, June 20, Tolley to Brehm, July 10, Englund to Brehm, July 24, Brehm to Englund, July 31, Brehm to Allin, July 31, R. T. Melvin to W. A. Hartman, June 5, Englund to I. O. Schaub, July 8, Warburton to William A. Schoenfeld, September 28, 1939, Englund to Tolley, December 12, 1938, Tolley to Thomas Cooper, December 26, 1939, FitzGerald to Willard, June 25, FitzGerald to Allin, July 29, Roy

E. Haight to FitzGerald, September 20, Allin to Haight, October 30, 1940, Ralph H. Rogers to Allin, May 23, Allin to Rogers, May 21, 1941, *ibid.*

52. Tolley to J. C. Blair, July 10, 1939, *ibid.*
53. Blair to Allin, June 17, 1939, *ibid.*
54. Virgil B. Fielder to Allin, December 20, Allin to Fielder, December 22, 1941, *ibid.*
55. Allin to Landerholm, August 25, 1939, *ibid.*
56. Kimball Young to Carl Taylor, December 21, 1939, *ibid.*
57. Tolley to Thomas Cooper, July 10, December 14, 26, Cooper to Tolley, December 18, 1939, January 18, W. A. Hartman to Allin, March 25, April 30, Allin to Cooper, April 10, 1940, *ibid.*
58. Cooper to Allin, May 14, June 5, 1940, *ibid.*
59. Allin to Cooper, June 10, 1940, *ibid.*
60. Cooper to Allin, June 25, 1940, *ibid.*
61. FitzGerald to Cooper, July 8, 1940, *ibid.*
62. Wilson to Cooper, August 9, 1940, Allin to Theo L. Vaughan, January 28, 1941, Cooper to Wilson, January 7, Cooper to J. Edwin Losey, November 7, Losey to Conrad Taeuber, November 10, 1942, *ibid.*
63. J. E. Wills to W. A. Hartman, September 18, 1939, Wilson to Brehm, January 28, Hartman to FitzGerald, April 11, 16, Wills to Allin, April 14, 1941, *ibid.*
64. Meeting of the Field Men, March 28, 1939, P. V. Kepner, August 1, 1941, J. D. Black speech before Graduate School of Public Administration, Harvard University, November 17, Taeusch to Tolley, July 29, November 20, 1942, *ibid.*; "Notes on Meeting of the Washington Committee on BAE Field Programs," January 30, 1943, HF.
65. Jack Blackmore and Alexander Moskowitz, "Analysis of Planning Procedures," April 17, 1941, NA, RG 83.
66. Allin to W. S. Middaugh, March 11, 1942, *ibid.*
67. "Address by M. L. Wilson," *Proceedings of the Association of Land-Grant Colleges and Universities, Fifty-Second Annual Convention*, November 14–16, 1938, 89.
68. Englund to Tolley, December 12, 1938, NA, RG 83.
69. L. E. Sawyer to M. M. Kelso, September 13, 1938, *ibid.*
70. Interview with Allin; Willard to Allin, March 17, 1942, Allin to Carl Tjerandsen, March 4, 1940, NA, RG 83.
71. Tolley to Englund, August 9, Willard to Allin, September 1, Gladwin E. Young to Allin, September 3, 1939, James W. Coddington to Allin, January 11, ERF, March 14, J. W. Bateman to Wilson, June 22, Allin to Bateman, July 1, Bateman to J. G. Lee, Jr., and Wilson, July 2, Wilson to H. P. Rusk, September 5, Wilson to Thomas Cooper, August 9, 1940, *ibid.*; Wilson and Hutson, OHC; interviews with J. D. Black, Wilson, Wallace, and Benedict; Lord, *Wallaces*, 382.
72. "Statement on Land-Use Planning by Special Subcommittee," November 8, 1940, "Report on the Progress of Land-Use Planning during 1939," NA, RG 83.
73. Virgil Hurlburt to Allin, May 31, 1939, *Agricultural Planning in a World*

at War, January, 1942, *ibid.*; "Planning by Farmers," M. S. McDowell to Wilson, October 8, 1940, NA, RG 16; Ellery A. Foster and Harold A. Vogel, "Cooperative Land-Use Planning — A New Development in Democracy," *Farmers in a Changing World*, 1144–50; *Report of the Chief of the Bureau of Agricultural Economics 1940*, 11–28.

74. Willard to Tolley, August 1, 1942, NA, RG 83.

75. E. J. Kyle to Tolley, January 19, 1940, *ibid.*

76. Neal C. Gross, "A Post Mortem on County Planning," *JFE*, XXV (August, 1943), 653–57.

77. Allin, "Next Steps," March 21, 1940, NA, RG 83.

78. B. W. A., November 10, 1936, Allin to H. W. Gilbertson, November 26, 1938, NA, RG 16; interview with Elliott.

79. Wallace, "The Importance of Planning in the Development of Agricultural Programs," March 20, 1939, Wilson to B. H. Crocheron, January 23, 1941, NA, RG 83; Tolley, *The Farmer Citizen at War*, 195 ff.; interview with Elliott.

80. Tolley, *Farmer Citizen at War*, 128 ff.; Elliott, " 'We, the People . . . ,' " *Land Policy Review*, II (May–June, 1939), 6–8; "Community Organization for Land-Use Planning in Idaho," Carl Taylor to Davis McEntire, March 22, Taylor to Varden Fuller, October 12, 1940, "Conference on Community Organization, Leadership, and County Land-Use Planning," October 3, 1939, NA, RG 83.

81. *Ibid.*, General Correspondence, Project-Planning Process Study; Carl Taylor to All Area Leaders, September 17, November 30, "Study of Organization and Participation in the County Land-Use Planning Program," July 12, 1940, NA, RG 83.

82. Meeting of Field Men, March 28, 1939, W. A. Hartman to P. O. Davis, February 16, Varden Fuller to Carl Taylor, October 4, Taylor to Willard, October 30, 1940, *ibid.*; J. Joe Reed to Herbert Folken, August 24, 1940, NA, RG 16.

83. "Conference on Community Organization, Leadership, and County Land-Use Planning," October 3, 1939, NA, RG 83.

84. Statement on Land-Use Planning by Special Subcommittee, November 8, 1940, *ibid.*

85. Allin, "Agricultural Land Planning from the Federal Point of View," May 12, 1941, *ibid.*; interviews with Allin, Elliott, and Carl Taylor.

86. Wilson to author, August 10, 1956.

87. Meeting of Field Men, March 28, 1939, J. R. Greenbaum to W. A. Hartman, October 4, 1940, NA, RG 83; Bryce Ryan, "Democratic Telesis and County Agricultural Planning," *JFE*, XXII (November, 1940), 698; Black, "BAE," *JFE*, 1947, 1039–40; interviews with Black, Wallace, and Englund.

88. W. W. Burr and W. H. Brokaw to Wallace, March 9, 1940, NA, RG 83.

89. Wilson to Asher Hobson, June 19, 1939, NA, RG 16.

90. Allin, "County Planning Project — A Cooperative Approach," *JFE*, XXII (February, 1940), 298–99; Wilson, "The Place of the Department of Agriculture in the Evolution of Agricultural Policy," NA, RG 83.

91. Tolley, *Farmer Citizen at War*, 174–75.

92. Gray, "Evolution of the Land Program of the USDA," March 22, 1939, NA, RG 83.

93. Gray, "Memorandum on Local Planning," December 9, 1938, *ibid*.

94. M. M. Kelso, "Notes on Bureau Organization as Related to Local Area Planning," December 16, 1938, *ibid*.

95. Allin to H. W. Hochbaum, January 31, 1939, NA, RG 16; Tolley to Allin, June 12, 1940, NA, RG 83; Tolley, *Farmer Citizen at War*, Chap. 7.

96. Harold Laski, "The Limitations of the Expert," *Harper's Magazine*, CLXII (December, 1930), 102, 109.

97. Carl Tjerandsen to Allin, November 9, 1940, NA, RG 83.

98. Allin to Elliott, April 20, 1943, *ibid*.

99. Englund to Tolley, June 7, 1941, *ibid*.

100. Robert S. Lynd, *Knowledge for What? The Place of Social Science in American Culture*, 9.

101. Wilson to Lynd, July 10, 1939, NA, RG 16; see also Tolley, OHC.

102. Wilson to H. E. Babcock, May 25, Wilson to John W. Nason, June 30, 1939, NA, RG 16; John M. Gaus and Leon O. Wolcott, *Public Administration and the United States Department of Agriculture*, 303–4; Allin, "County Planning Project," *JFE*, 1940, 298–99.

103. Correspondence for 1939, NA, RG 16, Under Secretary; and NA, RG 83, General Correspondence, Young; Young to J. A. Geddes, October 9, 1939, NA, RG 83; Tolley, *Farmer Citizen at War*, 254; Baker, *Century of Service*, 239.

104. Wilson to L. J. Fletcher, August 24, 1934, NA, RG 16.

105. Wilson to Selig Perlman, May 4, Wilson to Jay Whitson, November 2, 1936, *ibid.*; Taylor to Elliott, March 24, 1937, March 26, J. C. Ellickson to Taylor, March 22, Taylor to Tolley, November 14, 1938; Kimball Young to Taylor, June 9, 20, J. E. Hulett, Jr., to Young, October 25, 1939, NA, RG 83; Wilson, OHC; interview with Taylor.

106. Young to Taylor, June 9, 30, Taylor to Young, July 11, 1939, "Research Methodology," March 28, 1945, NA, RG 83; Likert, "Democracy in Agriculture — Way and How?" in *Farmers in a Changing World*, 999–1001.

107. Harry Alpert, "The Growth of Social Research in the United States," in Daniel Lerner, ed., *The Human Meaning of the Social Sciences*, 79–80.

108. Donald Blaisdell to Richard W. Hogue, November 10, 1938, NA, RG 16; Taylor to Wilson, January 22, 1941, NA, RG 83; Wilson, "Beyond Economics," in *Farmers in a Changing World*, 922–37; and Wilson, "The Democratic Process and the Formulation of Agricultural Policy," *Social Forces*, XIX (October, 1940), 1–11.

109. Tolley, "Contributions of Agricultural Economics to the General Welfare," *JFE*, 1939, 20.

110. Wilson to Donald R. Murphy, June 2, 1939, NA, RG 16.

111. Kimball Young, "Memorandum on Social Psychology," September 28, 1939, NA, RG 83.

112. Wilson to John Tibby, December 21, 1937, NA, RG 16; Tolley, *Farmer Citizen at War*, 245–48.

113. Likert, "Democracy in Agriculture," in *Farmers in a Changing World*, 999; O. B. Conaway to O. C. Stine, February 10, 1943, HF.
114. "Address by M. L. Wilson," *Proceedings of the Association of Land-Grant Colleges and Universities, Fifty-second Annual Convention*, 89.
115. Taeusch to Wilson, June 26, 1940, Taeusch to Roy I. Kimmel, December 4, 1941, Statement on Objectives of the Division of Program Study and Discussion, NA, RG 83; Taeusch, "Schools of Philosophy for Farmers," in *Farmers in a Changing World*, 1115–17, 1119–20.
116. *Ibid.*, 1117–19; Taeusch to Wilson, February 5, Taeusch to Englund, June 12, 1940, Wilson to Directors of Extension, January 11, Taeusch to Kimmel, December 4, 1941, NA, RG 83; Wilson to Stringfellow Barr, January 23, 1941, NA, RG 16.
117. Taeusch, "Schools of Philosophy for Farmers," in *Farmers in a Changing World*, 1113–14; Taeusch to Warburton, January 17, Taeusch to Wilson, December 18, 1940, January 31, 1941, NA, RG 83. On one extension director's contempt for the schools of philosophy, see Lord, *The Agrarian Revival*, 183–85.
118. Paul L. Vogt to H. W. Hochbaum, January 5, Taeusch to Wilson, February 5, December 2, 1940, NA, RG 83.
119. Taeusch, "Statement on Objectives of the Division of Program Study and Discussion," *ibid.*
120. Taeusch to Englund, June 12, Taeusch to Tolley, July 16, 1940, *ibid.*
121. Taeusch to Tolley, November 8, 1940, February 26, 1941, Copy of Suggested Letter to State BAE Representatives, Allin and Taeusch to State BAE Representatives and Field Representatives of the Division of Program Study and Discussion, March 4, 1941, *ibid.*
122. Taeusch to Roy I. Kimmel, December 4, 1941, *ibid.*
123. Wilson, OHC; interviews with Allin and Englund; Black and Westcott, *Rural Planning*, 125.
124. "Experimenting by Districts," NA, RG 83; Allin to Tolley, May 29, 1936, NA, RG 16.
125. Summary of Documents Dealing with Agricultural Planning, NA, RG 83.
126. Allin to Philip M. Glick, April 6, 1939, *ibid.*
127. Wilson to W. R. Ronald, August 3, 1934, NA, RG 16; Wilson, "The Place of the Department of Agriculture in the Evolution of Agricultural Policy," December 11, 1936, NA, RG 83.
128. *Ibid.*
129. Wilson to N. S. Boardman, September 28, 1937, NA, RG 16.
130. Wilson to Jay Whitson, November 2, 1936, *ibid.*
131. Wilson, "The Place of the Department of Agriculture in the Evolution of Agricultural Policy," December 11, 1936, NA, RG 83.
132. House, Subcommittee of the Committee on Appropriations, *Hearings, Agriculture Department Appropriation Bill for 1940*, 76th Cong., 1st Sess., 1939, 876; Allin to W. T. Hicks, May 29, 1940, Wallace to D. W. Bell, November 25, 1938, NA, RG 83; "Rough Draft of Statement on Departmental Reorganization for Use by the Secretary at the Appropri-

ations Hearings," NA, RG 16; Hardin, "BAE under Fire," *JFE*, XXVIII (August, 1946), 641.

133. Wallace, "The Importance of Planning in the Development of Agricultural Programs," March 20, 1939, Rudolph Evans to Wallace, December 12, Director Memorandum to State Offices, December 12, 1939, NA, RG 83; Tolley and Wilson, OHC; interview with Wallace; Black, "BAE," *JFE*, 1947, 1033.

134. Tolley, OHC; Black and Westcott, *Rural Planning*, 145.

135. Tolley to E. J. Kyle, February 6, 1940, NA, RG 83; Tolley, OHC.

136. Tolley, *Report of the Chief of the Bureau of Agricultural Economics 1940*, 9.

137. "Organization and Activities of the Division of State and Local Planning, 1939–1940," Ralph H. Rogers to Allin, December 13, 1940, Tolley *et al.* to Chairmen of State Agricultural Planning Committees, August 5, Wilson to B. H. Crocheron, August 2, 1941, NA, RG 83; Allin, "County Planning Project," *JFE*, 1940, 297, 300–301; interviews with Allin and Carl Taylor.

Notes to Chapter 11

1. Campbell, *Farm Bureau*, 102.

2. McConnell, *Agrarian Democracy*, 79.

3. Campbell, *Farm Bureau*, 4, Chap. 6; McConnell, *Agrarian Democracy*, 185; Robert L. Tontz, "Membership of General Farm Organizations, United States, 1874–1960," *AH*, XXXVIII (July, 1964), 147, 156.

4. The best account of the split between the Roosevelt Administration and the Farm Bureau is in Campbell, *Farm Bureau*, Chap. 10.

5. See, for example, O'Neal to Roosevelt, September 28, 1936, NA, RG 16.

6. AFBF, *Official News Letter*, December 20, 1938.

7. Eric Englund to Milton Eisenhower, January 20, 1939, NA, RG 83.

8. Excerpts from the Meeting of the AFBF, June 3, 4, 1940, R. W. Blackburn to Farm Bureau Presidents, March 21, 1941, *ibid.*; Francis Johnson to Iowa County Farm Bureau Presidents, August 22, 1940, HF.

9. Summary of AFB Report on Coordination of Agricultural Programs, November 8, 1940, NA, RG 16.

10. House, Subcommittee of the Committee on Appropriations, *Hearings, Agriculture Department Appropriation Bill for 1942*, 77th Cong., 1st Sess., 1941, II:407–13, 416–18, 470–79, 483–521 (hereafter, House, *Hearings for 1942*); AFBF, *Official News Letter*, February 11, 1941.

11. Campbell, *Farm Bureau*, 178; see also McConnell, *Agrarian Democracy*, 118–19, and William J. Block, *The Separation of the Farm Bureau and the Extension Service: Political Issue in a Federal System*, 35.

12. House, *Hearings for 1942*, II:527–30.

13. *Ibid.*, II:396, 417 ff., 436–37, 481, 482, 484, 512, 519; Cannon to Waldo Frasier, May 30, 1941, NA, RG 16; AFBF, *Official News Letter*, February 25, June 17, 1941; House, *Report No. 176*, 77th Cong., 1st Sess.,

1941; Senate, Subcommittee of the Committee on Appropriations, *Hearings, Agriculture Department Appropriation Bill*, 77th Cong., 1st Sess., 1941, 2, 9 (hereafter, Senate, *Hearings for 1942*).

14. Hardin, "BAE under Fire," *JFE*, 1946, 644.
15. Wilson to Samuel Guard, February 28, 1936, NA, RG 16.
16. Wilson to C. E. Brehm, September 20, 1940, *ibid.*
17. Wilson to O'Neal and Ogg, September 21, 1940, NA, RG 83.
18. Wilson, speech, "The Extension Service Marches On," *ibid.*
19. Wilson to C. E. Brehm, September 23, 1940, *ibid.*; R. T. Nelson to Reuben Bingham, February 7, 1941, NA, RG 16.
20. O'Neal to C. E. Brehm, September 13, 1940, L. R. Simons to H. C. Ramsower, January 10, 1941, Meeting of the Board of Directors, AFBF, December 7, 1940, *ibid.*
21. Wilson to Appleby, September 19, 1940, *ibid.*
22. October 27, 1940, RL, OF 1350.
23. "The Farm Bureau-State Extension Service Proposal of Farm Program Administration," March 16, 1941, NA, RG 16.
24. O'Neal to Roosevelt, November 30, 1940, RL, OF 1350; Campbell, *Farm Bureau*, 183–85; Albertson, *Roosevelt's Farmer*, 173–74, 184.
25. *Ibid.*, 189–92; McConnell, *Agrarian Democracy*, 120–21; Bureau of Agricultural Economics, Tolley to W. A. Jump, March 8, Englund to Charles L. McNary, March 17, 1941, NA, RG 83; various documents, March-May, 1941, NA, RG 16, Subject File, Immediate Office of the Secretary, Organization; House, *Hearings for 1942*, I:4, 261–67, 274–77, II:470–79, 507–9, 521–39; Senate, *Hearings for 1942*, 9–11, 72–80.
26. *Ibid.*, 378–81; unidentified document, March 18, 1942, NA, RG 83, General Correspondence, AFBF.
27. Campbell, *Farm Bureau*, 168.
28. Tolley to Hutcheson, July 10, 1942, NA, RG 83.
29. Senate, *Hearings for 1942*, 374, 378.
30. Allin to Hutcheson, September 20, October 24, 1940, NA, RG 83.
31. Allin to Wilson, January 17, 1941, *ibid.*
32. Simons to H. C. Ramsower, January 19, Simons to Grover B. Hill, July 17, 1941, NA, RG 16; R. J. Baldwin to Clark L. Brody, March 22, Simons to Hutcheson *et al.*, April 28, Simons to Directors of Extension, March 18, Simons to Tolley, March 19, 1941, NA, RG 83.
33. Simons to Wagner and Mead, March 18, 1941, *ibid.*
34. Senate, *Hearings for 1942*, 218–21, 359, 370–81, 440–41; R. J. Baldwin to Clark L. Brody, March 22, Ross J. Silkert to Gladwin E. Young, March 22, H. J. Reed to Simons, April 4, 1941, NA, RG 83.
35. Englund to Tolley, April 5, "Present and Proposed Defense Activities of the BAE," November 14, 1941, *ibid.*
36. Wilson to State Directors of Extension, January 13, Tolley Memorandum for Heads of Divisions, January 14, 1941, *Agricultural Planning in a World at War*, January, 1942, 46–52, Status of Inter-Bureau Coordinating Committees, August 31, 1942, *ibid.*
37. Tolley to E. D. Smith, July 31, 1941, *ibid.*

38. Tolley Memorandum for Appleby, May 29, 1941, and draft of May 26, draft of letter Secretary to Bureau Chiefs, n.d., *ibid.*

39. Appleby to Baldwin, *et al.*, June 4, 1941, NA, RG 16; Wilson and Tolley to State Extension Directors, June 4, 1941, NA, RG 83.

40. Hardin, "BAE under Fire," *JFE*, 1946, 643–44; *Report of the Chief of Agricultural Economics, 1940*, 66, 68.

41. Brief of the Agency Comments on Appleby Memorandum, NA, RG 83.

42. Wilson and Tolley to State Extension Directors, June 4, 1941, *ibid.*

43. Hutcheson to Wilson *et al.*, June 14, 1941, "Excerpts from the Minutes of the Meeting of the Committee on Extension Organization and Policy, June 13, 1941," Hutcheson to Subcommittee on Extension Organization and Policy, *ibid.*

44. John D. Black to Wickard, June 18, 1941, NA, RG 16.

45. Senate, *Report 149*, 77th Cong., 1st Sess., 1941; House, *Report 786*, 77th Cong., 1st Sess., 1941; *Public Law 144*; *CR*, 77th Cong., 1st Sess., 2881 (April 2, 1941) ; Senate, Subcommittee of the Committee on Appropriations, *Hearings, Agriculture Department Appropriation Bill for 1943*, 77th Cong., 2d Sess., 1942, 121, 126 (hereafter, Senate, *Hearings for 1943*) ; Englund to Tolley, June 19, Tolley to State Extension Directors, June 19, FitzGerald to Rex Willard, June 20, Tolley to Hutcheson, July 15, Tolley to Simons, July 19, Simons to Wilson, August 4, 1941, NA, RG 83.

46. *Agricultural Planning in a World at War*, January, 1942, 18, 20–21, 34, John D. Black lecture, Graduate School of Public Administration, Harvard University, November 17, 1942, *ibid.*; Baker, *Century of Service*, 285–86; House, Subcommittee of the Committee on Appropriations, *Hearings, Agriculture Department Appropriation Bill for 1943*, 77th Cong., 2d Sess., 1942, I, 4–5 (hereafter, House, *Hearings for 1943*).

47. Albertson, *Roosevelt's Farmer*, 148–49; Wilson, OHC.

48. Tolley, *ibid.*; Black lecture, Graduate School of Public Administration, Harvard University, November 17, 1942, NA, RG 83; Black, "BAE," *JFE*, 1947, 1033, 1035.

49. Albertson, *Roosevelt's Farmer*, 50, 78–79, 85, 131, 252; Ickes, *Diary*, III, 452; Tolley and Samuel Bledsoe, OHC.

50. *Ibid.*; Wickard to Tolley, July 17, 1941, *Agricultural Planning in a World at War*, January, 1942, 54–55, K. J. Nicholson to Tolley, September 10, 1941, NA, RG 83; Albertson, *Roosevelt's Farmer*, 178–79, 188–89, 208–12, 230, 233–34, 238; Benedict, *Farm Policies*, 402–7, 431–37, 441–42; Baker, *Century of Service*, 281–83, 304, 324–25; Walter W. Wilcox, *The Farmer in the Second World War*, Chap. 5; Bela Gold, *Wartime Economic Planning in Agriculture*, 69–75, 83, 95; Wilson, "Nutritional Science and Agricultural Policy," *JFE*, 1942, 197–99; Stine, OHC.

51. Albertson, *Roosevelt's Farmer*, 252, 291; Tolley, OHC; Allin to W. S. Middaugh, March 11, Gladwin Young to State BAE Representatives, March 14, 1942, NA, RG 83.

52. Tolley to Secretary, January 7, 1942, *ibid.*

53. Allin, Staff Memoranda, July 3, 29, Allin to William A. Hartman, August 7, Hartman to Allin, October 29, Ralph H. Rogers to Allin, November 3, 1941, Allin to Regional and State BAE Representatives, January 2, Tolley to Secretary, January 5, "Some Typical Quotations from the States," Memorandum No. 921, Supp. 1, January 7, Allin to Fred V. Kepner, January 28, Allin to J. Edwin Losey, January 31, Jules F. Ferry to Allin, February 6, Allin to Fred Wallace, February 9, 10, W. Bassett Orr to Allin, February 28, 1942, *ibid.*; Tolley, OHC.

54. Tolley to Wickard, January 19, 1942, NA, RG 83.

55. Tolley to Secretary, February 4, 1942, and Allin draft of February 1, *ibid.*

56. "The Work of the Bureau of Agricultural Economics, Budget Year 1943," *ibid.*

57. Gladwin Young to State BAE Representatives, March 14, 1942, *ibid.*; House, *Hearings for 1943*, I:339–40.

58. Tolley to Staff of BAE, February 16, 1942, NA, RG 83.

59. Allin to Regional and State BAE Representatives, March 3, 1942, *ibid.*

60. House, *Hearings for 1943*, II:607–74.

61. *Ibid.*, II:639–45; House, *Hearings for 1942*, II:434–36, 499–505, 518; *CR*, 77th Cong., 1st Sess., 1670–71 (March 3, 1941); 77th Cong., 2d Sess., 1890 (March 3, 1942).

62. Hardin, "BAE under Fire," *JFE*, 1946, 647; Tontz, "Membership of General Farm Organizations," *AH*, 1964, 156; Arthur Moore, "Earl Smith: Farmers' Boss," *Atlantic Monthly*, CLXXV (January, 1945), 85–90; Campbell, *Farm Bureau*, 180–83; AFBF, *Official News Letter*, February 11, 1941.

63. *CR*, 77th Cong., 2d Sess., 1895 (March 3, 1942), 1993 (March 5, 1942); Senate, *Hearings for 1943*, 114, 124.

64. *CR*, 77th Cong., 2d Sess., 1993 (March 5, 1942); 77th Cong., 1st Sess., 1916–17 (March 6, 1941).

65. *CR*, 77th Cong., 2d Sess., 1994–95, 1997 (March 5, 1942).

66. AFBF, *Official News Letter*, September 23, December 16, 1941.

67. *CR*, 77th Cong., 2d Sess., 2006, 2015–17 (March 6, 1942); unidentified document, March 18, 1942, NA, RG 83, General Correspondence, AFBF.

68. *CR*, 77th Cong., 2d Sess., 1994–97 (March 5, 1942); *NYT*, March 6, 7, 14, 22, July 2, 4, 7, 1942. At first, *The New York Times* identified Dirksen with the "economy bloc" but then recognized his ties with the Farm Bureau. On Cannon and Dirksen, see Gardner Jackson to Stephen Early, July 2, 1942, RL, OF 1568: "Those two men under the guidance of Ed O'Neal and Earl Smith of the Farm Bureau are at the bottom of the present situation."

69. AFBF, *Official News Letter*, March 10, 24, 1942.

70. Senate, *Hearings for 1943*, 729–30.

71. *Ibid.*, 113–35; Tolley to BAE Staff Members, March 17, Englund, "A Suggestion for the Secretary's Consideration Relating to the BAE Appropriation," March 23, James C. Foster to Allin, July 8, 1942, NA, RG 83;

Tolley to Senator Harry S Truman, March 18, 1942, Truman, Library, Senatorial Files.

72. Allin to W. S. Middaugh, March 11, 1942, NA, RG 83.

73. House, *Hearings for 1943*, II:480, 700–760; Senate, *Hearings for 1943*, 6, 69–71.

74. Albertson, *Roosevelt's Farmer*, 271, 277–78, 286; Baldwin, "FSA," 473–80, 507 ff., 518–22; RL, OF 1, first half of 1942.

75. Milton Eisenhower to Wickard, December 10, 1941, NA, RG 16.

76. Senate, *Hearings for 1943*, 127.

77. Hardin, "BAE under Fire," *JFE*, 1946, 644–45; J. Edwin Losey to Allin, January 20, W. Bassett Orr to Allin, February 28, 1942, NA, RG 83; John R. Hutcheson, "Re-defining the Extension Job and Field of Action," *Proceedings of the Association of Land-Grant Colleges and Universities, November 10–12, 1941*, 182–83.

78. In Tennessee, where the relations between the Farm Bureau and the extension service in their work with the Tennessee Valley Authority provided the farm organization with a model for its ideas about the administration of farm programs, the extension director had supported the BAE in 1941, but in 1942 the president of the University of Tennessee, who was also president of the land-grant college organization, endorsed the Farm Bureau proposals about the role that the extension service should play in handling the farm programs. James D. Hoskins, "A Unified Command and Democracy in Agriculture," *Proceedings of the Association of Land-Grant Colleges and Universities, October 28–30, 1942*, 24–32; McConnell, *Agrarian Democracy*, 123–24.

79. Allin to Regional and State BAE Representatives, December 2, 1941, NA, RG 83.

80. There was some friction between Allin and Simons in 1942, but the latter regretted the congressional action. Simons to Tolley, January 5, Allin to W. S. Middaugh, January 8, Simons to Tolley, July 22, Jules F. Ferry to Allin, May 25, H. C. Ramsower to Wilson, July 9, Hutcheson to Tolley, July 6, Allin to J. C. Taylor, July 22, W. E. Rawlings to Members of State Agricultural Program Planning Committee, July 24, Tolley to William A. Schoenfield, July 27, Black lecture, Graduate School of Public Administration, Harvard University, November 17, C. B. Hutchinson to Roscoe E. Bell, July 23, 1942, Raymond C. Smith to S. B. Show, January 28, 1943, *ibid.*; Hardin, *Freedom in Agricultural Education*, 251.

81. Tolley, OHC; Senate, *Hearings for 1943*, 914–15, 918.

82. *Ibid.*, 868–90, 906–12, 940–47; RL, OF 327, 1350, 1568; Albertson, *Roosevelt's Farmer*, 274–75, 317.

83. Senate, *Hearings for 1943*, 923, 940–42, 945.

84. *Ibid.*, 1034; *NYT*, February 14, 1942.

85. Senate, *Hearings for 1943*, 124–25.

86. *Ibid.*, 122, 127; Wayne S. Cole, *Senator Gerald P. Nye and American Foreign Relations.*

87. Senate, *Hearings for 1943*, 69–70; *CR*, 77th Cong., 2d Sess., 4182–83 (May 14, 1942), 5061 (June 9, 1942); Senate, 77th Cong., 2d Sess., *Report 1323*.

88. AFBF, *Official News Letter*, May 19, June 16, 1942; O'Neal letter of June 8, 1942, Hope Papers.

89. House, 77th Cong., 2d Sess., *Report 2288*; *Report 2218*; *Public Law 674*; *NYT*, June 26, 1942.

90. *CR*, 77th Cong., 2d Sess., 5624 (June 26, 1942).

91. Banfield, "Organization for Policy Planning," *JFE*, 1952, 28–29.

92. Gross, "A Post Mortem on County Planning," *JFE*, 1943, 644–61.

93. McConnell, *Agrarian Democracy*, 117.

94. John Black, *Federal-State-Local Relations in Agriculture*, 16.

95. Black and Westcott, *Rural Planning*, 397.

96. Hardin, "Political Planning: Possibilities, Limitations, and Aberrations," in Harold G. Holcrow *et al.*, eds., *Modern Land Policy*, 261.

97. Allin to Elliott, April 20, 1943, NA, RG 83.

98. W. Robert Parks, "Political and Administrative Guide Lines in Developing Public Agricultural Policies," *JFE*, XXXIII (May, 1951), 166.

99. Black, "BAE," *JFE*, 1947, 1035.

100. Allin to Tolley, June 12, 1942, NA, RG 83.

101. Draft of letter by Allin, June 17, 1942, NA, RG 16.

102. D. A. FitzGerald to Samuel Bledsoe, June 17, 1942, *ibid.*

103. Taeusch to Tolley, June 12, 1941, James C. Moore to Harold A. Vogel, July 17, 1942, Taeusch to O'Neal, October 25, 1943, NA, RG 83.

104. Unidentified document, March 18, 1942, *ibid.*

105. W. S. Middaugh to State BAE Representatives, April 16, W. A. Hartman to Allin, July 18, John Muehlbeier to Allin, July 23, BAE Representatives of Northeast to Tolley and Allin, August 10, 1942, *ibid.*

106. Jules F. Ferry to Allin, May 25, 1942, *ibid.*

107. Allin to W. S. Middaugh, March 11, 1942, *ibid.*

108. Tolley, OHC; Gladwin Young to State BAE Representatives, March 14, Tolley to H. C. Ramsower, June 25, July 14, Tolley to Allin, July 3, Allin to Regional and State BAE Representatives, July 3, Hugo Schwartz to Regional Supervisors, July 4, 10, 1942, NA, RG 83; Notes on Meeting of the Washington Committee on BAE Field Programs, January 30, 1943, HF.

NOTES TO CHAPTER 12

1. Michael Straight to Tolley, February 25, 1942, NA, RG 83.

2. John D. and Ewart Lewis, "The Farmer Helps to Plan," *New Republic*, CV (October 20, 1941), 504–5.

3. "Hamstringing the BAE," *ibid.*, CVII (August 24, 1942), 213.

4. Baldwin to Tolley, February 25, 1942, NA, RG 83.

5. Albertson, *Roosevelt's Farmer*, 327, 343, 345; McConnell, *Agrarian Democracy*, 106; O'Neal press release, June 23, 1942, RL, OF 1568; Tolley, *The Farmer Citizen at War*, 61, Chap. 6.

6. Baldwin, "FSA," 522–35; Benedict, *Farm Policies*, 492–93; McConnell, *Agrarian Democracy*, 109–10; RL, OF 1568 for 1943; R. W. Hudgens to Donald R. Murphy, November 11, 1943, J. H. Bankhead to Clinton Anderson, November 14, 1945, NA, RG 16.

7. Hewes, *Boxcar*, 203.

8. Daniels Memorandum for Roosevelt, September 4, Roosevelt to Baldwin, September 6, 1943, RL, OF 1568.

9. William J. Block, *The Separation of the Farm Bureau and the Extension Service: Political Issue in a Federal System*, 46–55.

10. Tolley, *The Farmer Citizen at War*, 113–14; Tolley, OHC.

11. Interview with Taylor; USDA Press Release, October 5, 1935, HF.

12. *Ibid.*; Taylor to Arthur Chew, December 8, 1943, NA, RG 83; Taylor, "Techniques of Community Study and Analysis as Applied to Modern Civilized Societies," in Ralph Linton, ed., *The Science of Man in the World Crisis*, 421; Taylor, "Subsistence Homesteads Program," *JFE*, 1935, 720–31; Edmund de S. Brunner, "Sociology Tomorrow," *Rural Sociology*, XI (June, 1946), 95–96.

13. Taylor, "Research and Planning in the Field of Farm Population and Rural Life," January 30, 1939, NA, RG 83.

14. Interview with Taylor; Taylor to Wilson, January 31, 1938, Conrad Taeuber to Allin, July 6, 1943, "War Production Goals and Their Attainment," February 13, 1942, *ibid.*

15. Taylor, "Program and Activities of the Division of Farm Population and Rural Life, 1938," *ibid.*

16. Taylor to Sherman Johnson, November 27, 1939, April 10, 1940, Taylor to F. F. Elliott, December 15, 1939, *ibid.*

17. Douglas Ensminger to Taylor, May 16, 1940, *ibid.*

18. Conrad Taeuber to Taylor, November 20, 1939, *ibid.*

19. Taylor, "Report of the Subcommittee of the Executive Committee on Participation of Sociologists in the National Emergency," *American Sociological Review*, VII (February, 1942), 89.

20. Taylor to Alexander, March 4, 1937, NA, RG 16; Taylor to Gray, December 1, 1938, NA, RG 83.

21. Taylor, "Land Utilization," *JFE*, 1937, 594.

22. Taylor to Allin, February 18, 1939, NA, RG 83.

23. Interview with Taylor; Taylor to Regional Leaders, May 21, 1946, FRC, RG 83; Taylor, "The Work of the Division of Farm Population and Rural Life," *Rural Sociology*, IV (June, 1939), 222–25, 228; Taeuber, "Some Recent Developments in Sociological Work in the Department of Agriculture," *American Sociological Review*, X (April, 1945), 169–70; Robin M. Williams, Jr., "Review of Current Research in Rural Sociology," *Rural Sociology*, XI (June, 1946), 106–7, 114.

24. Taylor to Walter McKain, Jr., January 5, 1944, NA, RG 83; Taylor, "Social Theory and Social Action," *Rural Sociology*, V (March, 1940), 17–31; Taylor, "Social Science and Social Action in Agriculture," *Social Forces*, XX (December, 1941), 154–59; Taylor, with discussion by Robert Redfield and Samuel A. Stouffer, "Sociology and Common

Sense," *American Sociological Review*, XII (February, 1947), 1–10;
William H. Sewell, with comments by Taylor, "Needed Research in
Sociology," *Rural Sociology*, XV (June, 1950), 116–17, 121–22, 129;
Roscoe C. Hinkle, Jr., and Gisela J. Hinkle, *The Development of Modern
Sociology: Its Nature and Growth in the United States*, 46–49; Edmund
de S. Brunner, *The Growth of a Science: A Half Century of Rural Soci-
ological Research in the United States*, 18–20.

25. A. G. Black to Appleby, June 4, William T. Ham Memorandum for
    Appleby, June 15, Wallace to Roy Hendrickson *et al.*, September 3, 1937,
    NA, RG 16.

26. Taeuber to Taylor, November 23, 1938, Taylor to Elliott, March 8, 1941,
    NA, RG 83.

27. Taylor to A. G. Black, June 25, 1937, Taylor to Englund, April 1, 1938,
    Olaf Larson to Taylor, June 17, 1940, Larson to Robert Buck, May 15,
    1942, *ibid.*

28. Taylor to David Meeker, June 22, William T. Ham to Taylor, June 21,
    1940, *ibid.*; interview with Taylor.

29. Taylor to Area Leaders, January 23, Taeuber, June 17, 1942, NA, RG 83.

30. Taylor to John Fischer, October 4, 1940, *ibid.*

31. Acting Administrator, FSA, to Tolley, October 16, Arthur Raper to
    George Mitchell, December 5, 1942, Taylor to Bushrod Allin and Peter
    De Vries, October 6, 1944, *ibid.*; interview with Taylor.

32. Roy F. Hendrickson to Taylor, April 21, December 1, 1937, NA, RG 83;
    John Thurston to W. A. Jump, May 9, 1944, NA, RG 16.

33. Tolley to George F. Dunning, April 14, 1944, NA, RG 83.

34. Kimball Young to Taylor, June 29, 1942, *ibid.*

35. Taylor to Peter De Vries, March 17, 1944, *ibid.*; Brunner, *The Growth
    of a Science*, 10, 13–14, 18–22, 26–27; Conrad Arensberg, "The Com-
    munity Study Method," *American Journal of Sociology*, LX (September,
    1954), 120–21; Walter Goldschmidt, "Social Class in America — A
    Critical Review," *American Anthropologist*, LII (October–December,
    1950), 484; Pauline H. Young, *Scientific Social Surveys and Research*,
    54–56.

36. Taylor to Regional Leaders, January 26, 1944, NA, RG 83.

37. For a more detailed and a documented version of this episode, see Rich-
    ard S. Kirkendall, "Social Science in the Central Valley of California: An
    Episode," *California Historical Society Quarterly*, XLIII (September,
    1964), 195–218.

38. Clawson to Lippert S. Ellis, August 5, 1944, Federal Records Center,
    South San Francisco, RG 83; Clawson to Tolley, July 10, September 20,
    1945, NA, RG 83; Taylor, with discussion by Clawson, "The Sociolo-
    gists' Part in Planning the Columbia Basin," *American Sociological Re-
    view*, XI (June, 1946), 321–29.

39. Tolley to Rex E. Willard, August 6, Drummond Jones to J. R. Hutcheson,
    August 21, O. V. Wells to Virgil Parr, November 3, 1942, "Agriculture
    Department: IBCC on Postwar Programs," Raymond C. Smith to Earle
    Rugg, March 17, Wilson to State Directors of Extension, August 10,

Gladwin E. Young to Tolley, September 27, 1943, Tolley to W. A. Minor, August 13, 1945, NA, RG 83; Raymond C. Smith to the Secretary, October 2, 1945, Anderson Papers (Truman Library, Independence, Missouri).

40. Allin to Tolley, April 20, Raymond C. Smith to Scott Russell, December 12, 1943, NA, RG 83; Mordecai Ezekiel to Felix A. Grisette, April 14, 1944, NA, RG 16.

41. Taylor to Tolley, March 4, 1944, NA, RG 83; Raymond C. Smith to W. A. Minor, October 19, 1945, NA, RG 16; B. H. Crocheron to S. B. Show, May 25, 1945, FRC, RG 83.

42. Tolley, OHC; Wickard Memorandum, May 13, 1941, "Agriculture in Postwar Adjustment," James G. Maddox to Elliott, August 10, 1945, Elliott, "American Agriculture after the War," August 21, 1942, George S. Wehrwein to Tolley, November 8, 1944, Tolley to Wallace, May 29, John Brewster to Servicemen in the Division of Land Economics, November 14, 1945, NA, RG 83; Allin and Smith testimony before Senate Special Committee on Postwar Economic Policy and Planning, NA, RG 16; Tolley, "Probable Trends for American Food Production after the War," *Proceedings of the Association of Land-Grant Colleges and Universities, October, 1944*, 159; Maddox, "What's Ahead for the Farmer," *Harper's Magazine*, CXC (March, 1945), 321–26; USDA, *What Peace Can Mean to American Farmers; Post-War Agriculture and Employment*, Misc. Pub. No. 562, May, 1945.

43. Ezekiel: OHC; *$2500 a Year: From Scarcity to Abundance; Jobs for All Through Industrial Expansion*; "Lines of Action in Economic Reconstruction," *Antioch Review*, I (September, 1941), 328–42; "Statistical Investigations of Saving, Consumption and Investment," *American Economic Review*, XXXII (March, 1942), 22–49; *ibid.* (June, 1942), 272–307; correspondence in NA, RG 16, Subject File, Immediate Office of the Secretary, Economics, especially Ezekiel to Hansen, July 6, 1939, and reply, July 21.

44. Ezekiel correspondence, NA, RG 16, Subject File, Immediate Office of the Secretary, Businessmen and Ezekiel.

45. Ezekiel Memoranda for the Secretary, September 15, December 12, 1937, HF; Arthur P. Chew to Mary A. Huss, March 17, 1938, NA, RG 16.

46. Ezekiel to Wilson, February 6, 1936, Ezekiel to John M. Chapman, June 14, 1938, Ezekiel to Wickard, January 26, 1942, *ibid.*

47. Henry Jarrett to Paul W. Chapman, August 8, 1945, NA, RG 83; Ezekiel, OHC.

48. Raymond C. Smith to W. R. Ogg, August 28, William A. D. Millron to Raymond C. Smith, November 25, 1943, USDA Press Release, May 5, Wickard to Reed F. Murray, December 9, 1944, NA, RG 83.

49. Tolley, OHC; Stephen Kemp Bailey, *Congress Makes a Law: The Story Behind the Employment Act of 1946*, 21, 24, 45, 55, 63–68, 77–78, 160.

50. Tolley to Division Heads, August 11, 1942, Allin to Tolley, February 19, 1943, NA, RG 83; USDA, *What Peace Can Mean to American Farmers*, 2.

51. F. L. Thomsen to Allin, July 14, 1943, NA, RG 83.

52. The basic documents on the plan and the development of it are available in HF and NA, RG 83, General Correspondence, Conversion Program, Allin, and Elliott; see also Stine, OHC.

53. Raymond C. Smith to Chairmen, Postwar Regional Committees, May 16, Smith to W. S. Middaugh, July 11, 1945, NA, RG 83.

54. BAE, "A Conversion Program for the Cotton South," April, 1945, *ibid.*

55. Henry Jarrett to Elliott, June 9, Jarrett to Corwin D. Edwards, August 2, Jarrett to Paul W. Chapman, August 8, Ezekiel to Helen Fuller, August 18, Elliott to Alexander Nunn, August 20, 28, 1945, *ibid.*; Hardin, "BAE under Fire," *JFE*, 1946, 657–58.

56. John Black, "BAE," *JFE*, 1947, 1036; see also John D. Millett, *The Process and Organization of Government Planning*, 81–82.

57. Raymond C. Smith to W. S. Middaugh, July 11, 1945, NA, RG 83.

58. Tolley to John V. Van Sickle, June 26, 1945, *ibid.*

59. In addition to the Conversion Program file in the National Archives, see Raymond C. Smith to Gordon R. Salmond *et al.*, May 21, 1945, NA, RG 83; "Cotton's Future," *Business Week*, December 9, 1944, 26, 28; *NYT*, December 5, 1944, May 15, 1945; *National Union Farmer*, June 1, July 15, 1945; House, Subcommittee of the Committee on Appropriations, *Hearings, Agriculture Department Appropriation Bill for 1946*, 79th Cong., 1st Sess., 1945, 14–16, 37 (hereafter, House, *Hearings for 1946*).

60. Henry Jarrett, Notes on Conversion Program Meetings in South, June 22, 1945, NA, RG 83; House, Subcommittee of the Committee on Appropriations, *Hearings, Agriculture Department Appropriation Bill for 1947*, 79th Cong., 2d Sess., 1946, 56, 252, 256 (hereafter, House, *Hearings for 1947*); *NYT*, December 6, 8, 9, 14, 18, 25, 1944; Arthur W. Baum, "They Say He's a Dangerous Man," *Saturday Evening Post*, CCXVII (May 5, 1945), 14 ff.; "Will Clayton's Cotton," *Fortune*, XXXII (November and December, 1945); "Adjustments in Southern Agriculture with Special Reference to Cotton," *JFE*, XXVIII (February, 1946), 341–79; Reo Christenson, *The Brannan Plan: Farm Politics and Policy*, 13–14, 45–46.

61. Peter F. Drucker, "Exit King Cotton," *Harper's Magazine*, CXCII (May, 1946), 477, 480.

62. Patton to Tolley, September 7, 1945, NA, RG 83.

63. *National Union Farmer*, June 1, July 1, 15, August 15, 1945; Patton Statement to the Eisenhower Committee. Patton sent the statement to Tolley with "Kindest personal regards," July 31, 1945, NA, RG 83.

64. Drucker, "Exit King Cotton," *Harper's Magazine*, 1946, 477; "New Farm Policies," *New Republic*, CXII (April 16, 1945), 496.

65. Paul Greer to Tolley, August 8, 1945, NA, RG 83.

66. Wilcox, *The Farmer in the Second World War*, 132–34, 225, 253–62, 373; Benedict, *Farm Policies*, 408–10, 450–52; Albertson, *Roosevelt's Farmer*, 361, 386; *NYT*, September 19, 25, 1945; Statement of O'Neal to President Truman, September 24, 1945, TL, OF 524.

67. John R. Hutcheson to Tolley, May 17, Jarrett to Elliott, June 9, Jarrett, Notes on Conversion Program Meetings in South, Jarrett to Paul W. Chapman, August 8, Alexander Nunn to Elliott, August 22, Wilhelm Anderson to David H. Eddy, September 6, Anderson to Elliott, June 1, Jarrett to Elliott, May 31, 1945, NA, RG 83.

68. *NYT*, May 24, 1945; Ovid Martin column, June 30, 1945, and article on Anderson "As Secretary," copies in Anderson Papers; Jack H. Pollock, "America's New Food Czar," *Liberty Magazine*, August 4, 1945.

69. Anderson to Albert S. Goss, October 30, Anderson to Eugene Cervi, November 18, 1946, NA, RG 16; Anderson to Luther H. Hodges, June 7, 1945, Anderson Papers.

70. W. Harry King to Anderson, June 4, 1945, *ibid.* An unidentified article on Anderson in these papers suggests that "in approaching his new job, he appears to have been torn between his 'smart' instinct to lean heavily upon Hutson, and his impulsiveness to show USDA who was boss. The second trait prevailed. . . ." An interview with Wilson strengthened my confidence in this interpretation. Compare Anderson's letter of June 7 to his friend Luther Hodges, the Vice President of Marshall Field and Co., asking him to serve as a consultant and to assist with the reorganization: "In this capacity I would want you to work on the assumption that you acquired a vast new plant which was sorely disorganized and urgently in need of being pulled together so as to function efficiently. . . . The viewpoint that you will bring, in my opinion, is highly essential since it is not encumbered by a knowledge of the way the Department of Agriculture operates."

71. Eisenhower to Anderson, May 31, June 9, September 20, 27, Anderson to Eisenhower, June 4, 1945, *ibid.*, and NA, RG 16.

72. Eisenhower to Anderson, May 31, 1945, Anderson Papers.

73. Eisenhower to Anderson, August 9, 1945, *ibid.*; Memorandum to Servicemen in the Division of Land Economics, September 4, 1945, NA, RG 83.

74. Likert to Tolley, July 20, 1945, *ibid.*

75. Anderson Statement for "Congressional Record on the Air," radio program, June 4, Will Clayton to Anderson, July 3, 1945, Anderson Papers; Anderson, "Work Conquers All Things: Full Employment First Requisite for Farm Prosperity," *Vital Speeches*, XI (August 15, 1945), 661–64; *NYT*, August 16, October 6, 1945; "Farm Cutbacks," *Business Week*, August 25, 1945, 21–22; Arthur P. Chew, "What's Ahead for Agriculture," *New Republic*, CXIII (September 17, 1945), 337–39; Anderson, "Is the Farmer Heading for Trouble Again?" *Saturday Evening Post*, CCXVIII (December 22, 1945), 18 ff.; House, *Hearings for 1947*, 251–52.

76. Anderson, Memphis speech, November 12, 1945, Anderson Papers.

77. Anderson to Dan Burross, November 19, 1945, *ibid.*

78. Patton to Truman, August 8, 1945, TL, OF 1-Misc.; Patton to Anderson, November 23, 1945, NA, RG 16.

79. Interviews with Murray Benedict, Eric Englund, and Bushrod Allin; Meeting of Policy and Program Committee, March 26, 1947, Anderson

Papers; Louis Bean, OHC; Black, "BAE," *JFE*, 1947, 1035–36; Eisenhower to Members of the USDA Committee on Organization, September 20, 1945, NA, RG 16.

80. Senate, Subcommittee of the Committee on Appropriations, *Hearings, Agricultural Appropriation Bill for 1947*, 79th Cong., 2d Sess., 1946, 528–29 (hereafter, Senate, *Hearings for 1947*) ; *National Union Farmer*, November 1, 1945.

81. Patton to Anderson, October 4, 1945, NA, RG 16.

82. *National Union Farmer*, August 1, October 15, November 1, 1945.

83. W. Harry King to Anderson, June 4, 1945, Anderson Papers.

84. Anderson to Dan Burross, November 19, 1945, *ibid.*; Anderson to Albert S. Goss, October 30, Anderson to E. E. Varce, November 20, 1946, NA, RG 16.

85. Patton to Anderson, October 4, 1945, *ibid.*

86. Anderson to Patton, October 10, 1945, *ibid.*

87. Tontz, "Memberships of General Farm Organizations," *AH*, 1964, 147, 150, 155–56; Louis Bernard Schmidt, "The Role and Techniques of Agrarian Pressure Groups," *AH*, XXX (April, 1956), 51.

88. Patton to Roosevelt, April 7, 1941, M. W. Thatcher to Drew Pearson, March 1, 1943, Thatcher to Wickard, October 1, 1944, NA, RG 16; Phil Murray to General Watson, February 25, 1942, RL, OF 1; Gladys Talbott Edwards, *The Farmers Union Triangle*, 54–55, 59, 138, 158; Russell Smith, "Big Business and the Farm Bloc," *Antioch Review*, IV (June, 1944), 189–204; William P. Tucker, "The Farmers Union: The Social Thought of a Current Agrarian Movement," *Southwestern Social Science Quarterly*, XXVII (June, 1946), 45–53; McCune, *The Farm Bloc*, Chap. 11; McCune, *Who's Behind Our Farm Policy?* 45–52.

89. C. C. Teague to Fred A. Sexauer, January 30, Teague to Ezra Taft Benson *et al.*, February 5, O'Neal to Teague, February 23, May 3, 1943, Teague Papers; O'Neal Press Release, June 23, 1942, RL, OF 1568; Kile, *Farm Bureau*, 292–93, 296. For a discussion of the role of the Farmers Union in the "Lib-Lab" lobby as opposed to the Farm Bureau's ties by 1945 with groups like the United States Chamber of Commerce and the National Association of Manufacturers, see Bailey, *Congress Makes a Law*, esp. 21–24, 75–77, 118, Chaps. 5, 7.

90. Martin column, June 30, 1945, unidentified article on Anderson, Carl V. Rice to Anderson, June 13, 1945, Anderson Papers; Pollock, "America's New Food Czar," *Liberty Magazine*, August 4, 1945.

91. Baldwin to Anderson, June 10, 1946, Patton to Anderson, October 12, J. H. Bankhead to Anderson, November 15, 1945, Anderson to Imogene Rousseau, January 24, O'Neal to Anderson, May 24, June 14, Anderson to Eugene Cervi, November 18, Anderson to J. Frank Hobbs, November 20, 1946, NA, RG 16; Bean, OHC.

92. The documents on this project are in NA, RG 83, General Correspondence, Farm Population and Reorganization — BAE.

93. Taylor to Area Leaders, December 3, 1943, Taylor to Frank Alexander,

May 19, Taylor to Kimball Young, June 27, 1944, Linden S. Dodson to
H. S. Long, May 23, 1945, Clawson to Earl Bell, September 24, Bell to
Clawson, November 23, 1945, NA, RG 83.

94. Taylor to Regional Leaders, January 10, 1945, *ibid.*
95. William H. Nichols, *Southern Tradition and Regional Progress*, 145–
46. Nichols points to "the dismissal of Dean Carl Taylor, a liberal
rural sociologist, of North Carolina State College in 1931," for his
"forays into the neglected social and economic areas" as one demonstration that the southern schools' "normal sense of 'the appropriate' was
well-founded." On that episode, W. J. Cash wrote: "So late as 1931
Dr. Carl Taylor was dismissed from his post as dean at the North Carolina State College of Agriculture and Engineering mainly because his
activities in behalf of free speech and civil liberty had antagonized the
cotton-mill magnates who dominated it." Cash, *The Mind of the South*,
327.
96. Taylor to Harold T. Christensen, January 20, Alexander to Dr. Wayland
J. Hayes, January 27, Alexander to Theodore Schultz, February 19,
Alexander to Jewell Garland, April 12, Ralph R. Nichols to Wayne C.
Neely, October 12, Alexander to Taylor, November 29, December 5,
Taylor to Congressman Abernethy, December 4, Taylor to Roy Roberts,
December 28, 1945, Elva McCaffrey to Carey McWilliams, May 3, 1946,
NA, RG 83; House, *Hearings for 1947*, 236.
97. W. H. Elliott to Allin, February 4, 1942, Taylor to Paul V. Kepner, Au-
gust 24, 1943, NA, RG 83.
98. Interview with Taylor; *CR*, 79th Cong., 2d Sess., 2073 (March 8, 1946);
National Union Farmer, March 1, 1946; Hardin, *Freedom in Agricultural
Education*, 184.
99. Enclosure with Dan R. McGehee to Anderson, November 15, 1945,
NA, RG 16.
100. House, *Hearings for 1947*, 239.
101. McGehee to Anderson, November 15, 1945.
102. On Anderson's friendship with McGehee, see McGehee to Anderson,
February 27, 1946, September 2, 1947, Anderson Papers.
103. Lindsay Warren to Matthew J. Connelly, October 5, Truman to Whittington, October 16, 1945, TL, OF 285–A.
104. Note relating to Anderson's response to McGehee, NA, RG 83; early
draft of reply, NA, RG 16.
105. Anderson to McGehee, December 5, 1945, NA, RG 83.
106. *National Union Farmer*, March 1, 1946; House, *Hearings for 1947*,
236–39, 241, 284; Senate, *Hearings for 1947*, 109.
107. Taylor to Abernethy, December 4, 5, 1945, NA, RG 83; *CR*, 79th Cong.,
2d Sess., 2073 (March 8, 1946).
108. Taylor to Clawson, July 19, 1943, NA, RG 83.
109. Raymond C. Smith to Taylor, January 24, 1946, *ibid.*
110. Wilhelm Anderson to Elliott, March 27, 1946, *ibid.*
111. Anderson Memoranda, December 12, 1945, Secretary to Chief, BAE,

January 2, 1946, *ibid.*; The 1947 Budget of Department of Agriculture; Estimates and Allowances, December 15, 1945, TL, OF 1; *NYT*, December 14, 1945; House, *Hearings for 1947*, 182–84.

112. See items December, 1945, to March, 1946, in NA, RG 16, Subject File, Immediate Office of the Secretary, Organization.
113. Patton to Anderson, December 27, 1945, *ibid.*

NOTES TO CHAPTER 13

1. House, *Hearings for 1947*, 1654.
2. *Ibid.*, 1644–45.
3. Senate, *Hearings for 1947*, 655.
4. House, *Hearings for 1947*, 1628, 1654.
5. Hardin, "BAE under Fire," *JFE*, 1946, 641.
6. House, *Hearings for 1947*, 1655.
7. *Ibid.*, 1646, 1653.
8. Lippert S. Ellis to Tolley, April 1, 1946, NA, RG 83.
9. House, *Hearings for 1947*, 186, 204; see also 206–7, 226.
10. *Ibid.*, 225.
11. *Ibid.*, 19.
12. *Ibid.*, 255; CR, 79th Cong., 2d Sess., 2015 (March 7, 1946).
13. Senate, *Hearings for 1947*, 93–101.
14. *CR*, 79th Cong., 2d Sess., 2007 (March 7, 1946).
15. *Ibid.*, 2073 (March 8, 1946).
16. House, *Hearings for 1947*, 235, 238–40, 284.
17. Elliott to Congressman William M. Whittington, March 25, 1946, NA, RG 83.
18. House, *Hearings for 1947*, 235, 239, 241.
19. Kile, *Farm Bureau*, 323–26.
20. V. O. Key, Jr., attributed Tarver's defeat in the primary election later in 1946 to the CIO. Key, *Southern Politics in State and Nation*, 657.
21. *CR*, 77th Cong., 2d Sess., 2015–16 (March 7, 1946).
22. *Ibid.*, 2062–63 (March 8, 1946). The BAE was aware of this political weakness of the plan. One member had pointed out to Elliott that "indirect subsidies to American cotton growers in the form of parity prices may be less vulnerable to political attack than direct subsidies from public funds. . . . The economic advantages of direct over indirect subsidies are easily shown but the uncertainty of the availability of funds for direct subsidies might well be considered openly and frankly in formulating a program for the South." L. D. Howell to Elliott, June 7, 1945, NA, RG 83.
23. *CR*, 79th Cong., 2d Sess., 2015 (March 7, 1946); Senate, *Hearings for 1947*, 96.
24. House, *Hearings for 1947*, 232, 234.
25. *CR*, 79th Cong., 2d Sess., 2015 (March 7, 1946), 2073 (March 8, 1946). Dirksen served as Republican floor manager for the Republican attack upon the BAE.

26. *Ibid.*, 2007 (March 7, 1946).

27. Hardin, "BAE under Fire," *JFE*, 1946, 649.

28. Hardin, *Freedom in Agricultural Education*, 165.

29. House, *Hearings for 1947*, 282.

30. Hardin, "BAE under Fire," *JFE*, 1946, 649–50; Hardin, *Freedom in Agricultural Education*, 164–65.

31. House, *Hearings for 1946*, 179, 182–84.

32. House, *Hearings for 1947*, 187.

33. *Ibid.*, 203. On conflict within the department about how much attention it should and could devote to the interests of consumers, see Meeting of Committee to Study Policies and Programs for Postwar Agriculture, May 15, 1945, NA, RG 83.

34. House, *Hearings for 1947*, 282, 289, 291.

35. *Ibid.*, 229, 230–31, 233, 289, 291.

36. *Ibid.*, 264.

37. *Ibid.*, 223, 268, 291–94.

38. Hardin, "BAE under Fire," *JFE*, 1946, 663.

39. *CR*, 79th Cong., 2d Sess., 2007 (March 7, 1946), 2071–73 (March 8, 1946).

40. Millett, *Government Planning*, 81; Lippert S. Ellis to Tolley, April 1, 1946, NA, RG 83.

41. House, *Hearings for 1947*, 19–20, 261; *CR*, 79th Cong., 2d Sess., 2007 (March 7, 1946).

42. House, *Report 1659, Department of Agriculture Appropriation Bill, Fiscal Year 1947*, 79th Cong., 2d Sess., 1946.

43. House, *Hearings for 1947*, 19, 33, 50–54, 184, 251–52; *CR*, 79th Cong., 2d Sess., 2073 (March 8, 1946); Hardin, "BAE under Fire," *JFE*, 1946, 655–56, 659–60, 668.

44. House, *Hearings for 1947*, 20; see also Christenson, *The Brannan Plan*, 57, 190.

45. Latham White to Anderson, April 4, Anderson to Walter L. Randolph, June 21, 1946, Anderson Papers; House, *Hearings for 1947*, 57–59; Hardin, "BAE under Fire," *JFE*, 1946, 639.

46. Senate, *Hearings for 1947*, 8–9, 54, 89–93, 99–103, 106–10; Anderson to Senator Richard Russell, May 22, 1946, NA, RG 83.

47. House, *Hearings for 1947*, 286–87.

48. E. L. Markel to Sheridan Downey and Tolley, May 15, 1946, NA, RG 83.

49. Senate, *Hearings for 1947*, 670.

50. Welch to Taylor, May 7, Alexander to Taylor, April 8, 1946, NA, RG 83.

51. Senate, *Hearings for 1947*, 531–32, 649–51.

52. Theodore Schultz, "Some Guiding Principles in Organizing Agricultural Economics Research," *JFE*, XXXVI (February, 1954), 18. On "The Iowa Margarine Incident" of 1943, which involved an attack by the Farm Bureau upon social scientists, see Hardin, *Freedom*, Chap. 10, and Schultz to Charles E. Friley, September 15, Schultz to Joseph H. Willits, September 22, 1943, Taylor Papers. More recently, Schultz had been attacked by one of Anderson's critics, Walter L. Randolph, the presi-

dent of the Alabama Farm Bureau. At a Triple-A meeting in Biloxi, Mississippi, on March 28, 1946, according to a report by one of Anderson's representatives, Randolph reported that a wag had said that Schultz's book, *Agriculture in an Unstable Economy*, "should be titled 'Agriculture by an Unstable Economist'" and "went on to say both Schultz and the Secretary of Agriculture were advocating lower prices for farm products." Randolph was not sure whether Schultz wrote his book after reading Anderson's speeches or Anderson composed the speeches after reading Schultz's book. "In this connection he went on in a semi-facetious vein and said that apparently Schultz had a lot more influence on the agricultural policies of the Department than many people thought." Latham White to Anderson, April 4, 1946, Anderson Papers.

53. Noble Clark to Gladwin E. Young, March 19, 1946, NA, RG 83.
54. Hardin, "BAE under Fire," *JFE*, 1946, 667.
55. Senate, *Hearings for 1947*, 529–30.
56. *Ibid.*, 528–29; Eisenhower to Anderson, April 2, 1946, NA, RG 16.
57. Tolley to Eisenhower, April 8, Anderson to Eisenhower, April 10, *ibid.*
58. Tontz, "Memberships of General Farm Organizations," *AH*, 1964, 155; E. J. Haselrud to Wilson, January 16, 1937, Glenn J. Talbott to Anderson, July 30, 1945, NA, RG 16; Haselrud to C. W. Warburton, June 22, Haselrud to Allin, July 15, 21, 1939, Haselrud to Tolley, February 6, Haselrud to Extension Specialists, June 4, 1940, NA, RG 83.
59. Obed A. Wyum to Langer, April 12, 1946, *ibid.*
60. *National Union Farmer*, March 1, 1946.
61. See Bailey, *Congress Makes a Law*, esp. 167–71, 226, 233.
62. Senate, *Agricultural Appropriation Bill, 1947*, 79th Cong., 2d Sess., 1946, Report 1334; *CR*, 79th Cong., 2d Sess., 6099, 6107 (June 1, 1946); AFBF, *Official News Letter*, May 29, 1946.
63. Appleby to M. C. Latta, June 21, 1945, TL, Bill File; *CR*, 79th Cong., 2d Sess., 6666–68, 6673 (June 11, 1946), 7043–45 (June 18, 1945). Appleby had been appointed Under Secretary of Agriculture by Wallace, had battled constantly with Wickard, and had, after losing his former position of importance in the department, resigned in February, 1944, and moved to the Bureau of the Budget. Albertson, *Roosevelt's Farmer*, 154–56, 387.
64. AFBF, *Official News Letter*, July 10, 1946; see also Hardin, "BAE under Fire," *JFE*, 1946, 666–67.
65. Eisenhower to Anderson, May 13, 1946, NA, RG 16.
66. Tolley, OHC; interviews with Taylor, Wilson, and Ezekiel; Tolley to Clinton Anderson, May 15, 1946, NA, RG 83; Tolley Memorandum, May 10, USDA Press Release, May 10, 1946, FRC, RG 83. On Tolley's work in international economics, Walter W. Wilcox has written: "[Tolley] probably was the outstanding man in the United States government from the standpoint of his vision of the relief feeding problem as it actually developed. While the War Food Administration was dropping one food consumption restriction after another in the summer and fall of 1944 in the fear of accumulating surpluses, Tolley pointed out that current gov-

ernment policies would lead to an international crisis when relief feeding became necessary." Wilcox, *The Farmer in the Second World War*, 283.

67. Tolley to BAE staff, May 14, 1946, NA, RG 83.

68. W. Harry King to Anderson, June 4, 1945, Latham White to Anderson, April 8, 1946, Anderson Papers; Stine, OHC.

69. As a consequence of the inherently controversial character of the social sciences, the BAE under Wells could not escape controversy. Finally, Secretary Benson destroyed the agency in 1953. Hardin, *Freedom in Agricultural Education*, 155–59, 175–82; Christenson, *The Brannan Plan*, 14, 26 ff., 34, 38, 82, 96, 128, 192; Kirkendall, "Social Science in the Central Valley," *California Historical Society Quarterly*, 1964, 206–10; O. V. Wells *et al.*, "The Fragmentation of the BAE," *JFE*, LIV (February, 1954), 1–21.

70. Patton to Truman, May 2, 1946, TL, OF 1-Misc.

71. In addition to the large volume of correspondence in *ibid.*, see "Mr. Anderson Should Bow Himself Out," *Commonweal*, XLIV (May 31, 1946), 157.

72. Anderson to Eugene Cervi, November 18, 1946, NA, RG 16; Christenson, *The Brannan Plan*, 159, 201. Outside the Administration, Anderson's strongest support at this time came from the organized milk producers, including Charles W. Holman and his National Cooperative Milk Producers Federation. Holman to the President, May 22, 1946, TL, OF 1-Misc. Anderson's interest in letting some farm prices drop was hampering his efforts to cultivate the Farm Bureau. Paul Mallon column, February 21, 1946, Mitchell, S.D., *Gazette*, February 21, 1946, in Anderson Papers.

73. Truman to Patton, May 4, 1946, TL, OF 1-Misc.

74. J. Joseph Huthmacher, "Urban Liberalism and the Age of Reform," *MVHR*, XLIX (September, 1962), 231–41.

75. Interviews with Taylor, Wilson, and Ezekiel; Taylor, "The Point Four Program," *American Sociological Review*, XVI (February, 1951), 73–74. "The research activities of various federal agencies withered on the vine following 1945, so that in recent years the accomplishments of the rural sociological personnel remaining in the U.S. Department of Agriculture make a poor showing alongside the achievements between 1935 and 1945," a leading rural sociologist has written. The "remarkable amount of work rural sociologists have done in other countries since 1945 . . . is probably the most significant development in rural sociology during the last decade." T. Lynn Smith, "Rural Sociology in the United States and Canada: A Trend Report," *Current Sociology*, VI (1957), 16–18.

76. Taylor, "The Social Responsibilities of the Social Sciences — the National Level," *American Sociological Review*, XI (August, 1946), 391–92; Taylor to Walter U. Fuhriman, October 31, 1946, NA, RG 83. The prohibition on "cultural surveys" persisted, thus seriously restricting Taylor's work and qualifying any claims that most farm leaders had to a role as champions of intellectual freedom. Interview with Taylor; Farm Foundation, *Human Relations in Agriculture and Farm Life: The Status of*

Sociology in the Land-Grant Colleges, 44–46. Although Taylor found new opportunities for service and believed that during his career the discipline had become more useful, he remained concerned that sociologists were "not often called upon to render advice, counsel and guidance in social policy. . . . Apparently, even the fruitful development of the past forty years still leaves us classified somewhat as esoteric intellectuals." Taylor, "Developments in Sociology during the Past Forty Years," *Sociology and Social Research*, XL (July–August, 1956), 412–13.

77. Tolley, "The Philosophy of Agricultural Adjustment," December 11–12, 1935, Wilson Papers.

Notes to Conclusion

1. Elliott, " 'We, the People . . . ,' " *Land Policy Review*, 1939, 8.
2. Lester G. Seligman, "Presidential Leadership: The Inner Circle and Institutionalization," *The Journal of Politics*, XVIII (August, 1956), 410–26.
3. See the address by the first chairman of the CEA, Edwin G. Nourse, "Economics in the Public Service," and Truman's response to it, as recorded in his note to Nourse, February 13, 1947, TL, OF 985.
4. William E. Leuchtenburg, *The Perils of Prosperity 1914–1932*, 103; Prothro, *The Dollar Decade*.
5. Dale E. Hathaway, *Government and Agriculture: Public Policy in a Democratic Society*, 399–400. See his excellent discussion of the changing nature of "the process of policy formation" (183–236).

BIBLIOGRAPHY

Books and Pamphlets

Advisory Committee on Economic and Social Research of the Social Science Research Council, *Research Method and Procedure in Agricultural Economics*. 2 vols., mimeo, 1928.

Albertson, Dean, *Roosevelt's Farmer: Claude R. Wickard in the New Deal*. New York, Columbia University Press, 1961.

Bailey, Stephen Kemp, *Congress Makes a Law: The Story Behind the Employment Act of 1946*. New York, Vintage Books, 1964.

Baker, Gladys L., *The County Agent*. Chicago, The University of Chicago Press, 1939.

———, Wayne D. Rasmussen, Vivian Wiser, and Jane M. Porter, *Century of Service: the first 100 years of the United States Department of Agriculture*. Washington, D.C., United States Department of Agriculture, 1963.

Baritz, Loren, *Servants of Power: A History of the Use of Social Science in American Industry*. Middletown, Conn., Wesleyan University Press, 1960.

Benedict, Murray, *Farm Policies of the United States, 1790–1950: A Study of Their Origins and Development*. New York, The Twentieth Century Fund, 1953.

Black, John D., *Agricultural Reform in the United States*. New York, McGraw-Hill Book Company, 1929.

———, ed., *Research in Farm Management — Scope and Method*. New York, Social Science Research Council, 1932.

———, *Federal-State-Local Relations in Agriculture*. Washington, D.C., National Planning Association, 1950.

———, and George William Westcott, *Rural Planning in One Country: Worces-*

ter County, Massachusetts. Cambridge, Mass., Harvard University Press, 1959.

Block, William J., *The Separation of the Farm Bureau and the Extension Service: Political Issue in a Federal System.* Urbana, University of Illinois Press, 1960.

Blum, John, *From the Morgenthau Diaries.* Boston, Houghton Mifflin Company, 1959.

Bremner, Robert H., *From the Depths: The Discovery of Poverty in the United States.* New York, New York University Press, 1956.

Brunner, Edmund de S., *The Growth of a Science: A Half Century of Rural Sociological Research in the United States.* New York, Harper and Brothers, 1957.

Campbell, Christiana M., *The Farm Bureau and the New Deal: A Study of the Making of National Farm Policy, 1933–1940.* Urbana, The University of Illinois Press, 1962.

Case, H. C. M., and D. B. Williams, *Fifty Years of Farm Management.* Urbana, The University of Illinois Press, 1957.

Cash, W. J., *The Mind of the South.* New York, Doubleday Anchor Books, 1956.

Cavin, James P., ed., *Economics for Agriculture: Selected Writings of John D. Black.* Cambridge, Mass., Harvard University Press, 1959.

Chambers, Clarke A., *California Farm Organizations.* Berkeley, University of California Press, 1952.

Christenson, Reo, *The Brannan Plan: Farm Politics and Policy.* Ann Arbor, The University of Michigan Press, 1959.

Childs, Marquis, *I Write from Washington.* New York, Harper and Brothers, 1942.

Cole, Wayne S., *Senator Gerald P. Nye and American Foreign Relations.* Minneapolis, The University of Minnesota Press, 1962.

Commager, Henry Steele, *The American Mind: An Interpretation of American Thought and Character since the 1880's.* New Haven, Conn., Yale University Press, 1950.

Commons, John R., *Labor and Administration.* New York, The Macmillan Company, 1913.

——, *Myself.* New York, The Macmillan Company, 1934.

Conkin, Paul K., *Tomorrow a New World: The New Deal Community Program.* Ithaca, N.Y., Cornell University Press, 1959.

Cremin, Lawrence A., *The Transformation of the School: Progressivism in American Education, 1876–1957.* New York, Alfred A. Knopf, 1961.

Curti, Merle, ed., *American Scholarship in the Twentieth Century.* Cambridge, Mass., Harvard University Press, 1953.

——, *American Paradox: The Conflict of Thought and Action.* New Brunswick, N.J., Rutgers University Press, 1956.

——, and Vernon Carstensen, *The University of Wisconsin: A History, 1848–1925.* 2 vols., Madison, The University of Wisconsin Press, 1949.

Davis, Joseph S., *Wheat and the AAA.* Washington, D.C., The Brookings Institution, 1935.

The Domestic Allotment Plan. Chicago, The Millers National Federation, 1932.

Dykeman, Wilma, and James Stokely, *The Seeds of Southern Change: The Life of Will Alexander*. Chicago, The University of Chicago Press, 1962.

Edwards, Gladys Talbott, *The Farmers Union Triangle*. Jamestown, N.D., Farmers Union Educational Service, 1941.

Emmet, Boris, and John E. Jeuck, *Catalogues and Counters: A History of Sears, Roebuck and Company*. Chicago, The University of Chicago Press, 1950.

Ezekiel, Mordecai, *$2500 a Year: From Scarcity to Abundance*. New York, Harcourt, Brace and Company, 1936.

———, *Jobs for All through Industrial Expansion*. New York, Alfred A. Knopf, 1939.

———, and Louis Bean, *The Economic Bases of the Agricultural Adjustment Act*. Washington, D.C., Government Printing Office, 1933.

Farley, James A., *Jim Farley's Story: The Roosevelt Years*. New York. McGraw-Hill Book Company, 1948.

Farm Foundation, *Human Relations in Agriculture and Farm Life: The Status of Sociology in the Land-Grant Colleges*. Chicago, The Farm Foundation, 1946.

Fine, Sidney, *Laissez Faire and the General Welfare State: A Study of Conflict in American Thought, 1865–1901*. Ann Arbor, The University of Michigan Press, 1956.

Finkelstein, Louis, *American Spiritual Autobiographies: Fifteen Self-Portraits*. New York, Harper and Brothers, 1948.

Fite, Gilbert C., *George N. Peek and the Fight for Farm Parity*. Norman, University of Oklahoma Press, 1954.

———, *Peter Norbeck: Prairie Statesman*. University of Missouri Studies, XXII:2. Columbia, University of Missouri Press, 1948.

Frank, Jerome, *Save America First: How to Make Our Democracy Work*. New York, Harper and Brothers, 1938.

Freidel, Frank, *Franklin D. Roosevelt: The Triumph*. Boston, Little, Brown and Company, 1956.

Fusfeld, Daniel R., *The Economic Thought of Franklin D. Roosevelt and the Origins of the New Deal*. New York, Columbia University Press, 1956.

Gabriel, Ralph Henry, *The Course of American Democratic Thought*. 2d ed., New York, Ronald Press Co., 1956.

Galbraith, John Kenneth, *American Capitalism: The Concept of Countervailing Power*. Sentry Edition, Boston, Houghton Mifflin Company, 1962.

Gardner, Charles M., *The Grange — Friend of the Farmer*. Washington, D.C., National Grange, 1949.

Garwood, Ellen Clayton, *Will Clayton, A Short Biography*. Austin, University of Texas Press, 1958.

Gaus, John M., and Leon O. Wolcott, *Public Administration and the United States Department of Agriculture*. Chicago, Public Administration Service, 1940.

Gold, Bela, *Wartime Economic Planning in Agriculture*. New York, Columbia University Press, 1949.

Goldman, Eric, *Rendezvous with Destiny: A History of Modern American Reform.* New York, Alfred A. Knopf, 1953.

Gosnell, Harold F., *Champion Campaigner: Franklin D. Roosevelt.* New York, The Macmillan Company, 1952.

Griswold, A. Whitney, *Farming and Democracy.* New York, Harcourt, Brace and Company, 1948.

Hardin, Charles M., *The Politics of Agriculture: Soil Conservation and the Struggle for Power in Rural America.* Glencoe, The Free Press, 1952.

————, *Freedom in Agricultural Education.* Chicago, The University of Chicago Press, 1955.

Hargreaves, Mary Wilma M., *Dry Farming in the Northern Great Plains, 1900–1925.* Cambridge, Mass., Harvard University Press, 1957.

Hathaway, Dale E., *Government and Agriculture: Public Policy in a Democratic Society.* New York, The Macmillan Company, 1963.

Hays, Samuel P., *Conservation and the Gospel of Efficiency: The Progressive Conservation Movement, 1890–1920.* Cambridge, Mass., Harvard University Press, 1959.

Hewes, Laurence, *Boxcar in the Sand.* New York, Alfred A. Knopf, 1957.

Hinkle, Roscoe C., Jr., and Gisela J. Hinkle, *The Development of Modern Sociology: Its Nature and Growth in the United States.* Garden City, L.I., Doubleday, Doran, 1954.

Hofstadter, Richard, *Social Darwinism in American Thought.* Rev. ed., Boston, Beacon Press, 1955.

————, *Anti-intellectualism in American Life.* New York, Alfred A. Knopf, 1963.

Holcrow, Harold G., *et al.*, eds., *Modern Land Policy.* Urbana, University of Illinois Press, 1960.

Howe, Irving, and Lewis Coser, *The American Communist Party: A Critical History.* New York, Praeger, 1962.

Ickes, Harold L., *The Secret Diary of Harold L. Ickes.* 3 vols., New York, Simon and Schuster, Inc., 1953–54.

Jesness, O. B., ed., *Readings in Agricultural Policy.* Philadelphia, Blakiston Company, 1949.

Kempton, Murray, *Part of Our Time: Some Ruins and Monuments of the Thirties.* New York, Simon and Schuster, Inc., 1955.

Key, V. O., Jr., *Southern Politics in State and Nation.* New York, Vintage Books, 1949.

Kile, Orville M., *The Farm Bureau Through Three Decades.* Baltimore, The Waverly Press, 1950.

La Follette, Robert M., *La Follette's Autobiography: A Personal Narrative of Political Experiences.* Madison, The Robert M. La Follette Co., 1911.

Lerner, Daniel, ed., *The Human Meaning of the Social Sciences.* New York, Meridian Books, Inc., 1959.

Leuchtenburg, William E., *The Perils of Prosperity 1914–1932.* Chicago, The University of Chicago Press, 1958.

Lindley, Ernest K., and Jay Franklin (The Unofficial Observer), *The New Dealers.* New York, Simon and Schuster, Inc., 1934.

Linton, Ralph, ed., *The Science of Man in the World Crisis.* New York, Columbia University Press, 1945.

Lord, Russell, *Agrarian Revival: A Study of Agricultural Extension.* New York, American Association for Adult Education, 1939.

———, *The Wallaces of Iowa.* Boston, Houghton Mifflin Company, 1947.

Lynd, Robert S., *Knowledge for What? The Place of Social Science in American Culture.* Princeton, Princeton University Press, 1939.

McConnell, Grant, *The Decline of Agrarian Democracy.* Berkeley, University of California Press, 1953.

McCoy, Donald R., *Angry Voices: Left-of-Center Politics in the New Deal Era.* Lawrence, The University of Kansas Press, 1958.

McCune, Wesley, *The Farm Bloc.* New York, Doubleday, Doran, 1943.

———, *Who's Behind Our Farm Policy?* New York, Praeger, 1956.

McGeary, M. Nelson, *Gifford Pinchot: Forester-Politician.* Princeton, Princeton University Press, 1960.

MacKenzie, Findlay, ed., *Planned Society: Yesterday, Today, Tomorrow.* New York, Prentice-Hall, Inc., 1937.

Maxwell, Robert S., *La Follette and the Rise of the Progressives in Wisconsin.* Madison, The State Historical Society of Wisconsin, 1956.

Millett, John D., *The Process and Organization of Government Planning.* New York, Columbia University Press, 1947.

Moley, Raymond, *After Seven Years.* New York, Harper and Brothers, 1939.

Montana State College Extension Service, *An Agricultural Program for Montana.* Bozeman, Montana State College, 1927.

Myers, William Starr, ed., *The State Papers and Other Public Writings of Herbert Hoover.* 2 vols., New York, Doubleday, Doran, 1934.

Neilson, William Allan, ed., *Roads to Knowledge.* Chautauqua, N.Y., Norton, 1932.

Nichols, William H., *Southern Tradition and Regional Progress.* Chapel Hill, The University of North Carolina Press, 1960.

Nixon, Edgar B., comp. and ed., *Franklin D. Roosevelt and Conservation.* 2 vols., Hyde Park, Roosevelt Library, 1957.

Nourse, Edwin G., Joseph S. Davis, and John D. Black, *Three Years of the Agricultural Adjustment Administration.* Washington, D.C., The Brookings Institution, 1937.

Peek, George N., *Why Quit Our Own?* New York, Van Nostrand, 1936.

Prothro, James Warren, *The Dollar Decade: Business Ideas in the 1920's.* Baton Rouge, Louisiana State University Press, 1954.

Ratner, Joseph, ed., *Intelligence in the Modern World: John Dewey's Philosophy.* New York, Modern Library, 1939.

Rauch, Basil, *The History of the New Deal.* New York, Creative Age Press, 1944.

Robbins, Roy M., *Our Landed Heritage: The Public Domain, 1776–1936.* Princeton, Princeton University Press, 1942.

Rodgers, Cleveland, *Robert Moses, builder for democracy.* New York, Holt, 1952.

Rollins, Alfred B., Jr., *Roosevelt and Howe.* New York, Alfred A. Knopf, 1962.

Roosevelt, Eleanor, *This I Remember.* New York, Harper and Brothers, 1949.

Roosevelt, Elliott, ed., *F. D. R.: His Personal Letters, 1928–1945.* 2 vols., Duell, Sloan and Pearce, 1950.

Rosenman, Samuel I., ed., *The Public Papers and Addresses of Franklin D. Roosevelt.* 5 vols., New York, The Macmillan Company, 1938.

Rowe, Harold B., *Tobacco under the AAA.* Washington, D.C., The Brookings Institution, 1935.

Rudolph, Frederick, *The American College and University: A History.* New York, Alfred A. Knopf, 1962.

Saloutos, Theodore, *Farmer Movements in the South, 1865–1933.* Berkeley, The University of California Press, 1960.

————, and John D. Hicks, *Agricultural Discontent in the Middle West, 1900–1932.* Madison, The University of Wisconsin Press, 1951.

Salter, Leonard A., Jr., *A Critical Review of Research in Land Economics.* Minneapolis, The University of Minnesota Press, 1948.

Schlesinger, Arthur M., Jr., *The Age of Roosevelt.* 3 vols., Boston, Houghton Mifflin Company, 1957–1960.

Schultz, Theodore W., *Training and Recruiting of Personnel in the Rural Social Studies.* Washington, D.C., American Council on Education, 1941.

Shideler, James, *Farm Crisis, 1919–1923.* Berkeley, University of California Press, 1957.

Sternsher, Bernard, *Rexford Tugwell and the New Deal.* New Brunswick, N.J., Rutgers University Press, 1964.

Swain, Donald, *Federal Conservation Policy, 1921–1933.* Berkeley, The University of California Press, 1963.

Taylor, Henry C., and Anne Dewees Taylor, *The Story of Agricultural Economics in the United States, 1840–1932.* Ames, The Iowa State University Press, 1952.

Tolley, Howard Ross, *The Farmer Citizen at War.* New York, The Macmillan Company, 1943.

Tugwell, Rexford G., ed., *The Trend of Economics.* New York, Crofts, 1924.

————, *Industry's Coming of Age.* New York, Harcourt Brace, 1927.

————, *The Industrial Discipline and the Governmental Arts.* New York, Columbia University Press, 1933.

————, *The Democratic Roosevelt, A Biography of Franklin D. Roosevelt.* Garden City, L.I., Doubleday, Doran, 1957.

————, and Leon Keyserling, eds., *Redirecting Education.* 2 vols., New York, Columbia University Press, 1934–1935.

Vance, Maurice M., *Charles Richard Van Hise: Scientist Progressive.* Madison, The State Historical Society of Wisconsin, 1960.

Wallace, Henry A., *New Frontiers.* New York, Reynal and Hitchcock, 1934.

Wilbur, Lyman, and Arthur M. Hyde, *The Hoover Policies.* New York, Charles Scribner's Sons, 1937.

Wilcox, Walter W., *The Farmer in the Second World War.* Ames, The Iowa State College Press, 1947.

Wilson, M. L., *Farm Relief and the Domestic Allotment Plan.* Minneapolis, The University of Minnesota Press, 1933.

Woodruff, Archibald M., Jr., *Farm Mortgage Loans of Life Insurance Compa-nies*. New Haven, Conn., Yale University Press, 1957.

Young, Pauline H., *Scientific Social Surveys and Research*. 2d ed., New York, Prentice-Hall, Inc., 1949.

PUBLIC DOCUMENTS

U.S. Agricultural Adjustment Administration, *Agricultural Adjustment 1937–38: A Report of the Activities Carried on by the Agricultural Adjustment Administration*. 1939.

U.S. Bureau of Agricultural Economics, *Report of the Chief of Agricultural Economics*. 1940.

U.S. *Congressional Record*. 1930–1946.

U.S. Department of Agriculture, *Proceedings of the National Conference on Land Utilization*. 1932.

———, *Farmers in a Changing World: The Yearbook of Agriculture, 1940*. 1940.

———, *What Peace Can Mean to American Farmers; Post-War Agriculture and Employment*. Misc. Pub. No. 562, May, 1945.

U.S. House of Representatives, *Report 176*. 77th Cong., 1st Sess., 1941.

———, *Report 786*. 77th Cong., 1st Sess., 1941.

———, *Report 2218*. 77th Cong., 2d Sess., 1942.

———, *Report 2288*. 77th Cong., 2d Sess., 1942.

———, Subcommittee of the Committee on Appropriations, *Hearings, Agriculture Department Appropriation Bill for 1940*. 76th Cong., 1st Sess., 1939.

———, *Hearings, Agriculture Department Appropriation Bill for 1942*. 77th Cong., 1st Sess., 1941.

———, *Hearings, Agriculture Department Appropriation Bill for 1943*. 77th Cong., 2d Sess., 1942.

———, *Hearings, Agriculture Department Appropriation Bill for 1946*. 79th Cong., 1st Sess., 1945.

———, *Hearings, Agriculture Department Appropriation Bill for 1947*. 79th Cong., 2d Sess., 1946.

———, *Department of Agriculture Appropriation Bill, Fiscal Year 1947*. Report 1659. 79th Cong., 2d Sess., 1946.

U.S. Senate, *Industrial Prices and their Relative Inflexibility*. Report 13. 74th Cong., 1st Sess., 1935.

———, *Report 149*. 77th Cong., 1st Sess., 1941.

———, *Report 1323*. 77th Cong., 2d Sess., 1942.

———, Subcommittee of the Committee on Appropriations, *Hearings, Agriculture Department Appropriation Bill for 1943*. 77th Cong., 2d Sess., 1942.

———, *Hearings, Agricultural Appropriation Bill for 1947*. 79th Cong., 2d Sess., 1946.

———, *Agricultural Appropriation Bill, 1947*. Report 1334. 79th Cong., 2d Sess., 1946.

———, Subcommittee on Administration of Farm Programs of the Committee on Agriculture and Forestry, *Report, Abuses and Disruptions of the Elected Farmer Committee System.* 84th Cong., 2d Sess., 1956.

U.S. Laws, Statutes, etc., *Public Law 144.* 77th Cong., 1st Sess., 1941.

————, *Public Law 674.* 77th Cong., 2d Sess., 1942.

U.S. National Resources Board, *A Report on National Planning and Public Works in Relation to Natural Resources and Including Land Use and Water Resources with Findings and Recommendations, December 1, 1934.* 1934.

U.S. National Resources Committee, *Farm Tenancy: Report of the President's Committee.* 1937.

ARTICLES, ESSAYS, AND BOOK REVIEWS

Adams, R. L., "The Management of Large Farms." *Agricultural Engineering,* XII (September, 1931), 353–56.

"Adjustments in Southern Agriculture with Special Reference to Cotton." *Journal of Farm Economics.* XXVIII (February, 1946), 341–79.

Allin, Bushrod W., "Migration Required for Best Land Use." *Journal of Farm Economics,* XVIII (August, 1936), 493–99.

————, "County Planning Project — A Cooperative Approach." *Journal of Farm Economics,* XXII (February, 1940), 292–301.

————, "The Objectives and Methods of Agricultural Economics." *Journal of Farm Economics,* XXX (August, 1948), 545–52.

————, "Is Group Choice a Part of Economics?" *Quarterly Journal of Economics,* LXVII (August, 1953), 362–79.

Anderson, Clifford B., "The Metamorphosis of American Agrarian Idealism in the 1920's and 1930's." *Agricultural History,* XXXV (October, 1961), 182–88.

Anderson, Clinton P., "Work Conquers All Things: Full Employment First Requisite for Farm Prosperity." *Vital Speeches,* XI (August 15, 1945), 661–64.

————, "Is the Farmer Heading for Trouble Again?" *Saturday Evening Post,* CCXVIII (December 22, 1945), 18 ff.

Arensberg, Conrad, "The Community Study Method." *American Journal of Sociology,* LX (September, 1954), 109–24.

Banfield, Edward C., "Ten Years of the Farm Tenant Purchase Program." *Journal of Farm Economics,* XXXI (August, 1949), 469–86.

————, "Organization for Policy Planning in the U.S. Department of Agriculture." *Journal of Farm Economics,* XXXIV (February, 1952), 14–34.

Bates, J. Leonard, "Fulfilling American Democracy: The Conservation Movement, 1907–1921." *Mississippi Valley Historical Review,* XLIV (June, 1957), 29–57.

————, "Review of Samuel P. Hays, *Conservation and the Gospel of Efficiency: The Progressive Conservation Movement, 1890–1920.*" *American Historical Review,* LXV (July, 1960), 930–31.

Baum, Arthur W., "They Say He's a Dangerous Man." *Saturday Evening Post,* CCXVII (May 5, 1945), 14 ff.

Benedict, M. R., and M. L. Wilson, "Howard Ross Tolley, 1889–1958." *Journal of Farm Economics*, XLI (February, 1959), 1–2.

Black, Albert G., "Agricultural Policy and the Economist." *Journal of Farm Economics*, XVIII (May, 1936), 311–19.

———, "The Need for Generalists." *Journal of Farm Economics*, XVIII (November, 1936), 657–61.

———, "Some Current Problems in Agricultural Credit." *Journal of Farm Economics*, XXIII (February, 1941), 37–51.

Black, John D., "Doctrines Relating to the Agricultural Policy of the United States." *Proceedings of the Second International Conference of Agricultural Economists*, August, 1930.

———, "Public Participation in Planning Adjustments." *American Cooperation* (1932), 490–93.

———, "Planning, Control and Research in Agriculture after Recovery." *Journal of Farm Economics*, XVII (February, 1935), 20–35.

———, "Discussion." *Journal of Farm Economics*, XXI (February, 1939), 25–30.

———, "Review of Russell Lord, *The Wallaces of Iowa.*" *Journal of Farm Economics*, XXIX (August, 1947), 773–78.

———, "The Bureau of Agricultural Economics — The Years in Between." *Journal of Farm Economics*, XXIX (November, 1947), 1027–42.

Bolles, Blair, "The Sweetheart of the Regimenters." *American Mercury*, XXXIX (September, 1936), 84–86.

Brandt, Karl, "The Orientation of Agricultural Economics." *Journal of Farm Economics*, XXXVII (December, 1955), 793–806.

Brunner, Edmund de S., "Sociology Tomorrow." *Rural Sociology*, XI (June, 1946), 95–102.

Carey, James C., "The Farmers' Independence Council of America." *Agricultural History*, XXXV (April, 1961), 70–77.

Chew, Arthur P., "What's Ahead for Agriculture." *New Republic*, CXIII (September 17, 1945), 337–39.

Christgau, Victor, "Legislation Needed to Bring About Readjustments in Agriculture." *Proceedings of the Association of the Land-Grant Colleges and Universities*, XLIV (November, 1930), 123–130.

———, "A Plan to Control Agricultural Production." *American Cooperation* (1931), 55–60.

———, "Adjustment of Production in Agriculture." *Journal of Farm Economics*, XIII (January, 1931), 1–8.

Clapper, Raymond, " 'AAA' Family Row?" *Literary Digest*, CXXI (March 21, 1936), 9.

"Cotton's Future." *Business Week*, December 9, 1944, 26, 28.

Curti, Merle, "Intellectuals and Other People." *American Historical Review*, LX (January, 1955), 259–82.

Cutting, Malcolm, "Farm Relief by Factory Methods." *Nation's Business*, XVIII (February, 1930), 47 ff.

Davis, Chester C., "The Program of Agricultural Adjustment." *Journal of Farm Economics*, XVI (January, 1934), 88–96.

———, "The Agricultural Adjustment Act and National Recovery." *Journal of Farm Economics*, XVIII (May, 1936), 229–41.

———, "The Place of Farmers, Economists and Administrators in Developing Agricultural Policy." *Journal of Farm Economics*, XXII (February, 1940), 1–9.

Davis, I. G., "The Social Science Fellowships in Agricultural Economics and Rural Sociology." *Journal of Farm Economics*, XVI (July, 1934), 496–503.

Davis, Joseph S., "The Voluntary Domestic Allotment Plan for Wheat." *Wheat Studies of the Food Research Institute*, IX (November, 1932).

Drucker, Peter F., "Exit King Cotton." *Harper's Magazine*, CXCII (May, 1946), 473–80.

Elliott, F. F., "Progress and Problems in Regional Agricultural Planning from the National Point of View." *Journal of Farm Economics*, XVIII (February, 1936), 95–106.

———, " 'We, the People. . . .' " *Land Policy Review*, II (May–June, 1939), 1–9.

Ezekiel, Mordecai, "Lines of Action in Economic Reconstruction." *Antioch Review*, I (September, 1941), 328–42.

———, "Statistical Investigations of Saving, Consumption and Investment." *American Economic Review*, XXXII (March–June, 1942), 22–49, 272–307.

———, "The Shift in Agricultural Policy toward Human Welfare." *Journal of Farm Economics*, XXIV (May, 1942), 463–76.

"Farm Cutbacks." *Business Week*, August 25, 1945, 21–22.

Feuer, Lewis S., "John Dewey and the Back to the People Movement." *Journal of the History of Ideas*, XX (October–December, 1959), 545–68.

Fite, Gilbert C., "John A. Simpson: The Southwest's Militant Farm Leader." *Mississippi Valley Historical Review*, XXXV (March, 1949), 563–84.

———, "Farmer Opinion and the Agricultural Adjustment Act." *Mississippi Valley Historical Review*, XLVIII (March, 1962), 656–73.

———, Bushrod W. Allin, Richard S. Kirkendall, and Ross B. Talbott, "The United States Department of Agriculture as an Instrument of Public Policy." *Journal of Farm Economics*, XLII (December, 1960), 1048–1113.

Gates, Paul W., "Comments." *Agricultural History*, XXXVII (October, 1963), 214–16.

Gleason, John P., "The Attitude of the Business Community toward Agriculture during the McNary-Haugen Period." *Agricultural History*, XXXII (April, 1958), 127–38.

Goldschmidt, Walter, "Social Class in America — A Critical Review." *American Anthropologist*, LII (October–December, 1950), 483–98.

Gray, Lewis C., "Farm Ownership and Tenancy." *Proceedings of the Academy of Political Science in the City of New York*, XI (April, 1925), 369–78.

———, "The Social and Economic Implications of the National Land Program." *Journal of Farm Economics*, XVIII (May, 1936), 257–73.

———, "Disadvantaged Rural Classes." *Journal of Farm Economics*, XX (February, 1938), 71–85.

———, "Federal Purchase and Administration of Submarginal Land in the Great Plains." *Journal of Farm Economics*, XXI (February, 1939), 123–31.

Green, Robert M., "Farm Mortgage Delinquencies and Foreclosures." *Journal of Farm Economics*, XV (January, 1933), 14–26.

Gregory, Clifford, "The American Farm Bureau Federation and the A.A.A.," in Harwood L. Childs, ed., *Pressure Groups and Propaganda. Annals of the American Academy of Political and Social Science*, CLXXIX (May, 1935).

Gross, Neal C., "A Post Mortem on County Planning." *Journal of Farm Economics*, XXV (August, 1943), 644–61.

"Hamstringing the BAE." *New Republic*, CVII (August 24, 1942), 213.

Hardin, Charles M., "The Bureau of Agricultural Economics Under Fire: A Study in Valuation Conflicts." *Journal of Farm Economics*, XXVIII (August, 1946), 635–68.

———, "The Politics of Agriculture in the United States." *Journal of Farm Economics*, XXXII (November, 1950), 571–83.

Harriman, Henry I., "The Farm Problem." Mimeo, copy available in library of Wesleyan University, Middletown, Connecticut.

Heacock, Walter J., "William B. Bankhead and the New Deal." *Journal of Southern History*, XXI (August, 1955), 347–59.

Hoover, Calvin, "Agrarian Reorganization in the South." *Journal of Farm Economics*, XX (May, 1938), 474–81.

———, "What Changes in National Policy Does the South Need?" *Journal of Farm Economics*, XXII (February, 1940), 206–12.

Hoskins, James D., "A Unified Command and Democracy in Agriculture." *Proceedings of the Association of Land-Grant Colleges and Universities, October 28–30, 1942*, 1942.

Huffman, Roy E., "Montana's Contributions to New Deal Farm Policy." *Agricultural History*, XXXIII (October, 1959), 164–67.

Hutcheson, John R., "Redefining the Extension Job and Field of Action." *Proceedings of the Association of Land-Grant Colleges and Universities, November 10–12, 1941*, 1941.

Huthmacher, J. Joseph, "Urban Liberalism and the Age of Reform." *Mississippi Valley Historical Review*, XLIX (September, 1962), 231–41.

"Interview with Henry A. Wallace." *United States News and World Report*, January 8, 1954, 40–44.

Johnson, William R., "National Farm Organizations and the Reshaping of Agricultural Policy in 1932." *Agricultural History*, XXXVII (January, 1963), 35–42.

Kirkendall, Richard S., "Franklin D. Roosevelt and the Service Intellectual." *Mississippi Valley Historical Review*, XLIX (December, 1962), 459–63.

———, "L. C. Gray and the Supply of Agricultural Land." *Agricultural History*, XXXVII (October, 1963), 206–14.

———, "Social Science in the Central Valley of California: An Episode." *California Historical Society Quarterly*, XLIII (September, 1964), 195–218.

Laski, Harold, "The Limitations of the Expert." *Harper's Magazine*, CLXII (December, 1930), 101–10.

Lewis, John D., and Ewart Lewis, "The Farmer Helps to Plan." *New Republic*, CV (October 20, 1941), 504–5.

Lord, Russell, "Profiles — Rural New Yorker." *New Yorker*, XI (March 23–30, 1934), 20–24, 22–26.

Maddox, James G., "Suggestions for a National Program of Rural Rehabilitation." *Journal of Farm Economics*, XXI (November, 1939), 881–96.

——, "What's Ahead for the Farmer." *Harper's Magazine*, CXC (March, 1945), 321–26.

Means, Gardiner, "National Combinations and Agriculture." *Journal of Farm Economics*, XX (February, 1938), 53–57.

Moore, Arthur, "Earl Smith: Farmers' Boss." *Atlantic Monthly*, CLXXV (January, 1945), 85–90.

"Mr. Anderson Should Bow Himself Out." *Commonweal*, XLIV (May 31, 1946), 157.

Murphy, Paul L., "The New Deal Agricultural Program and the Constitution." *Agricultural History*, XXIX (October, 1955), 160–69.

"New Farm Policies." *New Republic*, CXII (April 16, 1945), 496.

Nowell, R. I., "Experience of the Resettlement Administration Program in the Lake States." *Journal of Farm Economics*, XIX (February, 1937), 206–20.

——, "Discussion." *Journal of Farm Economics*, XXIX (November, 1947), 1505–1510.

Parks, W. Robert, "Political and Administrative Guide Lines in Developing Public Agricultural Policies." *Journal of Farm Economics*, XXXIII (May, 1951), 157–68.

Pollock, Jack H., "America's New Food Czar." *Liberty Magazine*, August 4, 1945.

Proceedings of the Forty-ninth Annual Convention of the Association of Land-Grant Colleges and Universities, November 18–20, 1935.

Reed, William G., and Howard Ross Tolley, "Weather as a Risk In Farming." *Geographical Review*, II (July, 1916), 48–53.

"The Republican Brain Trust." *New Republic*, LXXXVI (April 22, 1936), 299–300.

Ryan, Bryce, "Democratic Telesis and County Agricultural Planning." *Journal of Farm Economics*, XXII (November, 1940), 691–700.

Schmidt, Louis Bernard, "The Role and Techniques of Agrarian Pressure Groups." *Agricultural History*, XXX (April, 1956), 49–58.

Schultz, Theodore, "Some Guiding Principles in Organizing Agricultural Economics Research." *Journal of Farm Economics*, XXXVI (February, 1954), 18–21.

Seligman, Lester G., "Presidential Leadership: The Inner Circle and Institutionalization." *The Journal of Politics*, XVIII (August, 1956), 410–26.

Sewell, William H., with comments by Carl C. Taylor, "Needed Research in Sociology." *Rural Sociology*, XV (June, 1950), 115–30.

Shannon, David A., "Was McCarthy a Political Heir of La Follette?" *Wisconsin Magazine of History*, XLV (Autumn, 1961), 3–9.

Sillars, Malcolm O., "Henry A. Wallace's Editorials on Agricultural Discontent, 1921–1928." *Agricultural History*, XXVI (October, 1952), 132–40.

Slichter, Gertrude Almy, "Franklin D. Roosevelt and the Farm Problem,

1929–1932." *Mississippi Valley Historical Review*, XLIII (September, 1956), 238–58.

Smith, Russell, "Big Business and the Farm Bloc." *Antioch Review*, IV (June, 1944), 189–204.

Smith, T. Lynn, "Rural Sociology in the United States and Canada: A Trend Report." *Current Sociology*, VI (1957), 5–18.

Soth, Lauren K., "Making Economics Understandable." *Journal of Farm Economics*, XXVIII (August, 1946), 852–59.

Soule, George, "Planning for Agriculture." *New Republic*, LXVIII (October 7, 1931), 204–6.

Swing, Raymond Gram, "The Purge of the AAA." *The Nation*, CXL (February 20, 1935), 216–17.

Taeuber, Conrad, "Some Recent Developments in Sociological Work in the Department of Agriculture." *American Sociological Review*, X (April, 1945), 169–75.

Taeusch, Carl F., "Adequate Perspectives." *Journal of Adult Education*, IX (October, 1937), 410–13.

Taylor, Carl C., "Research Needed as a Guidance to the Subsistence Homesteads Program." *Journal of Farm Economics*, XVI (April, 1934), 310–14.

———, "Social and Economic Significance of the Subsistence Homesteads Program—From the Point of View of a Sociologist." *Journal of Farm Economics*, XVII (November, 1935), 720–31.

———, "Land Utilization: The Social Aspects of Land Adjustment Problems." *Journal of Farm Economics*, XIX (May 1937), 588–94.

———, "The Work of the Division of Farm Population and Rural Life." *Rural Sociology*, IV (June, 1939), 221–28.

———, "Social Theory and Social Action." *Rural Sociology*, V (March, 1940), 17–31.

———, "Social Science and Social Action in Agriculture." *Social Forces*, XX (December, 1941), 154–59.

———, "Report of the Subcommittee of the Executive Committee on Participation of Sociologists in the National Emergency." *American Sociological Review*, VII (February, 1942), 88–90.

———, with discussion by Marion Clawson, "The Sociologists' Part in Planning the Columbia Basin." *American Sociological Review*, XI (June, 1946), 321–29.

———, "The Social Responsibilities of the Social Sciences — the National Level." *American Sociological Review*, XI (August, 1946), 321–30.

———, with discussion by Robert Redfield and Samuel A. Stouffer, "Sociology and Common Sense." *American Sociological Review*, XII (February, 1947), 1–10.

———, "The Point Four Program." *American Sociological Review*, XVI (February, 1951), 73–74.

———, "Developments in Sociology during the Past Forty Years." *Sociology and Social Research*, XL (July–August, 1956), 412–13.

Taylor, Henry C., "L. C. Gray, Agricultural Historian and Land Economist." *Agricultural History*, XXVI (October, 1952), 165.

Taylor, Paul, "Perspectives on Housing Migratory Agricultural Laborers." *Land Economics*, XXVII (August, 1951), 198–201.

Tolley, Howard Ross, "Recent Developments in Research Methods and Procedure in Agricultural Economics." *Journal of Farm Economics*, XII (April, 1930), 213–30.

——, "Research in Local and National Outlook Work." *Journal of Farm Economics*, XII (October, 1930), 588–94.

——, "The Program Planning Division of the Agricultural Adjustment Administration." *Journal of Farm Economics*, XVI (April, 1934), 582–90.

——, "Discussion." *Journal of Farm Economics*, XVII (February, 1935), 35–37.

——, "Objectives in National Agricultural Policy." *Journal of Farm Economics*, XX (February, 1938), 24–36.

——, "Contributions of Agricultural Economics to the General Welfare." *Journal of Farm Economics*, XXI (February, 1939), 8–21.

——, "Probable Trends for American Food Production after the War." *Proceedings of the Association of Land-Grant Colleges and Universities, October, 1944*, 1944.

Tontz, Robert L., "Legal Parity: Implementations of the Policy of Equality for Agriculture, 1929–1954." *Agricultural History*, XXIX (October, 1954), 174–81.

——, "Origin of the Base Period Concept of Parity — A Significant Value Judgement in Agricultural Policy." *Agricultural History*, XXXII (January, 1958), 3–13.

——, "Memberships of General Farm Organizations, United States, 1874–1960." *Agricultural History*, XXVIII (July, 1964), 143–56.

Tucker, William P., "The Farmers Union: The Social Thought of a Current Agrarian Movement." *Southwestern Social Science Quarterly*, XXVII (June, 1946), 45–53.

——, "Populism Up-to-Date: The Story of the Farmer's Union." *Agricultural History*, XXI (October, 1947), 198–208.

"Tugwell: New Deal's Leading 'Red' Gets Job in Wall Street." *News Week*, VIII (November 28, 1936), 16–17.

"Tugwell to the Wolves." *New Republic*, LXXXV (December 25, 1935), 186–87.

Tugwell, Rexford G., "Economic Theory and Practice." *American Economic Review*, XIII (sup.) (March, 1923), 107–9.

——, "Notes on the Life and Work of Simon Nelson Patten." *Journal of Political Economy*, XXXI (April, 1923), 154–208.

——, "Problem of Agriculture." *Political Science Quarterly*," XXXIX (December, 1924), 549–91.

——, "Chameleon Words." *New Republic*, XLVIII (August 27, 1926), 17.

——, "What Will Become of the Farmer?" *The Nation*, CXXIV (June 15, 1927), 664–66.

——, "Platforms and Candidates." *New Republic*, LV (May 20, 1928), 44–45.

————, "Experimental Control in Russian Industry." *Political Science Quarterly*, XLIII (June, 1928), 161–87.

————, "Reflections on Farm Relief." *Political Science Quarterly*, XLIII (December, 1928), 481–97.

————, "Farm Relief and a Permanent Agriculture." *Annals of the American Academy*, CXLII (March, 1929), 271–82.

————, "Agricultural Policy of France." *Political Science Quarterly*, XLV (June–December, 1930), 214–30, 405–28, 524–47.

————, "Human Nature and Social Economy." *Journal of Philosophy*, XXVII (August 14–28, 1930), 449–57, 477–92.

————, "The Theory of Occupational Obsolescence." *Political Science Quarterly*, XLVI (June, 1931), 171–227.

————, "The Principle of Planning and the Institution of Laissez Faire." *American Economic Review*, XXII (sup.) (March, 1932), 75–92.

————, "The Place of Government in a National Land Program." *Journal of Farm Economics*, XVI (January, 1934), 55–69.

————, "Relief and Reconstruction." *National Conference of Social Work*, 1934, 32–48.

————, "Needed Social and Political Adjustment." *Vital Speeches*, I (November 18, 1934), 98–103.

————, "National Significance of Recent Trends in Farm Population." *Social Forces*, XIV (October, 1935), 1–7.

————, "The Progressive Task Today and Tomorrow." *Vital Speeches*, II (December 2, 1935), 130–35.

————, "Our New National Domain." *Scribner's Magazine*, XCIX (March, 1936), 167–78.

————, "Down to Earth." *Current History*, XLIV (July, 1936), 32–38.

————, "Changing Acres." *Current History*, XLIV (September, 1936), 57–63.

————, "Grass Did Not Grow." *Fortune*, XIV (October, 1936), 114 ff.

————, "The Future of National Planning." *New Republic*, LXXXIX (December 6, 1936), 164.

————, "Cooperation and Resettlement." *Current History*, XLV (February, 1937), 71–76.

————, "Is a Farmer-Labor Alliance Possible?" *Harper's Magazine*, CLXXIV (May, 1937), 651–61.

————, "After the New Deal." *New Republic*, XCIX (July 26, 1939), 323–25.

————, "The Preparation of a President." *Western Political Quarterly*, I (June, 1948), 131–53.

————, "A Planner's View of Agriculture's Future." *Journal of Farm Economics*, XXXI (February, 1949), 29–47.

————, "The Resettlement Idea." *Agricultural History*, XXXIII (October, 1959), 159–64.

Venkataramani, M. S., "Norman Thomas, Arkansas Sharecroppers, and the Roosevelt Agricultural Policies, 1933–1937." *Mississippi Valley Historical Review*, XLVII (September, 1960), 229–40.

Wallace, Henry A., "The Farmer and Social Discipline." *Journal of Farm Economics*, XVI (January, 1934), 1–12.

————, "Farm Economists and Agricultural Planning." *Journal of Farm Economics*, XVIII (February, 1938), 1–11.

Wehrwein, G. S., "An Appraisal of Resettlement." *Journal of Farm Economics*, XIX (February, 1937), 190–202.

Wells, O. V., "Agricultural Planning and the Agricultural Economist." *Journal of Farm Economics*, XX (August, 1938), 753–64.

————, *et al.*, "The Fragmentation of the BAE." *Journal of Farm Economics*, LIV (February, 1954), 1–21.

Wilcox, W. W., "Discussion." *Journal of Farm Economics*, XXI (February, 1939), 44–45.

"Will Clayton's Cotton." *Fortune*, XXXII (November and December, 1945).

Williams, Robin M., Jr., "Review of Current Research in Rural Sociology." *Rural Sociology*, XI (June, 1946), 103–14.

Wilson, M. L., "The Source Material of Economic Research and Points of View in its Organization." *Journal of Farm Economics*, VIII (January, 1926), 1–15.

————, "The Fairway Farms Project." *Journal of Land and Public Utility Economics*, II (April, 1926), 156–71.

————, "Research Studies in Economics of Large-scale Farming in Montana." *Agricultural Engineering*, X (January, 1929), 3–12.

————, "Experimental Method in Economic Research." *Journal of Farm Economics*, XI (October, 1929), 578–83.

————, "Research in the Field of Agricultural Adjustments." *Proceedings of the Western Farm Economics Association*, V (June, 1931), 93–108.

————, "Economic Planning as Applied to Agriculture." *Proceedings of the Western Farm Economics Association*, VI (August, 1932), 73–79.

————, "A Land-Use Program for the Federal Government." *Journal of Farm Economics*, XV (April, 1933), 217–35.

————, "The Place of Subsistence Homesteads in our National Economy." *Journal of Farm Economics*, XVI (January, 1934), 73–84.

————, "The Report on Land of the National Resources Board." *Journal of Farm Economics*, XVII (February, 1935), 39–50.

————, "Validity of the Fundamental Assumptions Underlying the Agricultural Adjustment Act." *Journal of Farm Economics*, XVIII (February, 1936), 12–26.

————, "Agricultural Conservation — An Aspect of Land Utilization." *Journal of Farm Economics*, XIX (February, 1937), 3–12.

————, "New Horizons in Agricultural Economics." *Journal of Farm Economics*, XX (February, 1938), 1–7.

————, "Address." *Proceedings of the Association of Land-Grant Colleges and Universities, Fifty-Second Annual Convention*, November 14–16, 1938.

————, "The Problems of Poverty in Agriculture." *Journal of Farm Economics*, XXII (February, 1940), 10–29.

————, "The Democratic Process and the Formulation of Agricultural Policy." *Social Forces*, XIX (October, 1940), 1–11.

————, "Nutritional Science and Agricultural Policy." *Journal of Farm Economics*, XXIV (February, 1942), 188–205.

Wilson, William H., "How the Chamber of Commerce Viewed the NRA: A Re-examination." *Mid-America*, XLIV (April, 1962), 95–108.

Zeuch, W. E., "The Subsistence Homesteads Program from the Viewpoint of an Economist." *Journal of Farm Economics*, XVII (November, 1935), 710–19.

UNPUBLISHED STUDIES

Baldwin, Sidney G., "The Farm Security Administration: A Study in Politics and Administration." Ph.D. dissertation, Syracuse University, 1955.

Friedman, Robert P., "The Public Speaking of Arthur M. Hyde." Ph.D. dissertation, University of Missouri, 1954.

Kirkendall, Richard S., "The New Deal Professors and the Politics of Agriculture." Ph.D. dissertation, University of Wisconsin, 1958.

Maddox, James G., "The Farm Security Administration." Ph.D. dissertation, Harvard University, 1950.

NEWSPAPERS AND OTHER PERIODICALS

Agricultural Leaders Digest, 1934.
American Farm Bureau Federation, *Official News Letter*, 1938–1946.
Bureau Farmer, 1933–1934.
Farmers Equity Union News, 1936.
Farm Journal, 1935–1938.
Hagerstown, Maryland, *Herald*, November 29, 1935.
Kiplinger Agricultural Letter, November 14, 1936.
Minneapolis Tribune, July 15, 1932.
Missouri Farmer, 1933–1934.
National Grange Monthly, 1934–1936.
National Union Farmer, 1945–1946.
New York Herald-Tribune, November 11, 1934.
The New York Times, 1930–1946.
Pacific Rural Press, 1933–1934.
Progressive Farmer and Southern Ruralist, 1933.
Rural New Yorker, 1933–1935.
Rio, Wisconsin, *Journal*, February 28, 1935.
St. Paul Dispatch, July 16, 1932.
Wallaces' Farmer and Iowa Homestead, 1930–1932.
Wisconsin Agriculturist and Farmer, 1933–1936.

MANUSCRIPT COLLECTIONS

Agricultural Adjustment Administration. Record Group 145, National Archives, Washington, D.C.

Agricultural Economics, Bureau of. Record Group 83, National Archives,

Washington, D.C., and Federal Records Center, South San Francisco, California

Agriculture, Secretary of.   Record Group 16, National Archives, Washington, D.C.

Anderson, Clinton P.   Truman Library, Independence, Missouri

Fragmentary Papers of Persons and Organizations. Group 31, Roosevelt Library, Hyde Park, New York

Frank, Jerome. Yale University, New Haven, Connecticut

Hirth, William. Western Historical Manuscripts Collection, University of Missouri, Columbia

Historical Files, Economic and Statistical Analysis Division, Economic Research Service. United States Department of Agriculture, Washington, D.C.

Hope, Clifford.   Kansas State Historical Society, Topeka

Peek, George N.   Western Historical Manuscripts Collection, University of Missouri, Columbia

Rainey, Henry T.   Library of Congress

Resettlement Administration and Farm Security Administration. Record Group 96, National Archives, Washington, D.C.

Ronald, W. R.   Memoir, Gilbert C. Fite Copy, University of Oklahoma

Roosevelt, Franklin D.   Roosevelt Library, Hyde Park, New York

Taylor, Henry C.   The State Historical Society of Wisconsin, Madison

Teague, C. C.   Bancroft Library, University of California, Berkeley

Truman, Harry S.   Truman Library, Independence, Missouri

Tugwell, Rexford G.   Diary, 1932–1933, Group 21, Roosevelt Library, Hyde Park, New York

Wilson, M. L.   Montana State College, Bozeman

PERSONAL CORRESPONDENCE

Baker, Gladys L.   October 28, 1965, to the author.
Wilson, M. L.   August 10, 1956, to the author.

INTERVIEWS
By the author

Allin, Bushrod W.
Appleby, Paul
Baker, Gladys L.
Benedict, Murray R.
Black, John D.
Christgau, Victor
Darrow, Wayne
Elliott, F. F.
Englund, Eric
Ezekiel, Mordecai
Hedge, Porter

James, De Los
Packard, Walter
Stedman, Alfred D.
Taeusch, Carl F.
Taylor, Carl C.
Taylor, Paul
Tugwell, Rexford G.
Wallace, Henry A.
Wiecking, Ernst H.
Wilson, M. L.

From Oral History Collection, Columbia University, New York

Bean, Louis
Bledsoe, Samuel B.
Ezekiel, Mordecai
Hutson, John
Taber, Louis
Tolley, Howard Ross
Stine, O. C.
Wilson, M. L.

INDEX